THE PRESBYTERIAN HYMNAL

THE PRESBYTERIAN HYMNAL

HYMNS, PSALMS,
AND
SPIRITUAL SONGS

Westminster/John Knox Press
Louisville, Kentucky

Unless otherwise indicated, scripture quotations are from the New Revised Standard Version Bible, © 1987 by the Division of Christian Education of the National Council of the Churches of Christ in the U.S.A., and are used by permission.

"Lord, have mercy," hymns 565, 573; "Glory to the Father," hymn 567; "Our Father in heaven," hymn 571; "Lord, have mercy upon us," hymns 572, 574; "Holy, holy, holy Lord," hymns 568, 581; and "Lift up your hearts," page 13, are from *Prayers We Have in Common*, copyright © 1970, 1971, and 1975 by International Consultation on English Texts. All rights reserved.

Revised Apostles' Creed, page 14; Nicene Creed, page 15; Lord's Prayer, page 16; and "Glory to God in the highest," hymns 566, 575, are copyright © 1987 by English Language Liturgical Consultation. All rights reserved.

"Great Prayer of Thanksgiving," page 13; "Christ has died," hymn 569; "Dying you destroyed our death," hymn 582; and "Jesus, remember me," hymn 599, are excerpts from the English translation of *The Roman Missal* © 1973, International Committee on English in the Liturgy, Inc. All rights reserved.

Published by Westminster/John Knox Press, 100 Witherspoon Street, Louisville, Kentucky 40202-1396.

PRINTED IN THE U.S.A. ON ACID-FREE PAPER.
15   14   13   12

Library of Congress Cataloging-in-Publication Data

The Presbyterian hymnal.

1. Hymns, English—United States. 2. Presbyterian Church (U.S.A.)—Hymns.
M2130.P8   1990   89-28142
ISBN 0-664-10097-X (Pew ed.)
ISBN 0-664-10099-6 (Leather ed.)
ISBN 0-664-10096-1 (Accompanist ed.)
ISBN 0-664-10098-8 (Large type ed.)
ISBN 0-664-10110-0 (Ecumenical ed.)

ORGANIZATION OF THE HYMNAL

TOPICAL HYMNS

PREFACE

The General Assemblies of 1980 and 1983 directed that a hymnal be developed "using inclusive language and sensitive to the diverse nature" of the church. The Program Agency and the General Assembly Mission Board responded by creating a hymnbook committee of eighteen persons, reflecting the breadth and diversity of the church. The group included hymnologists and professional musicians. Members of the committee, which was established in accordance with General Assembly guidelines, were from small and large churches and represented the ethnic diversity of the denomination. They sought to affirm the centrality of the sacraments, ecumenical and mission dimensions, the perspectives of women, and the concerns of youth and age.

The committee began its work in April 1985 and concluded the selection process in July 1989. Members of the Theology and Worship Unit, present at the final meeting, approved the Hymnal Committee's work and commend *The Presbyterian Hymnal: Hymns, Psalms, and Spiritual Songs* to the church at large.

Seventeen meetings were held, along with countless subcommittee meetings. The locations reached across the church, from San Francisco to Newark and from San Antonio to Pittsburgh. When schedules permitted, local forums were held so the committee could interpret its work as well as meet with and hear from Presbyterians of all viewpoints.

Presbyterians live in a church and a world much changed since *The Hymnbook* (1955) and *The Worshipbook* (1972) were published. Political, social, theological, cultural, and economic changes have brought a different day, a different constituency, and a different agenda to the church. In light of such developments, the committee made conscious efforts to recognize various racial and ethnic musical traditions in the church and to express them, taking into account their influence on past, present, and future hymnody. Committee members consulted groups outside the committee who were asked to suggest music from their traditions. Members of racial and/or ethnic groups (African-American, Asian, Native American, and Hispanic) brought hymns to the committee for discussion, referral to subcommittees, and possible inclusion. The committee also examined materials solicited and contributed from the gospel tradition and from evangelical publications.

The aim of the committee has been to provide a book for congregational singing with the expectation that all who use it may be enriched by hymns from gospel, evangelical, Reformed, racial, and ethnic traditions in the church. May Presbyterians be renewed and revived in singing their faith, that worship may call the church in this day to obey Jesus Christ.

Melva W. Costen, Chairperson   Betty Peek
Andrew Blunt   Sofia Porter
Jackie Chambless   John Rodland (deceased October 1989)
Lesley A. Davies   José A. Rodriguez
Charles R. Ehrhardt   Robert Stigall
Jane Parker Huber   Barbara Stout
May Murakami Nakagawa   John Weaver
David C. Partington   Sharon K. Youngs
Joy F. Patterson   James R. Sydnor, Consultant

Bonnie Karnes, Administrative Assistant
Robert H. Kempes, Administrative Staff
James G. Kirk, Consultant and Secretary
LindaJo McKim, Editor

INTRODUCTION

As the Presbyterian hymnal committee began its work in the spring of 1985, the immediate task was to develop a rationale for choosing the hymns that would be included in the collection. The committee was determined not to perform this task in a vacuum. Through the use of a brief questionnaire it sought to reach as many persons across the church as possible. Replies as to what the church wanted in a hymnal came in by the hundreds and were carefully reviewed. This process contributed to the development of a survey for Presbyterian Panel members and church musicians. In addition, questions were asked of racial and ethnic churches. As anticipated, the Panel brought significant data to the committee. As a result of this information, the committee adopted working guidelines which have served to assure that the hymnal:

- Is singable and playable
- Includes 600 hymns, psalms, and spiritual songs, and some service music—hymns old and new, traditional and contemporary, ethnically diverse, and offering expressions of faith both corporate and individual
- Includes hymns relating to Reformed doctrines, the lectionary, seasons of the church year, sacraments, ordinances, and the ministry and mission of the church
- Embraces the diversity of our historical traditions while providing a prophetic vision for the future
- Expresses a full range of biblical images for the Persons of the Trinity
- Is inclusive of all God's people—sensitive to age, race, gender, physical limitations, and language
- Has a complete set of indexes as helps for leaders and participants in worship

The next step in the process was to develop a list of hymns from the two most recent Presbyterian collections, *The Worshipbook* (1972) and *The Hymnbook* (1955). To this core were added the Hymn Society of America's hymns recommended for ecumenical use.

The two major subcommittees, music and text, separately reviewed each suggested hymn, made revisions when needed to comply with the guidelines, and brought recommendations to the full committee for discussion and vote. Every recommended hymn was sung through in its entirety before a vote was taken. This ensured the full participation of the committee in every decision.

Once the basic core list was approved, the committee began searching for new hymns. All major hymn collections published in the past ten years were studied. More than 2,500 unsolicited and unpublished new hymns were reviewed, as well as hundreds of referred hymns, including many by authors and composers of the present generation.

ORGANIZATION

One of the unique features of the new hymnal is its organization. The collection is divided into four sections:

The first of these is the church year. For the first time in our history Presbyterians have a hymnal that opens with an Advent hymn. As the church year begins, we open the hymnal to the front and move through its pages as we follow the life of Christ.

The psalms, which have long been a traditional element of Presbyterian worship, come next. At some points in our history they have been more used than at others. Today's emphasis on the use of scripture in worship through the lectionary readings has brought renewed interest in psalmody. Contemporary composers and authors have provided a wealth of fresh material and forms. The psalm subcommittee reviewed hundreds of ancient and modern psalm versions in order to ensure that the church would recover this Presbyterian and Reformed tradition for today. All the psalms included appear in the three-year lectionary for Sunday worship.

The third section is the largest and is arranged topically. Included are creedal topics: hymns about God, Jesus Christ, and the Holy Spirit, for example. Among its other hymns are those used in particular aspects of worship, including the sacraments and ordinances of the church.

The final section consists of service music. Included are pieces recommended for Sunday morning worship as well as those canticles used in morning and evening prayer.

INSTRUCTIONS

Throughout the collection there are music and text instructions. These appear as asterisk (*) and/or italicized information. There are optional musical instructions, suggested instrumentations, and possible wording changes.

When a tune is new to the Presbyterian tradition, the committee has a metronome range to indicate the tempo, e.g.: (♩ = 76–84).

Also included are footnotes suggesting alternate keys, alternate harmonizations, or other tunes to which a particular text may be sung.

Throughout the collection cue-size notes indicate optional use.

The word "fauxbourdon" is applied to a harmonization in which the melody appears in the tenor voice and should be sung in unison by the congregation while the accompanist plays that setting.

When a hymn has a direct scriptural reference, that reference appears on the top of the page opposite the running head. When there is more than one reference, the symbol of an open Bible 📖 appears next to the reference. Additional references may be found in the scriptural index. Simple allusions do not appear on the hymn page, but are confined to the index.

Most of the psalms are set metrically; however, some are pointed for singing. These also may be read responsively. The texts to these responsorial psalms are from the *New Revised Standard Version Bible*. The texts are pointed with a grave accent (`) at the mediant cadence and an acute accent (´) at the final cadence. Occasionally, when the tone contains a flex, this is indicated by a horizontal line over the affected syllable (‾).

When chanting the psalms, one must never fall into the trap of automatically stressing the first note of the cadence. At times the stress will fall on another syllable just before the cadence. The natural word stress must be maintained in order to ensure an intelligible performance. The text must always dominate the music. The example below, from Psalm 33, illustrates these principles. The stressed syllables are "joice," "Lord," and "righ." In performance the first cadence becomes:

Re - joice   in   the   Lord,   Ò   you   righ - teous.

The Presbyterian Church (U.S.A.) owes a great deal to the members of the hymnal committee, who volunteered their time and energies to the hymnal project.

The editor wishes to express gratitude to the following people for their unique contributions made on behalf of the hymnal: to Robert C. Dentan for his division of the psalms for responsive reading; to Robert Batastini for his pointing of the psalms for singing; and to Samuel Yun and Myung Ja Yue for their transliteration of Korean characters.

The talented women and men who offered their expertise in the editing and production process are also to be thanked.

September 1989   LJM

AIDS TO WORSHIP

SERVICE FOR THE LORD'S DAY

ASSEMBLE IN GOD'S NAME

Gathering of the People
Call to Worship
Hymn of Praise, Psalm, or Spiritual
Confession and Pardon
Act of Praise
The Peace

PROCLAIM GOD'S WORD

Prayer for Illumination or Prayer for the Day
First Lesson
Psalm
Second Lesson
Hymn, Spiritual, or Anthem
Gospel Lesson
Sermon
Creed or Affirmation of Faith
Hymn or Spiritual
(Baptism or an Ordinance of the Church)
Prayers of Intercession
Offering

GIVE THANKS TO GOD

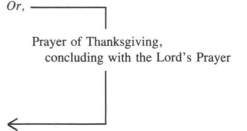

Preparation of the Table

Great Prayer of Thanksgiving,
   concluding with the Lord's Prayer

Breaking of the Bread

Communion of the People

Or,

Prayer of Thanksgiving,
   concluding with the Lord's Prayer

GO IN GOD'S NAME

Hymn, Spiritual, or Psalm
Charge and Blessing
Going Forth

GREAT PRAYER OF THANKSGIVING

The Lord be with you.
And also with you.
Lift up your hearts.
We lift them to the Lord.
Let us give thanks to the Lord our God.
It is right to give our thanks and praise.

*The minister gives thanks appropriate to the occasion,
remembering God's mighty acts of salvation. The congregation
then sings or says the song of praise sung without ceasing
by the hosts of heaven and by the faithful from every time
and place:*

Holy, holy, holy Lord, God of power and might,
heaven and earth are full of your glory.
   Hosanna in the highest.
Blessed is he who comes in the name of the Lord.
   Hosanna in the highest.

*The minister continues the thanksgiving, recalling Christ's
work of redemption and gift of the Sacrament. One of the
following memorial acclamations is then sung or said by the
congregation:*

Christ has died,		**When we eat this bread and drink**
Christ is risen,	*Or,*	**this cup, we proclaim your death,**
Christ will come again.		**Lord Jesus, until you come in glory.**

Or, Or,

We remember his death,	**Dying you destroyed our death,**
we proclaim his resurrection,	**rising you restored our life.**
we await his coming in glory.	**Lord Jesus, come in glory.**

*The action of the Holy Spirit is sought, and petitions are
offered that we may know the unity we have in Christ and be
empowered for service.*

The prayer concludes with praise to the Triune God.

Amen.
Our Father . . .

THE APOSTLES' CREED (Traditional)

I believe in God the Father Almighty, Maker of heaven and earth,

And in Jesus Christ his only Son our Lord; who was conceived by the Holy Ghost, born of the Virgin Mary, suffered under Pontius Pilate, was crucified, dead, and buried; he descended into hell; the third day he rose again from the dead; he ascended into heaven, and sitteth on the right hand of God the Father Almighty; from thence he shall come to judge the quick and the dead.

I believe in the Holy Ghost; the holy catholic church; the communion of saints; the forgiveness of sins; the resurrection of the body; and the life everlasting. Amen.

THE APOSTLES' CREED (Ecumenical)

I believe in God, the Father almighty, creator of heaven and earth.

I believe in Jesus Christ, God's only Son, our Lord, who was conceived by the Holy Spirit, born of the Virgin Mary, suffered under Pontius Pilate, was crucified, died, and was buried; he descended to the dead. On the third day he rose again; he ascended into heaven, he is seated at the right hand of the Father, and he will come to judge the living and the dead.

I believe in the Holy Spirit, the holy catholic Church, the communion of saints, the forgiveness of sins, the resurrection of the body, and the life everlasting. Amen.

EL CREDO DE LOS APOSTOLES (Spanish)

Creo en Dios Padre Todopoderoso, Creador del cielo y de la tierra; y en Jesucristo, su único Hijo, Señor nuestro; que fue concebido del Espíritu Santo, nació de la virgen María, padeció bajo el poder de Poncio Pilato; fue crucificado, muerto y sepultado; descendió a los infiernos; al tercer día resucitó de entre los muertos; subió al cielo y está sentado a la diestra de Dios Padre Todopoderoso; y desde allí vendrá al fin del mundo a juzgar a los vivos y a los muertos.

Creo en el Espíritu Santo, la Santa Iglesia Universal, la comunión de los santos, el perdón de los pecados, la resurrección del cuerpo y la vida perdurable. Amén.

SAH DOH SHIN KYUNG (Korean)

Chun nung ha sah chun jee rul mahn duh shin ha nah nim ah buh jee rul nae gah mid sah oh myu, Keu way ah dul oo ree joo Yesu Christo rul mid sah oh nee ee nun sung shin uh ro eeng tae ha sah dong jung nyu Maria eh geh nah she go, Pontiu Pilato eh geh go nahn ul bah duh sah, Seep ja gah eh mot pah kyu juk uh she go, Chang sah hahn jee sah hul mahn eh chuk un jah gah oon deh suh dah she sah rah nah she myu, Ha nul eh oh ruh sah, Chun nun ha shin ha nah nim oo pyun eh ahn jah keh she dah gah, Chu ree ro suh sahn jah wa chuk un jah rul shim pahn ha ruh oh she ree rah. Sung shin ul mid sah oh myu, Kuh ruk hahn kong hoe wa sung doh gah suh ro kyo tong ha nun gut gwa chway rul sah ha yuh joo she nun gut gwa, Mohm ee dah she sah nun gut gwa, Young won he sah nun guh sul mid sah om nah ee dah. Amen.

THE NICENE CREED (Traditional)

We believe in one God the Father Almighty, Maker of heaven and earth, and of all things visible and invisible;

And in one Lord Jesus Christ, the only-begotten Son of God, begotten of the Father before all worlds, God of God, Light of Light, Very God of Very God, begotten, not made, being of one substance with the Father by whom all things were made; who for us men, and for our salvation, came down from heaven, and was incarnate by the Holy Spirit of the Virgin Mary, and was made man, and was crucified also for us under Pontius Pilate. He suffered and was buried, and the third day he rose again according to the Scriptures, and ascended into heaven, and sitteth on the right hand of the Father. And he shall come again with glory to judge both the quick and the dead, whose kingdom shall have no end.

And we believe in the Holy Spirit, the Lord and Giver of Life, who proceedeth from the Father and the Son, who with the Father and the Son together is worshiped and glorified, who spoke by the prophets. And we believe one holy catholic and apostolic church. We acknowledge one baptism for the remission of sins. And we look for the resurrection of the dead, and the life of the world to come. Amen.

THE NICENE CREED (Ecumenical)

We believe in one God, the Father, the Almighty, maker of heaven and earth, of all that is, seen and unseen.

We believe in one Lord, Jesus Christ, the only Son of God, eternally begotten of the Father, God from God, Light from Light, true God from true God, begotten, not made, of one Being with the Father; through him all things were made. For us and for our salvation he came down from heaven, was incarnate of the Holy Spirit and the Virgin Mary and became truly human. For our sake he was crucified under Pontius Pilate; he suffered death and was buried. On the third day he rose again in accordance with the Scriptures; he ascended into heaven and is seated on the right hand of the Father. He will come again in glory to judge the living and the dead, and his kingdom will have no end.

We believe in the Holy Spirit, the Lord, the giver of life, who proceeds from the Father (and the Son), who with the Father and the Son is worshiped and glorified, who has spoken through the prophets. We believe in one holy catholic and apostolic Church. We acknowledge one baptism for the forgiveness of sins. We look for the resurrection of the dead, and the life of the world to come. Amen.

THE LORD'S PRAYER (Traditional)

Our Father who art in heaven, hallowed be thy name. Thy kingdom come, thy will be done, on earth as it is in heaven. Give us this day our daily bread; and forgive us our debts, as we forgive our debtors; and lead us not into temptation, but deliver us from evil. For thine is the kingdom and the power and the glory, forever. Amen.

THE LORD'S PRAYER (Ecumenical)

Our Father in heaven,
  hallowed be your name,
  your kingdom come,
  your will be done,
    on earth as in heaven.
Give us today our daily bread.
Forgive us our sins
  as we forgive those who sin against us.
Save us from the time of trial
  and deliver us from evil.

For the kingdom, the power, and the glory are yours
  now and for ever. Amen.

EL PADRE NUESTRO (Spanish)

Padre nuestro, que estás en los cielos, santificado sea tu nombre. Venga tu reino. Sea hecha tu voluntad, como en el cielo, así también en la tierra.

El pan nuestro de cada día, dánoslo hoy.

Y perdónanos nuestras deudas, como también nosotros perdonamos a nuestros deudores.

Y no nos dejes caer en tentación, mas líbranos del mal. Porque tuyo es el reino, el poder, y la gloria, por todos los siglos. Amén.

JOO GEE DOH MOON (Korean)

Ha neul eh geh shin oo ree ah buh jee, Ee rum ul kuh ruk ha geh ha op see myu, Nah rah ee im ha op see myu, Dduh see ha neul eh suh ee roon gut gah chee ddahng eh suh do ee ru uh jee ee dah. Oh neul nahl oo ree eh geh eel yong hahl yahng sig ul joo op see go, Oo ree gah oo ree eh geh chway jee un jah rul sah ha yuh joon gut gah chee oo ree eh chway rul sah ha yuh joo op see go, Oo ree rul she hum eh deul jee mahl geh ha op see go, Dah mahn ark eh suh koo ha op so suh. Nah rah wa kwon seh wa young Kwahng ee ah buh jee kkeh young won he ees sah om nah ee dah. Amen.

CHRISTIAN YEAR

Come, Thou Long-Expected Jesus 1

STUTTGART 8.7.8.7

Charles Wesley, 1744

Witt's *Psalmodia Sacra*, 1715; alt.

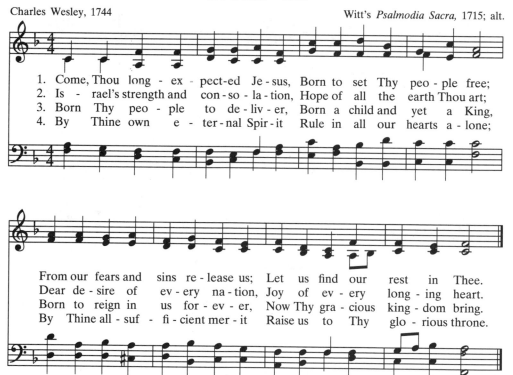

1. Come, Thou long-ex-pect-ed Je-sus, Born to set Thy peo-ple free;
2. Is-rael's strength and con-so-la-tion, Hope of all the earth Thou art;
3. Born Thy peo-ple to de-liv-er, Born a child and yet a King,
4. By Thine own e-ter-nal Spir-it Rule in all our hearts a-lone;

From our fears and sins re-lease us; Let us find our rest in Thee.
Dear de-sire of ev-ery na-tion, Joy of ev-ery long-ing heart.
Born to reign in us for-ev-er, Now Thy gra-cious king-dom bring.
By Thine all-suf-fi-cient mer-it Raise us to Thy glo-rious throne.

Alternate tune: HYFRYDOL, 2

2 Come, Thou Long-Expected Jesus

HYFRYDOL 8.7.8.7 D

Charles Wesley, 1744

Rowland Hugh Prichard, 1831

1. Come, Thou long-ex-pect-ed Je-sus, Born to set Thy
2. Born Thy peo-ple to de-liv-er, Born a child and

peo-ple free; From our fears and sins re-lease us;
yet a King, Born to reign in us for-ev-er,

Let us find our rest in Thee. Is-rael's strength and con-so-
Now Thy gra-cious king-dom bring. By Thine own e-ter-nal

la-tion, Hope of all the earth Thou art; Dear de-sire of
Spir-it Rule in all our hearts a-lone; By Thine all-suf-

ev-ery na-tion, Joy of ev-ery long-ing heart.
fi-cient mer-it Raise us to Thy glo-rious throne.

Alternate tune: STUTTGART, 1

Comfort, Comfort You My People

3

PSALM 42   8.7.8.7.7.7.8.8

Johannes Olearius, 1671
Trans. Catherine Winkworth, 1863; alt.

Genevan Psalter, 1551

1. Com-fort, com - fort you my peo - ple, Tell of peace, thus says our God;
2. For the her - ald's voice is call - ing In the des - ert far and near,
3. Make you straight what long was crook-ed, Make the rough - er plac - es plain;

Com-fort those who sit in dark-ness Bowed be-neath op - pres-sion's load.
Bid - ding us to make re - pent-ance Since the king-dom now is here.
Let your hearts be true and hum - ble, As be - fits God's ho - ly reign.

Speak you to Je - ru - sa - lem Of the peace that waits for them;
O that warn - ing cry o - bey! Now pre-pare for God a way;
For the glo - ry of the Lord Now o'er earth is shed a - broad;

Tell them that their sins I cov - er, And their war - fare now is o - ver.
Let the val - leys rise in meet-ing And the hills bow down in greet-ing.
And all flesh shall see the to - ken That God's word is nev - er bro - ken.

4 Creator of the Stars of Night

CONDITOR ALME SIDERUM LM

Latin hymn, 9th century
Trans. John Mason Neale, 1851
As in *The Hymnal 1940;* alt.

Sarum plainsong, Mode IV, 9th century
Harm. C. Winfred Douglas, 1943

1. Cre - a - tor of the stars of night, Your peo - ple's ev - er -
2. When this old world drew on toward night, You came, but not in
3. At Your great name, O Je - sus, now All knees must bend, all
4. To God the Fa - ther, God the Son, And God the Spir - it,

last - ing light, O Christ, Re - deem - er of us all,
splen - dor bright, Not as a mon - arch, but the child
hearts must bow: All things on earth with one ac - cord,
Three in One, Praise, hon - or, might, and glo - ry be

We pray You, hear us when we call.
Of Ma - ry, blame - less moth - er mild.
Like those in heaven, shall call You Lord.
From age to age e - ter - nal - ly. A - men.

Let All Mortal Flesh Keep Silence 5

PICARDY 8.7.8.7.8.7

From Liturgy of St. James, 4th century
Trans. Gerard Moultrie, 1864

French carol
Harm. *The English Hymnal*, 1906

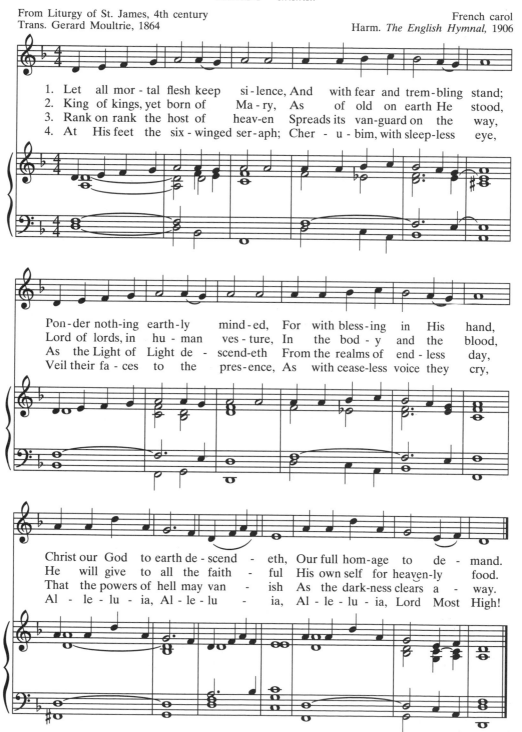

1. Let all mor-tal flesh keep si-lence, And with fear and trem-bling stand;
2. King of kings, yet born of Ma-ry, As of old on earth He stood,
3. Rank on rank the host of heav-en Spreads its van-guard on the way,
4. At His feet the six-winged ser-aph; Cher-u-bim, with sleep-less eye,

Pon-der noth-ing earth-ly mind-ed, For with bless-ing in His hand,
Lord of lords, in hu-man ves-ture, In the bod-y and the blood,
As the Light of Light de-scend-eth From the realms of end-less day,
Veil their fa-ces to the pres-ence, As with cease-less voice they cry,

Christ our God to earth de-scend - eth, Our full hom-age to de - mand.
He will give to all the faith - ful His own self for heav-en-ly food.
That the powers of hell may van - ish As the dark-ness clears a - way.
Al - le-lu - ia, Al-le-lu - ia, Al - le-lu - ia, Lord Most High!

6 Jesus Comes with Clouds Descending

HELMSLEY   8.7.8.7.4.4.4.7

Thomas Olivers, 1763
Harm. Ralph Vaughan Williams, 1906

Charles Wesley, 1758; alt.

1. Je - sus comes with clouds de - scend-ing; See the
2. Ev - ery eye shall then be - hold You Robed in
3. Yes, A - men! Let all a - dore You High on

Lamb for sin - ners slain! Thou - sand, thou - sand
awe - some ma - jes - ty; Those who jeered and
your e - ter - nal throne; Crowns and em - pires

saints at - tend - ing Join to sing the glad re -
mocked and sold You, Pierced and nailed You to the
fall be - fore You, Claim the king - dom for Your

frain: Al - le - lu - ia!   Al - le - lu - ia!
tree,   Shamed and griev - ing,   Shamed and griev - ing,
own: Come, Lord Je - sus,   Come, Lord Je - sus,

Al - le - lu - ia!   Christ the Lord re - turns to reign!
Shamed and griev - ing,   Shall their true Mes - si - ah see.
Come, Lord Je - sus,   Ev - er - last - ing Christ, come down!

Lord Christ,
When First You Came to Earth

7

MIT FREUDEN ZART   8.7.8.7.8.8.7

Walter Russell Bowie, 1928; alt.

Bohemian Brethren's *Kirchengesang,* 1566

1. Lord Christ, when first You came to earth, Up-on a cross they bound You, And mocked Your sav-ing king-ship then By thorns with which they crowned You; And still our wrongs may weave You now New thorns to pierce that

2. O won-drous love, which found no room In life, where sin de-nied You, And, doomed to death, must bring to doom The power which cru-ci-fied You, Till not a stone was left on stone, And all a na-tion's

3. New ad-vent of the love of Christ, Shall we a-gain re-fuse You, Till in the night of hate and war We per-ish as we lose You? From old un-faith our souls re-lease To seek the king-dom

4. O wound-ed hands of Je-sus, build In us Your new cre-a-tion; Our pride is dust, our vaunt is stilled, We wait Your rev-e-la-tion. O Love that tri-umphs o-ver loss, We bring our hearts be-

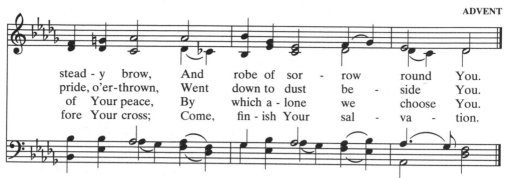

stead - y brow, And robe of sor - row round You.
pride, o'er-thrown, Went down to dust be - side You.
of Your peace, By which a - lone we choose You.
fore Your cross; Come, fin - ish Your sal - va - tion.

This tune in a higher key, 483

Psalm 24:7–10

Lift Up Your Heads, Ye Mighty Gates 8

TRURO LM

Georg Weissel, 1642
Trans. Catherine Winkworth, 1855

Thomas Williams, 1789
Harm. Lowell Mason (1792–1872)

1. Lift up your heads, ye might - y gates, Be - hold, the
2. Fling wide the por - tals of your heart; Make it a
3. Re - deem - er, come! I o - pen wide My heart to

King of glo - ry waits; The King of kings is
tem - ple, set a - part From earth - ly use for
Thee; here, Lord, a - bide. Let me Thy in - ner

draw - ing near; The Sav - ior of the world is here!
heaven's em - ploy, A - dorned with prayer, and love, and joy.
pres - ence feel; Thy grace and love in me re - veal.

9 O Come, O Come, Emmanuel

VENI EMMANUEL   LM with refrain

Latin, c. 12th century
Stanzas 1–2 trans. John Mason Neale, 1851; alt. 1854
Stanza 3 trans. Henry Sloane Coffin, 1916

Adapt. Thomas Helmore, 1854
Accomp. John Weaver, 1988

1. O come, O come, Em-man-u-el, And ran-som cap-tive Is-ra-el, That mourns in lone-ly ex-ile here Un-til the Son of God ap-pear.
2. O come, Thou Day-spring, come and cheer Our spir-its by Thine ad-vent here; Dis-perse the gloom-y clouds of night, And death's dark shad-ows put to flight. Re-joice! Re-joice!
3. O come, De-sire of na-tions, bind All peo-ples in one heart and mind; Bid en-vy, strife, and dis-cord cease; Fill the whole world with heav-en's peace.

Em - man - u - el Shall come to thee, O Is - ra - el!

Matthew 3:1–3

On Jordan's Bank the Baptist's Cry 10

WINCHESTER NEW LM

Charles Coffin, 1736
Trans. John Chandler, 1837; alt.

Musikalisches Handbuch, 1690
Harm. William Henry Monk, 1847; alt.

1. On Jor - dan's bank the Bap - tist's cry An -
2. Then cleansed be ev - ery life from sin; Make
3. We hail You as our Sav - ior, Lord, Our
4. All praise to You, e - ter - nal Son, Whose

noun - ces that the Lord is nigh; A - wake and heark - en,
straight the way for God with - in, And let us all our
ref - uge, and our great re - ward; O let Your face up -
ad - vent has our free - dom won, Whom with the Fa - ther

for he brings Glad tid - ings of the King of kings!
hearts pre - pare For Christ to come and en - ter there.
on us shine And fill the world with love di - vine.
we a - dore, And Ho - ly Spir - it, ev - er - more.

11 O Lord, How Shall I Meet You?

VALET WILL ICH DIR GEBEN   7.6.7.6 D

Paul Gerhardt, 1653
Trans. Catherine Winkworth and others, 1863; alt.

Melchior Teschner, 1614
Harm. William Henry Monk, 1861

1. O Lord, how shall I meet You, How wel - come You a - right?
2. Love caused Your in - car - na - tion, Love brought You down to me;
3. A glo - rious crown You give me, A trea - sure safe on high,

Your peo - ple long to greet You, My hope, my heart's de - light!
Your thirst for my sal - va - tion Pro - cured my lib - er - ty.
That will not fail nor leave me As earth - ly rich - es fly.

O kin - dle, Lord most ho - ly, A lamp with - in my breast,
O love be - yond all tell - ing, That led You to em - brace
My heart shall bloom for - ev - er For You with prais - es new,

To do in spir - it low - ly All that may please You best.
In love all loves ex - cel - ling Our lost and fall - en race.
And from Your name shall nev - er With - hold the hon - or due.

People, Look East

12

BESANÇON 8.7.9.8.8.7

Eleanor Farjeon (1881–1965)
As in *Oxford Book of Carols*, 1964

French folk melody
Harm. Martin Shaw (1875–1958)

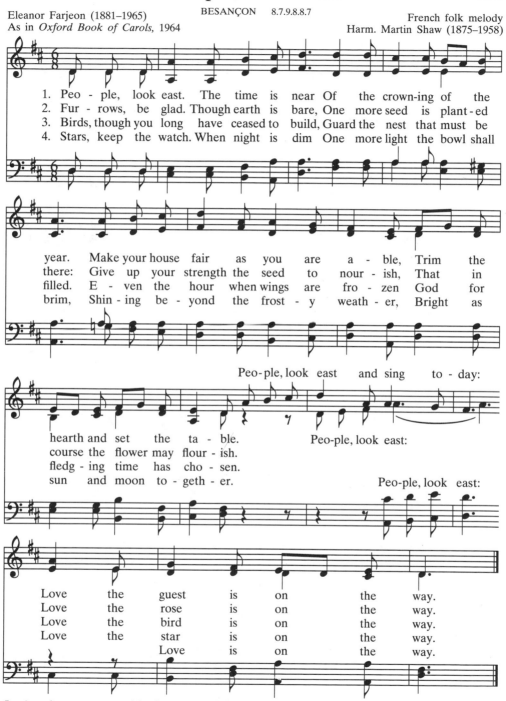

1. Peo - ple, look east. The time is near Of the crown-ing of the
2. Fur - rows, be glad. Though earth is bare, One more seed is plant-ed
3. Birds, though you long have ceased to build, Guard the nest that must be
4. Stars, keep the watch. When night is dim One more light the bowl shall

year. Make your house fair as you are a - ble, Trim the
there: Give up your strength the seed to nour - ish, That in
filled. E - ven the hour when wings are fro - zen God for
brim, Shin - ing be - yond the frost - y weath - er, Bright as

Peo - ple, look east and sing to - day:

hearth and set the ta - ble. Peo - ple, look east:
course the flower may flour - ish.
fledg - ing time has cho - sen.
sun and moon to - geth - er. Peo - ple, look east:

Love the guest is on the way.
Love the rose is on the way.
Love the bird is on the way.
Love the star is on the way.
Love is on the way.

5. Angels, announce with shouts of mirth   With the word, the Lord is coming.
   Christ who brings new life to earth.   People, look east and sing today:
   Set every peak and valley humming   Love the Lord is on the way.

13 Prepare the Way

BEREDEN VÄG FÖR HERRAN 7.6.7.6.7.7 with refrain

Frans Mikael Franzen (1771–1847)
Adapt. Charles P. Price, 1980; alt. 1989

Then Swenska Psalmboken, 1697
Arr. *American Lutheran Hymnal*, 1930

1. Pre - pare the way, O Zi - on, Your Christ is draw - ing near!
2. Christ brings God's rule, O Zi - on; He comes from heaven a - bove.
3. Fling wide your gates, O Zi - on; Your Sav - ior's rule em - brace.

Let ev - ery hill and val - ley A lev - el way ap - pear.
His rule is peace and free - dom, And jus - tice, truth, and love.
And tid - ings of sal - va - tion Pro - claim in ev - ery place.

Greet One who comes in glo - ry, Fore - told in sa - cred sto - ry.
Lift high your praise re - sound - ing, For grace and joy a - bound - ing.
All lands will bow re - joic - ing, Their ad - o - ra - tion voic - ing.

Text: Adaptation © 1985 Charles P. Price. Used by permission.

Refrain

O blest is Christ that came In God's most ho - ly name.

♩ =63–69

Savior of the Nations, Come

14

NUN KOMM, DER HEIDEN HEILAND   7.7.7.7

Attr. Ambrose of Milan, 4th century
Para. Martin Luther, 1524
Trans. William Morton Reynolds, 1850

Based on plainsong melody
Eyn Enchiridion, Erfurt, 1524
As in *Songs of Syon,* 1910

1. Sav - ior of the na - tions, come, Vir - gin's Son, make here Your home.
2. From the God-head forth You came, And re - turn un - to the same,
3. You, the cho - sen Ho - ly One, Have o'er sin the vic - tory won.
4. Bright-ly does Your man - ger shine, Glo - rious is its light di - vine.

Mar - vel now, O heaven and earth, That the Lord chose such a birth.
Cap - tive lead-ing death and hell. High the song of tri - umph swell!
Bound-less shall Your king - dom be; When shall we its glo - ries see?
Let not sin o'er - cloud this light; Ev - er be our faith thus bright.

15 Rejoice! Rejoice, Believers

LLANGLOFFAN 7.6.7.6 D

Laurentius Laurenti, 1700
Trans. Sarah Borthwick Findlater, 1854
Alt. *The Hymnal 1982*

Welsh folk melody
Evans' *Hymnau a Thonau*, 1865
As in *English Hymnal*, 1906

1. Re - joice! Re - joice, be - liev - ers, And let your lights ap - pear;
2. See that your lamps are burn - ing, Re - plen - ish them with oil;
3. Our hope and ex - pec - ta - tion, O Je - sus, now ap - pear;

The eve - ning is ad - vanc - ing And dark - er night is near.
Look now for your sal - va - tion, The end of sin and toil.
A - rise, Thou sun so longed for, A - bove this sha - dowed sphere!

The Bride-groom is a - ris - ing And soon He will draw nigh;
The mar - riage feast is wait - ing, The gates wide o - pen stand;
With hearts and hands up - lift - ed, We plead, O Lord, to see

Up, watch with ex - pec - ta - tion, At mid - night comes the cry.
A - rise, O heirs of glo - ry, The Bride-groom is at hand!
The day of earth's re - demp - tion, And ev - er be with Thee!

The Angel Gabriel from Heaven Came 16

GABRIEL'S MESSAGE 10.10.12.10

Para. Sabine Baring-Gould (1834–1924)

Basque carol
Arr. by Edgar Pettman and John Wickham

1. The an - gel Ga - bri - el from heav - en came, His
2. "For know a bless - ed moth - er you shall be, All
3. Then gen - tle Ma - ry meek - ly bowed her head, "To
4. Of her, Em-man - u - el, the Christ, was born In

wings as drift - ed snow, his eyes as flame; "All
gen - er - a - tions praise con - tin - ual - ly, Your
me be as it pleas - es God," she said, "My
Beth - le - hem, all on a Christ - mas morn, And

hail," said he, "O low - ly maid - en Ma - ry,"
Son shall be Em - man - u - el, by seers fore - told."
soul shall laud and mag - ni - fy God's ho - ly name."
Chris - tian folk through-out the world will ev - er say:

Most

high - ly fa - vored la - dy, Glo - ri - a!

J. = 63–69

17 "Sleepers, Wake!" A Voice Astounds Us

WACHET AUF   Irregular

Philipp Nicolai, 1599
Trans. Carl P. Daw, Jr., 1982

Attr. Philipp Nicolai, 1599
Harm. Johann Sebastian Bach, 1731

1. "Sleep-ers, wake!" A voice as - tounds us; The shout of ram-part
2. Zi - on hears the watch-men sing - ing, Her heart with joy - ful
3. Lamb of God, the heavens a - dore You; Let saints and an - gels

guards sur - rounds us: "A - wake, Je - ru - sa - lem, a - rise!"
hope is spring - ing; She wakes and hur - ries through the night.
sing be - fore You, As harps and cym - bals swell the sound.

Mid - night's peace their cry has bro - ken, Their ur - gent sum - mons
Forth He comes, her Bride-groom glo - rious In strength of grace, in
Twelve great pearls, the cit - y's por - tals: Through them we stream to

clear - ly spo - ken: "The time has come, O maid - ens wise!
truth vic - to - rious: Her star is risen, her light grows bright.
join the im - mor - tals As we with joy Your throne sur - round.

Rise up, and give us light; The Bride-groom is in sight.
Now come, most wor-thy Lord, God's Son, In-car-nate Word,
No eye has known the sight, No ear heard such de-light:

Al - le - lu - ia! Your lamps pre-pare and has-ten there,
Al - le - lu - ia! We fol-low all and heed Your call
Al - le - lu - ia! There-fore we sing to greet our King;

That you the wed-ding feast may share."
To come in-to the ban-quet hall.
For-ev-er let our prais-es ring.

18 The Desert Shall Rejoice

STERLING   6.6.8.8

Gracia Grindal, 1983

Joy F. Patterson, 1988

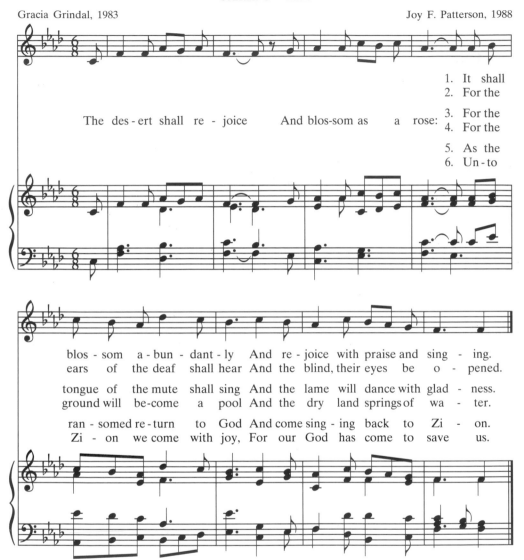

1. It shall
2. For the
3. For the
4. For the
5. As the
6. Un-to

The des-ert shall re-joice   And blos-som as   a   rose:

blos - som a - bun - dant - ly And re - joice with praise and sing - ing.
ears of the deaf shall hear And the blind, their eyes be o - pened.

tongue of the mute shall sing And the lame will dance with glad - ness.
ground will be - come a pool And the dry land springs of wa - ter.

ran - somed re - turn to God And come sing - ing back to Zi - on.
Zi - on we come with joy, For our God has come to save us.

To a Maid Engaged to Joseph

19

ANNUNCIATION   7.6.7.6.7.6

Gracia Grindal, 1984

Rusty Edwards, 1984

1. To a maid en-gaged to Jo-seph, The an-gel Ga-briel came.
2. "For you are high-ly fa-vored By God, the Lord of all,
3. But Ma-ry was most trou-bled To hear the an-gel's word.

4. "Fear not, for God is with you, And you shall bear a child.
5. "How shall this be?" said Ma-ry, "I am not yet a wife."
6. As Ma-ry heard the an-gel, She won-dered at his words.

"Fear not," the an-gel told her, "I come to bring good news.
Who e-ven now is with you. You are on earth most blest,
What was the an-gel say-ing? It trou-bled her to hear,

His name shall be called Je-sus, God's off-spring from on high.
The an-gel an-swered quick-ly "The power of the Most High
"Be-hold, I am your hand-maid," She said un-to her God.

Good news I come to tell you, Good news, I say, good news.
You are most blest, most bless-ed, God chose you, you are blest!"
To hear the an-gel's mess-age, It trou-bled her to hear.

And He shall reign for - ev - er, For - ev - er reign on high."
Will come up-on you short-ly; Your child will be God's child."
"So be it, I am read-y Ac-cord-ing to your Word."

20 Watchman, Tell Us of the Night

ABERYSTWYTH   7.7.7.7 D

John Bowring, 1825; alt. 1972

Joseph Parry, 1879

1. Watch-man, tell us of the night, What its signs of prom-ise are.
2. Watch-man, tell us of the night, High-er yet that star as-cends.
3. Watch-man, tell us of the night, For the morn-ing seems to dawn.

Trav-eler, o'er yon moun-tain's height, See that glo-ry - beam-ing star.
Trav-eler, bless-ed - ness and light, Peace and truth its course por-tends.
Trav-eler, dark-ness takes its flight, Doubt and ter-ror are with-drawn.

Watch-man, does its beau-teous ray Aught of joy or hope fore-tell?
Watch-man, will its beams a - lone Gild the spot that gave them birth?
Watch-man, let your wan-derings cease; Has-ten to your qui-et home.

Trav-eler, yes; it brings the day, Prom-ised day of Is-ra-el.
Trav-eler, a - ges are its own; See, it bursts o'er all the earth.
Trav-eler, lo, the Prince of Peace, Lo, the Son of God is come!

May be sung antiphonally.

This tune in a higher key, 303

Alternate tune: ST. GEORGE'S WINDSOR, 551

All My Heart Today Rejoices

21

WARUM SOLLT' ICH   8.3.3.6 D

Paul Gerhardt, 1653
Trans. Catherine Winkworth, 1858; alt.

Johann Georg Ebeling, 1666

1. All my heart to-day re-joic - es, As I hear,
2. Hark! A voice from yon-der man - ger, Soft and sweet,
3. Come, then, let us has-ten yon - der; Here let all,

Far and near, Sweet-est an-gel voic - es:
Does en - treat: "Flee from woe and dan - ger;
Great and small, Kneel in awe and won - der;

"Christ is born," their choirs are sing - ing, Till the air,
Come and see; from all that grieves you You are freed;
Love Him who with love is yearn - ing; Hail the star

Ev - ery - where, Now with joy is ring - ing.
All you need I will sure - ly give you."
That from far Bright with hope is burn - ing!

22 Angels, from the Realms of Glory

REGENT SQUARE   8.7.8.7.8.7

Stanzas 1–3, James Montgomery, 1816, 1825
Stanza 4, *Salisbury Hymn Book*, 1857

Henry Thomas Smart, 1867

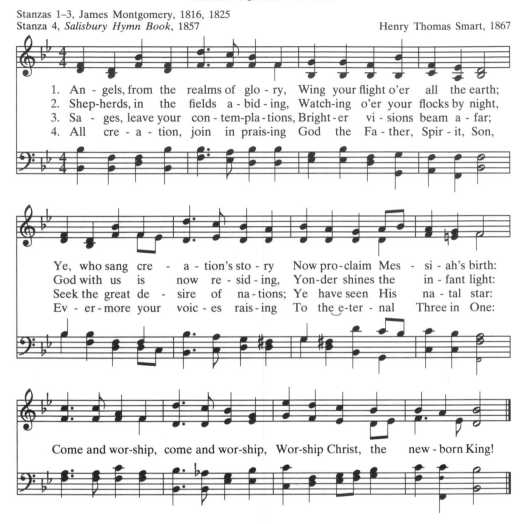

1. An - gels, from the realms of glo - ry, Wing your flight o'er all the earth;
2. Shep-herds, in the fields a - bid - ing, Watch-ing o'er your flocks by night,
3. Sa - ges, leave your con - tem-pla - tions, Bright-er vi - sions beam a - far;
4. All cre - a - tion, join in prais-ing God the Fa - ther, Spir - it, Son,

Ye, who sang cre - a - tion's sto - ry Now pro-claim Mes - si - ah's birth:
God with us is now re - sid - ing, Yon-der shines the in - fant light:
Seek the great de - sire of na - tions; Ye have seen His na - tal star:
Ev - er - more your voic - es rais-ing To the e-ter - nal Three in One:

Come and wor-ship, come and wor-ship, Wor-ship Christ, the new - born King!

Angels We Have Heard on High

23

French carol
Trans. James Chadwick (1813–1882); alt.

GLORIA 7.7.7.7 with refrain

French carol
Arr. Edward Shippen Barnes, 1937

1. An-gels we have heard on high, Sweet-ly sing-ing o'er the plains,
2. Shep-herds, why this ju-bi-lee? Why your joy-ous strains pro-long?
3. Come to Beth-le-hem and see Him whose birth the an-gels sing;

And the moun-tains in re-ply Ech-o-ing their joy-ous strains.
What the glad-some tid-ings be Which in-spire your heaven-ly song?
Come, a-dore on bend-ed knee Christ, the Lord, the new-born King.

Refrain

Glo - - - ri-a in ex-cel-sis De-o; Glo - - - - ri-a in ex-cel-sis De - o.

24   Away in a Manger

CRADLE SONG   11.11.11.11

Stanzas 1–2, *Little Children's Book*
for Schools and Families, c. 1885
Stanza 3, Gabriel's *Vineyard Songs*, 1892

William James Kirkpatrick, 1895

1. A - way in a man-ger, no crib for His bed, The lit - tle Lord
2. The cat - tle are low-ing, the poor Ba - by wakes, But lit - tle Lord
3. Be near me, Lord Je - sus; I ask Thee to stay Close by me for -

Je - sus laid down His sweet head. The stars in the bright sky looked
Je - sus, no cry - ing He makes. I love Thee, Lord Je - sus, look
ev - er and love me, I pray. Bless all the dear chil - dren in

down where He lay, The lit - tle Lord Je - sus, a - sleep on the hay.
down from the sky, And stay by my side un - til morn-ing is nigh.
Thy ten - der care, And fit us for heav-en to live with Thee there.

Away in a Manger

MUELLER   11.11.11.11

Stanzas 1–2, *Little Children's Book*
for Schools and Families, c. 1885
Stanza 3, Gabriel's *Vineyard Songs,* 1892

Attr. James R. Murray, 1887
Harm. John Weaver, 1986

25

1. A - way in a man-ger, no crib for His bed, The lit - tle Lord
2. The cat - tle are low-ing, the poor Ba - by wakes, But lit - tle Lord
3. Be near me, Lord Je - sus; I ask Thee to stay Close by me for -

Je - sus laid down His sweet head. The stars in the sky looked
Je - sus, no cry - ing He makes. I love Thee, Lord Je - sus, look
ev - er and love me, I pray. Bless all the dear chil - dren in

down where He lay, The lit - tle Lord Je - sus, a - sleep on the hay.
down from the sky, And stay by my side un - til morn-ing is nigh.
Thy ten - der care, And fit us for heav - en to live with Thee there.

26 Break Forth, O Beauteous Heavenly Light

ERMUNTRE DICH   8.7.8.7.8.8.7.7

Johann Rist, 1641
Trans. John Troutbeck, 1873

Johann Schop, 1641
Harm. Johann Sebastian Bach, 1734

Break forth, O beau-teous heaven-ly light, And ush-er in the

morn - ing. You shep-herds, shud-der not with fright, But

hear the an-gel's warn - ing. This Child, now weak in

in-fan-cy, Our con-fi-dence and joy shall be; The

power of Sa-tan break - ing, Our peace e-ter-nal mak - ing.

Gentle Mary Laid Her Child

27

TEMPUS ADEST FLORIDUM   7.6.7.6 D

Joseph Simpson Cook, 1919

Piae Cantiones, 1582
Arr. Ernest C. MacMillan, 1930

1. Gen-tle Ma-ry laid her child Low-ly in a man-ger;
2. An-gels sang a-bout His birth, Wise men sought and found Him;
3. Gen-tle Ma-ry laid her child Low-ly in a man-ger;

There He lay, the un-de-filed, To the world a stran-ger.
Heav-en's star shone bright-ly forth, Glo-ry all a-round Him.
He is still the un-de-filed, But no more a stran-ger.

Such a babe in such a place, Can He be the Sav-ior?
Shep-herds saw the won-drous sight, Heard the an-gels sing-ing;
Son of God, of hum-ble birth, Beau-ti-ful the sto-ry;

Ask the saved of all the race Who have found His fa-vor.
All the plains were lit that night, All the hills were ring-ing.
Praise His name in all the earth, Hail the King of glo-ry!

28 Good Christian Friends, Rejoice

IN DULCI JUBILO   6.6.7.7.7.8.5.5

Medieval Latin
Trans. and para. John Mason Neale, 1853; alt.

German folk tune, 14th century
Harm. David Hugh Jones, 1953

1. Good Chris-tian friends, re - joice   With heart, and soul, and voice;
2. Good Chris-tian friends, re - joice   With heart, and soul, and voice;
3. Good Chris-tian friends, re - joice   With heart, and soul, and voice;

Give ye heed to what we say: Je - sus Christ is born to - day;
Now ye hear of end - less bliss: Je - sus Christ was born for this!
Now ye need not fear the grave: Je - sus Christ was born to save!

Ox and ass be - fore Him bow, And He is in the man - ger now.
He hath o - pened heav - en's door, And we are blest for - ev - er-more.
Calls you one and calls you all To gain the ev - er - last - ing hall.

Christ is born to - day!   Christ is born to - day!
Christ was born for this!   Christ was born for this!
Christ was born to save!   Christ was born to save!

Music: Harmonization copyright, MCMLV, by John Ribble: renewed, 1983; adapted from *The Hymnbook,* published by Westminster Press.

Go, Tell It on the Mountain

29

GO TELL IT   7.6.7.6 with refrain

African-American spiritual
Arr. John W. Work III, 1940
Harm. and adapt. Melva Wilson Costen, 1987

Stanzas, John W. Work II (1872–1925)

Refrain

Go,   tell it on the moun - tain   O-ver the hills and   ev - ery - where;

Fine

Go,   tell it on the moun - tain That Je - sus Christ is   born!

1. While shep-herds kept their watch-ing   O'er   si - lent flocks by   night,
2. The   shep-herds feared and   trem-bled   When lo! a - bove the   earth,
3. Down   in a   low - ly   man - ger   The hum - ble Christ was   born,

D.C.

Be - hold through-out the heav-ens There shone a ho - ly   light.
Rang   out the   an - gel   cho - rus   That hailed our Sav - ior's   birth.
And   God   sent   us sal - va - tion That bless - ed Christ-mas   morn.

30 Born in the Night, Mary's Child

(MARY'S CHILD) 7.6.7.6

Geoffrey Ainger, 1964; alt.

Geoffrey Ainger, 1964
Harm. Richard D. Wetzel, 1972

1. Born in the night, Ma-ry's Child, A long way from Your home;
2. Clear shin-ing light, Ma-ry's Child, Your face lights up our way;
3. Truth of our life, Ma-ry's Child, You tell us God is good;
4. Hope of the world, Ma-ry's Child, You're com-ing soon to reign;

Com - ing in need, Mary's Child, Born in a bor-rowed room.
Light of the world, Mary's Child, Dawn on our dark-ened day.
Yes, it is true, Mary's Child, Shown on your cross of wood.
King of the earth, Mary's Child, Walk in our streets a - gain.

31 Hark! The Herald Angels Sing

MENDELSSOHN 7.7.7.7 D with refrain

Felix Mendelssohn, 1840
Arr. William Hayman Cummings, 1855

Charles Wesley, 1739; alt.

1. Hark! The her - ald an-gels sing, "Glo - ry to the new-born King.
2. Christ, by high - est heaven a - dored, Christ, the ev - er - last - ing Lord!
*3. Hail the heaven-born Prince of Peace! Hail the sun of right-teous-ness!

Peace on earth, and mer - cy mild, God and sin - ners rec - on - ciled!"
Late in time be - hold Him come, Off - spring of the vir - gin's womb.
Light and life to all He brings, Risen with heal - ing in His wings.

Joy - ful, all ye na - tions, rise, Join the tri - umph of the skies;
Veiled in flesh the God-head see; Hail the in - car - nate De - i - ty,
Mild He lays His glo - ry by, Born that we no more may die,

With the an-gel - ic host pro-claim, "Christ is born in Beth-le-hem!"
Pleased in flesh with us to dwell, Je - sus, our Em - man - u - el.
Born to raise us from the earth, Born to give us sec - ond birth.

Hark! The her - ald an - gels sing, "Glo - ry to the new-born King!"

*Descant and alternate harmonization for stanza 3, 32

32

Stanza 3, alternate arrangement*

Descant

Melody

3. Hail the heaven - born Prince of Peace! Hail the sun of

righ-teous-ness! Light and life to all He brings, Risen with heal - ing

in His wings. Mild He lays His glo - ry by, Born that we no

*Desc. and harm. David Willcocks, 1961

Sheng Ye Qing, Sheng Ye Jing
Holy Night, Blessed Night

33

Mandarin carol
Weiyu Zhu and Jingren Wu, 1921
Para. Kathleen Moody

7.8.9.8 with refrain

Qigui Shy, 1982
Arr. Pen-li Chen, 1987

Refrain

Sheng - ye qing, sheng - ye jing,
Ho - ly night, bless - ed night,

1. Ming - xing can - lan tian - di
2. Tian - shy xian - xian, mu - ren
3. Jiu - zhu Ye - su jin jiang -

1. Stars shine bright - ly, earth is
2. An - gels sing praise, shep - herds
3. Christ has come down, dwells with

ning.
jing,
sheng;

still.
fear,
us.

Shui su shan mian wan lai wu sheng,
Jin - qin yu - zheng, man tian he - yun,
Bo - ai, xi - sheng, gong - yi, he - ping

Hills and val - leys, field and wood-lands,
Earth and heav - en ring with prais - es,
Sac - ri - fice, love, peace and jus - tice

Qing - yun liao - rao yong zhe Bo - li - heng Ke - dian
Ha - li - lu - ya shan - hai yu qi - ming, Chuan - bao
Sheng rong he - hua you ru ry chu-sheng, En - guang

All sur-round the small town Beth - le - hem. In a
Al - le - lu - ia all cre - a - tion sings. Tell the
Shine up - on us like the morn-ing sun. Grace and

ma - cao dan-sheng tian - ing.
jia - in: Jiu - zhu jiang - sheng.
hui - yao, zhao-che qian - kun!

man - ger Christ the Lord sleeps.
good news: Christ is born now.
glo - ry bless the whole world.

34 In Bethlehem a Babe Was Born

DISCOVERY   Irregular with refrain

Barbara Mays, 1986

Barbara Mays, 1986
Harm. John Weaver, 1988

1. In Beth - le-hem a Babe was born With love e - nough for all.
2. Roy - al - ty and shep-herds came To wor - ship from a - far,
3. The mys - ter - y of Beth - le - hem Was long a - go, they say,

While king-doms slept, the Lord came down To grace a man - ger stall.
Guid - ed through the long cold night By one per - sis - tent star.
But, mir - a - cle of mir - a - cles, The Ba - by lives to - day

And with a glo - rious light An - gels ap - peared that night,
As each be - held the Son, Strang-ers be - came as one,
In each new heart that hears Love com-ing through the years,

Sing-ing, "Come, come, Christ is born! Come, come, world for-lorn.

The Child of peace and sac - ri - fice is wait - ing to be found."

Matthew 2:13–16

35 In Bethlehem a Newborn Boy

IN BETHLEHEM LM

Rosamond E. Herklots, 1969

Wilbur Held, 1983

1. In Beth - le - hem a new - born boy Was hailed with songs of
2. (The) sol - diers sought the child in vain: Not yet was he to
3. (Still) rage the fires of hate to - day, And in - no - cents the
4. (Lord) Je - sus, through our night of loss Shines out the won - der
5. (May) that great love our lives con - trol And con - quer hate in

praise and joy. Then warn - ing came of dan - ger near: King
share our pain; But down the a - ges rings the cry Of
price must pay, While ach - ing hearts in ev - ery land Cry
of your cross, The love that can - not cease to bear Our
ev - ery soul, Till, pledged to build and not de - stroy, We

1–4
Her - od's troops would soon ap - pear.
those who saw their chil - dren die.
out, "We can - not un - der - stand!"
hu - man an - guish ev - ery - where.
share your pain ánd find your joy.

5

2. The
3. Still
4. Lord
5. May

♩=48–52

In the Bleak Midwinter

CRANHAM   Irregular

Christina Rossetti, c. 1872; alt.

Gustav Theodore Holst, 1906

1. In the bleak mid - win - ter, Frost - y wind made moan,
2. Our God, heaven can - not hold Him, Nor earth sus - tain;
3. An - gels and arch - an - gels May have gath - ered there,
4. What can I give Him, Poor as I am?

Earth stood hard as i - ron, Wa - ter like a stone;
Heaven and earth shall flee a - way When He comes to reign:
Cher - u - bim and ser - a - phim Thronged the air;
If I were a shep - herd, I would bring a lamb;

Snow had fall - en, snow on snow, Snow on snow,
In the bleak mid - win - ter A sta - ble - place suf - ficed
But His moth - er on - ly, In her maid - en bliss,
If I were a wise man, I would do my part;

In the bleak mid - win - ter, Long a - go.
The Lord God in - car - nate, Je - sus Christ.
Wor - shiped the be - lov - ed With a kiss.
Yet what I can I give Him: Give my heart.

37 Infant Holy, Infant Lowly

W ŻŁOBIE LEŻY   4.4.7.4.4.7.4.4.4.4.7

Polish carol
Trans. and para. Edith M. G. Reed, 1925

Polish carol
Harm. A. E. Rusbridge (1917–1969)

1. In - fant ho - ly, In - fant low - ly, For His bed a cat - tle stall;
2. Flocks were sleep-ing; Shep-herds keep-ing Vig - il till the morn-ing new.

Ox - en low - ing, Lit - tle know - ing Christ the babe is Lord of all.
Saw the glo - ry, Heard the sto - ry, Tid - ings of a gos-pel true.

Swift are wing - ing An - gels sing - ing, No - els ring - ing,
Thus re - joic - ing, Free from sor - row, Prais - es voic - ing

Tid - ings bring - ing: Christ the babe is Lord of all.
Greet the mor - row: Christ the babe was born for you.

Music: Harmonization by A. E. Rusbridge (1917–1969). Used by permission of Rosalind Rusbridge.

It Came Upon the Midnight Clear

CAROL   CMD

Edmund Hamilton Sears, 1849   Richard Storrs Willis, 1850

1. It   came   up-on   the   mid-night clear, That   glo - rious song   of   old,
2. Still through the clo - ven   skies they come, With   peace-ful   wings un - furled,
3. And ye,   be-neath life's crush-ing   load, Whose forms are   bend-ing   low,
4. For   lo,   the days   are   has-tening on,   By   proph-et   bards fore - told,

From an - gels bend - ing   near the earth, To   touch their harps of   gold:
And   still their heaven-ly   mu - sic floats O'er   all   the wea - ry   world:
Who toil a - long   the climb-ing   way With   pain - ful   steps and   slow,
When with the ev - er - cir - cling years Comes round the   age   of   gold;

"Peace on   the   earth, good will to   all,   From heaven's all - gra - cious King":
A - bove   its   sad   and low - ly plains They bend   on hov - ering wing,
Look now! for glad   and gold-en hours Come swift - ly   on   the   wing:
When peace shall o - ver   all the earth Its   an - cient splen-dors   fling,

The world in   sol - emn still-ness lay,   To   hear the an - gels   sing.
And ev - er   o'er   its   Ba - bel sounds The   bless-ed an - gels   sing.
O   rest be - side   the   wea - ry road, And   hear the an - gels   sing.
And the whole world give back the song Which now the an - gels   sing.

39 Joyful Christmas Day Is Here

KURISUMASU   13.9.12.13.13.9

Toshiaki Okamoto (b. 1907)
Trans. Sandra Fukunaga and Hidemi Ito, 1981

Toshiaki Okamoto (b. 1907)

1. Joy - ful, joy - ful, joy - ful, joy - ful, Christ-mas day is here;
2. Joy - ful, hap - py, joy - ful, hap - py, Christ-mas day is here;

Ding, ding, dong, dong, Hear the church bells ring.
Ding, ding, dong, dong, Christ-mas day is here.

May be sung as a canon.

Chime through-out the land, He was born in Beth-le - hem;
Chime through-out the land, He was born in Beth-le - hem;

Ba - by Je - sus came in - to this world on Christ-mas day.
Ba - by Je - sus came in - to this world on Christ-mas day.

Hap - py, hap - py, hap - py, hap - py, Christ-mas day is here;
Sing to - geth - er, cel - e - brate; Christ is born to - day.

Ding, ding, dong, dong, Hear the church bells ring.
Ding, ding, dong, dong, Christ-mas day is here.

♩=84–92

40 Joy to the World!

ANTIOCH   CM with repeat

Isaac Watts, 1719; alt.

Attr. George Frederick Handel, 1742
Arr. Lowell Mason, 1836

1. Joy to the world! the Lord is come: Let earth re-
2. Joy to the world! the Sav - ior reigns: Let us our
3. No more let sins and sor - rows grow, Nor thorns in -
4. He rules the world with truth and grace, And makes the

ceive her King; Let ev - ery heart pre - pare Him room,
songs em - ploy; While fields and floods, rocks, hills, and plains
fest the ground; He comes to make His bless - ings flow
na - tions prove The glo - ries of His righ - teous - ness,

And heaven and na - ture sing, And heaven and na - ture
Re - peat the sound-ing joy, Re - peat the sound-ing
Far as the curse is found, Far as the curse is
And won - ders of His love, And won - ders of His
And heaven and na - ture sing,

And

sing, And heaven, and heaven and na - ture sing.
joy, Re - peat, re - peat the sound-ing joy.
found, Far as, far as the curse is found.
love, And won - ders, won - ders of His love.

heaven and na - ture sing,

O Come, All Ye Faithful

41

ADESTE FIDELES 6.6.10.5.6 with refrain

John Francis Wade (c. 1740–1743)
Trans. Frederick Oakeley, 1841

John Francis Wade (c. 1740–1743)
Harm. *The English Hymnal,* 1906

1. O come, all ye faith-ful, Joy-ful and tri-um-phant, O
2. Yea, Lord, we greet Thee, Born this hap-py morn-ing,
*3. Sing, choirs of an-gels, Sing in ex-ul-ta-tion!

come ye, O come ye to Beth-le-hem!
Je-sus, to Thee be all glo-ry given;
Sing, all ye cit-i-zens of heaven a-bove!

Come, and be-hold Him, Born the King of an-gels!
Word of the Fa-ther, Now in flesh ap-pear-ing!
Glo-ry to God, all Glo-ry in the high-est!

Refrain

O come, let us a-dore Him, O come, let us a-dore Him, O come, let us a-dore Him, Christ, the Lord!

Alternate harmonization and descant for stanza 3, 42

42

Stanza 3, alternate arrangement*

3. Sing, choirs of an - gels, Sing in ex - ul - ta - tion!

Sing, all ye cit - i - zens of heaven a - bove!

Glo - ry

Glo - ry to God, all glo - ry in the high - est! O

**Desc. and harm. David Willcocks, 1961*

43 O Little Town of Bethlehem

FOREST GREEN   CMD

Phillips Brooks, 1868

English folk melody
Arr. Ralph Vaughan Williams, 1906

1. O lit - tle town of Beth - le - hem, How still we see thee lie!
2. For Christ is born of Ma - ry; And gath - ered all a - bove,
3. How si - lent - ly, how si - lent - ly, The won - drous gift is given!
4. O ho - ly Child of Beth - le - hem, De - scend to us, we pray;

A - bove thy deep and dream-less sleep The si - lent stars go by.
While mor-tals sleep, the an - gels keep Their watch of won-dering love.
So God im-parts to hu - man hearts The bless-ings of His heaven.
Cast out our sin and en - ter in, Be born in us to - day.

Yet in thy dark streets shin - eth The ev - er - last - ing light;
O morn-ing stars, to - geth - er Pro - claim the ho - ly birth!
No ear may hear His com - ing, But in this world of sin,
We hear the Christ-mas an - gels The great glad tid - ings tell;

The hopes and fears of all the years Are met in thee to - night.
And prais - es sing to God the King, And peace to all on earth.
Where meek souls will re - ceive Him, still The dear Christ en-ters in.
O come to us, a - bide with us, Our Lord Em - man - u - el!

This tune in a higher key, 292

Music: Arrangement from the *English Hymnal,* 1906. Used by permission of Oxford University Press.

O Little Town of Bethlehem

ST. LOUIS   8.6.8.6.7.6.8.6

44

Phillips Brooks, 1868

Lewis Henry Redner, 1868

1. O lit - tle town of Beth - le - hem, How still we see thee lie!
2. For Christ is born of Ma - ry; And gath - ered all a - bove,
3. How si - lent - ly, how si - lent - ly, The won - drous gift is given!
4. O ho - ly Child of Beth - le - hem, De - scend to us, we pray;

A - bove thy deep and dream-less sleep The si - lent stars go by.
While mor - tals sleep, the an - gels keep Their watch of won-dering love.
So God im - parts to hu - man hearts The bless - ings of His heaven.
Cast out our sin and en - ter in, Be born in us to - day.

Yet in thy dark streets shin - eth The ev - er - last - ing light;
O morn-ing stars, to - geth - er Pro - claim the ho - ly birth!
No ear may hear His com - ing, But in this world of sin,
We hear the Christ-mas an - gels The great glad tid - ings tell;

The hopes and fears of all the years Are met in thee to - night.
And prais - es sing to God the King, And peace to all on earth.
Where meek souls will re - ceive Him, still The dear Christ en - ters in.
O come to us, a - bide with us, Our Lord Em - man - u - el!

A La Ru
45 O Sleep, Dear Holy Baby

A LA RU   Irregular

Hispanic folk song
Trans. John Donald Robb, 1954

Hispanic folk melody
Arr. John Donald Robb, 1954

1. Duér-
2. No

1. O
2. You

me - te, Ni - ño lin - do,   en los bra - zos del a -
te - mas al rey He - ro - des   que na - da te ha de ha -

sleep, dear ho - ly Ba - by,   with Your head a - gainst my
need not fear King Her - od,   he will bring no harm to

mor   mien - tras   que duer-me y des - can - sa   la
cer;   en los   bra - zos de tu ma - dre   y ahí

breast;   mean-while the pangs of my sor - row   are
You;   so rest in the arms of Your moth - er,   who

Guitar and keyboard should not sound together.

pe - na de mi do - lor.
na - die te ha de o-fen - der.
soothed and put to rest.
sings You a la ru.

*A la ru, a la

mé, a la ru, a la mé, a la

ru, a la mé, a la ru, a la ru, a la mé.

*These syllables have no meaning.

46 On This Day Earth Shall Ring

PERSONENT HODIE   6.6.6.6.6 with refrain

Piae Cantiones, 1582
Trans. Jane Marion Joseph (1894–1929)

Piae Cantiones, 1582
Arr. Gustav Theodore Holst, 1924

1. On this day earth shall ring With the song
2. His the doom, ours the mirth; When He came
3. God's bright star, o'er His head, Wise men three
4. On this day an-gels sing; With their song

chil-dren sing To the Lord, Christ our King, Born on earth to
down to earth Beth-le-hem saw His birth; Ox and ass be-
to Him led, Kneel-ing low by His bed, Lay their gifts be-
earth shall ring, Prais-ing Christ, heav-en's King, Born on earth to

Refrain

save us; Him the Fa-ther gave us.
side Him From the cold would hide Him.
fore Him, Praise Him and a-dore Him. *Id-e-o - o - o,
save us; Peace and love He gave us.

R.H.
L.H.
R.H.

*Therefore, glory to God in the highest.

Id-e-o - o - o, Id-e-o glo-ri-a in ex-cel-sis De-o!

Still, Still, Still

47

STILL, STILL, STILL   3.6.9.8.3.6

Austrian carol
Trans. George K. Evans (b. 1917)

Austrian melody
Arr. Walter Ehret (b. 1918)

1. Still, still, still, He sleeps this night so chill! The
2. Sleep, sleep, sleep, He lies in slum-ber deep While

Vir-gin's ten-der arms en-fold-ing, Warm and safe the Child are hold-ing.
an-gel hosts from heaven come wing-ing, Sweet-est songs of joy are sing-ing.

Still, still, still, He sleeps this night so chill.
Sleep, sleep, sleep, He lies in slum-ber deep.

48 Lo, How a Rose E'er Blooming

ES IST EIN' ROS'   7.6.7.6.6.7.6

German carol, 15th century
Trans. Theodore Baker (1851–1934)
Alt. *Rejoice in the Lord*, 1985

Alte Catholische Geistliche
Kirchengesäng, Cologne, 1599
Arr. Michael Praetorius, 1609

1. Lo, how a rose e'er bloom-ing From ten-der stem hath sprung,
2. I - sa - iah 'twas fore - told it, The rose I have in mind,

Of Jes-se's lin-eage com - ing, By faith - ful proph - ets sung.
With Ma - ry we be - hold it, The vir - gin moth - er kind.

It came a flower - et bright, A - mid the cold of
To show God's love a - right She bore for us a

win - ter, When half spent was the night.
Sav - ior, When half spent was the night.
was the

Once in Royal David's City

49

IRBY   8.7.8.7.7.7

Cecil Frances Alexander, 1848; alt.

Henry John Gauntlett, 1849
Harm. Arthur Henry Mann, 1919

1. Once in roy - al Da - vid's cit - y Stood a low - ly
2. He came down to earth from heav - en Who is God and
3. Je - sus is our child - hood's pat - tern, Day by day like
4. And our eyes at last shall see Him, Through His own re -

cat - tle shed, Where a moth - er laid her ba - by
Lord of all, And His shel - ter was a sta - ble,
us He grew; He was lit - tle, weak and help - less,
deem - ing love, For that Child so dear and gen - tle

In a man - ger for His bed. Ma - ry was that moth - er
And His cra - dle was a stall. With the poor, op-pressed, and
Tears and smiles like us He knew; And He feels for all our
Is our Lord in heaven a - bove; And He leads His chil - dren

mild, Je - sus Christ her lit - tle child.
low - ly, Lived on earth our Sav - ior ho - ly.
sad - ness, And He shares in all our glad - ness.
on To the place where He is gone.

Music: Harmonization by A. H. Mann, reprinted by permission of Novello and Company Limited.

50 Rise Up, Shepherd, and Follow

African-American spiritual

African-American spiritual

Unison

1. There's a star in the East on Christ - mas morn,
2. If you take good heed to the an - gel's words,

Harmony   *Unison*

Rise up, shep-herd, and fol - low, It will lead to the place where the
Rise up, shep-herd, and fol - low, You'll for - get your flocks, you'll for -

Harmony

Christ was born, Rise up, shep-herd, and fol - low.
get your herds, Rise up, shep-herd, and fol - low.

Refrain

Fol - low, fol - low, Rise up, shep-herd, and fol - low,

Fol-low the Star of Beth-le - hem, Rise up, shep-herd, and fol-low.

See Amid the Winter's Snow

51

HUMILITY   7.7.7.7 with refrain

Edward Caswall, 1858

John Goss, 1871

1. See a - mid the win - ter's snow, Born for us on earth be - low,
2. Say, you ho - ly shep - herds, say, Tell your joy - ful news to - day.
3. "As we watched at dead of night, There ap-peared a won - drous light;

See, the gen - tle Lamb ap - pears, Prom-ised from e - ter - nal years.
Why have you now left your sheep On the lone-ly moun - tain steep?
An - gels sing-ing 'Peace on earth' Told us of the Sav - ior's birth."

Refrain

Hail that ev - er - bless-ed morn, Hail re-demp-tion's hap - py dawn,

Sing through all Je - ru - sa-lem: Christ is born in Beth-le - hem.

♩=88–96

Hitsuji Wa
Sheep Fast Asleep

52

KŌRIN   8.7.8.7.8.7.8.6

Japanese hymn
Genzō Miwa, 1907
Trans. John Moss, 1957; alt.

Chûgorô Torii, 1941

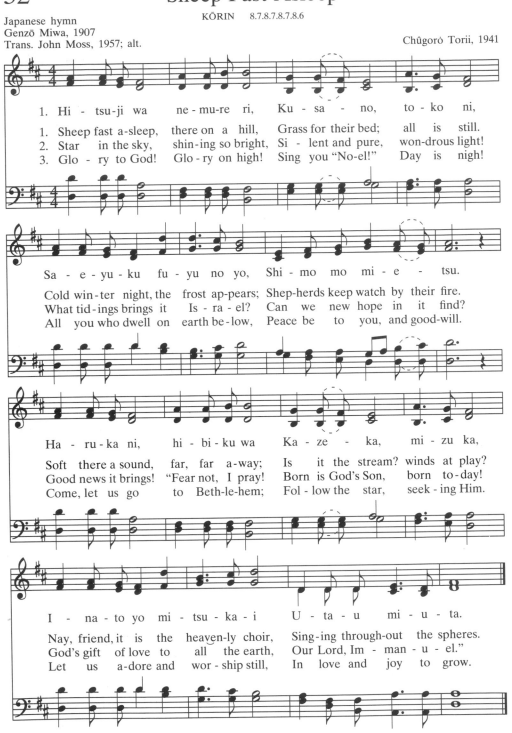

1. Hi - tsu-ji wa   ne - mu-re ri,   Ku - sa - no,   to - ko ni,
1. Sheep fast a-sleep,   there on a hill,   Grass for their bed;   all is still.
2. Star in the sky,   shin-ing so bright,   Si - lent and pure,   won-drous light!
3. Glo - ry to God!   Glo - ry on high!   Sing you "No-el!"   Day is nigh!

Sa - e - yu - ku fu - yu no yo,   Shi - mo mo mi - e - tsu.
Cold win-ter night, the   frost ap-pears;   Shep-herds keep watch by their fire.
What tid-ings brings it   Is - ra - el?   Can we new hope in it find?
All you who dwell on   earth be-low,   Peace be   to you, and good-will.

Ha - ru - ka ni,   hi - bi - ku wa   Ka - ze - ka,   mi - zu ka,
Soft there a sound,   far, far a-way;   Is it the stream? winds at play?
Good news it brings!   "Fear not, I pray!   Born is God's Son,   born to-day!
Come, let us go   to Beth-le-hem;   Fol - low the star,   seek - ing Him.

I - na - to yo mi - tsu - ka - i   U - ta - u   mi - u - ta.
Nay, friend, it is the   heaven-ly choir,   Sing-ing through-out the spheres.
God's gift of love to   all the earth,   Our Lord, Im - man - u - el."
Let us a-dore and   wor - ship still,   In love and joy to grow.

♩=76–84

Text and Music: Permission #1430 granted by the Hymnal Committee, United Church of Christ in Japan. Translation © 1963 John A. Moss. All rights reserved. Used by permission.

2. Mahiru ni otoranu Kushiki hikari,
   Misora no kanata ni Terikakaya ku.
   Sukui wo motarasu Kami no miko no
   Umareshi yorokobi Tsuguru hoshi ka.

3. Ame ni wa misakae Kami ni areya,
   Tsuchi ni wa odayaka Hito ni areto
   Mukashi no shirabe wo Ima ni kaeshi,
   Utaeya, tomora yo, Koemo takaku.

What Child Is This 53

GREENSLEEVES   8.7.8.7 with refrain

William Chatterton Dix, c. 1871

English ballad, 16th century
Arr. *Christmas Carols New and Old,* 1871

1. What Child is this, who, laid to rest, On Ma-ry's lap is sleep-ing?
2. Why lies He in such mean es-tate Where ox and ass are feed-ing?
3. So bring Him in-cense, gold, and myrrh; Come, one and all, to own Him.

Whom an-gels greet with an-thems sweet While shep-herds watch are keep-ing?
Good Chris-tian, fear; for sin-ners here The si-lent Word is plead-ing.
The King of kings sal-va-tion brings; Let lov-ing hearts en-throne Him.

This, this is Christ the King, Whom shep-herds guard and an-gels sing;

Haste, haste to bring Him laud, the Babe, the Son of Ma-ry!

This tune can be sung in the original mode by sharping all C's in the soprano and alto parts.

54 From Heaven Above

VOM HIMMEL HOCH LM

Martin Luther, 1535
Trans. Inter-Lutheran Commission on Worship
for *Lutheran Book of Worship*, 1978; alt.

Schumann's *Geistliche Lieder*, 1539
Harm. Hans Leo Hassler (1564–1612)

1. From heaven a - bove to earth I come To bring good
news to ev - ery - one! Glad tid - ings of great
joy I bring To all the world, and glad - ly sing:

2. To you this night is born a child Of Ma - ry,
cho - sen vir - gin mild; This new - born child of
low - ly birth Shall be the joy of all the earth.

3. This is the Christ, God's Son most high, Who hears your
sad and bit - ter cry; He will Him - self your
Sav - ior be And from all sin will set you free.

4. "Glo - ry to God in high - est heaven, Who un - to
us the Christ has given." With an - gels sing the
Sav - ior's birth, A glad new year to all the earth.

Text: Copyright © 1978 *Lutheran Book of Worship*. Reprinted by permission of Augsburg Fortress.

55 That Boy-Child of Mary

BLANTYRE Irregular

Tom Colvin, 1967

Malawi melody
Adapt. Tom Colvin, 1967

Refrain

That boy-child of Ma - ry was born in a sta - ble,

A man-ger His cra - dle in Beth - le - hem.

1. What shall we call Him, child of the man - ger?
2. His name is Je - su, God ev - er with us,
3. How can He save us, how can He help us,
4. Gift of the Fa - ther, to hu - man moth - er,
5. One with the Fa - ther, He is our Sav - ior,
6. Glad - ly we praise Him, love and a - dore Him,

D.C. al Fine

What name is giv - en in Beth - le - hem?
God giv - en for us, in Beth - le - hem.

Born here a - mong us, in Beth - le - hem?
Makes Him our broth - er of Beth - le - hem.

Heav - en - sent Help - er of Beth - le - hem.
Give our - selves to Him, of Beth - le - hem.

56 The First Nowell

THE FIRST NOWELL   Irregular with refrain

English carol, 17th century

English carol
Sandys' *Christmas Carols,* 1833

1. The first Now-ell the an-gel did say Was to cer-tain poor
2. They look-ed up and saw a star Shin-ing in the
3. And by the light of that same star, Three wise men
4. This star drew nigh to the north-west; O'er Beth-le-

shep-herds in fields as they lay; In fields where they lay a-keep-ing their
east be-yond them far, And to the earth it gave great
came from coun-try far; To seek for a king was their in-
hem it took its rest; And there it did both stop and

Refrain

sheep, On a cold win-ter's night that was so deep.
light, And so it con-tin-ued both day and night.
tent, And to fol-low the star wher-ev-er it went.   Now-ell,   Now-
stay, Right o-ver the place where Je-sus lay.

ell, Now-ell, Now-ell, Born is the King of Is-ra-el.

Refrain may be omitted except after final stanza.

5. Then entered in those wise men three,
   Fell reverently upon their knee,
   And offered there in His presence,
   Their gold, and myrrh, and
      frankincense.
   (Refrain)

6. Then let us all with one accord
   Sing praises to our heavenly Lord,
   That hath made heaven and earth of
      nought,
   And with His blood our life hath bought.
   (Refrain)

Arr. Healey Willan, 1926

Music: Used by permission of Oxford University Press, Inc.

57 The Snow Lay on the Ground

VENITE ADOREMUS   10.10.10.10 with refrain

English melody
Adapt. C. Winfred Douglas (1867–1944)
Harm. Leo Sowerby, 1941

Anglo-Irish carol; alt.

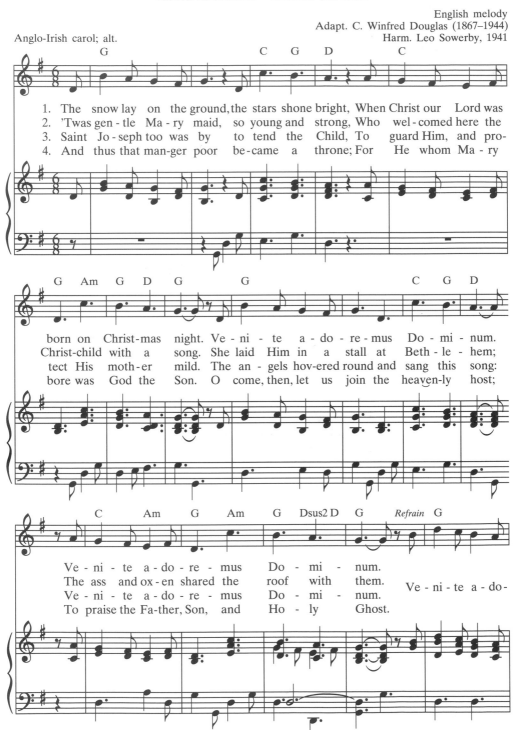

1. The snow lay on the ground, the stars shone bright, When Christ our Lord was born on Christ-mas night. Ve - ni - te a - do - re - mus Do - mi - num. Ve - ni - te a - do - re - mus Do - mi - num.
2. 'Twas gen - tle Ma - ry maid, so young and strong, Who wel - comed here the Christ-child with a song. She laid Him in a stall at Beth - le - hem; The ass and ox - en shared the roof with them.
3. Saint Jo - seph too was by to tend the Child, To guard Him, and pro - tect His moth - er mild. The an - gels hov-ered round and sang this song: Ve - ni - te a - do - re - mus Do - mi - num.
4. And thus that man-ger poor be-came a throne; For He whom Ma - ry bore was God the Son. O come, then, let us join the heaven-ly host; To praise the Fa-ther, Son, and Ho - ly Ghost.

Refrain   Ve - ni - te a - do -

Music: Harmonization © 1941. Used by permission of Ronald Stalford, executor of the estate of Leo Sowerby.

re - mus Do - mi - num. Ve - ni - te a - do - re - mus Do - mi - num.

♩.=88–96

Luke 2:10–14

While Shepherds Watched Their Flocks **58**

WINCHESTER OLD CM

Nahum Tate, 1700; alt. 1987

Este's *Psalmes,* 1592
Desc. Alan Gray, 1923

Descant

6. "All glo - ry be to God on high, And to the earth be peace:

1. While shep - herds watched their flocks by night, All seat - ed on the ground,
2. "Fear not," said he, for might - y dread Had seized their trou - bled mind;
3. "To you, in Da - vid's town this day, Is born of Da - vid's line
4. "The heaven - ly Babe you there shall find To hu - man view dis - played,

Good will to all from high - est heaven Be - gin and nev - er cease."

The an - gel of the Lord came down, And glo - ry shone a - round.
"Glad tid - ings of great joy I bring To you and hu - man - kind.
The Sav - ior, who is Christ the Lord, And this shall be the sign:
All hum - bly wrapped in swath - ing bands, And in a man - ger laid."

5. Thus spoke the seraph, and forthwith
   Appeared a shining throng
   Of angels praising God, who thus
   Addressed their joyful song:

6. "All glory be to God on high,
   And to the earth be peace:
   Good will to all from highest heaven
   Begin and never cease!"

Alternate tune: CHRISTMAS, 59

59 While Shepherds Watched Their Flocks

CHRISTMAS   CM with repeat

George Frederick Handel, 1728
Arr. Lowell Mason, 1821

Nahum Tate, 1700; alt. 1987

1. While shep-herds watched their flocks by night, All seat-ed
2. "Fear not," said he, for might-y dread Had seized their
3. "To you, in Da-vid's town this day, Is born of
4. "The heaven-ly Babe you there shall find To hu-man

on the ground, The an-gel of the Lord came down,
trou-bled mind; "Glad tid-ings of great joy I bring
Da-vid's line The Sav-ior, who is Christ the Lord,
view dis-played, All hum-bly wrapped in swath-ing bands,

And glo-ry shone a-round, And glo-ry shone a-round.
To you and hu-man-kind, To you and hu-man-kind.
And this shall be the sign, And this shall be the sign:
And in a man-ger laid, And in a man-ger laid."

5. Thus spoke the seraph, and forthwith
   Appeared a shining throng
   Of angels praising God, who thus
   Addressed their joyful song,
   Addressed their joyful song:

6. "All glory be to God on high,
   And to the earth be peace:
   Good will to all from highest heaven
   Begin and never cease!
   Begin and never cease!"

Alternate tune: WINCHESTER OLD, 58

Silent Night, Holy Night

STILLE NACHT   Irregular

Joseph Mohr, 1818
Trans. John Freeman Young, 1863

Franz Xaver Gruber, 1818

1. Si - lent night, ho - ly night! All is calm, all is bright, Round yon
2. Si - lent night, ho - ly night! Shep-herds quake at the sight, Glo - ries
3. Si - lent night, ho - ly night! Son of God, love's pure light Ra - diant
4. Si - lent night, ho - ly night! Won-drous star, lend thy light; With the

vir - gin moth-er and child! Ho - ly In - fant, so ten - der and mild,
stream from heav-en a - far, Heaven-ly hosts sing: "Al - le - lu - ia;
beams from Thy ho-ly face, With the dawn of re - deem - ing grace,
an - gels let us sing, Al - le - lu - ia to our King;

Sleep in heav-en-ly peace, Sleep in heav-en-ly peace.
Christ the Sav - ior is born, Christ the Sav - ior is born."
Je - sus, Lord, at Thy birth, Je - sus, Lord, at Thy birth.
Christ the Sav - ior is born, Christ the Sav - ior is born.

1. Stille Nacht, heilige Nacht!
   Alles schläft, einsam wacht
   Nur das traute, hochheilige Paar.
   Holder Knabe im lockigen Haar,
   Schlaf' in himmlischer Ruh',
   Schlaf' in himmlischer Ruh'!

2. Stille Nacht, heilige Nacht!
   Hirten erst kundgemacht
   Durch der Engel Alleluja,
   Tönt est laut von fern und nah:
   Christ der Retter ist da,
   Christ der Retter ist da!

3. Stille Nacht, heilige Nacht!
   Gottes Sohn, o wie lacht
   Lieb' aus deinem göttlichen Mund,
   Da uns schlägt die rettende Stund':
   Christ, in deiner Geburt,
   Christ, in deiner Geburt!

61 'Twas in the Moon of Wintertime

UNE JEUNE PUCELLE   8.6.8.6.8.8 with refrain

Native American (Huron)
Jean de Brébeuf, c. 1641
English text: Jesse Edgar Middleton, 1926

French carol, 16th century

1. 'Twas in the moon of win-ter-time, When all the birds had fled,
2. With-in a lodge of bro-ken bark The ten-der Babe was found;
3. O chil-dren of the for-est free, O you of Man-i-tou,

That might-y Gitch-i Man-i-tou Sent an-gel choirs in-
A rag-ged robe of rab-bit skin En-wrapped His beau-ty
The Ho-ly Child of earth and heaven Is born to-day for

stead. Be - fore their light the stars grew dim And won-dering
round. The chiefs from far be - fore Him knelt With gifts of
you. Come kneel be - fore the ra - diant boy Who brings you

hunt - ers   heard   the   hymn:
fox   and   bea - ver   pelt: Je - sus, your   King, is   born,
beau - ty,   peace, and   joy.

Je - sus   is   born.   In   ex - cel - sis   glo - ri - a.

62 Bring We the Frankincense of Our Love

EPIPHANY SONG 9.8.9.8 with refrain

H. Kenn Carmichael, 1976
Arr. Clayton D. Lein, 1976,
and John Weaver, 1989

H. Kenn Carmichael, 1976

1. Bring we the frank-in-cense of our love To the feet of the ho-ly Child, Ev-er re-mem-ber-ing God's great gift Of a love that is un-de-filed.
2. Bring we the myrrh of hu-mil-i-ty To the throne of the Son of God, Ev-er re-call-ing the pu-ri-ty Of His life when the earth He trod.
3. Ev-er se-cure in His change-less-ness, Though the king-doms of earth may fall, Bring we the gold of our faith-ful-ness To the King who is Lord of all.

Refrain

Ho-ly the In-fant and ho-ly the moth-er And ho-ly and pre-cious the gifts that we bring; Praise to the Fa-ther and

praise to the Spir-it And praise to Christ Je - sus our King.

♩=112–120

As with Gladness Men of Old 63

DIX 7.7.7.7.7.7

Conrad Kocher, 1838
Abr. William Henry Monk, 1861
Harm. *The English Hymnal*, 1906

William Chatterton Dix, c. 1858

1. As with glad-ness men of old Did the guid-ing star be-hold;
2. As with joy-ful steps they sped To that low-ly man-ger bed,
3. As they of-fered gifts most rare At that man-ger rude and bare;
4. Ho-ly Je-sus, ev-ery day Keep us in the nar-row way;

As with joy they hailed its light, Lead-ing on - ward, beam-ing bright;
There to bend the knee be-fore Him whom heaven and earth a - dore;
So may we with ho-ly joy, Pure, and free from sin's al - loy,
And, when earth-ly things are past, Bring our ran - somed souls at last

So, most gra-cious Lord, may we Ev - er-more be led to Thee.
So may we with will - ing feet Ev - er seek Thy mer - cy seat.
All our cost-liest trea - sures bring, Christ, to Thee, our heaven-ly King.
Where they need no star to guide, Where no clouds Thy glo - ry hide.

De Tierra Lejana Venimos
From a Distant Home

Matthew 2:1–12

64

ISLA DEL ENCANTO   12.12 with refrain

Puerto Rican carol
Trans. George K. Evans and Walter Ehret

Puerto Rican melody

1. De tie-rra le-ja - na ve-ni-mos a ver - te,
2. Al re-cién na-ci - do que es Rey de los rey - es,

1. From a dis-tant home the Sav - ior we come seek - ing,
2. Glow-ing gold I bring the new-born babe so ho - ly,

Nos sir-ve de gui - a La Es-tre-lla de O-rien - te.
O - ro le re-ga - lo pa-ra or-nar sus sien - es.

Us-ing as our guide the star, so bright-ly beam - ing.
To-ken of His power to reign a - bove in glo - ry.

Estribillo
Refrain

O bri-llan-te es-tre - lla que a-nun - cias la au -
Glo-ria en las al - tu - ras al Hi - jo de

Love-ly east-ern star that tells us of God's
Glo - ry in the high - est to the Son of

ro - ra No nos fal - te nun - ca
Di - os, Glo - ria en las al - tu - ras
morn - ing, Heav-en's won - drous light, O
Heav - en, And up - on the earth be

tu luz bien - he - cho - ra.
nev - er cease thy shin - ing!

y en la tie-rra a - mor.
peace and love to all.

3. Como es Dios el Niño le regalo in-
cienso,
Perfume con alma que sube hasta el
cielo.
Estribillo

4. Al Niño del cielo que bajo a la tierra,
Le regalo mirra que inspira tristeza.
Estribillo

3. Frankincense I bring the Child of God's
own choosing,
Token of our prayers to heaven ever
rising.
Refrain

4. Bitter myrrh have I to give the infant
Jesus,
Token of the pain that He will bear to
save us.
Refrain

65 Midnight Stars Make Bright the Sky

HUAN-SHA-CH'I   7.7.7.7 D with refrain

Chinese hymn
Ching-chiu Yang, 1930
Trans. Mildred A. Wiant, 1966

Chi-fang Liang, 1934
Harm. Bliss Wiant, 1934

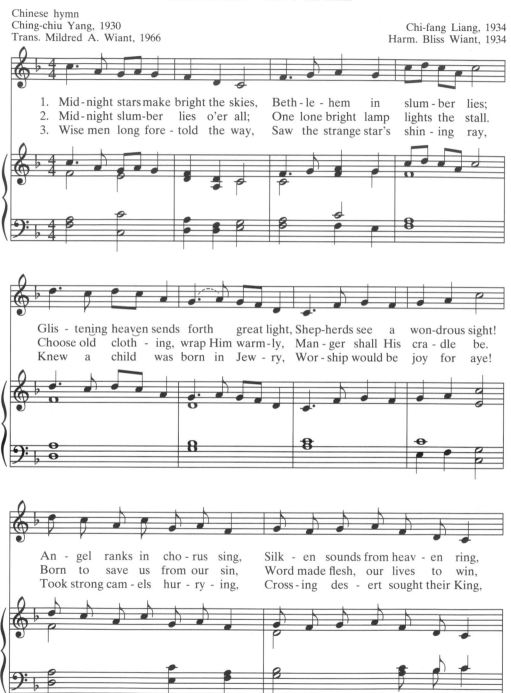

1. Mid-night stars make bright the skies, Beth-le-hem in slum-ber lies;
2. Mid-night slum-ber lies o'er all; One lone bright lamp lights the stall.
3. Wise men long fore-told the way, Saw the strange star's shin-ing ray,

Glis-tening heaven sends forth great light, Shep-herds see a won-drous sight!
Choose old cloth-ing, wrap Him warm-ly, Man-ger shall His cra-dle be.
Knew a child was born in Jew-ry, Wor-ship would be joy for aye!

An-gel ranks in cho-rus sing, Silk-en sounds from heav-en ring,
Born to save us from our sin, Word made flesh, our lives to win,
Took strong cam-els hur-ry-ing, Cross-ing des-ert sought their King,

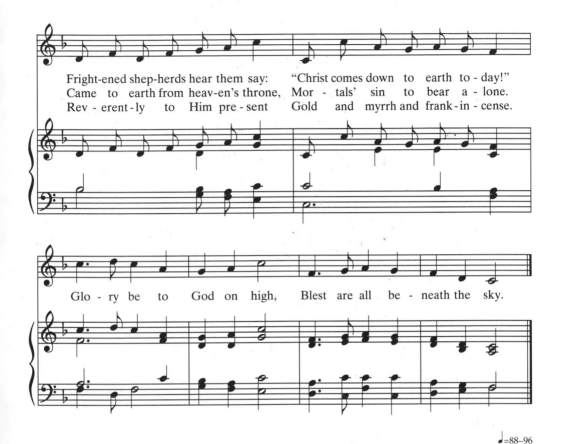

Fright-ened shep-herds hear them say: "Christ comes down to earth to - day!"
Came to earth from heav-en's throne, Mor - tals' sin to bear a - lone.
Rev - erent-ly to Him pre - sent Gold and myrrh and frank - in - cense.

Glo - ry be to God on high, Blest are all be - neath the sky.

♩=88–96

66   We Three Kings of Orient Are

THREE KINGS OF ORIENT   8.8.44.6 with refrain

John Henry Hopkins, Jr., 1857; alt.

John Henry Hopkins, Jr., 1857; alt.
Intro. Robert Stigall, 1988

All: 1. We three kings of O - ri - ent are,
Opt. solo: 2. Born a King on Beth - le - hem's plain,
Opt. solo: 3. Frank - in - cense to of - fer have I:
Opt. solo: 4. Myrrh is mine; its bit - ter per - fume
All: 5. Glo - rious now be - hold Him a - rise,

Optional Introduction

Bear - ing gifts we tra - verse a - far,   Field and foun - tain,
Gold I bring to crown Him a - gain,   King for ev - er,
In - cense owns a De - i - ty nigh;   Prayer and prais - ing
Breathes a life of gath - er - ing gloom;   Sor - rowing, sigh - ing,
King and God and Sac - ri - fice;   Al - le - lu - ia,

moor and moun - tain, Fol - low - ing yon - der star.
ceas - ing nev - er O - ver us all to reign.
we are rais - ing, Wor - ship - ing God Most High.
bleed - ing, dy - ing, Sealed in the stone - cold tomb.
Al - le - lu - ia Sounds through the earth and skies.

Music: Introduction © 1990 Robert Stigall. All rights reserved. Used by permission.

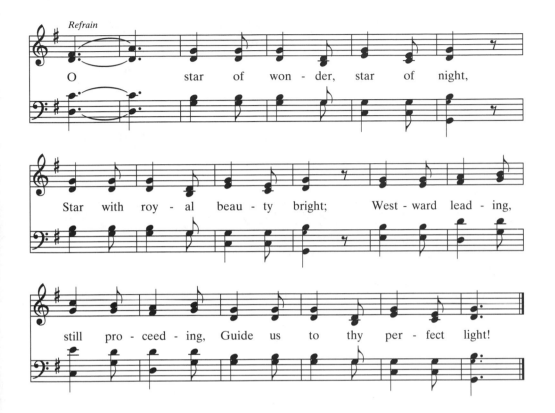

Refrain

O star of won-der, star of night,

Star with roy-al beau-ty bright; West-ward lead-ing,

still pro-ceed-ing, Guide us to thy per-fect light!

67 Brightest and Best of the Stars of the Morning

MORNING STAR 11.10.11.10

Reginald Heber, 1811; alt.   James Proctor Harding, 1892

1. Bright - est and best of the stars of the morn - ing,
2. Cold on His cra - dle the dew - drops are shin - ing,
3. Shall we then yield Him, in cost - ly de - vo - tion,
4. Vain - ly we of - fer each am - ple ob - la - tion,

Dawn on our dark - ness and lend us thine aid;
Low lies His head with the beasts of the stall;
O - dors of E - dom and of - ferings di - vine,
Vain - ly with gifts would His fa - vor se - cure;

Star of the east, the ho - ri - zon a - dorn - ing,
An - gels a - dore Him in slum - ber re - clin - ing,
Gems of the moun - tain and pearls of the o - cean,
Rich - er by far is the heart's ad - o - ra - tion,

Guide where our in - fant Re - deem - er is laid.
Mak - er and Mon - arch and Sav - ior of all!
Myrrh from the for - est, or gold from the mine?
Dear - er to God are the prayers of the poor.*

*Repeat stanza 1.

What Star Is This, with Beams So Bright 68

PUER NOBIS NASCITUR LM

Charles Coffin, 1736
Trans. John Chandler, 1837; alt.

Trier ms., 15th century
Adapt. Michael Praetorius, 1609
Harm. George Ratcliffe Woodward, 1910

1. What star is this, with beams so bright, More love-ly than the noon-day light? 'Tis sent to an-nounce a new-born King, Glad tid-ings of our God to bring.

2. 'Tis now ful-filled what God de-creed, "From Ja-cob shall a star pro-ceed"; And lo! the East-ern sa-ges stand To read in heaven the Lord's com-mand.

3. O Je-sus, while the star of grace Im-pels us on to seek Your face, Let not our sloth-ful hearts re-fuse The guid-ance of Your light to use.

4. To God the Fa-ther, God the Son, And Ho-ly Spir-it, Three in one, May ev-ery tongue and na-tion raise An end-less song of thank-ful praise.

69   O Morning Star, How Fair and Bright

WIE SCHÖN LEUCHTET   8.8.7.8.8.7.4.8.4.8

Philipp Nicolai, 1597
Alt. Johann Adolf Schlegel, 1768
Trans. Catherine Winkworth, 1863

Philipp Nicolai, 1599
Harm. Johann Sebastian Bach, 1740

1. O Morn-ing Star, how fair and bright Thou beam-est
2. Thou heaven-ly bright-ness! Light di-vine! O deep with-

forth in truth and light! O Sov-ereign meek and low-ly!
in my heart now shine, And make Thee there an al-tar!

Thou root of Jes-se, Da-vid's Son, My Lord and Sav-ior,
Fill me with joy and strength to be Thy mem-ber, ev-er

Thou hast won My heart to serve Thee sole-ly! Thou art ho-ly,
joined to Thee In love that can-not fal-ter! Toward Thee long-ing

Fair and glo - rious, all - vic - to - rious, Rich in bless - ing,
Doth pos - sess me; turn and bless me; Here in sad - ness

Rule and might o'er all pos - sess - ing.
Eye and heart long for Thy glad - ness!

BAPTISM OF THE LORD

Christ, When for Us You Were Baptized 70

CAITHNESS CM

F. Bland Tucker, 1979; alt. 1982

Scottish Psalter, 1635
Harm. *The English Hymnal*, 1906

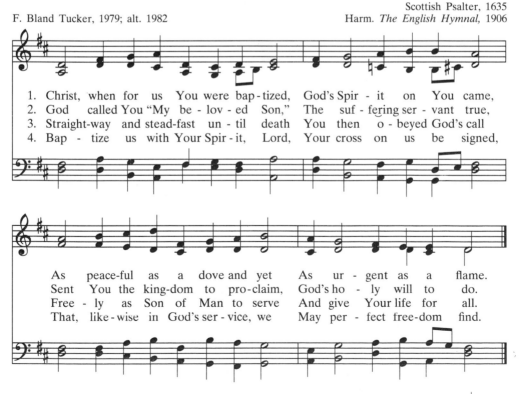

1. Christ, when for us You were bap - tized, God's Spir - it on You came,
2. God called You "My be - lov - ed Son," The suf - fering ser - vant true,
3. Straight-way and stead-fast un - til death You then o - beyed God's call
4. Bap - tize us with Your Spir - it, Lord, Your cross on us be signed,

As peace-ful as a dove and yet As ur - gent as a flame.
Sent You the king-dom to pro-claim, God's ho - ly will to do.
Free - ly as Son of Man to serve And give Your life for all.
That, like-wise in God's ser - vice, we May per - fect free-dom find.

Text: From The Hymnal 1982, © Church Pension Fund. Used by permission.

♩=92–100

71 Lord, When You Came to Jordan

GENEVAN 130   7.6.7.6 D

Brian Wren, 1979   Genevan Psalter, 1542

1. Lord, when You came to Jor - dan And asked to be bap - tized,
2. Was this God's crown-ing mo - ment Of all You had be - come,
3. Faith rests con - tent with ques - tions Of when and why and how,

What was Your vow and vi - sion Of love and sac - ri - fice?
The Spir - it's power and bless - ing: "Go now, You are My Son"?
But craves the gift of see - ing What God is do - ing now.

Was there a sud-den splen - dor Of proph-ets, priests, and kings,
Did scrip - ture join with scrip - ture In words of sharp sur - prise:
Lord, bring us to our Jor - dan Of new - ly o - pened eyes,

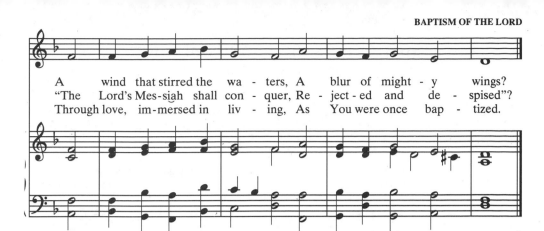

A wind that stirred the wa - ters, A blur of might - y wings?
"The Lord's Mes-siah shall con - quer, Re - ject - ed and de - spised"?
Through love, im-mersed in liv - ing, As You were once bap - tized.

Alternate tune: LLANGLOFFAN, 289

Matthew 3:13–16

When Jesus Came to Jordan

72

DE EERSTEN ZIJN DE LAATSTEN   7.6.7.6

Fred Pratt Green, 1973 · Frederik August Mehrtens (1922–1975)

1. When Je - sus came to Jor - dan To be bap - tized by John,
2. He came to share re - pen - tance With all who mourn their sins,
3. He came to share temp - ta - tion, Our ut - most woe and loss;
4. So when the dove de - scend - ed On him, the Ho - ly One,

He did not come for par - don, But as God's Ho - ly One.
To speak the vi - tal sen - tence With which good news be - gins.
For us and our sal - va - tion To die up - on the cross.
The hid - den years had end - ed, The age of grace be - gun.

Luke 9:28–36

73   Swiftly Pass the Clouds of Glory

GENEVA   8.7.8.7 D

Thomas H. Troeger, 1985   George Henry Day, 1940

1. Swift - ly pass the clouds of glo - ry, Heav-en's voice, the daz - zling light;
2. Glimpsed and gone the rev - e - la - tion, They shall gain and keep its truth,
3. Lord, trans-fig - ure our per-cep - tion With the pur - est light that shines,

Mo - ses and E - li - jah van - ish; Christ a - lone com-mands the height!
Not by build-ing on the moun-tain An - y shrine or sa - cred booth,
And re - cast our life's in - ten - tions To the shape of Your de - signs,

Pe - ter, James, and John fall si - lent, Turn - ing from the sum-mit's rise
But by fol - low - ing the Sav - ior Through the val - ley to the cross
Till we seek no oth - er glo - ry Than what lies past Cal - vary's hill

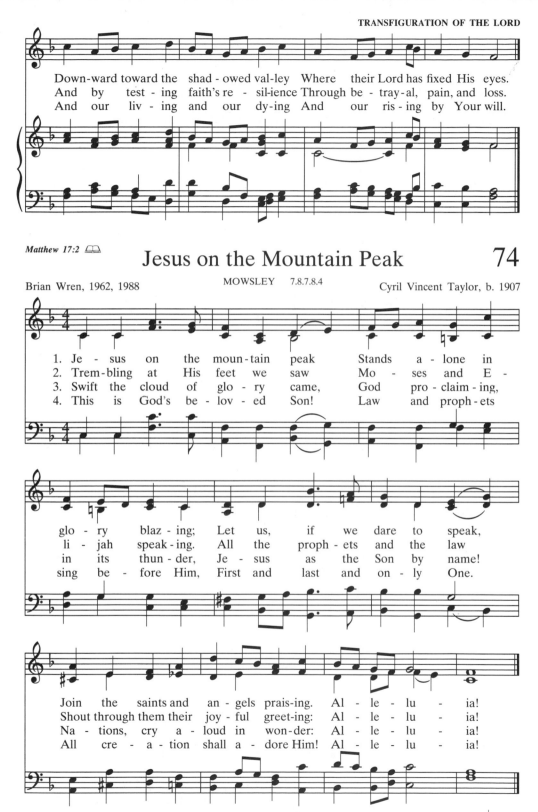

Matthew 17:2

Jesus on the Mountain Peak

74

MOWSLEY   7.8.7.8.4

Brian Wren, 1962, 1988

Cyril Vincent Taylor, b. 1907

Down-ward toward the shad-owed val-ley Where their Lord has fixed His eyes.
And by test-ing faith's re-sil-ience Through be-tray-al, pain, and loss.
And our liv-ing and our dy-ing And our ris-ing by Your will.

1. Je - sus on the moun-tain peak Stands a - lone in
2. Trem-bling at His feet we saw Mo - ses and E -
3. Swift the cloud of glo - ry came, God pro - claim - ing,
4. This is God's be - lov - ed Son! Law and proph - ets

glo - ry blaz-ing; Let us, if we dare to speak,
li - jah speak-ing. All the proph-ets and the law
in its thun-der, Je - sus as the Son by name!
sing be - fore Him, First and last and on - ly One.

Join the saints and an - gels prais-ing. Al - le - lu - ia!
Shout through them their joy - ful greet-ing: Al - le - lu - ia!
Na - tions, cry a - loud in won-der: Al - le - lu - ia!
All cre - a - tion shall a - dore Him! Al - le - lu - ia!

♩=88–96

75   O Wondrous Sight, O Vision Fair

DEO GRACIAS   LM

Trans. John Mason Neale, 1851; alt. 1861   "The Agincourt Song," England, c. 1415

1. O won-drous sight, O vi-sion fair Of glo-ry that the church shall share, Which Christ up-on the moun-tain shows, Where bright-er than the sun He glows!

2. From age to age the tale de-clare, How with the three dis-ci-ples there, Where Mo-ses and E-li-jah meet, The Lord holds con-verse high and sweet.

3. The law and proph-ets there have place, Two cho-sen wit-ness-es of grace; The Fa-ther's voice from out the cloud Pro-claims His on-ly Son a-loud.

4. With shin-ing face and bright ar-ray Christ deigns to man-i-fest to-day What glo-ry shall be theirs a-bove Who joy in God with per-fect love.

5. And faith-ful hearts are raised on high By this great vi-sion's mys-ter-y, For which in joy-ful strains we raise The voice of prayer, the hymn of praise.

My Song Is Love Unknown

76

LOVE UNKNOWN   6.6.6.6.4.4.4.4

Samuel Crossman, 1664

John Ireland, 1918

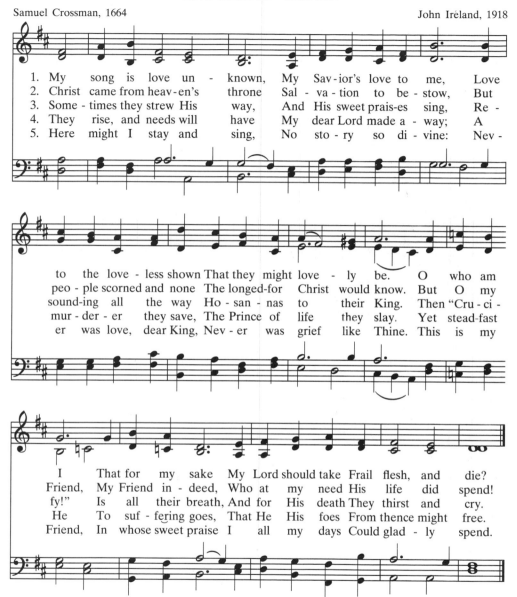

1. My song is love un - known, My Sav-ior's love to me, Love to the love - less shown That they might love - ly be. O who am I That for my sake My Lord should take Frail flesh, and die?

2. Christ came from heav-en's throne Sal - va - tion to be - stow, But peo - ple scorned and none The longed-for Christ would know. But O my Friend, My Friend in - deed, Who at my need His life did spend!

3. Some - times they strew His way, And His sweet prais-es sing, Re - sound-ing all the way Ho - san - nas to their King. Then "Cru - ci - fy!" Is all their breath, And for His death They thirst and cry.

4. They rise, and needs will have My dear Lord made a - way; A mur - der - er they save, The Prince of life they slay. Yet stead-fast He To suf - fering goes, That He His foes From thence might free.

5. Here might I stay and sing, No sto - ry so di - vine: Nev - er was love, dear King, Nev - er was grief like Thine. This is my Friend, In whose sweet praise I all my days Could glad - ly spend.

♩=52–56

77 Forty Days and Forty Nights

AUS DER TIEFE RUFE ICH   7.7.7.7

George Hunt Smyttan, 1856; alt.   Attr. Martin Herbst, 1676

1. For - ty days and for - ty nights You were fast - ing in the wild;
2. Shall not we Your sor - row share And from world - ly joys ab - stain,
3. Then if Sa - tan on us press, Flesh or spir - it to as - sail,
4. So shall we have peace di - vine: Ho - lier glad - ness ours shall be;

For - ty days and for - ty nights Tempt - ed, and yet un - de - filed.
Fast - ing with un - ceas - ing prayer, Strong with You to suf - fer pain?
Vic - tor in the wil - der - ness, Grant that we not faint nor fail!
Round us, too, shall an - gels shine, Such as served You faith - ful - ly.

5. Keep, O keep us, Savior dear,
   Ever constant by Your side;
   That with You we may appear
   At the eternal Eastertide.

♩=50–54

78 Alas! And Did My Savior Bleed

MARTYRDOM   CM

Hugh Wilson, c. 1800
Isaac Watts, 1707   Adapt. and harm. Robert Smith, 1825

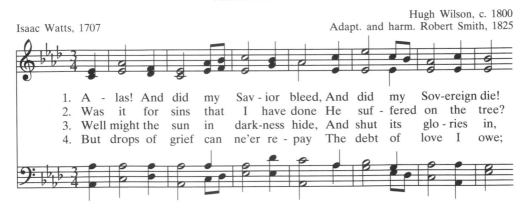

1. A - las! And did my Sav - ior bleed, And did my Sov - ereign die!
2. Was it for sins that I have done He suf - fered on the tree?
3. Well might the sun in dark - ness hide, And shut its glo - ries in,
4. But drops of grief can ne'er re - pay The debt of love I owe;

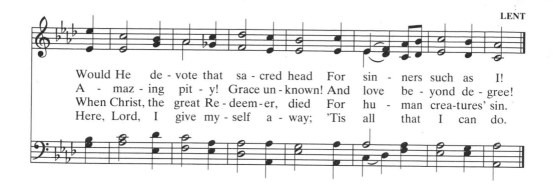

Would He de-vote that sa-cred head For sin-ners such as I!
A - maz - ing pit - y! Grace un-known! And love be - yond de - gree!
When Christ, the great Re-deem-er, died For hu - man crea-tures' sin.
Here, Lord, I give my-self a - way; 'Tis all that I can do.

Kind Maker of the World 79

A LA VENUE DE NOËL LM

Attr. Gregory the Great (540–604)
Vers. *The Hymnal 1940; alt. 1982*

Fleurs des noëls, 1535

1. Kind Mak-er of the world, O hear The fer-vent
2. Each heart is man - i - fest to Thee; Thou know-est
3. Spare us, O Lord, who now con - fess Our sins and
4. Give us the dis - ci - pline that springs From ab - sti -

prayer, with man - y a tear Poured forth by all the
our in - fir - mi - ty; Now we re-pent and
all our wick - ed - ness, And, for the glo ry
nence in out - ward things With in - ward fast - ing,

pen - i - tent Who keep this ho - ly fast of Lent!
seek Thy face; Grant un - to us Thy par - doning grace.
of Thy Name, Our weak-ened souls to health re - claim.
so that we In heart and soul may dwell with Thee.

5. Grant, O Thou blessed Trinity,
   Grant, O unchanging Unity,
   That this our fast of forty days
   May work our profit and Thy praise!

♩=72–80

80 Jesus Walked This Lonesome Valley

LONESOME VALLEY 8.8.10.8

American spiritual

American spiritual

1. Je - sus walked this lone-some val - ley, He had to
2. We must walk this lone-some val - ley, We have to
3. You must go and stand your tri - al, You have to

walk it by Him - self; O, no-bod-y else could walk it
walk it by our - selves; O, no-bod-y else can walk it
stand it by your - self, O, no-bod-y else can stand it

for Him, He had to walk it by Him - self.
for us, We have to walk it by our - selves.
for you, You have to stand it by your - self.

Luke 4:1–13

81 Lord, Who Throughout These Forty Days

ST. FLAVIAN CM

Claudia F. I. Hernaman, 1873; alt.

Day's *Psalter*, 1562

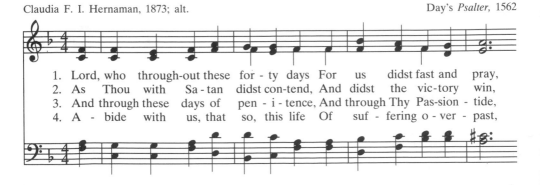

1. Lord, who through-out these for - ty days For us didst fast and pray,
2. As Thou with Sa - tan didst con-tend, And didst the vic - to-ry win,
3. And through these days of pen - i - tence, And through Thy Pas - sion - tide,
4. A - bide with us, that so, this life Of suf - fering o - ver - past,

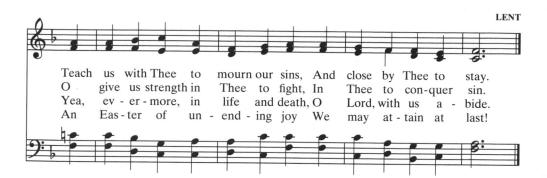

Teach us with Thee to mourn our sins, And close by Thee to stay.
O give us strength in Thee to fight, In Thee to con-quer sin.
Yea, ev-er-more, in life and death, O Lord, with us a-bide.
An Eas-ter of un-end-ing joy We may at-tain at last!

John 1:29

O Lamb of God Most Holy! 82

O LAMM GOTTES 7.7.7.7.7.7.7

Nikolaus Decius, c. 1541
Trans. Arthur Tozer Russell (1806–1874)

Nikolaus Decius, c. 1541

Stanzas 1,2,3

O Lamb of God most ho-ly! Who on the cross did suf-fer,

And pa-tient still and low-ly, Your-self to scorn did of-fer;

Our sins by You were tak-en, Or hope had us for-

sak-en:
1. Have mer-cy on us, Je - sus!
2. Have mer-cy on us, Je - sus!
3. Your peace be with us, Je - sus!

83 O Love, How Deep, How Broad, How High

DEO GRACIAS   LM

Attr. Thomas à Kempis (1380–1471)
Trans. Benjamin Webb and John Mason Neale, 1851; alt.

"The Agincourt Song," England, c. 1415
Based on E. Power Biggs, 1947
Arr. Richard Proulx (b. 1937)

Fanfare (may be introduction, interlude, and conclusion)

1. O love, how deep, how broad, how high, How
2. For us bap-tized, for us He bore His
3. For us to e - vil power be - trayed, Scourged,
4. For us He rose from death a - gain; For
5. All glo - ry to our Lord and God For

pass - ing thought and fan - ta - sy, That God, the Son of
ho - ly fast and hun-gered sore; For us temp-ta - tions
mocked, in pur - ple robe ar - rayed, He bore the shame-ful
us He went on high to reign; For us He sent the
love so deep, so high, so broad: The Trin - i - ty whom

God, should take Our mor - tal form for mor-tals' sake.
sharp He knew, For us the tempt - er o - ver - threw.
cross and death, For us gave up His dy - ing breath.
Spir - it here To guide, to strength - en, and to cheer.
we a - dore For - ev - er and for - ev - er - more.

Galatians 6:14

In the Cross of Christ I Glory 84

RATHBUN 8.7.8.7

John Bowring, 1825   Ithamar Conkey, 1849

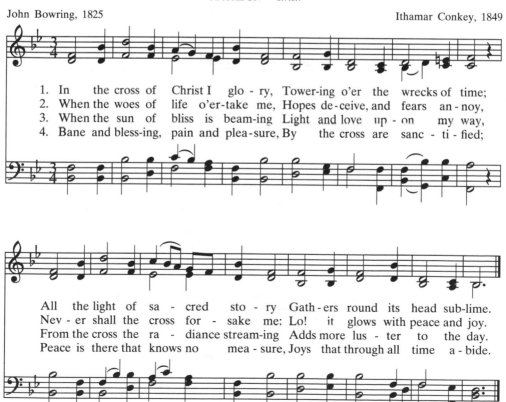

1. In the cross of Christ I glo - ry, Tower-ing o'er the wrecks of time;
2. When the woes of life o'er-take me, Hopes de-ceive, and fears an - noy,
3. When the sun of bliss is beam-ing Light and love up - on my way,
4. Bane and bless-ing, pain and plea-sure, By the cross are sanc - ti - fied;

All the light of sa - cred sto - ry Gath-ers round its head sub-lime.
Nev - er shall the cross for - sake me: Lo! it glows with peace and joy.
From the cross the ra - diance stream-ing Adds more lus - ter to the day.
Peace is there that knows no mea - sure, Joys that through all time a - bide.

85 What Wondrous Love Is This

WONDROUS LOVE   12.9.12.12.9

Walker's *Southern Harmony,* 1835
Harm. *Cantate Domino,* 1980

American folk hymn, c. 1811

1. What won-drous love is this, O my soul, O my soul,
2. To God and to the Lamb I will sing, I will sing,
3. And when from death I'm free, I'll sing on, I'll sing on,

What won - drous love is this, O my soul!
To God and to the Lamb, I will sing;
And when from death I'm free, I'll sing on;

What won - drous love is this that caused the Lord of bliss
To God and to the Lamb who is the great I Am,
And when from death I'm free, I'll sing and joy - ful be,

Music: Harmonization © World Council of Churches. Reprinted by permission.

To   bear the *heav - y   cross   for my   soul,   for my   soul,
While   mil - lions join the   theme,   I   will   sing,   I   will   sing;
And   through e - ter - ni - ty   I'll sing   on,   I'll sing   on,

To   bear the   *heav - y   cross   for my   soul!
While   mil - lions join the   theme,   I will   sing!
And   through e - ter - ni - ty   I'll sing   on!

*Or "dreadful curse" (as original text).

86 When We Are Tempted to Deny Your Son

PSALM 22   10.10.10.6

David W. Romig, 1965   Louis Bourgeois, 1542; abridged

1. When we are tempt-ed to de - ny Your Son,
2. When we are tempt-ed to be - tray Your Son,
3. When we for - get the cross that held Your Son,
4. When doubt ob - scures the vic - tory of Your Son,

Be - cause we fear the an - ger of the world,
Be - cause He leads us in a hard - er way,
And would a - void the bur - den of this life,
And faith is weak and all re - solve has fled,

And we are few who bear the in - sults hurled,
And makes de - mands we do not want to pay,
The cry for jus - tice and an end to strife,
Help us to know Him ris - en from the dead;

Your will, O God, be done.

Text: © 1972 by The Westminster Press; from *The Worshipbook—Services and Hymns.*

The Glory of These Forty Days

ERHALT UNS, HERR   LM

87

Gregory the Great (540–604)
Trans. Maurice F. Bell, 1906

Klug's *Geistliche Lieder,* 1543
Harm. Johann Sebastian Bach, 1725

1. The glo-ry of these for-ty days We
cel-e-brate with songs of praise; For Christ, by whom all
things were made, Him-self has fast-ed and has prayed.

2. A-lone and fast-ing, Mo-ses saw The
lov-ing God who gave the law; And to E-li-jah,
fast-ing, came The steeds and char-i-ots of flame.

3. So Dan-iel trained his mys-tic sight, De-
liv-ered from the li-on's might; And John, the Bride-groom's
friend, be-came The her-ald of Mes-si-ah's name.

4. Then grant that we like them be true, Con-
sumed in fast and prayer with You; Our spir-its strength-en
with Your grace, And give us joy to see Your face.

Text: From the *English Hymnal,* 1906. Used by permission of Oxford University Press.

♩=76–84

88 All Glory, Laud, and Honor

VALET WILL ICH DIR GEBEN   7.6.7.6 D

Theodulph of Orleans, c. 820
Trans. John Mason Neale, 1851; alt. 1859

Melchior Teschner, 1614
Arr. William Henry Monk, 1861

Refrain

All glo-ry, laud, and hon - or To Thee, Re-deem-er, King!

Fine

To whom the lips of chil - dren Made sweet ho-san-nas ring.

1. Thou art the King of Is - ra - el, Thou Da - vid's roy - al Son,
2. The peo - ple of the He - brews With palms be - fore Thee went;
3. To Thee, be - fore Thy pas - sion, They sang their hymns of praise;
4. Thou didst ac - cept their prais - es; Ac - cept the prayers we bring,

Repeat Refrain

Who in the Lord's name com - est, The King and bless-ed One.
Our praise and prayers and an - thems Be - fore Thee we pre - sent.
To Thee, now high ex - alt - ed, Our mel - o - dy we raise.
Who in all good de - light - est, Thou good and gra-cious King!

Hosanna, Loud Hosanna

ELLACOMBE   7.6.7.6 D

Jennette Threlfall, 1873

Gesangbuch der Herzogl. Wirtembergischen
Katholischen Hofkapelle, 1784; alt. 1868

1. Ho - san - na, loud ho - san - na, The lit - tle chil-dren sang;
2. From Ol - i - vet they fol - lowed 'Mid an ex - ult - ant crowd,
3. "Ho - san - na in the high - est!" That an - cient song we sing,

Through pil - lared court and tem - ple The joy - ful an - them rang;
The vic - tor palm branch wav - ing, And chant-ing clear and loud;
For Christ is our Re - deem - er, The Lord of heaven our King.

To Je - sus, who had blessed them Close fold - ed to His breast,
The Lord of earth and heav - en Rode on in low - ly state,
O may we ev - er praise Him With heart and life and voice,

The chil - dren sang their prais - es, The sim - plest and the best.
Nor scorned that lit - tle chil - dren Should on His bid-ding wait.
And in His bliss - ful pres - ence E - ter - nal - ly re - joice.

90 Ride On! Ride On in Majesty!

THE KING'S MAJESTY   LM

Henry Hart Milman, 1827   Graham George, 1939

1. Ride on! Ride on in maj - es - ty! Hark! all the tribes ho-san-na cry; O Sav-ior meek, pur-sue Thy road With palms and scat-tered gar-ments strowed.

2. Ride on! Ride on in maj - es - ty! In low-ly pomp ride on to die; O Christ, Thy tri-umphs now be-gin O'er cap-tive death and con-quered sin.

3. Ride on! Ride on in maj - es - ty! The wing-ed squad-rons of the sky Look down with sad and won-dering eyes To see the ap-proach-ing sac-ri-fice.

4. Ride on! Ride on in maj - es - ty! In low-ly pomp ride on to die; Bow Thy meek head to mor-tal pain, Then take, O God, Thy power, and reign.

Ride On! Ride On in Majesty!

ST. DROSTANE   LM

91

Henry Hart Milman, 1827

John Bacchus Dykes, 1862

1. Ride on! Ride on in maj - es - ty! Hark! all the tribes ho - san - na cry; O Sav - ior meek, pur - sue Thy road With palms and scat - tered gar - ments strowed.

2. Ride on! Ride on in maj - es - ty! In low - ly pomp ride on to die: O Christ, Thy tri - umphs now be - gin O'er cap - tive death and con - quered sin.

3. Ride on! Ride on in maj - es - ty! The wing - ed squad - rons of the sky Look down with sad and won - dering eyes To see the ap - proach-ing sac - ri - fice.

4. Ride on! Ride on in maj - es - ty! In low - ly pomp ride on to die; Bow Thy meek head to mor - tal pain, Then take, O God, Thy power, and reign.

92 Beneath the Cross of Jesus

ST. CHRISTOPHER 7.6.8.6.8.6.8.6

Elizabeth Cecilia Douglas Clephane, 1868

Frederick Charles Maker, 1881

1. Be - neath the cross of Je - sus I fain would take my stand,
2. Up - on the cross of Je - sus Mine eye at times can see

The shad - ow of a might - y rock With - in a wea - ry land;
The ver - y dy - ing form of One Who suf - fered there for me:

A home with - in the wil - der - ness, A rest up - on the way,
And from my strick - en heart with tears Two won - ders I con - fess:

From the burn - ing of the noon - tide heat, And the bur - den of the day.
The won - ders of re - deem - ing love And my un - wor - thi - ness.

Ah, Holy Jesus

HERZLIEBSTER JESU 11.11.11.5

Johann Heermann, 1630
Trans. Robert Bridges, 1899
Alt. *Psalter Hymnal,* 1987

Johann Crüger, 1640

1. Ah, ho-ly Je - sus, how have You of - fend - ed,
2. Who was the guilt - y? Who brought this up - on You?
3. For me, dear Je - sus, was Your in - car - na - tion,
4. There - fore, dear Je - sus, since I can - not pay You,

That mor-tal judg-ment has on You de - scend - ed? By foes de -
It is my trea - son, Lord, that has un - done You. 'Twas I, Lord
Your mor-tal sor - row, and Your life's ob - la - tion, Your death of
I do a - dore You, and will ev - er praise You, Think on Your

rid - ed, by Your own re - ject - ed, O most af - flict - ed!
Je - sus, I it was de - nied You; I cru - ci - fied You.
an - guish and Your bit - ter pas - sion, For my sal - va - tion.
pit - y and Your love un - swerv-ing, Not my de - serv - ing.

John 13:3–5

94 An Upper Room Did Our Lord Prepare

O WALY WALY   9.8.9.8

Fred Pratt Green, 1973

English folk melody
Harm. John Weaver, 1988

1. An up-per room did our Lord pre-pare For those He loved un-til the end: And His dis-ci-ples still gath-er there To cel-e-brate their ris-en Friend.
2. A last-ing gift Je-sus gave His own: To share His bread, His lov-ing cup. What-ev-er bur-dens may bow us down, He by His cross shall lift us up.
3. And af-ter sup-per He washed their feet, For ser-vice, too, is sac-ra-ment. In Christ our joy shall be made com-plete: Sent out to serve, as He was sent.
4. No end there is! We de-part in peace, He loves be-yond the ut-ter-most: In ev-ery room in our Fa-ther's house Christ will be there, as Lord and Host.

♩=54–58

He Never Said a Mumbalin' Word

Irregular

African-American spiritual

African-American spiritual

5. He bowed His head and died, and He never
   said a mumbalin' word;
   He bowed His head and died, and He never
   said a mumbalin' word.
   Not a word, not a word, not a word.

96

Calvary

9.9.9.8 with refrain

African-American spiritual

African-American spiritual

Refrain
Harmony

Cal - va - ry, Cal - va - ry, Cal - va -

ry, Cal - va - ry, Cal - va - ry,

Fine

Cal - va - ry, Sure-ly He died on Cal - va - ry.

Unison

1. Ev - ery time I think a-bout Je - sus, Ev - ery
2. Don't you hear the ham - mer ring - ing? Don't you
3. Don't you hear Him call - ing His Fa - ther? Don't you
4. Don't you hear Him say, "It is fin - ished"? Don't you

time I think a-bout Je - sus, Ev - ery time I
hear the ham - mer ring - ing? Don't you hear the
hear Him call - ing His Fa - ther? Don't you hear Him
hear Him say, "It is fin - ished"? Don't you hear Him

D.C.

think a-bout Je - sus,
ham - mer ring - ing?
call - ing His Fa - ther? Sure-ly He died on Cal - va - ry.
say, "It is fin - ished"?

Go to Dark Gethsemane

97

REDHEAD 76　7.7.7.7.7.7

James Montgomery, 1820, 1825; alt.　　　　　　　　　　　　　Richard Redhead, 1853

1. Go to dark Geth-se-ma-ne, All who feel the tempt-er's power;
2. Fol-low to the judg-ment hall; View the Lord of life ar-raigned;
3. Cal-vary's mourn-ful moun-tain climb; There, a-dor-ing at His feet,
4. Ear-ly has-ten to the tomb Where they laid His breath-less clay:

Your Re-deem-er's con-flict see, Watch with Him one bit-ter hour;
O the worm-wood and the gall! O the pangs His soul sus-tained!
Mark the mir-a-cle of time, God's own sac-ri-fice com-plete;
All is sol-i-tude and gloom. Who has tak-en Him a-way?

Turn not from His griefs a-way, Learn from Je-sus Christ to pray.
Shun not suf-fering, shame, or loss; Learn from Christ to bear the cross.
"It is fin-ished!" hear Him cry; Learn from Je-sus Christ to die.
Christ is risen! He meets our eyes. Sav-ior, teach us so to rise.

98 O Sacred Head, Now Wounded

PASSION CHORALE   7.6.7.6 D

Attr. Bernard of Clairvaux (1091–1153)
Trans. James Waddell Alexander, 1830

Hans Leo Hassler, 1601
Harm. Johann Sebastian Bach, 1729

1. O sa - cred head, now wound-ed, With grief and shame weighed down;
2. What Thou, my Lord, hast suf - fered Was all for sin - ners' gain:
3. What lan - guage shall I bor - row To thank Thee, dear - est friend,

Now scorn-ful - ly sur - round - ed With thorns, Thine on - ly crown;
Mine, mine was the trans - gres - sion, But Thine the dead - ly pain.
For this Thy dy - ing sor - row, Thy pit - y with - out end?

O sa - cred head, what glo - ry, What bliss till now was Thine!
Lo, here I fall, my Sav - ior! 'Tis I de - serve Thy place;
O make me Thine for - ev - er; And should I faint - ing be,

Yet, though de - spised and gor - y, I joy to call Thee mine.
Look on me with Thy fa - vor, Vouch - safe to me Thy grace.
Lord, let me nev - er, nev - er Out - live my love to Thee.

Throned Upon the Awful Tree

ARFON 7.7.7.7.7.7

French and Welsh melody
Arr. Hugh Davies, c. 1906

John Ellerton, 1875

1. Throned up-on the aw-ful tree, Lamb of God, Your
grief I see. Dark-ness veils Your an-guished face;
None its lines of woe can trace. None can tell what
pangs un-known Hold You si-lent and a-lone—
Till the Lamb of God may die.

2. Si-lent through those three dread hours, Wres-tling with the
e-vil powers, Left a-lone with hu-man sin,
Gloom a-round You and with-in, Till the ap-point-ed
time is nigh, Till the Lamb of God may die.

3. Hark, that cry that peals a-loud Up-ward through the
whelm-ing cloud! You, the Fa-ther's on-ly Son,
You, His own a-noint-ed one, You are ask-ing—
can it be— "Why have You for-sak-en Me?"

4. Lord, should fear and an-guish roll, Flood-ing o'er my
sin-ful soul, You, who once were thus be-reft
That Your own might ne'er be left, Teach me by that
bit-ter cry In the gloom to know You nigh.

100 When I Survey the Wondrous Cross

ROCKINGHAM LM

Second Supplement to Psalmody in Miniature, 1783
Harm. Edward Miller, 1790

Isaac Watts, 1707

1. When I sur - vey the won - drous cross On which the
2. For - bid it, Lord, that I should boast, Save in the
3. See, from His head, His hands, His feet, Sor - row and
4. Were the whole realm of na - ture mine, That were a

Prince of glo - ry died, My rich - est gain I
death of Christ my God; All the vain things that
love flow min - gled down; Did e'er such love and
pres - ent far too small; Love so a - maz - ing,

count but loss, And pour con - tempt on all my pride.
charm me most, I sac - ri - fice them to His blood.
sor - row meet, Or thorns com - pose so rich a crown?
so di - vine, De - mands my soul, my life, my all.

When I Survey the Wondrous Cross 101

HAMBURG LM

Isaac Watts, 1707

Lowell Mason, 1824

1. When I sur-vey the won-drous cross On which the Prince of glo-ry died, My rich-est gain I count but loss, And pour con-tempt on all my pride.
2. For-bid it, Lord, that I should boast, Save in the death of Christ my God; All the vain things that charm me most, I sac-ri-fice them to His blood.
3. See, from His head, His hands, His feet, Sor-row and love flow min-gled down; Did e'er such love and sor-row meet, Or thorns com-pose so rich a crown?
4. Were the whole realm of na-ture mine, That were a pres-ent far too small; Love so a-maz-ing, so di-vine, De-mands my soul, my life, my all.

102 Were You There?

WERE YOU THERE   Irregular

African-American spiritual
Arr. Melva Wilson Costen, 1987

African-American spiritual

1. Were you there when they cru-ci-fied my Lord? (Were you there?)
2. Were you there when they nailed Him to the tree? (Were you there?)
3. Were you there when they pierced Him in the side? (Were you there?)
4. Were you there when they laid Him in the tomb? (Were you there?)

Were you there when they cru-ci-fied my Lord?
Were you there when they nailed Him to the tree?
Were you there when they pierced Him in the side?   Oh!
Were you there when they laid Him in the tomb?

Some-times it caus-es me to trem-ble, trem-ble, trem-ble.

Were you there when they cru-ci-fied my Lord? (Were you there?)
Were you there when they nailed Him to the tree? (Were you there?)
Were you there when they pierced Him in the side? (Were you there?)
Were you there when they laid Him in the tomb? (Were you there?)

Deep Were His Wounds, and Red

MARLEE 6.6.6.6.8.8

103

William Johnson, 1953

Leland Bernhard Sateren, 1958

1. Deep were His wounds, and red, On cru - el Cal - va - ry,
2. He suf-fered shame and scorn And wretch-ed, dire dis-grace;
3. His life, His all, He gave When He was cru - ci - fied;

As on the cross He bled In bit - ter ag - o - ny. But they whom
For-sak - en and for-lorn, He hung there in our place. But all who
Our bur-dened souls to save, What fear - ful death He died! But each of

sin has wound-ed sore Find heal-ing in the wounds He bore.
would from sin be free Look to His cross for vic - to - ry.
us, though dead in sin, Through Christ e - ter - nal life may win.

♩=96–104

104 Christ Is Risen! Shout Hosanna!

HYMN TO JOY   8.7.8.7 D

Ludwig van Beethoven, 1824
Adapt. Edward Hodges (1796–1867); alt.

Brian Wren (b. 1936)

1. Christ is ris - en! Shout Ho - san - na! Cel - e - brate this day of days!
2. Christ is ris - en! Raise your spir - its From the cav - erns of de - spair.
3. Christ is ris - en! Earth and heav-en Nev - er - more shall be the same.

Christ is ris - en! Hush in won-der: All cre - a - tion is a - mazed.
Walk with glad-ness in the morn-ing. See what love can do and dare.
Break the bread of new cre - a - tion Where the world is still in pain.

In the des - ert all - sur-round-ing, See, a spread-ing tree has grown.
Drink the wine of res - ur - rec - tion, Not a ser - vant, but a friend,
Tell its grim, de - mon-ic cho - rus: "Christ is ris - en! Get you gone!"

Heal - ing leaves of grace a - bound-ing Bring a taste of love un-known.
Je - sus is our strong com-pan - ion. Joy and peace shall nev - er end.
God the First and Last is with us. Sing Ho - san - na, ev - ery-one!

Because You Live, O Christ

VRUECHTEN   Irregular

Shirley Erena Murray, 1987

Dutch melody, 17th century
Harm. Alice Parker, 1969

1. Be-cause You live, O Christ, The gar-den of the world has come to flow-er;
2. Be-cause You live, O Christ, The spir-it bird of hope is freed for fly-ing;
3. Be-cause You live, O Christ, The rain-bow of Your peace will span cre-a-tion,

The dark-ness of the tomb Is flood-ed with Your res-ur-rec-tion pow-er.
Our ca-ges of de-spair No long-er keep us closed and life-de-ny-ing.
The col-ors of Your love Will draw all hu-man-kind to ad-o-ra-tion.

Refrain

The stone has rolled a-way And death can-not im-pris-on!

O sing this Eas-ter Day, For Je-sus Christ has ris-en,

has ris-en, has ris-en, has ris-en!

106 Alleluia, Alleluia! Give Thanks

ALLELUIA NO. 1   8.8 with refrain

Donald Fishel, 1973
Arr. Betty Pulkingham
and Donald Fishel, 1979

Donald Fishel, 1973

Descant

Al - le - lu - ia, al - le -

Refrain E   C#m   F#m

Al-le - lu - ia, al-le - lu - ia! Give thanks to the

lu - ia, al - le - lu - ia!

B   E   C#m

ris - en Lord. Al - le - lu - ia, al - le - lu - ia! Give

1-4   *Final ending*

Praise to His Name.   Name.

F#m   B   E   E

praise to His Name.   Name.

1. Je - sus is Lord of all the earth.
2. Spread the good news o'er all the earth:
3. We have been cru - ci - fied with Christ.
4. Come, let us praise the liv - ing God,

He is the King of cre - a - tion.
Je - sus has died and has ris - en.
Now we shall live for ev - er.
Joy - ful - ly sing to our Sav - ior.

Al-le -

♩=80–88

107 Celebrate with Joy and Singing

EVELYN CHAPEL   8.7.8.7 D

Mary Jackson Cathey, 1986   R. Bedford Watkins, 1984

1. Cel - e - brate with joy and sing - ing, Al - le - lu - ia
2. Hon - or, glo - ry, praise, thanks-giv - ing Give we now to
3. Wor-ship now with shouts of glad-ness, For the Christ, the

be our song. Je - sus Christ has risen to save us,
God a - bove. With the cross and grave Christ bought us,
Ho - ly One, On this day of res - ur - rec - tion,

Prais-es to our Christ be - long. Through great love has come the vic-tory;
Let us now re - turn that love. By our lives of ded - i - ca-tion,
For the world new life has won. Let us pray and praise the Sav-ior,

Life, not death, can be our claim. Let us now de -
As we teach and tes - ti - fy, May we show Christ's
Trust the acts, be - lieve the word. Our sal - va - tion

clare Christ's great - ness, Spread good news, pro - claim Christ's name.
love a - round us, May it grow and pu - ri - fy.
has been pur - chased By our lov - ing, ris - en Lord.

♩=112–120

Christ Is Alive!   108

TRURO   LM

Brian Wren, 1968; rev.

Thomas Williams, 1789
Harm. Lowell Mason (1792–1872)

1. Christ is a - live! Let Chris - tians sing. The cross stands
2. Christ is a - live! No long - er bound To dis - tant
3. Not throned a - far, re - mote - ly high, Un - touched, un -
4. In ev - ery in - sult, rift, and war, Where col - or,

emp - ty to the sky. Let streets and homes with
years in Pal - es - tine, But sav - ing, heal - ing,
moved by hu - man pains, But dai - ly, in the
scorn, or wealth di - vide, Christ suf - fers still, yet

prais - es ring. Love, drowned in death, shall nev - er die.
here and now, And touch - ing ev - ery place and time.
midst of life, Our Sav - ior in the God - head reigns.
loves the more, And lives, where ev - en hope has died.

5. Christ is alive, and comes to bring   Till earth and sky and ocean ring
   Good news to this and every age,   With joy, with justice, love, and praise.

Cristo Vive
Christ Is Risen

1 Corinthians 15:12–23

ARGENTINA (Sosa)   8.7.8.7 D

Nicolas Martinez, 1960
Trans. Fred Kaan, 1972

Pablo Sosa, 1960; alt.
As in *Cantate Domino*, 1980

1. Cris - to vi - ve, fue-ra_el llan - to, Los la - men - tos
2. Que si Cris - to no vi - vie - ra Va - na fue - ra

1. Christ is ris - en, Christ is liv - ing, Dry your tears, be
2. If the Lord had nev - er ris - en, We'd have noth - ing

y el pe - sar! Ni la muer - te ni_el se - pul - cro
nues-tra fe. Mas se cum - ple Su pro - me - sa:

un - a - fraid! Death and dark - ness could not hold Him,
to be - lieve. But His prom - ise can be trust - ed:

Lo han po - di - do su - je - tar. No bus - quéis en - tre los
"Por - que vi - vo, vi - vi - réis." Si_en Ad - án en - tró la

Nor the tomb where He was laid. Do not look a - mong the
"You will live, be - cause I live." As we share the death of

muer-tos Al que siem - pre_ha de vi - vir. Cris - to
muer - te, Por Je - sús la vi - da_en - tró; No te -
dead for One who lives for - ev - er - more; Tell the
Ad - am, So in Christ we live a - gain. Death has

vi - ve! es - tas nue - vas Por do - quier de - jad o - ir.
máis, el triun-fo_es vues - tro: ¡El Se - ñor re - su - ci - tó!
world that Christ is ris - en, Make it known He goes be - fore.
lost its sting and ter - ror. Christ the Lord has come to reign.

3. Si_es verdad que de la muerte
El pecado_es aguijón,
No temáis pues Jesucristo
Nos da vida y salvación.
Gracias demos al Dios Padre
Que nos da seguridad.
Que quien cree en Jesucristo
Vive pro la_eternidad.

3. Death has lost its old dominion,
Let the world rejoice and shout!
Christ, the firstborn of the living,
Gives us life and leads us out.
Let us thank our God who causes
Hope to spring up from the ground.
Christ is risen, Christ is giving
Life eternal, life profound.

110 Christ Jesus Lay in Death's Strong Bands

CHRIST LAG IN TODESBANDEN   8.7.8.7.7.8.7.4

Martin Luther, 1524
Trans. Richard Massie, 1854; alt.

Geystliche gesangk Buchleyn, 1524
Adapt. and harm. Johann Sebastian Bach, c. 1707

1. Christ Je - sus lay in death's strong bands For our of - fens - es
2. It was a strange and dread - ful strife When life and death con -
3. Then let us feast this Eas - ter Day On the true bread of

giv - en; But now at God's right hand Christ stands And
tend - ed; The vic - to - ry re - mained with life; The
heav - en; The Word of grace hath purged a - way The

brings us life from heav - en; There-fore let us
reign of death was end - ed. Ho - ly Scrip - ture
old and wick - ed leav - en. Christ a - lone our

joy - ful be And sing to God right thank - ful - ly Loud
plain - ly saith That death is swal - lowed up by death; Its
souls will feed; Christ is our meat and drink in - deed; Faith

songs of al - le - lu - ia! Al - le - lu - ia!
sting is lost for - ev - er! Al - le - lu - ia!
lives up - on no oth - er! Al - le - lu - ia!

Good Christians All, Rejoice and Sing! 111

GELOBT SEI GOTT   8.8.8 with alleluias

Cyril A. Alington, 1931; alt.

Melchior Vulpius, 1609
As in *Pilgrim Hymnal,* 1958

1. Good Chris-tians all, re - joice and sing! Now is the tri - umph
2. The Lord of life is risen to - day! Bring flowers of song, be -
3. Praise we in songs of vic - to - ry That love, that life which
4. Thy name we bless, O ris - en Lord, And sing to - day with

of our King! To all the world glad news we bring:
deck the way; Let ev - ery tongue re - joice and say:
can - not die, And sing with hearts up - lift - ed high:
one ac - cord The life laid down, the life re - stored:

Al - le - lu - ia!   Al - le - lu - ia!   Al - le - lu - ia!

112 Christ the Lord Is Risen Again

CHRIST IST ERSTANDEN   7.7.7.7 with alleluias

German folk melody
Klug's *Geistliche Lieder*, 1533
Arr. Ethel Porter, 1958

Michael Weisse (c. 1480–1534)
Trans. Catherine Winkworth, 1858; alt. 1988

1. Christ the Lord is risen a-gain, Christ has bro-ken ev-ery chain.
2. He who slum-bered in the grave Is ex-alt-ed now to save;
3. He who bore all pain and loss, Com-fort-less up-on the cross,

Hark, the an-gels shout for joy, Sing-ing ev-er-more on high:
Now through Chris-ten-dom it rings That the Lamb is King of kings:
Lives in glo-ry now on high, Pleads for us and hears our cry:

Al - le-lu - ia! Al - le - lu - ia! Al - le -

lu - ia! Al - le - lu - ia!

Hark, the an-gels shout for joy,
Now through Chris-ten-dom it rings
Lives in glo-ry now on high,

Sing-ing ev-er-more on high:
That the Lamb is King of kings: Al - le-lu - ia!
Pleads for us and hears our cry:

Christ the Lord Is Risen Today!

113

LLANFAIR   7.7.7.7 with alleluias

Charles Wesley, 1739; alt.

Robert Williams, 1817
Harm. David Evans, 1927

1. "Christ the Lord is   risen to - day!"
2. Love's re - deem-ing   work is   done,
3. Lives   a - gain our   glo - rious King;
4. Hail,   the Lord of   earth and heaven!

Al - le - lu - ia!

All   cre - a - tion,   join to   say;
Fought the fight, the   bat - tle   won;
Where, O death, is   now your sting?
Praise to You by   both be   given;

Al - le - lu - ia!

Raise your joys and   tri - umphs high;
Death in vain for - bids   Him   rise;
Je - sus died, our   souls to   save;
Ev - ery knee to   You   shall bow,

Al - le - lu - ia!

Sing,   O heavens, and   earth re - ply,
Christ has   o - pened par - a - dise.
Where your vic - to - ry, O   grave?
Ris - en Christ, tri - um - phant now.

Al - le - lu - ia!

Music: Harmonization from the *Revised Church Hymnary 1927.* Used by permission of Oxford University Press.

114 Come, Ye Faithful, Raise the Strain

AVE VIRGO VIRGINUM   7.6.7.6 D

John of Damascus (c. 675–749)
Trans. John Mason Neale, 1859; alt.

Bohemian Brethren's *Gesangbuch,* 1544

1. Come, ye faith-ful, raise the strain Of tri-um-phant glad-ness;
2. 'Tis the spring of souls to-day; Christ hath burst His pris-on,

God hath brought forth Is-ra-el In-to joy from sad-ness;
And from three days' sleep in death As a sun hath ris-en.

Loosed from Phar-aoh's bit-ter yoke Ja-cob's sons and daugh-ters;
Now re-joice, Je-ru-sa-lem, And with true af-fec-tion

Led them, with un-moist-ened foot, Through the Red Sea wa-ters.
Wel-come in un-wea-ried strains Je-sus' res-ur-rec-tion!

Come, Ye Faithful, Raise the Strain 115

ST. KEVIN   7.6.7.6 D

John of Damascus (c. 675–749)
Trans. John Mason Neale, 1859; alt.

Arthur Seymour Sullivan (1842–1900); alt.

1. Come, ye faith-ful, raise the strain Of tri-um-phant glad-ness;
2. 'Tis the spring of souls to-day; Christ hath burst His pris-on,

God hath brought forth Is-ra-el In-to joy from sad-ness;
And from three days' sleep in death As a sun hath ris-en.

Loosed from Phar-aoh's bit-ter yoke Ja-cob's sons and daugh-ters;
Now re-joice, Je-ru-sa-lem, And with true af-fec-tion

Led them, with un-moist-ened foot, Through the Red Sea wa-ters.
Wel-come in un-wea-ried strains Je-sus' res-ur-rec-tion!

116 O Sons and Daughters, Let Us Sing!

O FILII ET FILIAE   8.8.8 with alleluias

Attr. Jean Tisserand (d. 1494)
Trans. John Mason Neale, 1852

French tune, 15th century
Airs sur les hymnes sacrez, odes et nöels, 1623

Al - le - lu - ia! Al - le - lu - ia! Al - le-lu - ia! Al -

le - lu - ia!

1. O   sons   and daugh - ters,   let   us   sing!
2. That   Eas - ter morn,   at   break   of   day,
3. An   an - gel clad   in   white   they   see,
4. That   night the a-pos - tles   met   in   fear;
5. On   this   most ho - ly   day   of   days,

The   King   of heaven, the   glo - rious King, O'er death and hell   rose
The   faith - ful wom - en   went their way To   seek the tomb   where
Who   sat   and spoke un - to   the three, "Your Lord goes on   to
A -   mong them came their   Lord most dear, And   said, "My peace   be
To   God   your hearts and   voic - es raise, In   laud and ju - bi -

Fine

tri - umph-ing.   Al - le - lu - ia!   Al - le - lu - ia!
Je - sus lay.   Al - le - lu - ia!   Al - le - lu - ia!
Gal - i - lee."   Al - le - lu - ia!   Al - le - lu - ia!
with   you here." Al - le - lu - ia!   Al - le - lu - ia!
lee   and praise. Al - le - lu - ia!   Al - le - lu - ia!

O Sons and Daughters, Let Us Sing!   117

Attr. Jean Tisserand (d. 1494)
Trans. John Mason Neale, 1852

The following stanzas may be used for the Second Sunday of Easter:

Alleluia! Alleluia!
Alleluia! Alleluia!

1. O sons and daughters, let us sing!
   The King of heaven, the glorious King,
   O'er death and hell rose triumphing.
   Alleluia! Alleluia!

2. That night the apostles met in fear;
   Among them came their Lord most dear,
   And said, "My peace be with you here."
   Alleluia! Alleluia!

3. When Thomas first the tidings heard,
   How they had seen the risen Lord,
   He doubted the disciples' word.
   Alleluia! Alleluia!

4. "My piercèd side, O Thomas, see;
   My hands, My feet, I show to thee;
   Not faithless, but believing be."
   Alleluia! Alleluia!

5. No longer Thomas then denied,
   He saw the feet, the hands, the side;
   "Thou art my Lord and God," he cried.
   Alleluia! Alleluia!

6. How blest are they who have not seen,
   And yet whose faith hath constant been,
   For they eternal life shall win.
   Alleluia! Alleluia!

Tune: O FILII ET FILIAE (opposite)

118 The Day of Resurrection!

LANCASHIRE   7.6.7.6 D

John of Damascus (c. 675–749)
Trans. John Mason Neale, 1862

Henry Thomas Smart, c. 1835

1. The day of res - ur - rec - tion! Earth, tell it out a - broad;
2. Our hearts be pure from e - vil, That we may see a - right
3. Now let the heavens be joy - ful, Let earth the song be - gin,

The Pass - o - ver of glad - ness, The Pass - o - ver of God.
The Lord in rays e - ter - nal Of res - ur - rec - tion light;
Let the round world keep tri - umph, And all that is there - in;

From death to life e - ter - nal, From this world to the sky,
And, lis - ten - ing to His ac - cents, May hear, so calm and plain,
Let all things seen and un - seen Their notes of glad-ness blend,

Our Christ hath brought us o - ver With hymns of vic - to - ry.
His own "All hail!" and, hear - ing, May raise the vic - tor strain.
For Christ the Lord is ris - en, Our joy that hath no end.

Alternate tune: ELLACOMBE, 89

The Strife Is O'er

119

VICTORY 8.8.8 with alleluias

Latin, c. 1695
Trans. Francis Pott, 1861

Giovanni Pierluigi da Palestrina, 1591
Adapt. William Henry Monk, 1861

Refrain (before stanza 1 and after stanza 4)

Al - le - lu - ia, al - le - lu - ia, al - le - lu - ia!

1. The strife is o'er, the bat - tle done, The vic - to -
2. The powers of death have done their worst, But Christ their
3. The three sad days are quick - ly sped, Christ ris - es
4. Lord, by Your wounds on Cal - va - ry From death's dread

ry of life is won; The song of tri - umph
le - gions hath dis - persed: Let shouts of ho - ly
glo - rious from the dead: All glo - ry to our
sting Your ser - vants free, That we may live e -

has be - gun. Al - le - lu - ia!
joy out - burst. Al - le - lu - ia!
ris - en Head! Al - le - lu - ia!
ter - nal - ly. Al - le - lu - ia!

120 Hail Thee, Festival Day!

SALVE FESTA DIES   7.9.7.7 with refrain

Venantius Honorius Fortunatus (c. 530–609)
Trans. *Lutheran Book of Worship,* 1978

Ralph Vaughan Williams, 1906

Refrain

Hail thee, fest - i - val day! Blest day to be hal-lowed for - ev - er;

Day when our Lord was raised, Break-ing the king-dom of death.   death.

First time only | 2

1. Christ, who was nailed to the cross,   Is   Lord and the Rul - er of na - ture;
3. God   the Al - might - y, the Lord,   The rul - er of earth and the heav - ens,
5. Spir - it   of life and of power,   Now flow in us, fount of our be - ing,

Text: Translation copyright © 1978 *Lutheran Book of Worship.* Used by permission of Augsburg Fortress.
Music: From the *English Hymnal,* 1906. Used by permission of Oxford University Press.

Repeat Refrain once after each stanza

All things cre - at - ed on earth Sing to the glo - ry of God:
Guard us from harm with - out; Cleanse us from e - vil with - in:
Light that en - light-ens us all, Life that in all may a - bide:

2. Rise from the grave now, O Lord, The au-thor of life and cre - a - tion.
4. Je - sus, the health of the world, En-light-en our minds, great Re-deem-er,
6. Praise to the giv - er of good! O Lov-er and Au - thor of con-cord,

Repeat Refrain once after each stanza

Tread-ing the path-way of death, New life You give to us all:
Son of the Fa - ther su-preme, On - ly be - got - ten of God:
Pour out Your balm on our days; Or - der our ways in Your peace:

121 That Easter Day with Joy Was Bright

PUER NOBIS NASCITUR   LM

Trier ms., 15th century

Latin hymn, 5th century
Trans. John Mason Neale, 1852; alt.

Adapt. Michael Praetorius, 1609
Harm. George Ratcliffe Woodward, 1910

1. That Eas - ter day with joy was bright, The sun shone
2. O Je - sus, King of gen - tle - ness, Do all our
3. From ev - ery weap - on death can wield, Your own re -

out with fair - er light, When, to their long - ing eyes re -
in - most hearts pos - sess, And we to You will ev - er
deemed for - ev - er shield; O Lord of all, with us a -

stored, The a - pos - tles saw their ris - en Lord.
raise The trib - ute of our grate - ful praise.
bide In this our joy - ful Eas - ter - tide.

Thine Is the Glory

122

JUDAS MACCABEUS   5.5.6.5.6.5.6.5 with refrain

Edmond Louis Budry, 1884
Trans. R. Birch Hoyle, 1923; alt.

George Frederick Handel, 1748

1. Thine is the glo-ry, Ris-en, con-quering Son; End-less is the
2. Lo! Je-sus meets us, Ris-en from the tomb; Lov-ing-ly He
3. No more we doubt Thee, Glo-rious Prince of life! Life is nought with-

vic-tory Thou o'er death hast won. An-gels in bright rai-ment
greets us, Scat-ters fear and gloom. Let the church with glad-ness
out Thee; Aid us in our strife. Make us more than con-querors

Rolled the stone a-way, Kept the fold-ed grave-clothes
Hymns of tri-umph sing, For the Lord now liv-eth;
Through Thy death-less love; Bring us safe through Jor-dan

Refrain (last time only)

Where Thy bod-y lay.
Death hath lost its sting.
To Thy home a-bove. Thine is the glo-ry, Ris-en, con-quering Son;

End-less is the vic-tory Thou o'er death hast won.

1 Corinthians 15:3–4

123 Jesus Christ Is Risen Today

EASTER HYMN   7.7.7.7 with alleluias

Stanzas 1–3, *Lyra Davidica*, 1708
Stanza 4, Charles Wesley, 1740

Lyra Davidica, 1708
Adapted from *The Compleat Psalmodist*, 1749
Desc. *Hymns Ancient and Modern*, 1955

1. Je - sus Christ is risen to - day, Al - le - lu - ia!
2. Hymns of praise then let us sing, Al - le - lu - ia!
3. But the pains which He en - dured, Al - le - lu - ia!
4. Sing we to our God a - bove, Al - le - lu - ia!

Our tri - um - phant ho - ly day, Al - le - lu - ia!
Un - to Christ, our heaven-ly King, Al - le - lu - ia!
Our sal - va - tion have pro - cured; Al - le - lu - ia!
Praise e - ter - nal as God's love; Al - le - lu - ia!

Who did once up - on the cross, Al - le - lu - ia!
Who en - dured the cross and grave, Al - le - lu - ia!
Now a - bove the sky He's King, Al - le - lu - ia!
Praise our God, ye heaven-ly host, Al - le - lu - ia!

Suf - fer to re - deem our loss. Al - le - lu - ia!
Sin - ners to re - deem and save. Al - le - lu - ia!
Where the an - gels ev - er sing. Al - le - lu - ia!
Fa - ther, Son, and Ho - ly Ghost. Al - le - lu - ia!

Spirit of God, Unleashed on Earth 124

KEDRON LM

Attr. Elkanah Kelsay Dare
As in Pilsbury's *United States Harmony*, 1799

John W. Arthur, 1972; alt.

1. Spir - it of God, un - leashed on earth With
2. You came in power, the church was born; O
3. With burn - ing words of vic - tory won In -

rush of wind and roar of flame! With tongues of fire saints
Ho - ly Spir - it, come a - gain! From liv - ing wa - ters
spire our hearts grown cold with fear, Re - vive in us bap -

spread good news; Earth, kin - dling, blazed its loud ac - claim.
raise new saints, Let new tongues hail the ris - en Lord.
tis - mal grace, And fan our smol - dering lives to flame.

𝅗𝅥 =58–63

125 Come, Holy Spirit, Our Souls Inspire

VENI CREATOR SPIRITUS   LM

Attr. Rabanus Maurus, 9th century
Trans. John Cosin, 1627; alt.

Plainsong, Mode VIII
Arr. Healey Willan (1880–1968)

1. Come, Ho - ly Spir - it, our souls in - spire, And light - en
2. Thy bless - ed unc - tion from a - bove Is com - fort,
3. Teach us to know the Fa - ther, Son, And Thee, of

with ce - les - tial fire; Thou the a - noint - ing
life, and fire of love; En - a - ble with per -
both, to be but one; That through the a - ges

Spir - it art, Who dost Thy seven - fold gifts im - part.
pet - ual light The dull - ness of our mor - tal sight.
all a - long This may be our end - less song:

Music: Reprinted with the permission of the executor of the estate of Healey Willan.

4. Praise to Thine e - ter - nal mer - it, Fa - ther,

Son, and Ho - ly Spir - it. A - men.

Come, Holy Spirit, Heavenly Dove 126

ST. AGNES   CM

Isaac Watts, 1707

John Bacchus Dykes, 1866

1. Come, Ho - ly Spir - it, heaven-ly Dove, With all Thy quick-ening powers;
2. In vain we tune our for - mal songs, In vain we strive to rise;
3. Dear Lord, and shall we ev - er live At this poor dy - ing rate?
4. Come, Ho - ly Spir - it, heaven-ly Dove, With all Thy quick-ening powers;

Kin - dle a flame of sa - cred love In these cold hearts of ours.
Ho - san-nas lan - guish on our tongues, And our de - vo - tion dies.
Our love so faint, so cold to Thee, And Thine to us so great!
Come, shed a - broad a Sav - ior's love, And that shall kin - dle ours.

127 Come, O Spirit

BOUNDLESS MERCY   7.6.7.6 D

John A. Dalles, 1983

Union Harmony, 1837
Harm. Hilton Rufty, 1934

1. Come, O Spir-it, with Your sound Like a wind, quick rush-ing;
2. Come, O Spir-it, with Your flame, Leap-ing tongues of fire;
3. Come, O Spir-it, fill Your church, Mak-ing strong our mis-sion;

Come from heaven and stir our hearts, Each dis-ci-ple touch-ing!
Come, and with Your glo-rious light All our thoughts in-spire!
Fill Your daugh-ters and Your sons With a might-y vi-sion,

Mold our ac-tions to Your will, You our ser-vice giv-ing;
Rest up-on each ser-vant's head Till each one is speak-ing
Till the great and glo-rious day When the whole cre-a-tion

Move with-in our fel-low-ship, Trans-form now our liv-ing!
Of our Christ, the Ho-ly One All the earth is seek-ing!
Sings Your praise as Lord and King, Giv-er of sal-va-tion!

Alternate tune: ST. KEVIN, 115

On Pentecost They Gathered   128

MUNICH   7.6.7.6 D

Neuvermehrtes Meiningisches Gesangbuch, 1693
Adapt. Felix Mendelssohn, 1847

Jane Parker Huber, 1981

1. On Pen-te-cost they gath-ered Quite ear-ly in the day,
2. The peo-ple all a-round them Were star-tled and a-mazed
3. God pours the Ho-ly Spir-it On all who would be-lieve,
4. O Spir-it, sent from heav-en On that day long a-go,

A band of Christ's dis-ci-ples, To wor-ship, sing, and pray.
To un-der-stand their lan-guage, As Christ the Lord they praised.
On wom-en, men, and chil-dren Who would God's grace re-ceive.
Re-kin-dle faith a-mong us In all life's ebb and flow.

A might-y wind came blow-ing, Filled all the swirl-ing air,
What un-i-ver-sal mes-sage, What great good news was here?
That Spir-it knows no lim-it, Be-stow-ing life and power.
O give us ears to lis-ten And tongues a-flame with praise,

And tongues of fire a-glow-ing In-spired each per-son there.
That Christ, once dead, is ris-en To van-quish all our fear.
The church, formed and re-form-ing, Re-sponds in ev-ery hour.
So folk of ev-ery na-tion Glad songs of joy shall raise.

129 Come, O Spirit, Dwell Among Us

EBENEZER   8.7.8.7 D

Janie Alford, 1979

Thomas John Williams, 1890

1. Come, O Spir-it, dwell a - mong us, Come with Pen - te-
2. We would raise our al - le - lu - ias For the grace of
3. Come, O Spir-it, dwell a - mong us; Give us words of

cos - tal power; Give the church a strong-er vi - sion,
yes - ter - years; For to - mor-row's un - known path - way,
fire and flame. Help our fee - ble lips to praise You,

Help us face each cru - cial hour. Built up - on a firm foun - da - tion,
Hear, O Lord, our hum - ble prayers. In the church's pil - grim jour-ney
Glo - ri - fy Your ho - ly name. Fa - ther, Son, and Ho - ly Spir - it,

Je - sus Christ, the Cor - ner - stone, Still the church is
You have led us all the way, Still in pres - ence
Three in one: what mys - ter - y! We would sing our

called to mis-sion That God's love shall be made known.
move be-fore us, Fire by night and cloud by day.
loud ho-san-nas Now and through e-ter-ni-ty.

Let Every Christian Pray 130

LAUDES DOMINI 6.6.6 D

Fred Pratt Green, 1970   Joseph Barnby, 1868

1. Let ev-ery Chris-tian pray, This day and ev-ery day,
2. The Spir-it brought to birth The church of Christ on earth
3. On-ly the Spir-it's power Can fit us for this hour:

Come, Ho-ly Spir-it, come! Was not the church we love
To seek and save the lost: God nev-er has with-drawn,
Come, Ho-ly Spir-it, come! In-struct, in-spire, u-nite,

Com-mis-sioned from a-bove? Come, Ho-ly Spir-it, come!
Since that tre-men-dous dawn, The gifts at Pen-te-cost.
And help us see Your light: Come, Ho-ly Spir-it, come!

131 Wind Who Makes All Winds That Blow

ABERYSTWYTH   7.7.7.7 D

Thomas H. Troeger, 1983

Joseph Parry, 1879

1. Wind who makes all winds that blow— Gusts that bend the sap-lings low,
2. Fire who fuels all fires that burn— Suns a-round which plan-ets turn,
3. Ho-ly Spir-it, Wind and Flame, Move with-in our mor-tal frame.

Gales that heave the sea in waves, Stir-rings in the mind's deep caves—
Bea-cons mark-ing reefs and shoals, Shin-ing truth to guide our souls—
Make our hearts an al-tar pyre, Kin-dle them with Your own fire.

Aim Your breath with stead-y power On Your church this day, this hour.
Come to us as once You came: Burst in tongues of sa-cred flame!
Breathe and blow up-on that blaze Till our lives, our deeds and ways,

Raise, re-new the life we've lost, Spir-it God of Pen-te-cost.
Light and Pow-er, Might and Strength, Fill Your church, its breadth and length.
Speak that tongue which ev-ery land By Your grace shall un-der-stand.

This tune in a lower key, 20

Text: From *New Hymns for the Lectionary;* © 1985, Thomas H. Troeger. By permission of Oxford University Press, Inc.

Come, Great God of All the Ages

132

ABBOT'S LEIGH   8.7.8.7 D

Mary Jackson Cathey, 1987

Cyril Vincent Taylor, 1941

1. Come, great God of all the a-ges, Make Your earth-ly mis-sion known;
2. Come, Christ Je-sus, flesh and spir-it, Sure foun-da-tion, cor-ner-stone,
3. Come, great Spir-it, in and with us, Tune our ears to hear Your call;
4. Come, O come, in cel-e-bra-tion, House-hold of the one true God,

Speak through ev-ery deed and per-son, Let Your way and will be shown.
Help us form the church e-ter-nal, May Your vi-sion be our own.
Through the mov-ing of Your pres-ence, Let re-deem-ing love re-call
In com-mit-ment and re-joic-ing Let us go where Christ has trod;

Guide the church to true com-mit-ment, Give di-rec-tion now, we ask;
Send a mes-sage to each fol-lower, Lead all peo-ple to Your way;
Min-is-try in ded-i-ca-tion, Love em-bod-ied in our deeds;
As we act in faith and rev-erence, Let us, Lord, the fu-ture see;

Fit us for the work of build-ing, Ded-i-cate us to the task.
Urge us to strong faith and ac-tion As we build the church to-day.
Chal-lenge us to do Your bid-ding, See Your pur-pose, fill all needs.
Place us in the church tri-um-phant, Now and for e-ter-ni-ty.

♩=88–96

133 All Glory Be to God on High

ALLEIN GOTT IN DER HÖH' 8.7.8.7.8.8.7

Nikolaus Decius, 1522
Trans. F. Bland Tucker, 1977; alt.

Nikolaus Decius, 1539
Harm. Hieronymus Praetorius (1560–1629)

1. All glo - ry be to God on high, And peace on earth from
2. O Lamb of God, Lord Je - sus Christ, Whom God the Fa - ther
3. You on - ly are the Ho - ly One, Who came for our sal -

heav - en, And God's good will un - fail - ing - ly Be to all
gave us, Who for the world was sac - ri - ficed Up - on the
va - tion, And on - ly You are God's true Son, Who was be -

Text: Translation used by permission of the Church Pension Fund.

peo - ple giv - en. We bless, we wor - ship You, we raise For
cross to save us; And as You sit at God's right hand And
fore cre - a - tion. You on - ly, Christ, as Lord we own And,

Your great glo - ry thanks and praise, O God, Al-might - y Fa - ther.
we for judg - ment there must stand, Have mer - cy, Lord, up - on us.
with the Spir - it, You a - lone Share in the Fa - ther's glo - ry.

♩.=54–58

Isaiah 45:7

134 Creating God, Your Fingers Trace

HANCOCK LM

Jeffery Rowthorn, 1979

Eugene W. Hancock, 1989

1. Cre-at-ing God, Your fin-gers trace The bold de-signs of
2. Sus-tain-ing God, Your hands up-hold Earth's mys-teries known or
3. Re-deem-ing God, Your arms em-brace All now de-spised for
4. In-dwell-ing God, Your gos-pel claims One fam-ily with a

far-thest space; Let sun and moon and stars and light
yet un-told; Let wa-ter's frag - ile blend with air,
creed or race; Let peace, de-scend - ing like a dove,
bil-lion names; Let ev-ery life be touched by grace

And what lies hid-den praise Your might.
En - a-bling life, pro-claim Your care.
Make known on earth Your heal - ing love.
Un - til we praise You face to face.

Text: Copyright © 1979 by The Hymn Society of America, Texas Christian University, Fort Worth, TX 76129.
All rights reserved. Used by permission.
Music: Copyright © 1989 by Hope Publishing Company, Carol Stream, IL 60188. All rights reserved.
Used by permission.

♩=46–50

God Is One, Unique and Holy

135

TRINITY   8.7.8.7.8.7

Brian Wren, 1983

Peter Cutts, 1983

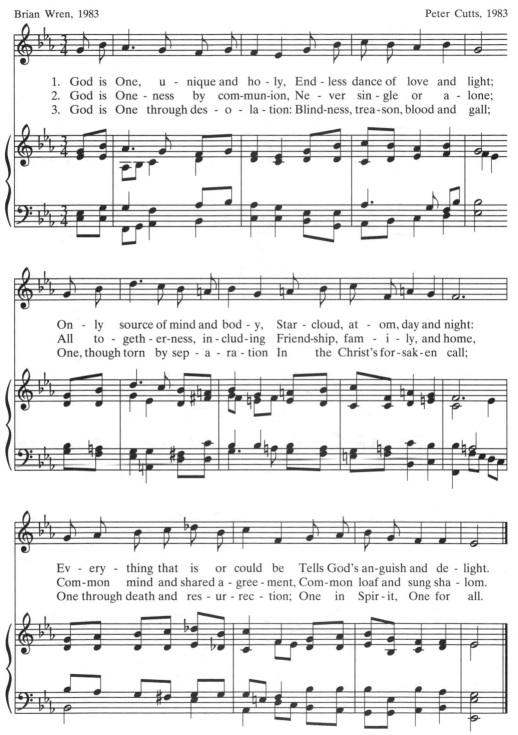

1. God is One, u - nique and ho - ly, End - less dance of love and light;
2. God is One - ness by com - mun - ion, Ne - ver sin - gle or a - lone;
3. God is One through des - o - la - tion: Blind - ness, trea - son, blood and gall;

On - ly source of mind and bod - y, Star - cloud, at - om, day and night:
All to - geth - er - ness, in - clud - ing Friend - ship, fam - i - ly, and home,
One, though torn by sep - a - ra - tion In the Christ's for - sak - en call;

Ev - ery - thing that is or could be Tells God's an - guish and de - light.
Com - mon mind and shared a - gree - ment, Com - mon loaf and sung sha - lom.
One through death and res - ur - rec - tion; One in Spir - it, One for all.

136 Sovereign Lord of All Creation

GENEVA 8.7.8.7 D

Stewart Cross (1928–1989) George Henry Day, 1940

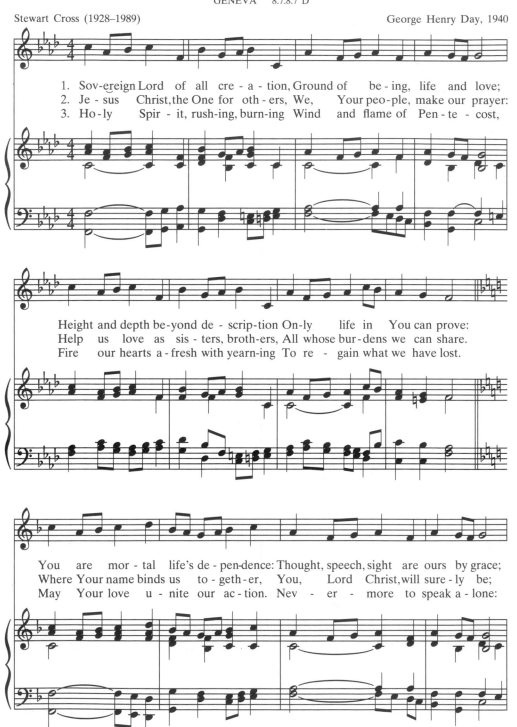

1. Sov-ereign Lord of all cre - a - tion, Ground of be - ing, life and love;
2. Je - sus Christ, the One for oth - ers, We, Your peo - ple, make our prayer:
3. Ho - ly Spir - it, rush-ing, burn-ing Wind and flame of Pen - te - cost,

Height and depth be-yond de - scrip-tion On-ly life in You can prove:
Help us love as sis - ters, broth-ers, All whose bur-dens we can share.
Fire our hearts a - fresh with yearn-ing To re - gain what we have lost.

You are mor - tal life's de - pen-dence: Thought, speech, sight are ours by grace;
Where Your name binds us to - geth - er, You, Lord Christ, will sure - ly be;
May Your love u - nite our ac - tion. Nev - er - more to speak a - lone:

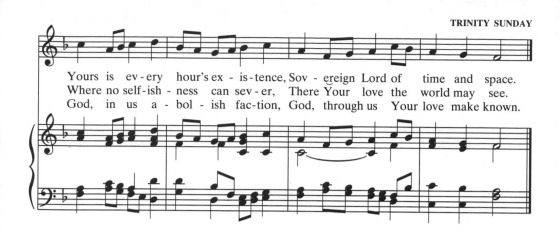

Yours is ev-ery hour's ex-is-tence, Sov-ereign Lord of time and space.
Where no self-ish-ness can sev-er, There Your love the world may see.
God, in us a-bol-ish fac-tion, God, through us Your love make known.

We All Believe in One True God 137

WIR GLAUBEN ALL' AN EINEN GOTT   8.7.7.7.7.7

Tobias Clausnitzer, 1668
Trans. Catherine Winkworth, 1863; alt.

Kirchengesangbuch, Darmstadt, 1699
As in *Allgemeines Choral-Melodienbuch*, 1793

1. We all be-lieve in one true God, Fa - ther, Son, and Ho - ly Ghost,
2. We all be-lieve in Je - sus Christ, Son of God and Ma-ry's son,
3. We all con-fess the Ho - ly Ghost, Who from both for - e'er pro-ceeds,

Ev - er - pres-ent help in need, Praised by all the heaven-ly host,
Who de - scend-ed from His throne And for us sal - va - tion won,
Who up - holds and com-forts us In all tri - als, fears, and needs.

By whose might-y power a - lone All is made and wrought and done.
By whose cross and death are we Res - cued from sin's mis - er - y.
Blest and Ho - ly Trin - i - ty, Praise for - ev - er be to Thee!

138 Holy, Holy, Holy! Lord God Almighty!

NICAEA   11.12.12.10

Reginald Heber (1783–1826)
As in *Hymns Written and Adapted*, 1827; alt.

John Bacchus Dykes, 1861
Desc. David McKinley Williams, 1948

Descant
4. Ho - ly,

1. Ho - ly, ho - ly, ho - ly! Lord God Al - might - y!
2. Ho - ly, ho - ly, ho - ly! all the saints a - dore Thee,
3. Ho - ly, ho - ly, ho - ly! though the dark-ness hide Thee,
4. Ho - ly, ho - ly, ho - ly! Lord God Al - might - y!

Ho - ly,

Ear - ly in the morn - ing our song shall rise to Thee;
Cast - ing down their gold - en crowns a - round the glass - y sea;
Though the eye of sin - ful - ness Thy glo - ry may not see,
All Thy works shall praise Thy name, in earth and sky and sea;

Ho - ly,

Ho - ly, ho - ly, ho - ly! mer - ci - ful and might - y!
Cher - u - bim and ser - a - phim fall - ing down be - fore Thee,
On - ly Thou art ho - ly; there is none be - side Thee
Ho - ly, ho - ly, ho - ly! mer - ci - ful and might - y!

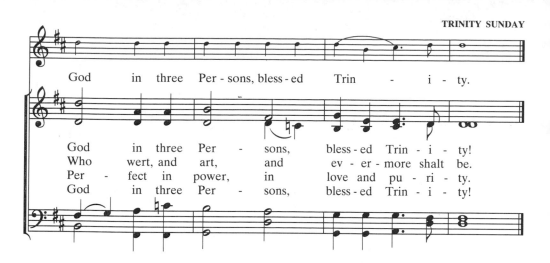

God in three Per - sons, bless - ed Trin - i - ty.

God in three Per - sons, bless - ed Trin - i - ty!
Who wert, and art, and ev - er - more shalt be.
Per - fect in power, in love and pu - ri - ty.
God in three Per - sons, bless - ed Trin - i - ty!

Come, Thou Almighty King 139

ITALIAN HYMN   6.6.4.6.6.6.4

Collection of Hymns for Social Worship, 1757; alt.   Felice de Giardini, 1769

1. Come, Thou Al - might - y King, Help us Thy name to sing,
2. Come, Thou In - car - nate Word, Gird on Thy might - y sword,
3. Come, Ho - ly Com - fort - er, Thy sa - cred wit - ness bear
4. To Thee, great One in Three, The high - est prais - es be,

Help us to praise: Fa - ther, all - glo - ri - ous, O'er all vic -
Our prayer at - tend: Come, and Thy peo - ple bless, And give Thy
In this glad hour: Thou who al - might - y art, Now rule in
Hence ev - er - more! Thy sov - ereign maj - es - ty May we in

to - ri - ous, Come, and reign o - ver us, An - cient of Days.
word suc - cess; Spir - it of ho - li - ness, On us de - scend.
ev - ery heart, And ne'er from us de - part, Spir - it of power.
glo - ry see, And to e - ter - ni - ty Love and a - dore.

140

Holy, Holy

HOLY, HOLY   Irregular

Jimmy Owens, 1972

Jimmy Owens, 1972

1. Ho - ly, ho - ly, ho - ly, ho - ly, Ho - ly,
2. Gra - cious Fa - ther, gra - cious Fa - ther, We're so
3. Pre - cious Je - sus, pre - cious Je - sus, We're so
4. Ho - ly Spir - it, Ho - ly Spir - it, Come and

ho - ly, Lord God Al - might - y;
blest to be Your chil - dren, gra - cious Fa - ther;
glad that You've re - deemed us, pre - cious Je - sus;
fill our hearts a - new, Ho - ly Spir - it;

And we lift our hearts be - fore You as a
And we lift our heads be - fore You as a
And we lift our hands be - fore You as a
And we lift our voice be - fore You as a

to - ken of our love, Ho - ly, ho - ly, ho - ly, ho - ly.
to - ken of our love, Gra - cious Fa - ther, gra - cious Fa - ther.
to - ken of our love, Pre - cious Je - sus, pre - cious Je - sus.
to - ken of our love, Ho - ly Spir - it, Ho - ly Spir - it.

Text and Music: Copyright © 1972, by Communiqué Music (Administered by CMI).

A Hymn of Glory Let Us Sing

141

DEO GRACIAS   LM

The Venerable Bede (673–735)
Stanzas 1–2 trans. Elizabeth Rundle Charles
(1828–1896); alt.
Stanza 3 trans. Benjamin Webb (1819–1885); alt.

"The Agincourt Song," England, c. 1415
Based on E. Power Biggs, 1947
Arr. Richard Proulx (b. 1937)

Fanfare (may be introduction, interlude, and conclusion)

1. A hymn of glo - ry let us sing, New
2. You are a pres - ent joy, O Lord, You
3. O ris - en Christ, as - cend-ed Lord, All

hymns through-out the world shall ring; By a new way none
will be ev - er our re - ward, And great the light in
praise to You let earth ac - cord. You are, while end - less

ev - er trod Christ takes His place, the throne of God!
You we see To guide us to e - ter - ni - ty.
a - ges run, With Fa - ther and with Spir - it One.

Music: From *Treasury of Early Organ Music,* © 1947 Mercury Music Corporation. Reprinted by permission of the publisher.
Arrangement copyright © 1985 by G.I.A. Publications, Inc., Chicago, Illinois. All rights reserved.

142   All Hail the Power of Jesus' Name!

CORONATION   8.6.8.6.8.6

Stanzas 1–3, Edward Perronet, 1779, 1780
Stanzas 2–3, alt. John Rippon, 1787
Stanza 4, John Rippon, 1787

Oliver Holden, 1793
Desc. Michael E. Young, 1979

Descant

4. O that with yon-der sa-cred throng We at His feet may fall!

1. All hail the power of Je - sus' name! Let an - gels pros-trate fall;
2. Ye cho-sen seed of Is-rael's race, Ye ran-somed from the fall,
3. Let ev - ery kin - dred, ev - ery tribe, On this ter - res - trial ball,
4. O that with yon - der sa - cred throng We at His feet may fall!

We'll join the song and crown Him Lord of all!

Bring forth the roy - al di - a - dem, And crown Him Lord of all!
Hail Him who saves you by His grace, And crown Him Lord of all!
To Him all maj - es - ty as - cribe, And crown Him Lord of all!
We'll join the ev - er - last-ing song, And crown Him Lord of all!

We'll join the song and crown Him Lord of all!

Bring forth the roy - al di - a - dem, And crown Him Lord of all!
Hail Him who saves you by His grace, And crown Him Lord of all!
To Him all maj - es - ty as - cribe, And crown Him Lord of all!
We'll join the ev - er - last-ing song, And crown Him Lord of all!

All Hail the Power of Jesus' Name!   143

DIADEM   8.6.6.8 with refrain

Stanzas 1–3, Edward Perronet, 1779, 1780
Stanzas 2–3 alt. John Rippon, 1787
Stanza 4, John Rippon, 1787

James Ellor, 1838

1. All hail the power of Je - sus' name! Let an - gels pros-trate
2. Ye cho - sen seed of Is - rael's race, Ye ran-somed from the
3. Let ev - ery kin - dred, ev - ery tribe, On this ter - res - trial
4. O that with yon - der sa - cred throng We at His feet may

fall, Let an - gels pros-trate fall; Bring forth the roy - al di - a -
fall, Ye ran - somed from the fall, Hail Him who saves you by His
ball, On this ter - res - trial ball, To Him all maj - es - ty as -
fall, We at His feet may fall! We'll join the ev - er - last - ing

dem,
grace, And crown Him,
cribe,
song, And crown Him,   crown Him,   crown Him,   crown Him,

crown

crown Him,   crown Him,   crown Him, And crown Him Lord of all!

Him,

144 Alleluia! Sing to Jesus!

HYFRYDOL   8.7.8.7 D

William Chatterton Dix, 1866   Rowland Hugh Prichard, 1831

1. Al - le - lu - ia! Sing to Je - sus! His the scep - ter,
2. Al - le - lu - ia! Not as or - phans Are we left in
3. Al - le - lu - ia! Bread of an - gels, Thou on earth our
4. Al - le - lu - ia! King e - ter - nal, Thee the Lord of

His the throne! Al - le - lu - ia! His the tri - umph,
sor - row now. Al - le - lu - ia! He is near us;
food, our stay. Al - le - lu - ia! Here the sin - ful
lords we own; Al - le - lu - ia! Born of Ma - ry,

His the vic - to - ry a - lone! Hark! the songs of peace - ful
Faith be - lieves nor ques - tions how. Though the cloud from sight re -
Flee to Thee from day to day. In - ter - ces - sor, friend of
Earth Thy foot - stool, heaven Thy throne. Thou with - in the veil hast

Zi - on Thun - der like a might - y flood; Je - sus out of
ceived Him, When the for - ty days were o'er, Shall our hearts for -
sin - ners, Earth's Re - deem - er, plead for me, Where the songs of
en - tered, Robed in flesh, our great High Priest; Thou on earth both

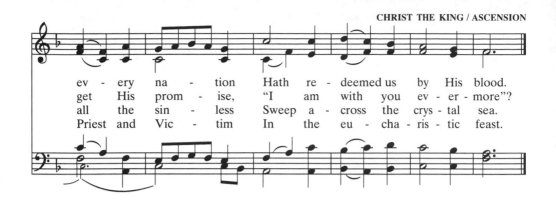

ev - ery na - tion Hath re - deemed us by His blood.
get His prom - ise, "I am with you ev - er - more"?
all the sin - less Sweep a - cross the crys - tal sea.
Priest and Vic - tim In the eu - cha - ris - tic feast.

Rejoice, Ye Pure in Heart! 145

MARION   SM with refrain

Edward Hayes Plumptre, 1865   Arthur Henry Messiter, 1883

1. Re - joice, ye pure in heart! Re - joice, give thanks, and sing!
2. Yes, on through life's long path, Still chant-ing as ye go;
3. At last the march shall end; The wea - ried ones shall rest;
4. Then on, ye pure in heart! Re - joice, give thanks, and sing!

Your fes - tal ban - ner wave on high, The cross of Christ your King.
From youth to age, by night and day, In glad-ness and in woe.
The pil - grims find their home at last, Je - ru - sa - lem the blest.
Your fes - tal ban - ner wave on high, The cross of Christ your King.

Refrain

Re - joice! re - joice! Re - joice, give thanks, and sing!

Re - joice! re - joice!

Alternate tune: VINEYARD HAVEN, 146

146 Rejoice, Ye Pure in Heart!

VINEYARD HAVEN   SM with refrain

Edward Hayes Plumptre, 1865   Richard Wayne Dirksen, 1974

1. Re - joice, ye pure in heart! Re - joice, give thanks, and sing!
2. Yes, on through life's long path, Still chant-ing as ye go;
3. At last the march shall end; The wea - ried ones shall rest;
4. Then on, ye pure in heart! Re - joice, give thanks, and sing!

Your fes - tal ban - ner wave on high, The cross of Christ your King.
From youth to age, by night and day, In glad-ness and in woe.
The pil - grims find their home at last, Je - ru - sa - lem the blest.
Your fes - tal ban - ner wave on high, The cross of Christ your King.

Refrain

Ho - san - na, ho - san - na! Re - joice, give thanks, and sing!

Alternate tune: MARION, 145

Blessing and Honor

147

O QUANTA QUALIA　　10.10.10.10

Paris *Antiphoner*, 1681

Horatius Bonar, 1866; alt.　　　　　　　　As in La Feillée's *Méthode du plain-chant,* 1808

1. Bless - ing and hon - or and glo - ry and power,
2. Hear through the heav - ens the sound of the Name,
3. Ev - er as - cend - ing the song and the prayer;
4. Give we the glo - ry and praise to the Lamb;

Wis - dom and rich - es and strength ev - er - more,
While rings the earth with Christ's glo - ry and fame;
Ev - er de - scend - ing the love that we share;
Take we the robe and the harp and the palm;

Give we to Christ who our bat - tle has won,
O - cean and moun - tain, stream, for - est, and flower
Bless - ing and hon - or and glo - ry and praise—
Sing we the song of the Lamb that was slain,

Whose are the king - dom, the crown, and the throne.
Ech - o these prais - es and tell of God's power.
This is the theme of the hymns that we raise.
Dy - ing in weak - ness but ris - ing to reign.

Philippians 2:5–11

148 At the Name of Jesus

KING'S WESTON   6.5.6.5 D

Caroline Maria Noel, 1890; alt. 1931

Ralph Vaughan Williams, 1925

1. At the name of Je - sus Ev - ery knee shall bow,
2. Hum-bled for a sea - son, To re-ceive a name
3. Bore it up tri - um - phant, With its hu - man light,
4. Chris-tians, this Lord Je - sus Shall re-turn a - gain,

Ev - ery tongue con - fess Him King of glo - ry now;
From the lips of sin - ners, Un - to whom He came,
Through all ranks of crea - tures, To the cen - tral height,
With His Fa - ther's glo - ry O'er the earth to reign;

'Tis the Fa - ther's plea - sure We should call Him Lord,
Faith-ful - ly He bore it Spot-less to the last,
To the throne of God - head, To the Fa - ther's breast;
For all wreaths of em - pire Meet up - on His brow,

Music: From *Enlarged Songs of Praise*, 1925. Used by permission of Oxford University Press.

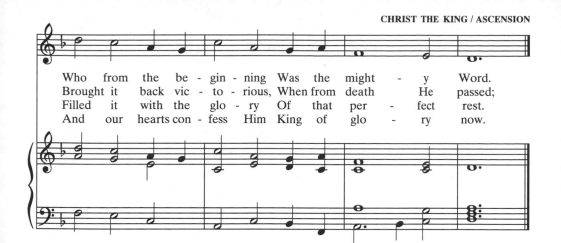

Who from the be - gin - ning Was the might - y Word.
Brought it back vic - to - rious, When from death He passed;
Filled it with the glo - ry Of that per - fect rest.
And our hearts con - fess Him King of glo - ry now.

Hebrews 2:9

The Head That Once Was Crowned 149

ST. MAGNUS CM

Thomas Kelly, 1820

Jeremiah Clark (1670–1707)
Playford's *Divine Companion*, 1709

1. The head that once was crowned with thorns Is crowned with glo - ry now;
2. The high - est place that heaven af - fords Is His, is His by right,
3. The joy of all who dwell a - bove, The joy of all be - low
4. To them the cross, with all its shame, With all its grace, is given;

A roy - al di - a - dem a - dorns The might - y vic - tor's brow.
The King of kings, and Lord of lords, And heaven's e - ter - nal Light:
To whom He man - i - fests His love, And grants His name to know.
Their name an ev - er - last - ing name, Their joy the joy of heaven.

5. They suffer with their Lord below,
They reign with Him above;
Their profit and their joy to know
The wonder of His love.

150 Come, Christians, Join to Sing

MADRID   6.6.6.6 D

Spanish folk melody
Arr. Benjamin Carr, 1824
Harm. David Evans, 1927

Christian Henry Bateman, 1843

1. Come, Chris-tians, join to sing   Al - le - lu - ia!   A - men!
2. Come, lift your hearts on high;   Al - le - lu - ia!   A - men!
3. Praise yet our Christ a - gain;   Al - le - lu - ia!   A - men!

Loud praise to Christ our King;   Al - le - lu - ia!   A - men!
Let prais - es fill the sky;   Al - le - lu - ia!   A - men!
Life shall not end the strain;   Al - le - lu - ia!   A - men!

Let all, with heart and voice,   Be - fore His throne re - joice;
He is our guide and friend;   To us He'll con - de - scend;
On heav-en's bliss - ful shore   His good - ness we'll a - dore,

Praise is His gra - cious choice;   Al - le - lu - ia!   A - men!
His love shall nev - er end;   Al - le - lu - ia!   A - men!
Sing - ing for - ev - er - more,   "Al - le - lu - ia!   A - men!"

Music: Harmonization from the *Revised Church Hymnary 1927.* Used by permission of Oxford University Press.

Crown Him with Many Crowns

151

DIADEMATA   SMD

Matthew Bridges, 1851   George Job Elvey, 1868

1. Crown Him with man - y crowns, The Lamb up - on His throne;
2. Crown Him the Lord of love; Be - hold His hands and side,
3. Crown Him the Lord of peace; Whose power a scep - ter sways
4. Crown Him the Lord of years, The Po - ten - tate of time;

Hark, how the heaven-ly an - them drowns All mu - sic but its own!
Rich wounds, yet vi - si - ble a - bove, In beau - ty glo - ri - fied:
From pole to pole, that wars may cease, Ab-sorbed in prayer and praise:
Cre - a - tor of the roll - ing spheres, In - ef - fa - bly sub - lime.

A - wake, my soul, and sing Of Him who died for thee,
No an - gel in the sky Can ful - ly bear that sight,
His reign shall know no end; And round His pierc - ed feet
All hail, Re - deem - er, hail! For Thou hast died for me;

And hail Him as thy match-less King Through all e - ter - ni - ty.
But down-ward bends his burn - ing eye At mys - ter - ies so bright.
Fair flowers of Par - a - dise ex - tend Their fra-grance ev - er sweet.
Thy praise shall nev - er, nev - er fail Through-out e - ter - ni - ty.

152 Earth's Scattered Isles and Contoured Hills

MEADVILLE   8.8.8.8.8.8

Para. Jeffery Rowthorn, 1974

Walter Pelz, 1977
Adapt. W. Thomas Jones, 1980

1. Earth's scat-tered isles and con-toured hills Which part the seas and
2. God's judg-ment passed on so-cial ills That thwart a-while di-
3. The con-stant care which Is-rael knew A-like in faith and
4. The light which shines through no-ble acts, The quest for truth dis-

mold the land, And vis-tas new-ly seen from space
vine in-tent, The flag-ging dreams of wea-ry folk
faith-less-ness, The sub-tle prov-i-dence which guides
pel-ling lies, The grace of Christ re-newed in us

That show a world awe-some and grand, All won-drous-
Whose brave new world lies torn and rent, In pain-ful
A pil-grim church through change and stress, In-spire us
So love lives on and dis-cord dies, All blend their

This tune in a higher key, 227

ly u - nite to sing:
form their mes-sage bring:
grate - ful - ly to sing: Take heart, take hope, the Lord is King!
song, good news to bring:

153 He Is King of Kings

HE IS KING   8.5.8.5 with refrain

African-American spiritual
Arr. Joseph T. Jones (1902–1983)
Adapt. Melva W. Costen, 1989

African-American spiritual

Refrain

(He is) King of kings, He is Lord of lords,

Je - sus Christ, the first and last, No one works like Him. O He is

No one works like Him.

Fine

1. He built His throne up in the air,
2. He pitched His tents on Ca - naan ground,
3. I know that my Re - deem - er lives,

No one works like Him, And called His saints from
No one works like Him, And broke op - pres - sive
No one works like Him, And by His love sweet

ev - ery - where,
king - doms down, No one works like Him. O He is
bless - ing gives,

Music: Adaptation © 1990 Melva W. Costen. All rights reserved. Used by permission. Dedicated to the memory of J. T. Jones.

Lord, Enthroned in Heavenly Splendor 154

BRYN CALFARIA 8.7.8.7.444.7.7

George Hugh Bourne, 1874; alt.

William Owen, 1852
Harm. *Christian Hymns,* 1977

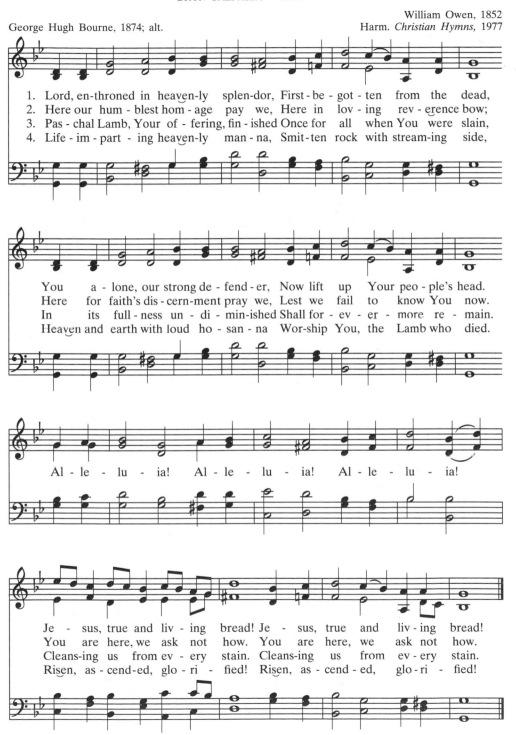

1. Lord, en-throned in heaven-ly splen-dor, First - be - got - ten from the dead,
2. Here our hum - blest hom - age pay we, Here in lov - ing rev - erence bow;
3. Pas - chal Lamb, Your of - fering, fin - ished Once for all when You were slain,
4. Life - im - part - ing heaven-ly man - na, Smit-ten rock with stream-ing side,

You a - lone, our strong de - fend - er, Now lift up Your peo - ple's head.
Here for faith's dis - cern-ment pray we, Lest we fail to know You now.
In its full - ness un - di - min-ished Shall for - ev - er - more re - main.
Heaven and earth with loud ho - san - na Wor-ship You, the Lamb who died.

Al - le - lu - ia! Al - le - lu - ia! Al - le - lu - ia!

Je - sus, true and liv - ing bread! Je - sus, true and liv - ing bread!
You are here, we ask not how. You are here, we ask not how.
Cleans-ing us from ev - ery stain. Cleans-ing us from ev - ery stain.
Risen, as - cend-ed, glo - ri - fied! Risen, as - cend - ed, glo - ri - fied!

♩=69–76

Revelation 1:18

155 Rejoice, the Lord Is King

DARWALL'S 148TH   6.6.6.6.8.8

John Darwall, 1770
Desc. Sidney Hugo Nicholson (1875–1947)

Charles Wesley, 1746

Descant

3. Re - joice in glo - rious hope! For Christ, the Judge, shall come

1. Re - joice, the Lord is King! Your Lord and King a - dore!
2. God's king-dom can - not fail, Christ rules o'er earth and heaven;
3. Re - joice in glo - rious hope! For Christ, the Judge, shall come

To glo - ri - fy the saints For their e - ter - nal home:

Re - joice, give thanks, and sing, And tri - umph ev - er - more:
The keys of death and hell Are to our Je - sus given:
To glo - ri - fy the saints For their e - ter - nal home:

Lift up your heart, lift up your voice! Re - joice, a - gain I say, re - joice!

Lift up your heart, lift up your voice! Re - joice, a - gain I say, re - joice!

This tune in a higher key and without descant, 430

You, Living Christ, Our Eyes Behold   156

PALACE GREEN   8.7.8.7.8.8.7

Edmund R. Morgan, 1950; alt. 1973   Michael Fleming, 1958

1. You, liv-ing Christ, our eyes be-hold A - mid Your church ap-pear-ing, All girt a-bout Your breast with gold, And bright ap-par-el wear-ing; Your coun-te-nance is burn-ing bright, A sun re-splen-dent in its might: Lord Christ, we see Your glo-ry.

2. Your glo-rious feet have sought and found Your own in ev-ery na-tion; With ev-er-last-ing voice You sound The call of our sal-va-tion; You search us still with eyes of flame, You know and call us all by name: Lord Christ, we see Your glo-ry.

3. O ris-en Christ, to-day a-live, A - mid Your church a-bid-ing, Who still Your blood and bod-y give, New life and strength pro-vid-ing, We join the heaven-ly com-pa-ny To sing Your praise tri-um-phant-ly, For we have seen Your glo-ry.

Jesús Es Mi Rey Soberano
157 Our King and Our Sovereign, Lord Jesus

MI REY Y MI AMIGO   Irregular

Vincente Mendoza, 1920
Trans. George P. Simmonds, 1966; alt. 1989

Vincente Mendoza, 1920; alt.

1. Je - sús   es   mi   Rey   so - be - ra - no,   Mi
2. Je - sús   es   mi a - mi - go an - he - la - do,   Y en

1. Our   King   and   our   sov - ereign, Lord   Je - sus,   With
2. Our   friend   whom   we   long   for,   O   Je - sus,   In

go - zo es can - tar   su   lo - or;   Es   Rey,   y   me   ve   cual her -
som - bras o en   luz   siem - pre   va   Pa - cien - te y   hu - mil - de a   mi

joy   we   will   sing forth Your   praise;   You   call   us   Your   sis - ters   and
sun - shine and storm   here   You   stay;   You   pa - tient - ly   walk   close   be -

ma - no,   Es   Rey   y   me im - par - te   su a - mor.   De -
la - do,   Y a - yu - da y   so - co - rro   me   da.   Por

broth - ers,   Your   love   You share with   us   al - ways.   You
side   us   To   com - fort   and   help   us   each   day;   From

jan - do   su   tro - no   de   glo - ria,   Me   vi - no a   sa - car   de   la es -
e - so   cons - tan - te   lo   si - go,   Por - que El es   mi   Rey   y   mi a -

gave   up   Your throne   in   God's glo - ry   To   save   us,   O   won - der - ful
You   noth - ing   ev - er   can   sev - er,   We'll   fol - low   You   now   and   for -

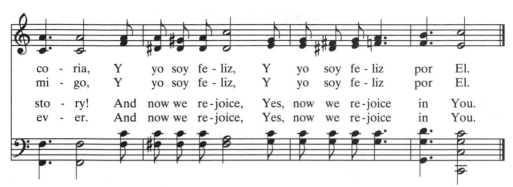

co - ria,   Y   yo soy fe - liz,   Y   yo soy fe - liz   por   El.
mi - go,   Y   yo soy fe - liz,   Y   yo soy fe - liz   por   El.
sto - ry! And now we re-joice, Yes, now we re-joice   in   You.
ev - er.   And now we re-joice, Yes, now we re-joice   in   You.

3. Señor, ¿qué pudiera yo darte
   Por tanta bondad para mí?
   ¿Me basta servirte y amarte?
   ¿Es todo entregarme yo a Ti?
   Entonces acepta mi vida,
   Que a Ti sólo queda rendida,
   Pues yo soy feliz,
   Pues yo soy feliz por Ti.

3. O what can we give You, Lord Jesus,
   For all you have done and still do?
   Is serving You here all that matters?
   Or saying we love only You?
   Yours only, to You consecrated,
   Our lives, Lord, are now dedicated;
   Dear Lord, we rejoice,
   Yes, Lord, we rejoice in You.

PSALMS

PSALM 1

158 The One Is Blest

DUNFERMLINE CM

The Psalter, 1912; alt. 1985

Scottish Psalter, 1615

1. The one is blest who, fear - ing God, Walks
2. How blest the one who in God's law Finds
3. That one is nour - ished like a tree Set
4. The wick - ed, like the driv - en chaff, Are

not where sin - ners meet, Who does not stand with
good - ness and de - light, And med - i - tates up -
by the riv - er's side; Its leaf is green, its
swept from off the land; They shall not gath - er

wick - ed ones, And shuns the scorn - ers' seat.
on that law With glad - ness day and night.
fruit is sure: The works of such a - bide.
with the just, Nor at the judg - ment stand.

5. The Lord will guard the righteous well,   The way of sinners, far from God,
   Their way to God is known;   Shall surely be o'erthrown.

Why Are Nations Raging

159

SALZBURG   7.7.7.7 D

Jacob Hintze, 1678
Harm. Johann Sebastian Bach (1685–1750)
As in *Hymns Ancient and Modern*, 1861

Fred R. Anderson, 1986; alt.

1. Why are na-tions rag - ing And con-spir-ing plots in vain?
2. But the Lord has scorn on them, Laugh-ing and en-throned on high.
3. God's de-cree un - to the King Tells us what the Lord did say:
4. There-fore, lead-ers of the earth, Serve the Lord with ho - ly fear;

Rul - ers of the world rise up, Weav-ing webs of death and pain.
God brings wrath up - on their work; Filled with an - ger God re-plies:
"You are My own ho - ly child; I've be - got-ten You this day.
Trem-bling come be - fore the throne Or God's an - ger will ap-pear.

Then a - gainst the Lord they cry, And a - gainst God's ho - ly Son,
"It is My own ho - ly will That the Christ on earth shall reign,
Ask of Me and I will make All the na - tions Your own stay.
Kiss God's feet in trem-bling awe Or the Lord will use the rod,

"Let us tear their bonds from us And with their con - trol be done."
And on Zi - on's ho - ly hill, My a - noint-ed I'll main-tain."
These pos-ses - sions You shall rule, Strong as i - ron smash-ing clay."
Mak - ing beg - gars of all kings. Blest are those who trust in God.

160　　　　PSALM 4

Psalm tone: St. Meinrad VII
Refrain: Helen L. Wright, 1984

Anthony Teague, 1979

Refrain

In the night I can take my rest, You a - lone keep my life se - cure.

1. When I call, You give heed, O Lord, righteous God;
   free me from my anguish, pity, héar my prayer.
2. How long will they all remain hàrd of heart?
   How long will their lies and their vanitý endure? *(R)*

3. **Remember, the Lord does wonders fòr the godly,**
   the Lord will hear when I call on the hóly name.
4. **Do not sìn but tremble;**
   as you lie on your bed, in silénce reflect. *(R)*

5. Offer praise and worshìp to God,
   put your trust iń the Lord.
6. Many sigh as they pray: Lord, show uś Your joy;
   when shall I see the light óf Your face? *(R)*

7. **In my heart You have poured the fullnèss of joy,**
   far richer than their harvests of gŕain and wine.
8. **In peace I lie down and sleep còmes at once,**
   for You, Lord, alone, keep my lífe secure. *(R)*

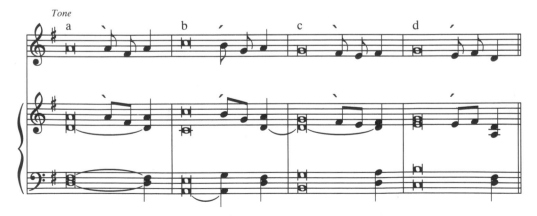

Tone

As Morning Dawns

WAREHAM LM

Fred R. Anderson, 1986   William Knapp, 1738

1. As morn - ing dawns, Lord, hear our cry. O sov - ereign
2. Be - fore You, Lord, the wick - ed fall, And none shall
3. Your stead - fast love shall wel - come all Who seek Your
4. Let all who seek You then re - joice, And sing to

God, now hear our sigh. As first light brings the
dwell with - in Your hall. The proud shall nev - er
house and on You call. O lead us, Lord, in
You with joy - ful voice. For You shall bless the

sun's warm rays, Ac - cept our sac - ri - fice of praise.
gain a place, Nor e - vil live to see Your face.
righ - teous - ness, As through this day Your name we bless.
righ - teous, Lord. For - ev - er be Your name a - dored.

Another harmonization of this tune, 421

162 O Lord, Our God, How Excellent

WINCHESTER OLD   CM

Fred R. Anderson, 1986

Este's *Psalmes*, 1592

1. O Lord, our God, how ex - cel - lent, How
2. The heav - ens shout Your hand - i - work; We
3. Yet You have made us less than gods, Sur -
4. In - to our hands You've placed all things: The

glo - rious is Your name. Your maj - es - ty sur -
stand be - neath in awe, To think the One who
pass - ing all but You, With heart and mind, with
earth, the sea; each place We're called to probe for

rounds the earth, And chil - dren sing Your fame.
made all things Should care for us at all.
strength and will, To search for what is true.
se - cret gifts And ven - ture in - to space.

5. O Lord, our God, how excellent,
How glorious is Your name,
Majestic in Your holiness.
We sing and praise Your fame.

This tune with descant, 58

Text: © 1986 Fred R. Anderson; from *Singing Psalms of Joy and Praise.* Used by permission.

Lord, Our Lord, Thy Glorious Name

163

GOTT SEI DANK DURCH ALLE WELT   7.7.7.7

The Psalter, 1912
As in *Rejoice in the Lord,* 1985

Freylinghausen's *Geistreiches Gesangbuch,* 1704; alt.

1. Lord, our Lord, Thy glo - rious name
   All Thy won - drous works pro - claim;
   In the heavens with ra - diant signs
   Ev - er - more Thy glo - ry shines.

2. In - fant lips Thou dost or - dain
   Wrath and ven - geance to re - strain;
   Weak - est means ful - fill Thy will,
   Might - y en - e - mies to still.

3. Moon and stars in shin - ing height
   Night - ly tell their Mak - er's might;
   Hu - man strength can not com - pare
   With the glo - ry pres - ent there.

4. What are we that we should be
   Loved and vis - it - ed by Thee,
   Raised to an ex - alt - ed height,
   Crowned with hon - or in Thy sight?

5. With dominion crowned we stand,
   O'er the creatures of Thy hand,
   All to us subjection yield
   In the sea and air and field.

6. Lord, our Lord, Thy glorious name,
   All Thy wondrous works proclaim;
   Thine the name of matchless worth,
   Excellent in all the earth.

164 Lord, Who May Dwell Within Your House

CHESHIRE CM

Christopher L. Webber, 1986

Este's *Psalmes*, 1592
As in *Songs of Syon*, 1910

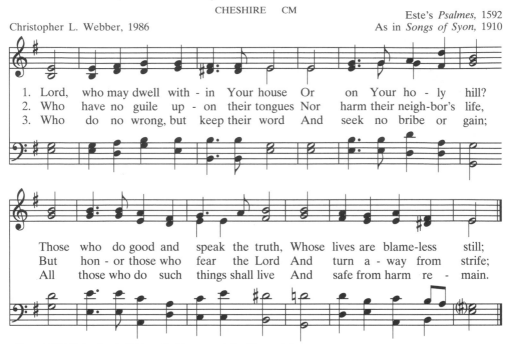

1. Lord, who may dwell with-in Your house Or on Your ho-ly hill?
2. Who have no guile up-on their tongues Nor harm their neigh-bor's life,
3. Who do no wrong, but keep their word And seek no bribe or gain;

Those who do good and speak the truth, Whose lives are blame-less still;
But hon-or those who fear the Lord And turn a-way from strife;
All those who do such things shall live And safe from harm re-main.

165 When in the Night I Meditate

The Psalter, 1912

ST. FLAVIAN CM

Day's *Psalter*, 1562

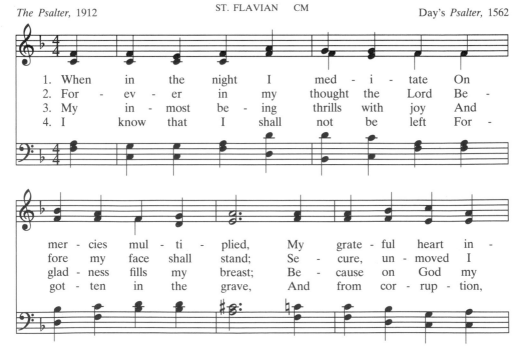

1. When in the night I med-i-tate On
2. For-ev-er in my thought the Lord Be-
3. My in-most be-ing thrills with joy And
4. I know that I shall not be left For-

mer-cies mul-ti-plied, My grate-ful heart in-
fore my face shall stand; Se-cure, un-moved I
glad-ness fills my breast; Be-cause on God my
got-ten in the grave, And from cor-rup-tion,

spires my tongue To bless the Lord, my guide.
shall re - main, With God at my right hand.
trust is stayed, My flesh in hope shall rest.
Thou, O Lord, Thy ho - ly one wilt save.

5. The path of life Thou showest me;
Of joy a boundless store
Is ever found at Thy right hand,
And pleasures evermore.

PSALM 19:1–6

The Heavens Above Declare God's Praise 166

CAITHNESS   CM

Christopher L. Webber, 1986

Scottish Psalter, 1635
Harm. *The English Hymnal,* 1906; alt.

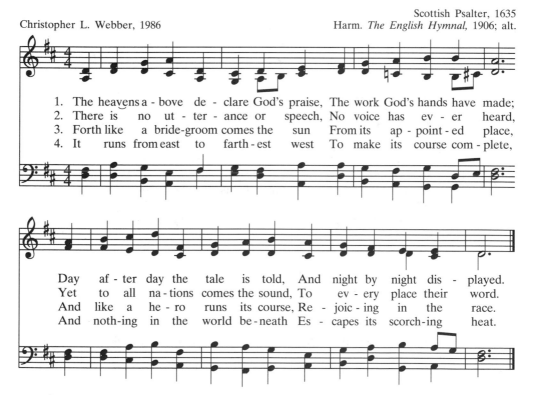

1. The heavens a - bove de - clare God's praise, The work God's hands have made;
2. There is no ut - ter - ance or speech, No voice has ev - er heard,
3. Forth like a bride-groom comes the sun From its ap - point - ed place,
4. It runs from east to farth - est west To make its course com - plete,

Day af - ter day the tale is told, And night by night dis - played.
Yet to all na - tions comes the sound, To ev - er - y place their word.
And like a he - ro runs its course, Re - joic - ing in the race.
And noth - ing in the world be - neath Es - capes its scorch - ing heat.

167 God's Law Is Perfect and Gives Life

HALIFAX   CMD

Christopher L. Webber, 1986

George Frederick Handel, 1748
Harm. C. Winfred Douglas, 1941

1. God's law is per-fect and gives life, Re-vives the wea-ry soul;
2. The fear of God is al-ways clean, En-dur-ing as the sun;
3. Your ser-vant finds en-light-en-ment By means of them, O Lord;
4. Lord, keep me from pre-sump-tuous sins; Let them not rule my soul;

God's tes-ti-mon-ies all are sure, Wis-dom for all to hold.
The judg-ments of the Lord are true And righ-teous, ev-ery one.
And in the keep-ing of Your law, There is a great re-ward.
Then I shall not com-mit great wrongs, I shall be sound and whole.

The stat-utes of the Lord are just And give the heart de-light;
And ev-en more to be de-sired Than gold, the fin-est gold,
But who can tell how of-ten they Of-fend un-know-ing-ly?
Let all my words and all my thoughts, My Lord, Re-deem-er, Might,

God's pre-cepts are dir-ect and pure And give the eyes clear sight.
And sweet-er than the hon-ey-comb, The words God spoke of old.
From all my se-cret faults, O Lord, I ask You to cleanse me.
Find fa-vor now, and al-ways win Ac-cept-ance in Your sight.

Psalm 20 is number 169

Lord, Why Have You Forsaken Me 168

CONDITOR ALME SIDERUM LM

Christopher L. Webber, 1986; alt.

Sarum plainsong, Mode IV, 9th century
Harm. C. Winfred Douglas, 1943

1. Lord, why have You for-sak-en me, And why are You so
2. Yet You are ho-ly, and the songs Of praise of Is-rael
3. But I am mocked and put to scorn, All those who see me
4. Yet You, O Lord, have been my God And on-ly hope since

far a-way From my com-plaint and my dis-tress
are Your throne; When our an-ces-tors called on You,
laugh and say, "You trust in God, so let us see
I was born; Trou-ble is near me, none can help;

Poured out be-fore You night and day?
You saved them, res-cued all Your own.
The help of God to whom you pray."
My Sav-ior, leave me not for-lorn.

169 In the Day of Need

SAMSON 12.9.12.11

Based on a paraphrase by Christopher M. Idle, 1969

Norman L. Warren, 1972

1. In the day of need may your an-swer be the Lord,
2. May the Lord God grant you suc-cess in all your plans,
3. Now I know the Lord will en-cour-age all be-loved,
4. There are some who boast of the weap-ons of the world,

May the God of Ja-cob strength-en you;
May God give you all your heart's de-sire;
God will hear and an-swer from on high;
But the power of God is all our pride;

May our Lord send help from the high and ho-ly place,
May we sing for joy when we see the bat-tle won;
Not a word shall fail of the prom-is-es once made,
Those who live by war shall one day col-lapse and fall,

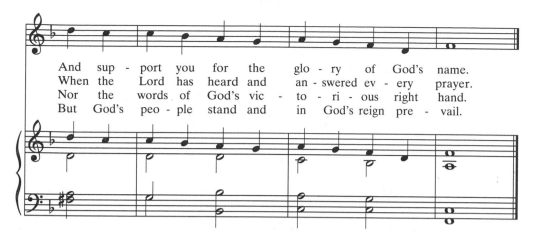

And sup - port you for the glo - ry of God's name.
When the Lord has heard and an - swered ev - ery prayer.
Nor the words of God's vic - to - ri - ous right hand.
But God's peo - ple stand and in God's reign pre - vail.

Psalm 22 is number 168

PSALM 23

The Lord's My Shepherd, I'll Not Want 170

CRIMOND CM

Scottish Psalter, 1650

Jessie Seymour Irvine, 1872
Harm. T. C. L. Pritchard, 1929

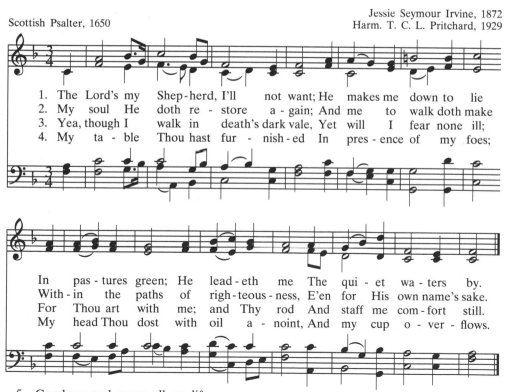

1. The Lord's my Shep-herd, I'll not want; He makes me down to lie
2. My soul He doth re - store a - gain; And me to walk doth make
3. Yea, though I walk in death's dark vale, Yet will I fear none ill;
4. My ta - ble Thou hast fur - nish - ed In pres - ence of my foes;

In pas - tures green; He lead-eth me The qui - et wa - ters by.
With - in the paths of righ-teous-ness, E'en for His own name's sake.
For Thou art with me; and Thy rod And staff me com - fort still.
My head Thou dost with oil a - noint, And my cup o - ver - flows.

5. Goodness and mercy all my life
   Shall surely follow me;
   And in God's house forevermore
   My dwelling place shall be.

Music: Harmonization from *The Scottish Psalter,* 1929. Used by permission of Oxford University Press.

171 The King of Love My Shepherd Is

ST. COLUMBA   8.7.8.7

Henry Williams Baker, 1868

Ancient Irish melody

1. The King of love my Shep - herd is, Whose good-ness fail - eth nev - er; I noth - ing lack if I am His And He is mine for - ev - er.

2. Where streams of liv - ing wa - ter flow My ran - somed soul He lead - eth, And where the ver - dant pas - tures grow, With food ce - les - tial feed - eth.

3. Per - verse and fool - ish oft I strayed, But yet in love He sought me, And on His shoul - der gent - ly laid, And home, re - joic - ing, brought me.

4. In death's dark vale I fear no ill With Thee, dear Lord, be - side me; Thy rod and staff my com - fort still, Thy cross be - fore to guide me.

5. Thou spreadest a table in my sight;
   Thy unction grace bestoweth;
   And O what transport of delight
   From Thy pure chalice floweth!

6. And so through all the length of days
   Thy goodness faileth never;
   Good Shepherd, may I sing Thy praise
   Within Thy house forever.

My Shepherd Will Supply My Need

172

RESIGNATION CMD

Para. Isaac Watts, 1719; alt. 1972

Walker's *Southern Harmony,* 1835
Harm. Dale Grotenhuis, 1986

1. My Shep-herd will sup-ply my need; Je-ho-vah is His name:
In pas-tures fresh He makes me feed, Be-side the liv-ing stream.
He brings my wan-dering spir-it back, When I for-sake His ways;
And leads me, for His mer-cy's sake, In paths of truth and grace.

2. When I walk through the shades of death Your pres-ence is my stay;
One word of Your sup-port-ing breath Drives all my fears a-way.
Your hand, in sight of all my foes, Does still my ta-ble spread;
My cup with bless-ings o-ver-flows, Your oil a-noints my head.

3. The sure pro-vi-sions of my God At-tend me all my days;
O may Your House be my a-bode, And all my work be praise.
There would I find a set-tled rest, While oth-ers go and come;
No more a strang-er, or a guest, But like a child at home.

173 PSALM 23

Robert J. Moore, 1984

Joseph Gelineau, 1963

Refrain

My shep-herd is the Lord, noth-ing in-deed shall I want.

1. The Lord is my Shepherd, I will never be in need. In the fresh green meadow my Shepherd
2. Guiding me to greener pastures, You are true to Your word. Though I walk through the darkest of shadows,
3. You spread a table be - fore me, be - fore all my foes. You a - noint my head with oil,
4. Surely goodness and kindness wait for me every day of my life. In the house of the Lord will I live,

will make me lie down,   and   to the still
what danger could I   fear?   You will

[*omit*
[*omit*

water will guide me,   find re - fresh-ment for my spir - it. *(R)*
always go with me,   Your rod and staff will lead me. *(R)*
        ]   fill my cup to ov - er - flow - ing. *(R)*
        ]   for - ev - er and for - ev - er. *(R)*

PSALM 23

174 The Lord's My Shepherd

DOMINUS REGIT ME   8.7.8.7

Para. Jane Parker Huber, 1988   John Bacchus Dykes, 1868

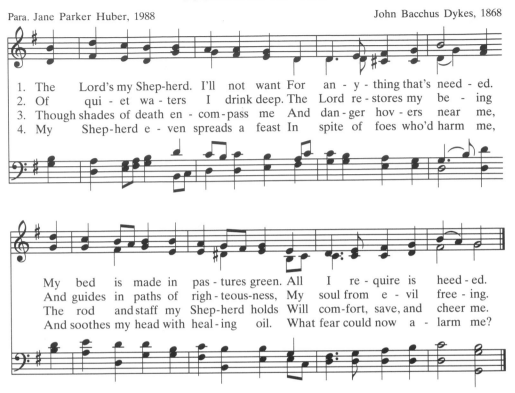

1. The Lord's my Shep-herd. I'll not want For an-y-thing that's need-ed.
2. Of qui-et wa-ters I drink deep. The Lord re-stores my be-ing
3. Though shades of death en-com-pass me And dan-ger hov-ers near me,
4. My Shep-herd e-ven spreads a feast In spite of foes who'd harm me,

My bed is made in pas-tures green. All I re-quire is heed-ed.
And guides in paths of righ-teous-ness, My soul from e-vil free-ing.
The rod and staff my Shep-herd holds Will com-fort, save, and cheer me.
And soothes my head with heal-ing oil. What fear could now a-larm me?

5. My cup is full, and more than full,   That I will live each night and day
   Such lavish love outpouring   My Shepherd Lord adoring.

Text: © 1990 Jane Parker Huber. Used by permission.

PSALM 23

175 The Lord's My Shepherd, All My Need

EVAN   CM

Christopher L. Webber, 1986; alt.   William Henry Havergal, 1846

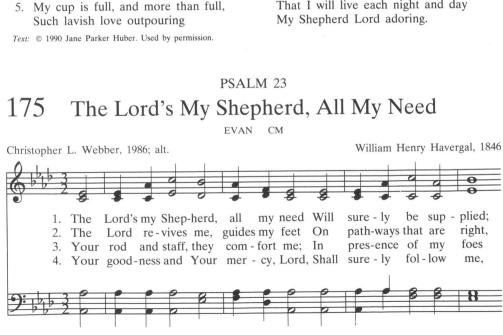

1. The Lord's my Shep-herd, all my need Will sure-ly be sup-plied;
2. The Lord re-vives me, guides my feet On path-ways that are right,
3. Your rod and staff, they com-fort me; In pres-ence of my foes
4. Your good-ness and Your mer-cy, Lord, Shall sure-ly fol-low me,

Text: © 1986 Christopher L. Webber. All rights reserved. Used by permission.

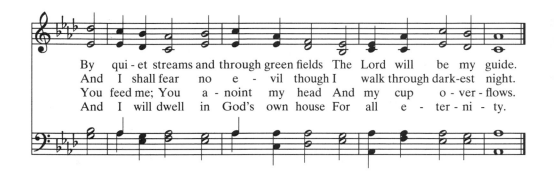

By   qui - et streams and through green fields The Lord will   be my guide.
And   I shall fear   no   e - vil though I   walk through dark-est night.
You   feed me; You   a - noint   my head And   my   cup   o - ver - flows.
And   I will dwell   in   God's own house For   all   e - ter - ni - ty.

PSALM 24

The Earth and All That Dwell Therein 176

CAITHNESS   CM

The Psalter, 1912; alt. 1986

Scottish Psalter, 1635
Harm. *The English Hymnal,* 1906

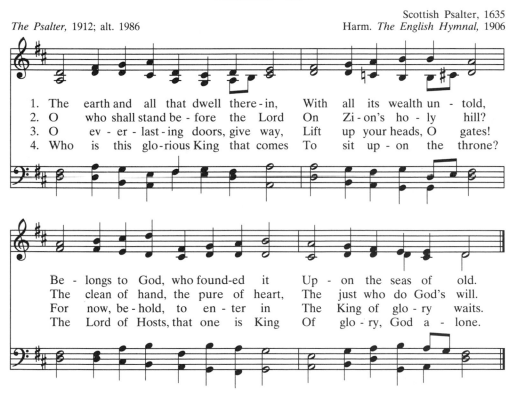

1. The   earth and all that dwell there - in,   With   all its wealth un - told,
2. O   who shall stand be - fore   the Lord   On   Zi - on's ho - ly   hill?
3. O   ev - er - last - ing doors, give way,   Lift   up your heads, O   gates!
4. Who   is this glo - rious King that comes   To   sit up - on   the   throne?

Be - longs to God, who found-ed   it   Up - on   the seas of   old.
The   clean of hand, the pure of heart,   The   just who do God's will.
For   now, be - hold, to en - ter in   The   King of glo - ry   waits.
The   Lord of Hosts, that one is King   Of   glo - ry, God a - lone.

177 Lift Up the Gates Eternal

Arlo D. Duba, 1984   PROMISED ONE   12.12.12.12   Israeli folk melody
Refrain: Willard F. Jabusch, 1966   Arr. John Ferguson, 1973

Refrain

Lift up the gates e - ter - nal, lift up your voic - es;

The King of glo - ry comes, the na - tion re - joic - es.

1. See, all the earth is God's, its peo - ple and na - tions;
2. Who can go up this moun-tain, who stand in prais - ing?
3. They shall re - ceive for - give - ness, and have God's bless - ing

4. Come, lift your voic - es high, be lift - ed to glo - ry;
5. Who is this glo - rious one, for whom we are wait - ing?

6. Come, lift your heads with joy; come, lift up your tow - er;
7. Who is this King of glo - ry of whom we're sing - ing?

Gradually increasing tempo can heighten the sense of joy and power in this psalm.

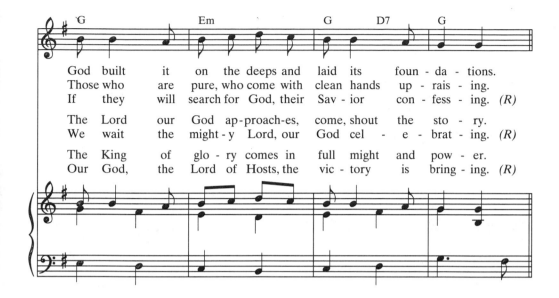

God built it on the deeps and laid its foun - da - tions.
Those who are pure, who come with clean hands up - rais - ing.
If they will search for God, their Sav - ior con - fess - ing. *(R)*

The Lord our God ap-proach-es, come, shout the sto - ry.
We wait the might - y Lord, our God cel - e - brat - ing. *(R)*

The King of glo - ry comes in full might and pow - er.
Our God, the Lord of Hosts, the vic - tory is bring - ing. *(R)*

178 Lord, to You My Soul Is Lifted

GENEVAN 25   8.7.8.7.7.8.7.8

Stanley Wiersma, 1980

Louis Bourgeois, 1551
Harm. Howard Slenk, 1985

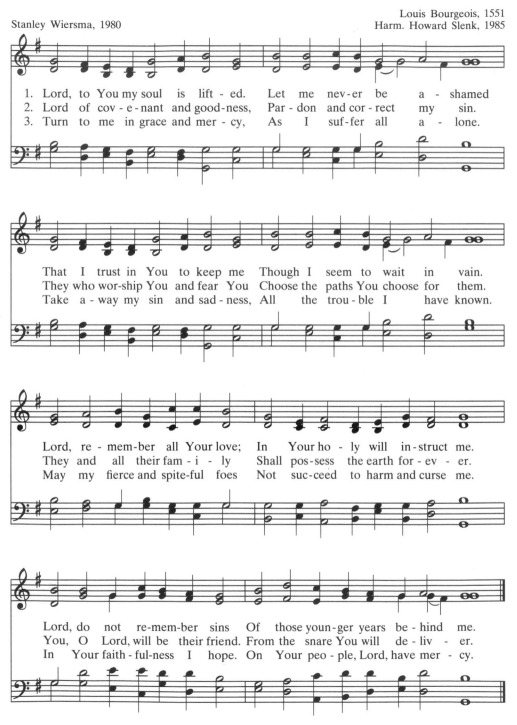

1. Lord, to You my soul is lift - ed. Let me nev-er be a - shamed
2. Lord of cov - e - nant and good-ness, Par - don and cor - rect my sin.
3. Turn to me in grace and mer - cy, As I suf-fer all a - lone.

That I trust in You to keep me Though I seem to wait in vain.
They who wor-ship You and fear You Choose the paths You choose for them.
Take a - way my sin and sad - ness, All the trou - ble I have known.

Lord, re - mem-ber all Your love; In Your ho - ly will in-struct me.
They and all their fam - i - ly Shall pos-sess the earth for - ev - er.
May my fierce and spite-ful foes Not suc-ceed to harm and curse me.

Lord, do not re-mem-ber sins Of those youn-ger years be - hind me.
You, O Lord, will be their friend. From the snare You will de - liv - er.
In Your faith-ful-ness I hope. On Your peo - ple, Lord, have mer - cy.

God Is My Strong Salvation

179

CHRISTUS, DER IST MEIN LEBEN   7.6.7.6

James Montgomery, 1822; alt. 1988   Melchior Vulpius, 1609

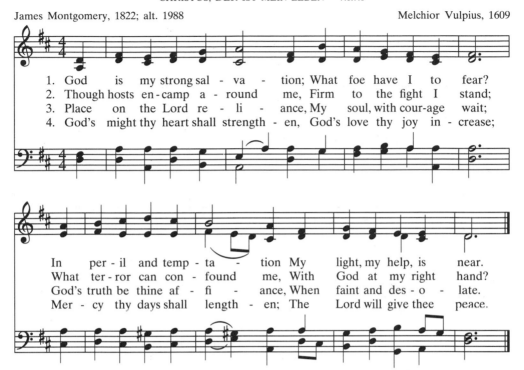

1. God is my strong salvation; What foe have I to fear?
2. Though hosts encamp around me, Firm to the fight I stand;
3. Place on the Lord reliance, My soul, with courage wait;
4. God's might thy heart shall strengthen, God's love thy joy increase;

In peril and temptation My light, my help, is near.
What terror can confound me, With God at my right hand?
God's truth be thine affiance, When faint and desolate.
Mercy thy days shall lengthen; The Lord will give thee peace.

180 The God of Heaven

GLORY   Irregular

Michael A. Perry, 1973; alt.   Norman L. Warren, 1973

1. The God of heav - en thun-ders,   Whose voice in ca - dent
2. The des - ert writhes in tem - pest,   Wind whips the trees to
3. The might-y God e - ter - nal   Is to the throne as -

ech - oes   Re-sounds a - bove the wa - ters,
fu - ry,   The light-ning splits the for - est
cend - ed,   And we who are God's peo - ple,

And all the world sings, "Glo - ry glo - ry, glo - ry!"
And flame dif - fus - es Glo - ry, glo - ry, glo - ry!
With - in these walls cry, "Glo - ry, glo - ry, glo - ry!"

Come Sing to God

ELLACOMBE   CMD

Fred R. Anderson, 1986

Gesangbuch der Herzogl. Wirtembergischen
Katholischen Hofkapelle, 1784; alt. 1868

1. Come sing to God, O liv-ing saints, Sing prais-es to God's name.
2. In my suc-cess I felt se-cure. How good You've been to me.
3. What good is gained by my dis-grace, What prof-it in de-feat?
4. You change my grief to joy-filled dance, My sor-rows You de-stroy.

God's an-ger is not per-ma-nent, God's love will nev-er wane.
I said that this is my own work, As-crib-ing all to me.
My grave can-not con-fess Your name, Nor praise for You re-peat.
In faith-ful-ness You hear my cry And fill my life with joy.

Though tears may tar-ry for the night With sighs of deep-est pain,
But when You turned a-side Your face, My life was filled with fears.
Now hear, O Lord, my plain-tive cry; Be mer-ci-ful to me.
And so to You my heart shall sing, My voice Your good-ness raise.

Yet joy comes with the morn-ing sun, A peace that is not vain.
I begged for help, to You I cried With loud and bit-ter tears.
Ac-cept my long-ing heart's re-quest And from death set me free.
You are my God, for-ev-er-more, My life shall sing Your praise.

182   PSALM 31:9–16

Ladies of the Grail
Refrain: Hal H. Hopson, 1983

Hal H. Hopson, 1985

Refrain

O Lord, You are my God, I trust in You.

1. Have mercy on me, O Lord, for I am in dis - tress.
2. For my life is spent with sorrow and my years with sighs.
3. In the face of all my foes I am a re - proach,
4. Those who see me in the street run far a - way from me.
5. I have heard the slander of the crowd, fear is all a - round me,
6. But as for me, I trust in You, Lord, I say: You are my God.
7. Let Your face shine up - on Your servant.

1. Tears have wasted my eyes, my.............throat, and my heart.
2. Af - fliction has broken
   down my strength and my.......bones waste a - way. *(R)*
3. An object of scorn to my
   neighbors and of..............fear to my friends.
4. I am like the dead, forgotten by
   all, like a....................thing thrown a - way. *(R)*
5. As they plot together against me, as they plan to take my life.
6. My life is in Your hands,
   deliver me from the ....hands of those who hate me.
7. [ ] Save me ....in Your love. *(R)*

In You, Lord, I Have Put My Trust 183

IN DICH HAB' ICH GEHOFFET   8.8.7.4.4.7

Adam Reissner, 1533
Trans. Catherine Winkworth, 1863; alt.

Sunderreiter's *Himmlische Harfen*, 1573

1. In You, Lord, I have put my trust; Leave me not help-less in the dust, Let me not be con-found-ed. Let in Your Word My faith, O Lord, Be al-ways firm-ly ground-ed.

2. O lis-ten, Lord, most gra-cious-ly And hear my cry, my prayer, my plea, Make haste for my pro-tec-tion; For woes and fear Sur-round me here. Help me in my af-flic-tion.

3. You are my strength, my shield, my rock, My for-tress that with-stands each shock, My help, my life, my tow-er, My bat-tle sword; Al-might-y Lord, What can re-sist Your pow-er?

4. With You, Lord, I have cast my lot; O faith-ful God, for-sake me not, To You my soul com-mend-ing. Lord, be my stay And lead the way Now and when life is end-ing.

184 How Blest Are Those

ES FLOG EIN KLEINS WALDVÖGELEIN 7.6.7.6 D

Fred R. Anderson, 1986

Memmingen ms., 17th century
Harm. George Ratcliffe Woodward, 1904

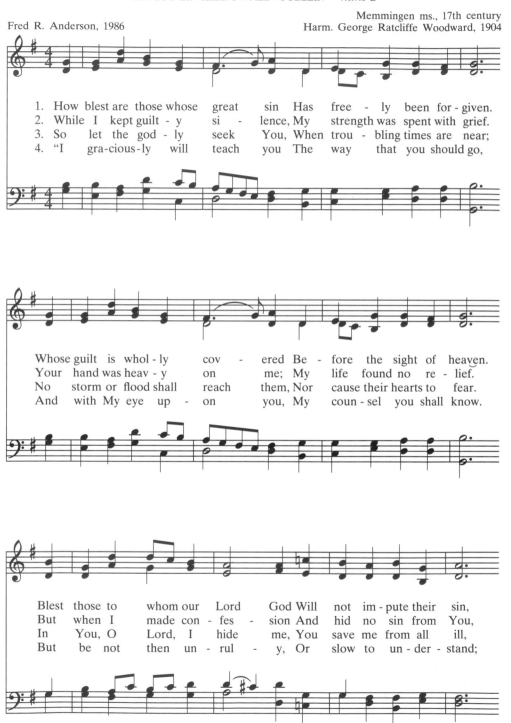

1. How blest are those whose great sin Has free - ly been for - given.
2. While I kept guilt - y si - lence, My strength was spent with grief.
3. So let the god - ly seek You, When trou - bling times are near;
4. "I gra-cious-ly will teach you The way that you should go,

Whose guilt is whol - ly cov - ered Be - fore the sight of heaven.
Your hand was heav - y on me; My life found no re - lief.
No storm or flood shall reach them, Nor cause their hearts to fear.
And with My eye up - on you, My coun - sel you shall know.

Blest those to whom our Lord God Will not im - pute their sin,
But when I made con - fes - sion And hid no sin from You,
In You, O Lord, I hide me, You save me from all ill,
But be not then un - rul - y, Or slow to un - der - stand;

Text: © 1986 Fred R. Anderson; from *Singing Psalms of Joy and Praise.* Used by permission.

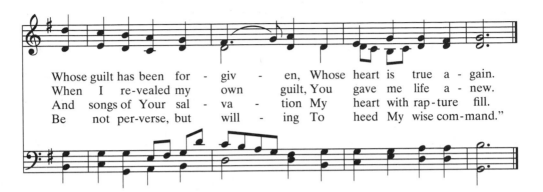

Whose guilt has been for - giv - en, Whose heart is true a - gain.
When I re-vealed my own guilt, You gave me life a - new.
And songs of Your sal - va - tion My heart with rap-ture fill.
Be not per-verse, but will - ing To heed My wise com-mand."

5. The sorrows of the wicked
   In number shall abound,
   But those who trust our own God
   Great mercy shall surround.

Then in the Lord be joyful,
In song lift up your voice;
Be glad in God, you righteous;
Rejoice, O saints, rejoice.

185

PSALM 33

Psalm tone: Laurence Bevenot, 1987
Refrain: Richard Proulx, 1987

Lord, let Your mer-cy be on us, as we place our trust in You.

[1] Rejoice in the Lord, Ò you righteous.
Praise befíts the upright.
[2] Praise the Lord wìth the lyre,
make melody to Him with the harp óf ten strings! *(R)*

**[3] Sing to Him à new song,
play skillfully on the strings, with loud shouts.
[4] For the word of the Lòrd is upright;
and all His work is dóne in faithfulness.** *(R)*

[5] He loves righteousnèss and justice;
the earth is full of the steadfast love óf the Lord.
[6] By the word of the Lord the heavèns were made,
and all their host by the breath óf His mouth. *(R)*

**[7] He gathered the waters of the sea as ìn a bottle;
He put the deeps ín storehouses.
[8] Let all the earth fèar the Lord,
let all the inhabitants of the world stand in áwe of Him.** *(R)*

[9] For He spoke, and it càme to be;
He commanded, and ít stood firm.
[10] The Lord brings the counsel of the natìons to nothing;
He frustrates the plans óf the peoples. *(R)*

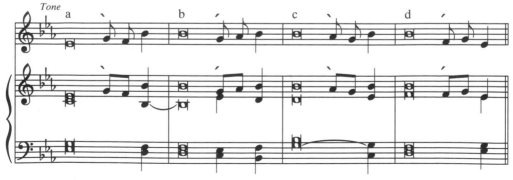

Thy Mercy and Thy Truth, O Lord 186

TALLIS' ORDINAL   CM

The Psalter, 1912; alt.   Thomas Tallis, c. 1567

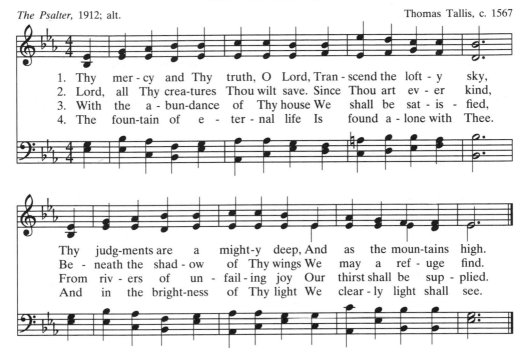

1. Thy mer-cy and Thy truth, O Lord, Tran-scend the loft-y sky,
2. Lord, all Thy crea-tures Thou wilt save. Since Thou art ev-er kind,
3. With the a-bun-dance of Thy house We shall be sat-is-fied,
4. The foun-tain of e-ter-nal life Is found a-lone with Thee.

Thy judg-ments are a might-y deep, And as the moun-tains high.
Be-neath the shad-ow of Thy wings We may a ref-uge find.
From riv-ers of un-fail-ing joy Our thirst shall be sup-plied.
And in the bright-ness of Thy light We clear-ly light shall see.

5. From those that know Thee may Thy love
   And mercy ne'er depart,
   And may Thy justice still protect
   And bless the upright heart.

Psalm 34 is number 187

187

Psalm Tone: St. Meinrad VIII
Refrain: Robert E. Kreutz

Para. Helen L. Wright, 1984

Refrain

Taste and see, taste and see the good-ness of the Lord.

1. Fear the Lord, you ho - ly ones,
2. Come, my chil - dren, and listen:
3. Then your tongue must not speak evil,
4. The eyes of the Lord are on the righteous,
5. The righteous cry out and God hears,
6. Though misfortunes of the good a - bound,
7. Their own evil brings death to the wicked,

And your needs will be sup - plied;
I will teach you the fear of the Lord.

Nor your lips say ly - ing words.
The ears of God hear their cry;

They are delivered from their dis - tress.
They are delivered from them all;
And those who hate good will be brought to ruin.

Psalm 36 is number 186

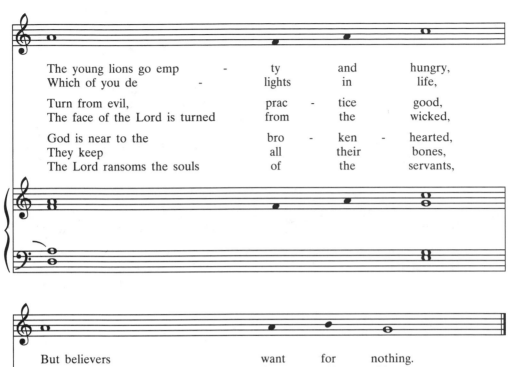

The young lions go emp - ty and hungry,
Which of you de - lights in life,

Turn from evil, prac - tice good,
The face of the Lord is turned from the wicked,

God is near to the bro - ken - hearted,
They keep all their bones,
The Lord ransoms the souls of the servants,

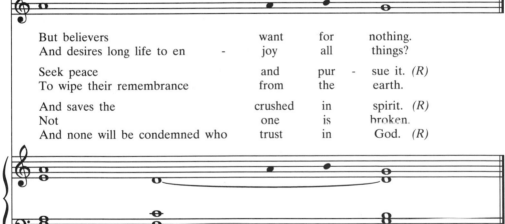

But believers want for nothing.
And desires long life to en - joy all things?

Seek peace and pur - sue it. *(R)*
To wipe their remembrance from the earth.

And saves the crushed in spirit. *(R)*
Not one is broken.
And none will be condemned who trust in God. *(R)*

188 Fret Not for Those Who Do Wrong Things

CULROSS   CM

Christopher L. Webber, 1986   Scottish Psalter, 1635

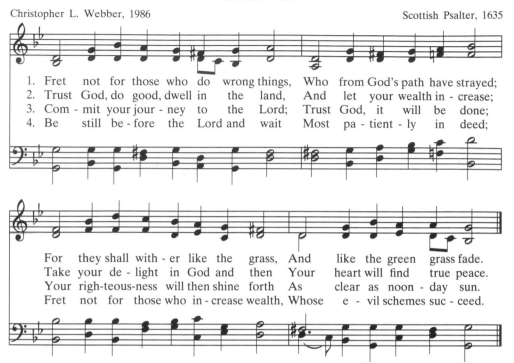

1. Fret not for those who do wrong things, Who from God's path have strayed;
2. Trust God, do good, dwell in the land, And let your wealth in - crease;
3. Com - mit your jour - ney to the Lord; Trust God, it will be done;
4. Be still be - fore the Lord and wait Most pa - tient - ly in deed;

For they shall with - er like the grass, And like the green grass fade.
Take your de - light in God and then Your heart will find true peace.
Your righ-teous-ness will then shine forth As clear as noon - day sun.
Fret not for those who in - crease wealth, Whose e - vil schemes suc - ceed.

5. Let neither rage nor anger gain
   In you the upper hand,
   For those who wait upon the Lord
   Shall soon possess the land.

PSALM 42:1–7

As Deer Long for the Streams

189

ROCKINGHAM   LM

Christopher L. Webber, 1986

Second Supplement to Psalmody in Miniature, 1783
Harm. Edward Miller, 1790

1. As deer long for the streams, O Lord, So my soul
2. My tears have been my con - stant food Poured out be -
3. I pour my soul out when I think How to God's
4. Why, O my soul, are you so full Of heav - i -

al - so seeks Your face; When will my soul, a -
fore You night and day, While all day long they
house I led the throng, All those who keep the
ness, why so down - cast? O put your trust in

thirst for God, Ap - pear be - fore the God of grace?
say to me, "Where is your God now when you pray?"
ho - ly days With voice of prayer and thank - ful song.
God, my help; I will give thanks to God at last.

190 PSALM 42

Psalm tone: Douglas Mews, 1986
Refrain: Joseph Gelineau, 1986

My soul is thirst-ing for the Lord: when shall I see God face to face?

¹As a deer longs for flòwing streams,
  so my soul longs for Yóu, O God.
²My soul thìrsts for God,
  for the líving God. *(repeat phrases c and d)*
When shall I come ànd behold
  the fáce of God? *(R)*

**³My tears have bèen my food
  [both] dáy and night,
while people say to mè continually,
  "Where ís your God?" *(R)***

⁴These things Ì remember,
  as I pour óut my soul:
how I went wìth the throng,
  and led them in procession
  to the hóuse of God, *(repeat phrases c and d)*
with glad shouts and songs òf thanksgiving,
  a multitude kéeping festival. *(R)*

**⁵Why are you cast down, Ò my soul,
  and why are you disquietéd within?
Hope in God; for I shall àgain praise Him,
  my help ⁶ ánd my God. *(R)***

My soul is cast dòwn within me;
  therefore I rémember You
from the land of Jordan ànd of Hermon,
  [and] fróm Mount Mizar.

7Deep càlls to deep
  at the thunder óf Your cataracts;
all Your waves ànd Your billows
  have gone óver me. *(R)*

8**By day the Lord commands His stèadfast love,**
  and at night His song ís with me, *(omit phrase c)*
a prayer to the God óf my life. *(R)*

9I say to Gòd, my rock,
  "Why have Yóu forgotten me?
Why must I walk àbout mournfully
  because the enemý oppresses me?" *(R)*

10**As with a deadly wound ìn my body,**
  my adversáries taunt me,
 while they say to mè continually,
"Where ís your God?" *(R)*

11Why are you cast down, Ò my soul,
  and why are you disquietéd within me?
Hope in God; for I shall àgain praise Him,
  my help ánd my God. *(R)*

PSALM 46

God Is Our Refuge and Our Strength 191

WINCHESTER OLD   CM

The Psalter, 1912; alt. 1988

Este's *Psalmes*, 1592

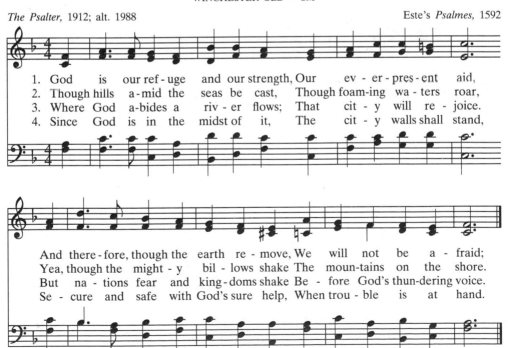

1. God is our ref-uge and our strength, Our ev-er-pres-ent aid,
2. Though hills a-mid the seas be cast, Though foam-ing wa-ters roar,
3. Where God a-bides a riv-er flows; That cit-y will re-joice.
4. Since God is in the midst of it, The cit-y walls shall stand,

And there-fore, though the earth re-move, We will not be a-fraid;
Yea, though the might-y bil-lows shake The moun-tains on the shore.
But na-tions fear and king-doms shake Be-fore God's thun-der-ing voice.
Se-cure and safe with God's sure help, When trou-ble is at hand.

This tune with descant, 58

192 God, Our Help and Constant Refuge

MICHAEL   8.7.8.7.3.3.7

Fred R. Anderson, 1986; alt.   Herbert Howells, 1930, 1977

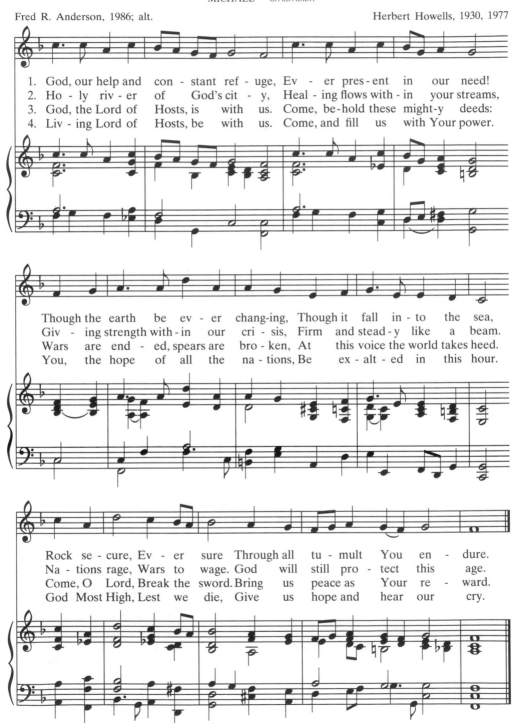

1. God, our help and con - stant ref - uge, Ev - er pres - ent in our need!
2. Ho - ly riv - er of God's cit - y, Heal - ing flows with - in your streams,
3. God, the Lord of Hosts, is with us. Come, be - hold these might - y deeds:
4. Liv - ing Lord of Hosts, be with us. Come, and fill us with Your power.

Though the earth be ev - er chang-ing, Though it fall in - to the sea,
Giv - ing strength with - in our cri - sis, Firm and stead - y like a beam.
Wars are end - ed, spears are bro - ken, At this voice the world takes heed.
You, the hope of all the na - tions, Be ex - alt - ed in this hour.

Rock se - cure, Ev - er sure Through all tu - mult You en - dure.
Na - tions rage, Wars to wage. God will still pro - tect this age.
Come, O Lord, Break the sword. Bring us peace as Your re - ward.
God Most High, Lest we die, Give us hope and hear our cry.

PSALM 46

TONE 8-g

Psalm tone: Richard Proulx, 1975
Refrain: A. Gregory Murray, 1963

193

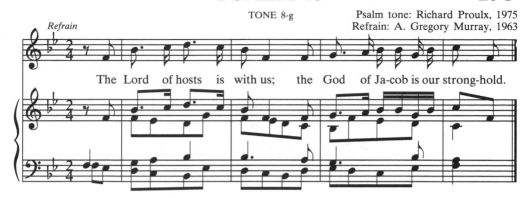

Refrain

The Lord of hosts is with us; the God of Ja-cob is our strong-hold.

¹God is our refuge and strèngth,
   a very present hélp in trouble.

²Therefore we will not fear though the earth should chànge,
   though the mountains shake in the héart of the sea;
³though its waters roar and fòam,
   though the mountains tremble wíth its tumult. *(R)*

⁴There is a river whose streams make glad the city of Gòd,
   the holy habitation óf the Most High.
⁵God is in the midst of the city, it shall not be mòved;
   God will help it whén the morning dawns.

⁶The nations are in an uproar, the kingdoms tòtter;
   He utters His vóice, the earth melts. *(R)*

⁷The Lord of hosts is wìth us;
   the God of Jacob ís our refuge.

⁸Come, behold the works of the Lòrd;
   see what desolations He has bróught on the earth.
⁹He makes wars cease to the end of the ēarth;
   He breaks the bow, and shatters the spèar;
   He búrns the shields with fire. *(R)*

¹⁰"Be still, and know that I am Gōd!
   I am exalted among the nàtions,
   I am exálted in the earth."

¹¹The Lord of hosts is wìth us;
   the God of Jacob ís our refuge. *(R)*

Tone

Use for three-line versicles.

194 Peoples, Clap Your Hands!

GENEVAN 47   10.10.10.10.10.10

Para. Joy F. Patterson, 1989

Genevan Psalter, 1551
Harm. Claude Goudimel, 1564

1. Peo - ples, clap your hands! Shout to God with joy!
2. God as - cends the throne with a joy - ful cry,

King of all the earth is the Lord Most High;
And with trum - pet sound has gone up on high;

All hu - man - i - ty stands in awe of God.
Sing your praise to God, sing with joy - ful voice!

With a might - y hand God brings na - tions low,
Rul - ers, peo - ples, now join to serve the Lord,

And be - neath our feet casts down ev - er - y foe;
For earth's might - y ones all be - long to God,

Our in - her - i - tance comes from God the Lord.
Who ex - alt - ed reigns: now with psalms re - joice!

PSALM 51

Have Mercy on Us, Living Lord

195

PTOMEY CM

Fred R. Anderson, 1986

Hal H. Hopson, 1983

1. Have mer - cy on us, liv - ing Lord, Re - mem - ber not our sin.
2. Our sin and guilt are heav - y, Lord, And e - vil in Your sight.
3. We're born in - to a guilt - y world And sin - ful in our ways.
4. So come and pu - ri - fy our lives, Our hearts with love re - deem.

Ac - cord - ing to Your stead - fast love   Come, cleanse us deep with - in.
A - gainst You on - ly have we sinned;   Your judg - ment, Lord, is right.
Lord, teach us wis - dom in our hearts   And lead us all our days.
Re - store us to Your life - filled ways.   Come, Lord, and make us clean.

5. Your Spirit place within our hearts
   That we may teach Your ways,
   And all the people of the earth
   Shall learn to sing Your praise.

6. You are not pleased with sacrifice,
   It brings You no delight.
   A humble spirit given in love
   Is pleasing in Your sight.

7. Rebuild Your people with Your love,
   Renew us every day;
   With hearts renewed, in all our work,
   Our lives shall sing Your praise.

196 PSALM 51

The Grail

David Clark Isele, 1979

Refrain Unison

The sac-ri-fice You ac-cept, O God, is a hum-ble spir-it.

1. Have mercy on me, O God, in Your kindness;
2. My offenses, truly I know them;
3. That You may be justified when You give sentence
4. Indeed, You love truth in the heart;
5. Make me hear rejoicing and gladness,
6. A pure heart create for me, O God,
7. Give me again the joy of Your help;
8. O rescue me, God, my helper,
9. For in sacrifice You take no de - light,
10. In Your goodness, show favor to Zion:

in Your com - passion blot out my of - fense.
my sin is always be - fore me.

and be without reproach when You judge,
then in the secret of my heart teach me wisdom.

that the bones You have crushed may thrill.
put a steadfast spirit with - in me.

with a spirit of fervor sus - tain me,
and my tongue shall ring out Your good - ness.

burnt offering from me You would re - fuse;
re - build the walls of Jeru - sa - lem.

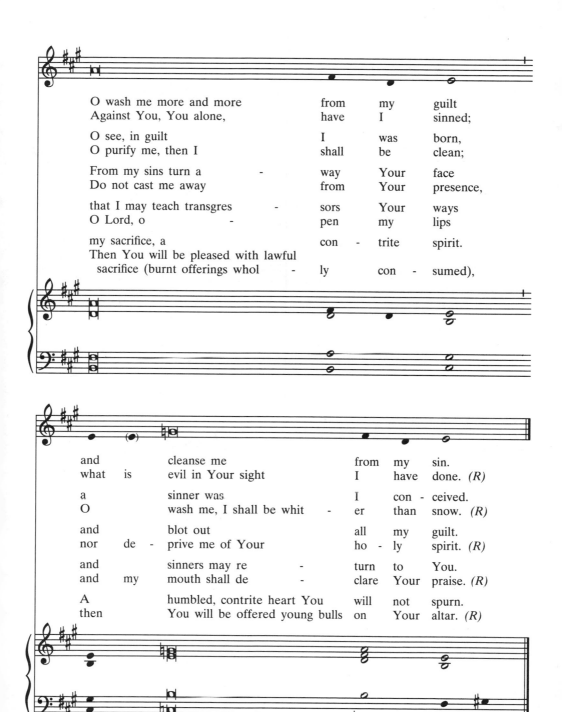

O wash me more and more   from   my   guilt
Against You, You alone,   have   I   sinned;

O see, in guilt   I   was   born,
O purify me, then I   shall   be   clean;

From my sins turn a - way   Your   face
Do not cast me away   from   Your   presence,

that I may teach transgres - sors   Your   ways
O Lord, o - pen   my   lips

my sacrifice, a con - trite   spirit.
Then You will be pleased with lawful
  sacrifice (burnt offerings whol - ly   con - sumed),

and   cleanse me   from   my   sin.
what is   evil in Your sight   I   have   done. *(R)*

a   sinner was   I   con - ceived.
O   wash me, I shall be whit - er   than   snow. *(R)*

and   blot out   all   my   guilt.
nor de - prive me of Your   ho - ly   spirit. *(R)*

and   sinners may re - turn to   You.
and my   mouth shall de - clare   Your   praise. *(R)*

A   humbled, contrite heart You   will   not   spurn.
then   You will be offered young bulls on   Your   altar. *(R)*

197 My Soul in Silence Waits for God

CHESHIRE   CM

The Psalter, 1912
Alt. Fred R. Anderson, 1984

Este's *Psalmes,* 1592
As in *Songs of Syon,* 1910

1. My soul in si - lence waits for God, Who
2. In God a - lone my hon - or rests, Who
3. All peo - ple are but van - i - ty, The
4. In your own strength, then, place no hope, For

my own hope has proved. A rock and strong - hold
brings de - liv - 'erance sure; My rock of strength is
best of us a lie; Both high and low es -
rich - es, have no lust; Though for a mo - ment

is my God, I nev - er shall be moved.
found in God, My ref - uge most se - cure.
tate com - bined Are light - er than a sigh.
they ap - peal, They are not worth your trust.

5. For truly God has spoken once,
   And twice to me made known:
   That strength and power belong to God,
   And unto God alone.

6. For so it is that sovereign grace
   Belongs to You, O Lord;
   For You according to our work
   Shall everyone reward.

Text: Alteration © 1990 Fred R. Anderson. Used by permission.

O God, You Are My God

198

ST. BRIDE   SM

Christopher L. Webber, 1986

Samuel Howard, 1762

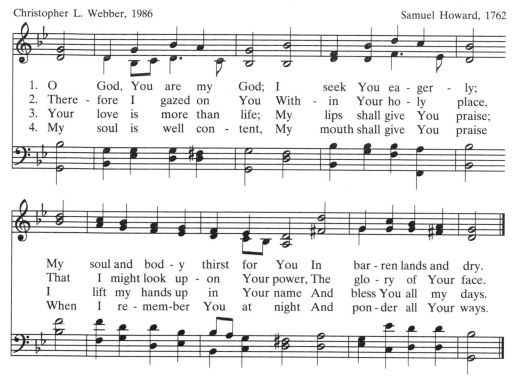

1. O   God, You are my   God; I   seek You ea - ger - ly;
2. There - fore I   gazed on   You With - in Your ho - ly   place,
3. Your   love is more than   life; My   lips shall give You praise;
4. My   soul is well con - tent, My   mouth shall give You praise

My   soul and bod - y   thirst for You In   bar - ren lands and dry.
That   I   might look up - on   Your power, The glo - ry of Your face.
I   lift my hands up   in   Your name And bless You all my   days.
When   I   re - mem - ber You at   night And pon - der all Your ways.

5. Your wings have sheltered me,
   My helper in the past;
   My soul, Lord, clings to You alone,
   Your right hand holds me fast.

Alternate tune: SOUTHWELL, 301

199 O Lord, You Are My God

ALBERTA 10.4.10.4.10.10

Para. John G. Dunn, 1983

William H. Harris, 1930

1. O Lord, You are my God, for You I long: Show me Your face.
2. My spir-it seeks Your glo-rious maj-es-ty: Show me Your face.
3. I pray to You and in Your help con-fide: Show me Your face.

Your life with-in me makes my spir-it strong: Lord of all grace.
Your con-stant love gives more than life to me: Lord of all grace.
You feed my soul and I am sat-is-fied: Lord of all grace.

For You I thirst like des-erts parched and dried.
Thus will I bless Your name through all my days,
O keep me in the shel-ter of Your throne;

With - in Your care my soul is sat - is - fied.
And lift my hands to You in thank - ful praise.
To You I cling, my joy, my God a - lone.

To Bless the Earth

200

CHRISTUS, DER IST MEIN LEBEN 7.6.7.6

The Psalter, 1912; alt.

Melchior Vulpius, 1609

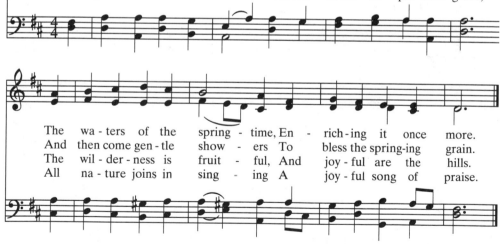

1. To bless the earth God sends us From heaven's a - bun-dant store
2. The seed by God pro - vid - ed Is sown o'er hill and plain,
3. God crowns the year with good - ness, The earth God's mer - cy fills,
4. With grain the fields are cov - ered, The flocks in pas-tures graze;

The wa - ters of the spring - time, En - rich-ing it once more.
And then come gen - tle show - ers To bless the spring-ing grain.
The wil - der - ness is fruit - ful, And joy - ful are the hills.
All na - ture joins in sing - ing A joy - ful song of praise.

201 Praise Is Your Right, O God, in Zion

GENEVAN 65   9.6.9.6 D

Stanley Wiersma, 1980

Harm. Dale Grotenhuis, 1985

1. Praise is Your right, O God, in Zi - on. To You we
pay our vows. When we Your peo - ple pray, You hear us,
All flesh to You will bow. When our trans-gres-sions o - ver-
whelm us, You gra-cious-ly for - give. How sat - is-fied Your
cho - sen ser - vants; With - in Your courts they live.

2. Your might - y acts work our sal - va - tion. All earth waits
hope - ful - ly. You have the strength to make the moun - tains,
To calm the storm - y sea. You calm the tu - mult of the
peo - ple. Such awe-some signs You do That earth, from sun - rise
to the sun - set, For joy cries out to You.

3. You bless the earth with streams and riv - ers, And with the
gen - tle rain. You set - tle ridg - es, soft - en fur - rows,
And bless the sprout - ing grain. You crown the year with am - ple
har - vest; A rich a - bun-dance springs. All flocks and grains and
hills and mead - ows, Yes, all cre - a - tion sings.

PSALM 67

Psalm tone: Laurence Bevenot, 1986
Refrain: Marie Kremer, 1986

202

Refrain

O God, O God, let all the na-tions praise You!

¹May God be gracious to ùs and bless us
   and make His face to shíne upon us,
²that Your way may be known ùpon earth,
   Your saving power amóng all nations. *(R)*

³**Let the peoples praise Yòu, O God;** *(omit phrases b and c)*
   let all the péoples praise You!

⁴Let the nations be glad and sìng for joy,
   for You judge the peoplés with equity *(omit phrase c)*
   and guide the nations úpon earth. *(R)*

⁵**Let the peoples praise Yòu, O God;** *(omit phrases b and c)*
   let all the péoples praise You!

⁶The earth has yielded ìts increase;
   God, our Gód, has blessed us.
⁷May God continùe to bless us;
   let all the ends of the éarth revere Him! *(R)*

Tone

a   b   c   d

203

God of Mercy, God of Grace

Henry F. Lyte, 1834; alt. 1984   IMPACT   7.7.7.7   David G. Wilson, 1973

1. God of mer-cy, God of grace, Show the bright-ness of Your face;
2. Let the peo-ple praise You, Lord, Be by all that live a-dored;
3. Let the na-tions shout and sing, Glo-ry to their Sav-ior bring;
4. Let the peo-ple praise You, Lord, Earth shall then its fruits af-ford;

Shine up-on us, Sav-ior, shine, Fill us with Your light di-vine.
At Your feet their trib-ute pay, And Your ho-ly will o-bey.
All be-low and all a-bove Sing Your praise with joy and love.
Shine up-on us, Sav-ior, shine, Fill us with Your light di-vine.

204   **PSALM 72**

Psalm tone: Laurence Bevenot, 1986
Refrain: John Schiavone, 1975

Refrain

Jus-tice shall flour-ish in God's time, and full-ness of peace for-ev-er.

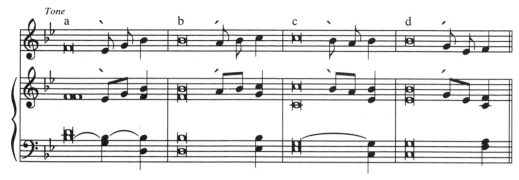

¹Give the king Your jùstice, O God,
    and Your righteousness tó a king's son.
²May he judge Your peoplè with righteousness,
    and Your póor with justice. *(R)*

³May the mountains yield prosperity fòr the people,
    and the hílls, in righteousness.
⁴May he defend the cause of the poor of the people,
    give deliverance tò the needy,
    and crush thé oppressor. *(R)*

⁵May he live while the sùn endures,
    and as long as the moon, throughout all génerations.
⁶May he be like rain that falls òn the mown grass,
    like showers that wáter the earth. *(R)*

⁷In his days may rìghteousness flourish
    and peace abound, until the moon ís no more.
⁸May he have dominion from sèa to sea,
    and from the River to the ends óf the earth. *(R)*

⁹May his foes bow dòwn before him,
    and his enemies líck the dust.
¹⁰May the kings of Tarshish and of the isles
    rendèr him tribute,
    may the kings of Sheba and Seba
    bríng gifts. *(R)*

¹¹May all kings fall dòwn before him,
    all nations gíve him service.
¹²For he delivers the needy whèn they call,
    the poor and those who háve no helper. *(R)*

¹³He has pity on the weak ànd the needy,
    and saves the lives óf the needy.
¹⁴From oppression and violence he redèems their life;
    and precious is their blood ín his sight. *(R)*

205 All Hail to God's Anointed

ROCKPORT 7.6.7.6 D

James Montgomery, 1821; alt. 1984

Thomas Tertius Noble, 1938

1. All hail to God's a - noint - ed, Great Da - vid's great - er Son!
2. You shall come down like show - ers Up - on the fruit - ful earth,
3. All rul - ers bow be - fore You, And gold and in - cense bring;
4. O'er ev - ery foe vic - to - rious, You on Your throne shall rest;

All hail, in time ap - point - ed, Your reign on earth be - gun!
And love, joy, hope, like flow - ers, Spring in Your path to birth:
All na - tions shall a - dore You, Your praise all peo - ple sing;
From age to age more glo - rious, All bless - ing and all blest:

You come to break op - pres - sion, To set the cap - tive free,
Be - fore You on the moun - tains Shall peace, the her - ald, go,
To You shall prayer un - ceas - ing And dai - ly vows as - cend;
The tide of time shall nev - er Your cov - e - nant re - move;

To take a - way trans - gres - sion And rule in eq - ui - ty.
And righ - teous-ness in foun - tains From hill to val - ley flow.
Your rule is still in - creas - ing, Your rule is with - out end.
Your name shall stand for - ev - er, Your change-less name of love.

Music: Copyright © 1941 by United Church Press. Used by permission.

O Hear Our Cry, O Lord

206

VINEYARD HAVEN   SM with refrain

Fred R. Anderson, 1986

Richard Wayne Dirksen, 1974

1. O hear our cry, O Lord; Now hear us as we pray.
2. En - throned a - bove all worlds, You shine with ho - ly light.
3. O Lord, the God of Hosts, Turn not Your face a - way.
4. O Lord, our God, re - turn; Bring peace in - to each home.

You guide us as a shep-herd leads, So keep us in Your way.
Lord, pour Your power up - on us all And save us with Your might.
Our tears have been both food and drink, Foes mock us night and day.
So let Your face shine on us all, Re - store us as Your own.

O come, Lord, come, Re - store and save us now.

207
How Lovely, Lord

MERLE'S TUNE   7.6.7.6 D

Arlo D. Duba, 1984   Hal H. Hopson, 1983

1. How love-ly, Lord, how love - ly Is Your a - bid - ing place;
2. In Your blest courts to wor - ship, O God, a sin - gle day
3. A sun and shield for - ev - er Are You, O Lord Most High;

My soul is long-ing, faint - ing, To feast up - on Your grace.
Is bet - ter than a thou - sand If I from You should stray.
You show-er us with bless - ings; No good will You de - ny.

The spar - row finds a shel - ter, A place to build her nest;
I'd rath - er keep the en - trance And claim You as my Lord
The saints, Your grace re - ceiv - ing, From strength to strength shall go,

And so Your tem - ple calls us With - in its walls to rest.
Than rev - el in the rich - es The ways of sin af - ford.
And from their life shall riv - ers Of bless - ing o - ver - flow.

208   PSALM 84

Psalm tone: Chrysogonus Waddell, 1986
Refrain: A. Gregory Murray, 1963

How love - ly is Your dwell-ing place, O Lord of hosts.

¹How lovely is Your dwèlling place, *(omit phrases b and c)*
  O Lord óf hosts.

²**My soul longs, indèed it faints**
  for the courts of thé Lord;
  my heart and my flesh sing fòr joy
  to the livíng God. *(R)*

³Even the sparrow fìnds a home,
    and the swallow a nest for hérself, *(repeat phrase b)*
    where she may lay hér young,
  at Your altars, O Lord òf hosts,
    my King and mý God. *(R)*

⁴Happy are those who live ìn Your house,
　　ever singing Yóur praise.
⁵Happy are those whose strength is ìn You,
　　in whose heart are the highways tó Zion.　*(R)*

⁶As they go through the valley of Baca
　　they make it a plàce of springs;
　　the early rain also covers it wíth pools.
⁷They go from strength tò strength;
　　the God of gods will be seen ín Zion.　*(R)*

⁸O Lord God of hosts, hèar my prayer;
　　give ear, O God óf Jacob.
⁹Behold our shield, Ò God;
　　look on the face of Your ánointed.　*(R)*

¹⁰For a day in Your còurts is better
　　than a thousánd elsewhere.
　I would rather be a doorkeeper in the house of mỳ God
　　than live in the tents óf wickedness.　*(R)*

¹¹For the Lord God is a sùn and shield;
　　He bestows favor ánd honor.
　No good thing does the Lord wìthhold
　　from those who walk úprightly.

¹²O Lòrd of hosts,　*(omit phrases b and c)*
　　happy is everyone who trusts ín You.　*(R)*

209 My Song Forever Shall Record

ST. PETERSBURG 8.8.8.8.8.8.8

The Psalter, 1912; alt.

Dimitri S. Bortniansky, 1825; alt.

1. My song for-ev-er shall re-cord The ten-der mer-cies
of the Lord; Thy faith-ful-ness will I pro-claim, And
ev-ery age shall know Thy name. I sing of mer-cies
that en-dure, For-ev-er build-ed firm and sure.

2. Al-might-y God, Thy loft-y throne Has jus-tice for its
cor-ner-stone; And shin-ing bright be-fore Thy face Are
truth and love and bound-less grace. The heavens shall join in
glad ac-cord To praise Thy won-drous works, O Lord.

3. The swell-ing sea o-beys Thy will; Its an-gry waves Thy
voice can still. The heavens and earth, by right di-vine, The
world and all there-in are Thine; The whole cre-a-tion's
won-drous frame Pro-claims its Mak-er's glo-rious name.

4. With bless-ing is the na-tion crowned Whose peo-ple know the
joy-ful sound; They in the light, O Lord, shall live, The
light Thy face and fa-vor give. Their fame and might to
Thee be-long, For in Thy fa-vor they are strong.

Our God, Our Help in Ages Past

210

ST. ANNE CM

Isaac Watts, 1719; alt.

Attr. William Croft, 1708

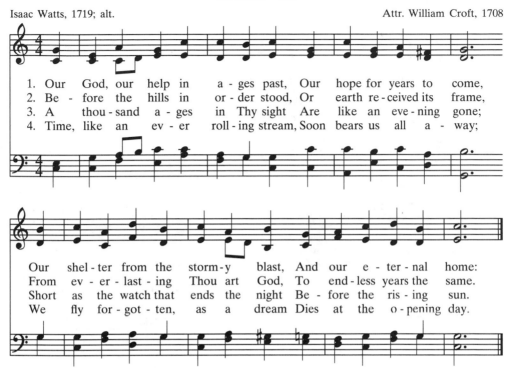

1. Our God, our help in a - ges past, Our hope for years to come,
2. Be - fore the hills in or - der stood, Or earth re - ceived its frame,
3. A thou - sand a - ges in Thy sight Are like an eve - ning gone;
4. Time, like an ev - er roll - ing stream, Soon bears us all a - way;

Our shel - ter from the storm - y blast, And our e - ter - nal home:
From ev - er - last - ing Thou art God, To end - less years the same.
Short as the watch that ends the night Be - fore the ris - ing sun.
We fly for - got - ten, as a dream Dies at the o - pening day.

5. Our God, our help in ages past,
   Our hope for years to come,
   Be Thou our guard while life shall last,
   And our eternal home.

211 Lord, You Have Been Our Dwelling Place

LOBT GOTT IN SEINEM HEILIGTUM   LM

Fred R. Anderson, 1986   Heinrich Schütz, 1628

1. Lord, You have been our dwell-ing place,
2. Your words can turn us back to dust,
3. Our years are but three-score and ten,
4. So teach us how to count our days,

A ref-uge
Our lives are
With spe-cial
That wis-dom

where our feet have trod.
frag-ile, like a dream.
health they reach four-score.
might fill all our time.

Be-fore You placed all things in
As grass which sprouts yet fades at
But still they're filled with pain and
Re-turn, O Lord, ac-cept our

space, From ev-er-last-ing You are God.
dusk We're born, we live, but pass un-seen.
sin, Soon gone, and then we live no more.
praise, That through our lives Your love may shine.

5. Establish, Lord, the work we do,
   And through it make Your glory known,
   That praise may ever come to You,
   And unto all Your love be shown.

Text: © 1986 Fred R. Anderson; from *Singing Psalms of Joy and Praise.* Used by permission.

Within Your Shelter, Loving God

212

ABBEY CM

John G. Dunn, 1982

Scottish Psalter, 1615

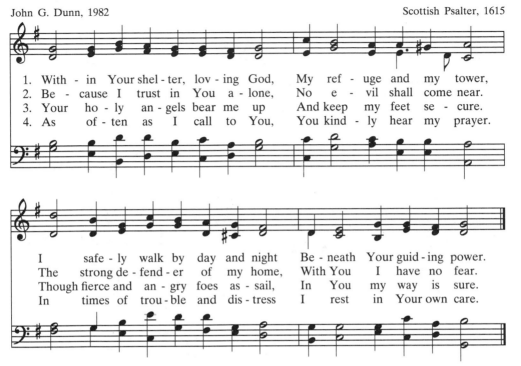

1. With - in Your shel - ter, lov - ing God, My ref - uge and my tower,
2. Be - cause I trust in You a - lone, No e - vil shall come near.
3. Your ho - ly an - gels bear me up And keep my feet se - cure.
4. As of - ten as I call to You, You kind - ly hear my prayer.

I safe - ly walk by day and night Be - neath Your guid - ing power.
The strong de - fend - er of my home, With You I have no fear.
Though fierce and an - gry foes as - sail, In You my way is sure.
In times of trou - ble and dis - tress I rest in Your own care.

5. All those who know Your name on earth
   Shall life abundant know.
   On all abiding in Your love
   Your saving grace bestow.

Text: © 1983 John G. Dunn, revised 1985. Used by permission.

213 God, Our Lord, a King Remaining

BRYN CALFARIA 8.7.8.7.444.7.7

John Keble, 1839; alt. 1988

William Owen, 1852

1. God, our Lord, a King re-main-ing, Robed in maj - es -
2. In its ev - er - last-ing sta - tion Earth is poised, to
3. With all tones of wa-ters blend-ing, Glo - rious is the
4. Lord, the words Your lips are tell - ing Are the per - fect

ty and light: You have robed Your - self, and reign - ing,
swerve no more; You have laid Your throne's foun - da - tion
break-ing deep; Glo - rious, beau - teous, with - out end - ing,
and the true. In Your high e - ter - nal dwell - ing,

Clothed Your - self with power and might. Al - le - lu - ia!
From all time where thought can soar. Al - le - lu - ia!
God, who reigns on heaven's high steep. Al - le - lu - ia!
Ho - li - ness shall live with You. Al - le - lu - ia!

Al - le - lu - ia! Al - le - lu - ia! God our King in depth and
Al - le - lu - ia! Al - le - lu - ia! Lord, You are for - ev - er -
Al - le - lu - ia! Al - le - lu - ia! Songs of o - cean nev - er
Al - le - lu - ia! Al - le - lu - ia! Lord, Your word is ev - er

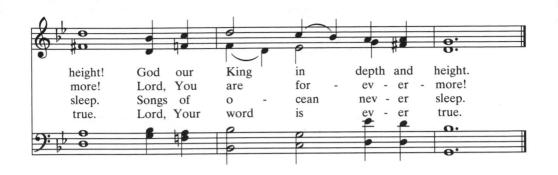

height! God our King in depth and height.
more! Lord, You are for - ev - er - more!
sleep. Songs of o - cean nev - er sleep.
true. Lord, Your word is ev - er true.

PSALM 95

O Come and Sing Unto the Lord 214

IRISH   CM

The Psalter, 1912; alt.

A Collection of Hymns and Sacred Poems, 1749

1. O come and sing un - to the Lord, To
2. Be - fore God's pres - ence let us come With
3. The Lord our God is King of kings, A -
4. To God the spa - cious sea be - longs; God

God our voic - es raise; Let us in our most
praise and thank - ful voice; Let us sing psalms to
bove all gods en - throned; The depths of earth and
made its waves and tides. And by God's hand the

joy - ful songs The Lord, our Sav - ior, praise.
God with grace, With grate - ful hearts re - joice.
moun - tains high By God a - lone are owned.
ris - ing land Was formed, and still a - bides.

5. O come, and bowing down to God   Yea, let us kneel before the Lord,
   Our worship let us bring;   Our Maker and our King.

215 Come, Sing with Joy to God

TO GOD WITH GLADNESS   Irregular

Para. Arlo D. Duba, 1984

David Clark Isele, 1979

1. Come, sing with joy to God, Our Rock and Sav - ior
2. The heights and depths of earth Are cra - dled in God's
3. Our God and Lord a - lone, Through all the years the
4. Lord, we would hear Your word, And not the test re -

praise; Come, en - ter in with shouts of joy, your voic - es
hand; The same al-might-y power made moun-tains, sea, and
same, You feed us, take us by the hand, call each by
peat Of Mas - sah with its man - na and the wa - ters

raise. O might - y God, You are the
land. Come, wor - ship God, come, kneel and
name. You are the shep - herd, we the
sweet. We ask for sight, Your rest re -

Lord, The God of gods by all a - dored.
bow Be - fore the Lord our Mak - er now.
sheep; Lord, shel - ter us, our foot - steps keep.
store, And we shall praise you ev - er - more.

O Sing a New Song to the Lord

216

GONFALON ROYAL LM

Charles H. Gabriel (1856–1932); alt.

Percy C. Buck, 1918

1. O sing a new song to the Lord, Sing, all the
   earth and bless that Name; From day to day God's praise re - cord,
   The Lord's re - deem - ing grace pro - claim.

2. Tell all the world God's won - drous ways; Tell hea - then
   na - tions far and near; Great is the Lord, and great God's praise;
   The Lord a - lone let na - tions fear.

3. The hea - then gods are i - dols vain; The shin - ing
   heavens the Lord sup - ports; Both light and hon - or lead the train,
   While strength and beau - ty fill the courts.

4. Let ev - ery tongue and ev - ery tribe Give to the
   Lord due praise and sing; All glo - ry un - to God as - cribe,
   Come, throng the courts, and of - ferings bring. Al - le - lu - ia!

Music: Used by permission of Oxford University Press.

217 O Sing a New Song

Helen L. Wright, 1983

Hal H. Hopson, 1983

Refrain

O sing a new song to the Lord, Sing to the Lord, Sing all the earth.

Verses

1. O sing a new song to the Lord,
2. Proclaim God's salvation day by day,
3. The Lord is great and worthy of all praise,
4. For the Lord made the heavens!
5. Let the heavens be glad, let the earth re - joice,
6. Shout for joy, all trees of the woods,

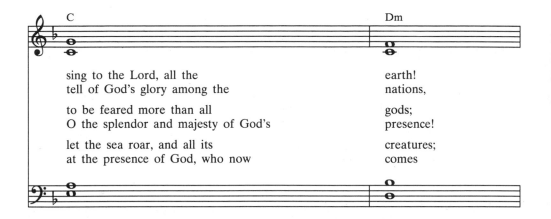

C   Dm

sing to the Lord, all the   earth!
tell of God's glory among the   nations,

to be feared more than all   gods;
O the splendor and majesty of God's   presence!

let the sea roar, and all its   creatures;
at the presence of God, who now   comes

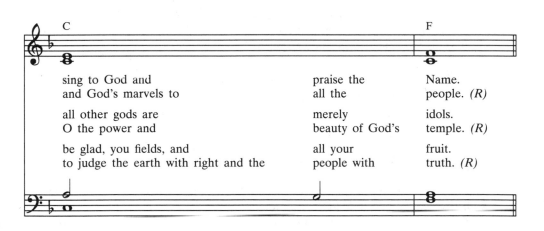

C   F

sing to God and   praise the   Name.
and God's marvels to   all the   people. *(R)*

all other gods are   merely   idols.
O the power and   beauty of God's   temple. *(R)*

be glad, you fields, and   all your   fruit.
to judge the earth with right and the   people with   truth. *(R)*

218 New Songs of Celebration Render

RENDEZ À DIEU 9.8.9.8 D

Erik Routley, 1972; alt. 1984

Louis Bourgeois, 1543; rev. 1551

1. New songs of cel - e - bra - tion ren - der To God who
2. Joy - ful - ly, heart - i - ly re - sound - ing, Let ev - ery
3. Riv - ers and seas and tor - rents roar - ing, Hon - or the

has great won - ders done; Love sits en - throned in age-less splen - dor;
in - stru - ment and voice Peal out the praise of grace a - bound - ing,
Lord with wild ac - claim; Moun - tains and stones, look up a - dor - ing,

Come and a - dore the might - y One. God has made known the great sal -
Call - ing the whole world to re - joice. Trum-pets and or - gans, set in
And find a voice to praise God's name. Right-teous, com - mand - ing, ev - er

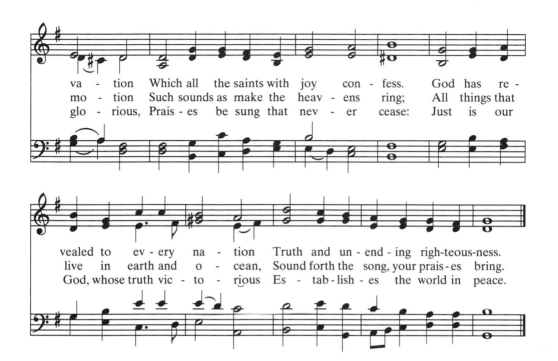

va - tion Which all the saints with joy con - fess. God has re -
mo - tion Such sounds as make the heav - ens ring; All things that
glo - rious, Prais - es be sung that nev - er cease: Just is our

vealed to ev - ery na - tion Truth and un - end - ing righ-teous-ness.
live in earth and o - cean, Sound forth the song, your prais - es bring.
God, whose truth vic - to - rious Es - tab - lish - es the world in peace.

219 To God Compose a Song of Joy

Ruth C. Duck, 1986

KEDDY   CM

Edwin R. Taylor, 1987

1. To God com - pose a song of joy; To God make
2. Be - fore the na - tions God re - veals A just and
3. In ev - ery cor - ner of the earth, God comes to

4. With trum - pet, with the sound of horns, With strings, yes,
5. Let seas in all their full - ness roar, And peo - ple
6. The God of jus - tice comes to save; Let earth make

mel - o - dy, Whose arm of strength does
righ - teous will, Re - mem - ber - ing in
save and free; Break forth with shouts of

with the lyre, With voic - es praise the
of all lands, Let moun - tains join and
mel - o - dy! For God will judge with

won - drous things, Whose hand brings vic - to - ry!
faith - ful love The house of Is - ra - el.
ho - ly joy; All lands, make mel - o - dy.

sov - ereign God, A lust - y, joy - ous choir.
shout for joy, Let riv - ers clap their hands.
righ - teous - ness And rule with eq - ui - ty.

All People That on Earth Do Dwell
220

OLD HUNDREDTH   LM

William Kethe, 1560   Attr. Louis Bourgeois (c. 1510–c. 1561)

1. All   peo-ple that on   earth   do   dwell, Sing   to   the Lord with
2. Know   that the Lord is   God   in - deed; With - out   our aid He
3. O   en - ter then His   gates with   praise, Ap - proach with joy His
4. For   why? The Lord our   God   is   good, His   mer - cy   is   for -

cheer - ful   voice;   Him   serve with mirth, His   praise   forth
did   us   make;   We   are   His   folk,   He   doth   us
courts   un - to;   Praise,   laud,   and   bless His   name   al -
ev - er   sure;   His   truth   at   all   times   firm - ly

tell,   Come   ye   be - fore   Him   and   re -   joice.
feed,   And   for   His   sheep He   doth   us   take.
ways,   For   it   is   seem - ly   so   to   do.
stood,   And   shall   from   age   to   age   en -   dure.

221

*Fauxbourdon setting**

Arr. John Dowland (1563–1626); alt.

PSALM 103

Psalm tone and Refrain: Richard Proulx, 1975

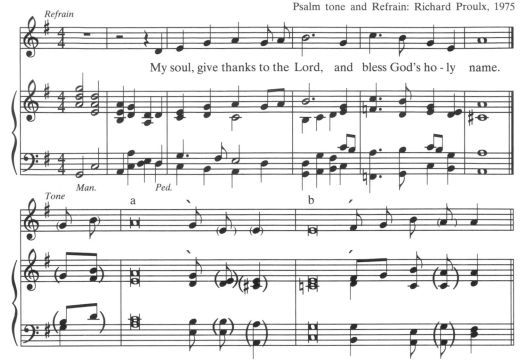

My soul, give thanks to the Lord, and bless God's ho-ly name.

¹Bless the Lord, O my sòul,
   and all that is within me,
   bléss His holy name. *(R)*

²**Bless the Lord, O my sòul,**
   and do not forget áll His benefits,
³**who forgives all your inìquity,**
   who heals all yóur diseases,
⁴**who redeems your life from the Pìt,**
   who crowns you with steadfast lóve and mercy,
⁵**who satisfies you with good as long as you lìve**
   so that your youth is renewed líke the eagle's. *(R)*

⁶The Lord works vindicàtion
   and justice for áll who are oppressed.

⁷**He made known His ways to Mòses,**
   His acts to the peoplé of Israel.

⁸The Lord is merciful and gràcious,
   slow to anger and aboundíng in steadfast love.

⁹**He will not always accùse,**
   nor will He keep His angér forever.
¹⁰**He does not deal with us according to our sìns,**
   nor repay us according to óur iniquities. *(R)*

¹¹For as the heavens are high above the èarth,
   so great is His steadfast love toward thóse who fear Him;

¹²as far as the east is from the wèst,
    so far He removes our transgréssions from us.

**¹³As a father has compassion for his chìldren,
    so the Lord has compassion for thóse who fear Him.** *(R)*

PSALM 103

O My Soul, Bless Your Redeemer   223

STUTTGART   8.7.8.7

Witt's *Psalmodia Sacra,* 1715
Para. in *The Book of Psalms,* 1871; alt. 1972, 1988   As in *Hymns Ancient and Modern,* 1861

1. O   my   soul,   bless   your   Re - deem - er;   All   with - in   me
2. God   for - gives   all   your   trans - gres - sions,   All   dis - eas - es
3. Far   as   east   from   west   is   dis - tant,   God   has   put   a -
4. As   it   was   with - out   be - gin - ning,   So   it   lasts   with -

bless   God's   name;   Bless   the   Sav - ior,   and   for - get   not
gen - tly   heals;   God   re - deems   you   from   de - struc - tion,
way   our   sin;   Like   the   pit - y   of   a   fa - ther
out   an   end;   To   their   chil - dren's   chil - dren   ev - er

All   God's   mer - cies   to   pro - claim;
And   with   you   so   kind - ly   deals.
Has   the   Lord's   com - pas - sion   been.
Shall   God's   righ - teous - ness   ex - tend:

5. Unto such as keep God's covenant
   And are steadfast in God's way;
   Unto those who still remember
   The commandments and obey.

6. Bless your Maker, all you creatures,
   Ever under God's control,
   All throughout God's vast dominion;
   Bless the Lord of all, my soul!

224 Bless the Lord, My Soul and Being

Fred R. Anderson, 1986 — RUSTINGTON 8.7.8.7 D — C. Hubert H. Parry, 1897

1. Bless the Lord, my soul and be-ing! Lord my God, You have such might.
2. Lord, You laid the earth's foun-da-tion That it would be al-ways sound.
3. Grass You cause to grow for cat-tle, Plants for us to cul-ti-vate.
4. Lord, how great are all Your work-ings, Wis-dom marks them through and through.

Cloaked with hon-or, grand and glo-rious, You are clothed with pur-est light.
By the word of Your com-mand-ing, You set forth each o-cean's bound.
Food You bring forth from our la-bor, Wine for joy and bread for plate.
All the earth is Your pos-ses-sion, Great and small be-long to You.

Stretch-ing out the heavens like tent cloth, You are cham-bered on the deep.
Springs gush forth at Your own bid-ding, Giv-ing drink to ev-ery field.
Trees You give the birds for shel-ter, Moun-tain rock and cave for beast.
Food You give in each due sea-son, At Your hand come all good things.

Rid-ing on the wings of wind-storm, Flame and fire Your bid-ding keep.
Bird and beast and all Your crea-tures In that cool-ness find thirst healed.
Sun and moon both mark the sea-sons, In their light we work and feast.
By Your Spir-it You cre-ate us; Lord, Your breath re-new-al brings.

5. May Your glory reign forever.
Lord, rejoice in all You make!
As You look on Your creation,
Mountains smoke, foundations shake.

May these words and thoughts be pleasing,
For in You my joy is found.
Bless the Lord, my soul and being!
With this song let praise abound.

Text: © 1986 Fred R. Anderson; from *Singing Psalms of Joy and Praise.* Used by permission.

Praise the Lord!

225

LAUDATE PUERI   Irregular

Marjorie Jillson, 1970

Heinz Werner Zimmermann, 1970

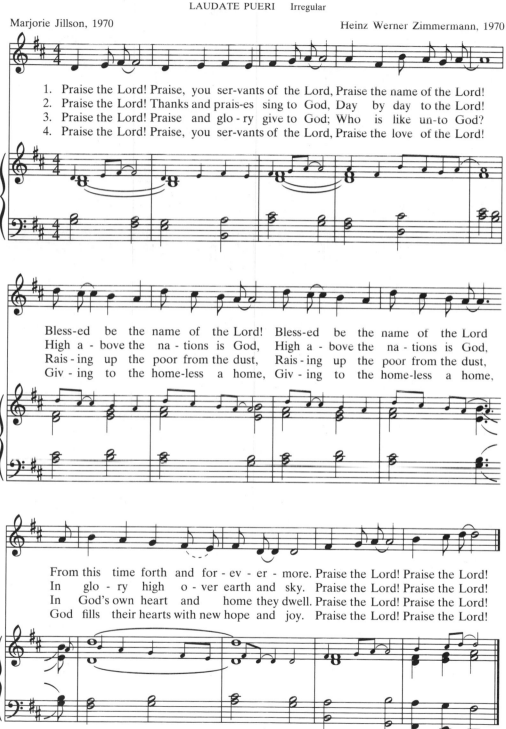

1. Praise the Lord! Praise, you ser-vants of the Lord, Praise the name of the Lord!
2. Praise the Lord! Thanks and prais-es sing to God, Day   by   day   to the Lord!
3. Praise the Lord! Praise   and glo - ry   give to God; Who   is   like un-to God?
4. Praise the Lord! Praise, you ser-vants of the Lord, Praise the love   of the Lord!

Bless-ed   be   the   name of the Lord!   Bless-ed   be   the   name of   the Lord
High a - bove the   na - tions is God,   High a - bove the   na - tions is God,
Rais - ing   up   the poor from the dust,   Rais - ing   up   the poor from the dust,
Giv - ing   to   the home-less   a   home,   Giv - ing   to   the home-less   a   home,

From this   time forth and for - ev - er - more. Praise the Lord! Praise the Lord!
In   glo - ry   high   o - ver earth and sky.   Praise the Lord! Praise the Lord!
In   God's own heart   and   home they dwell. Praise the Lord! Praise the Lord!
God   fills   their hearts with new hope and joy.   Praise the Lord! Praise the Lord!

226 Sing Praise Unto the Name of God

GENEVAN 36   8.8.8.8.8.8 D

Fred R. Anderson, 1983, 1989

Attr. Matthäus Greiter, 1525
Genevan Psalter, 1539

1. Sing praise un-to the name of God. Come, ser-vants,
2. You help the need-y in dis-tress, And give them

now and of-fer laud. Blest is Your name, O liv-ing Lord.
life that con-quers death, The great and small for You are one.

From this time forth and ev-er-more, O'er all the
You grant the home-less shel-tered space, And emp-ty

world from shore to shore, O may Your name be long a-dored.
peo-ple feel Your grace, That in all times Your will is done.

You, Lord, are rul - er of all lands; The works of
I'll praise the Lord with all my breath, And trust my

states are in Your hands. There is no oth - er like You, God;
Mak - er un - to death. Praise to the one who brings us life,

Your power is great, Your love is broad. All peo - ple
And holds us safe in cv - ery strife. For God has

live with - in Your power. Sing praise in this and ev - ery hour.
con-quered and is King; E - ter - nal One, to You we sing.

227 Not Unto Us, O Lord of Heaven

MEADVILLE   8.8.8.8.8.8

Walter Pelz, 1977
Adapt. W. Thomas Jones, 1980

The Psalter, 1912; alt.

1. Not un-to us, O Lord of heaven, But un-to You be
2. The id-ol gods of hea-then lands Are but the work of
3. Let Is-rael trust in God a-lone, The Lord whose grace and

glo-ry given. In love and truth You do ful-fill
hu-man hands; They can-not see, they can-not speak,
power are known; To God your full al - le-giance yield,

The coun-sels of Your sov-ereign will; Though na-tions
Their ears are deaf, their hands are weak; Like them shall
That one will be your help and shield; All those who

This tune in a lower key, 152

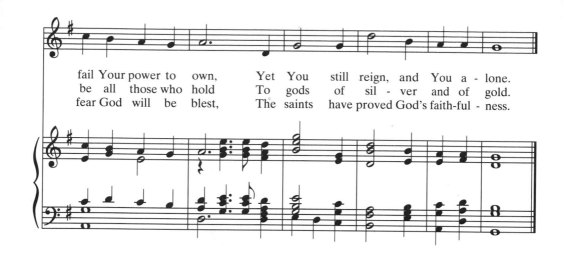

fail Your power to own, Yet You still reign, and You a - lone.
be all those who hold To gods of sil - ver and of gold.
fear God will be blest, The saints have proved God's faith-ful - ness.

PSALM 116

O Thou, My Soul, Return in Peace 228

MARTYRDOM CM

Stanzas 1–2, *Murrayfield Psalms,* 1950; alt.
Stanzas 3–6, *The Psalter,* 1912; alt.

Hugh Wilson, c. 1800
Adapt. and harm. Robert Smith, 1825

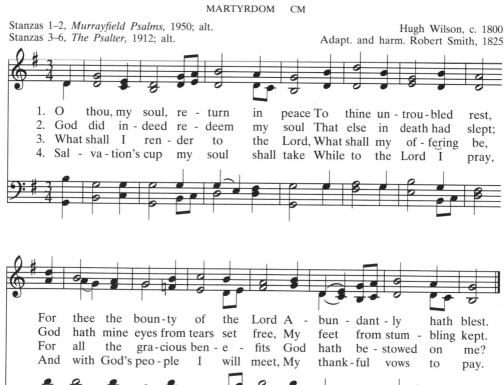

1. O thou, my soul, re - turn in peace To thine un - trou - bled rest,
2. God did in - deed re - deem my soul That else in death had slept;
3. What shall I ren - der to the Lord, What shall my of - fering be,
4. Sal - va - tion's cup my soul shall take While to the Lord I pray,

For thee the boun - ty of the Lord A - bun - dant - ly hath blest.
God hath mine eyes from tears set free, My feet from stum - bling kept.
For all the gra - cious ben - e - fits God hath be - stowed on me?
And with God's peo - ple I will meet, My thank - ful vows to pay.

5. Not lightly dost Thou, Lord, permit
   Thy chosen saints to die;
   From death Thou hast delivered me;
   Thy servant, Lord, am I.

6. Within God's house, the house of prayer,
   My soul shall bless the Lord,
   And praises to God's holy name
   Let all the saints accord.

229 From All That Dwell Below the Skies

LASST UNS ERFREUEN LM with alleluias

Isaac Watts, 1719

Geistliche Kirchengesäng, 1623; alt.
Harm. Ralph Vaughan Williams, 1906

1. From all that dwell be-low the skies Let the Cre-a-tor's praise a-
2. In ev-ery land be-gin the song, To ev-ery land the strains be-
3. E-ter-nal are Thy mer-cies, Lord; E-ter-nal truth at-tends Thy

rise: Al-le-lu-ia! Al-le-lu-ia! Let the Re-deem-er's
long: Al-le-lu-ia! Al-le-lu-ia! In cheer-ful sound all
word: Al-le-lu-ia! Al-le-lu-ia! Thy praise shall sound from

name be sung Through ev-ery land, in ev-ery tongue.
voic-es raise And fill the world with joy-ful praise. Al-le-lu-ia!
shore to shore, Till suns shall rise and set no more.

Al-le-lu-ia! Al-le-lu-ia! Al-le-lu-ia! Al-le-lu-ia!

Music: From the *English Hymnal,* 1906. Used by permission of Oxford University Press.

This Is the Day the Lord Hath Made   230

NUN DANKET ALL' UND BRINGET EHR'   CM

Isaac Watts, 1719; alt.   Johann Crüger, 1647

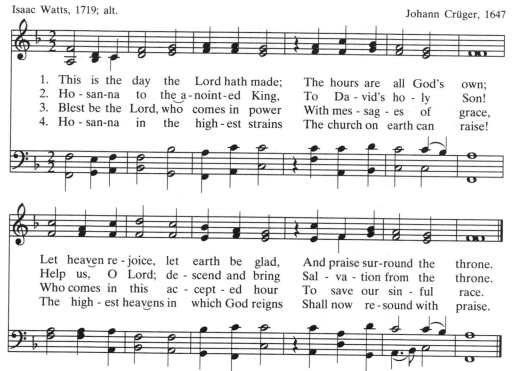

1. This is the day the Lord hath made; The hours are all God's own;
2. Ho - san - na to the a - noint - ed King, To Da - vid's ho - ly Son!
3. Blest be the Lord, who comes in power With mes - sag - es of grace,
4. Ho - san - na in the high - est strains The church on earth can raise!

Let heaven re - joice, let earth be glad, And praise sur - round the throne.
Help us, O Lord; de - scend and bring Sal - va - tion from the throne.
Who comes in this ac - cept - ed hour To save our sin - ful race.
The high - est heavens in which God reigns Shall now re - sound with praise.

231   PSALM 118:14–24

Psalm tone: Laurence Bevenot, 1986
Refrain: A. Gregory Murray, 1963

Al - le - lu - ia, al - le - lu - ia, al - le - lu - ia.

¹⁴The Lord is my strength ànd my might;
He has become mý salvation. *(omit phrase c)*
¹⁵There are glad songs of victory in the tents óf the righteous. *(R)*

"The right hand of the Lòrd does valiantly.
¹⁶ **the right hand of the Lord ís exalted,** *(omit phrase c)*
the right hand of the Lórd does valiantly." *(R)*

¹⁷I shall not die, but Ì shall live,
and recount the deeds óf the Lord.
¹⁸The Lord has punished mè severely,
but He did not give me overr to death. *(R)*

¹⁹**Open to me the gàtes of righteousness,**
that I may énter through them *(omit phrase c)*
and give thanks tó the Lord. *(R)*

²⁰This is the gate òf the Lord;
the righteous shall énter through it.
²¹I thank You that Yòu have answered me
and have become mý salvation. *(R)*

²²**The stone that the bùilders rejected**
has become thé chief cornerstone.
²³**This is thè Lord's doing;**
it is marvelous ín our eyes.

²⁴This is the day that the Lòrd has made; *(omit phrases b and c)*
let us rejoice ánd be glad in it. *(R)*

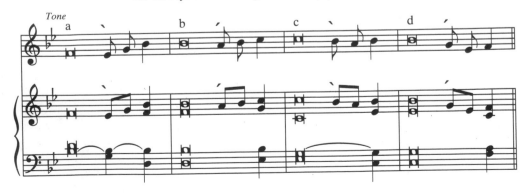

Tone
a   b   c   d

Psalm tone: Laurence Bevenot, 1986
Refrain: A. Gregory Murray, 1963

Refrain

Ho - san - na, ho - san - na, ho - san - na.

¹⁹Open to me the gàtes of righteousness,
    that I may énter through them *(omit phrase c)*
    and give thanks tó the Lord. *(R)*

²⁰This is the gate òf the Lord;
    the righteous shall énter through it.
²¹I thank You that Yòu have answered me
    and have become mý salvation. *(R)*

²²The stone that the bùilders rejected
    has become thé chief cornerstone.
²³This is thè Lord's doing;
    it is marvelous ín our eyes.

²⁴This is the day that the Lòrd has made; *(omit phrases b and c)*
    let us rejoice ánd be glad in it. *(R)*

²⁵Save us, we beseech Yòu, O Lord!
    O Lord, we beseech You, give ús success!
²⁶Blessed is the one who comes in the name òf the Lord!
    We bless You from the house óf the Lord. *(R)*

²⁷The Lòrd is God,
    and He has givén us light.
Bind the festal processìon with branches,
    up to the horns óf the altar. *(R)*

²⁸You are my God, and I will give thànks to You;
    You are my God, I wíll extol You.
²⁹O give thanks to the Lord, for Hè is good,
    for His steadfast love endúres forever. *(R)*

Tone

233 Blest Are the Uncorrupt in Heart

RICHMOND   CM

Thomas Haweis, c. 1792

Fred R. Anderson, 1986

Adapt. Samuel Webbe, Jr., 1808

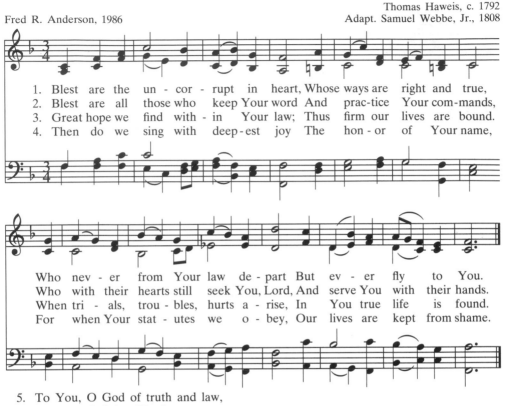

1. Blest are the un-cor-rupt in heart, Whose ways are right and true,
2. Blest are all those who keep Your word And prac-tice Your com-mands,
3. Great hope we find with-in Your law; Thus firm our lives are bound.
4. Then do we sing with deep-est joy The hon-or of Your name,

Who nev-er from Your law de-part But ev-er fly to You.
Who with their hearts still seek You, Lord, And serve You with their hands.
When tri-als, trou-bles, hurts a-rise, In You true life is found.
For when Your stat-utes we o-bey, Our lives are kept from shame.

5. To You, O God of truth and law,
To You, O living Word,
To You, O Comforter of life,
May now our praise be heard.

I to the Hills Will Lift My Eyes

234

DUNDEE CM

The Psalter, 1912; alt. 1988

Scottish Psalter, 1615

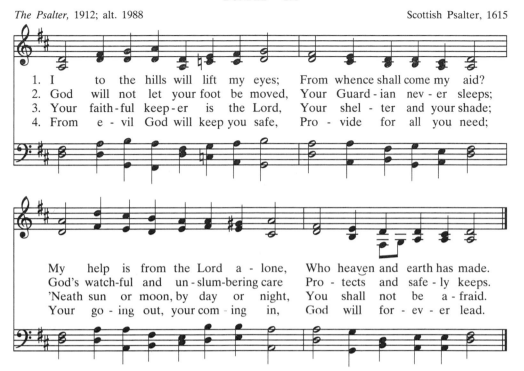

1. I to the hills will lift my eyes; From whence shall come my aid?
2. God will not let your foot be moved, Your Guard-ian nev-er sleeps;
3. Your faith-ful keep-er is the Lord, Your shel-ter and your shade;
4. From e-vil God will keep you safe, Pro-vide for all you need;

My help is from the Lord a-lone, Who heaven and earth has made.
God's watch-ful and un-slum-bering care Pro-tects and safe-ly keeps.
'Neath sun or moon, by day or night, You shall not be a-fraid.
Your go-ing out, your com-ing in, God will for-ev-er lead.

235 With Joy I Heard My Friends Exclaim

GONFALON ROYAL   LM

The Psalter, 1912; alt.   Percy C. Buck, 1918

1. With joy I heard my friends ex - claim, "Come, let us
2. How beau - ti - ful doth Zi - on stand, A cit - y
3. They come to learn the will of God, To pay their
4. For Zi - on's peace let prayer be made; May all that
5. For love of friends and kin - dred dear, My heart's de -

in God's tem - ple meet"; With - in thy gates, O Zi - on blest,
built com - pact and fair; The peo - ple of the Lord u - nite
vows, God's grace to own, For there is judg - ment's roy - al seat,
love thee pros - per well! With - in thy walls let peace a - bide,
sire is Zi - on's peace, And for the house of God, the Lord,

Shall ev - er stand our will - ing feet.
With joy and praise to wor - ship there.
Mes - si - ah's sure and last - ing throne.
And glad - ness with thy chil - dren dwell.
My lov - ing care shall nev - er cease. Al - le - lu - ia!

Music: Used by permission of Oxford University Press.

Now Israel May Say

236

OLD 124TH　10.10.10.10.10

The Psalter, 1912　　　　　　　　　　　　　　　　　　Genevan Psalter, 1551

1. Now Is - ra - el may say, and that in truth: If that the Lord had not our right main - tained, If that the Lord had not with us re - mained When cru - el foes a - gainst us rose to strive, We sure - ly had been swal-lowed up a - live.

2. Yea, when their wrath a - gainst us fierce-ly rose, The swell - ing tide had o'er us spread its wave, The rag - ing stream had then be-come our grave, The surg-ing flood, in proud-ly swell-ing roll, Most sure - ly then had o - ver-whelmed our soul.

3. Blest be the Lord, who made us not their prey; As from the snare a bird es - cap - eth free, Their net is rent and so es-caped are we; Our on - ly help is in God's ho - ly name, Who made the earth and all the heaven - ly frame.

237 When God Delivered Israel

SHEAVES 7.6.7.7.6.6

Michael A. Saward, 1973

Norman L. Warren, 1973

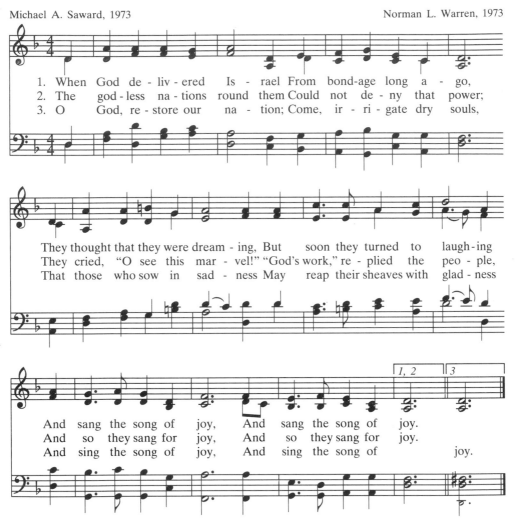

1. When God de-liv-ered Is-rael From bond-age long a-go,
2. The god-less na-tions round them Could not de-ny that power;
3. O God, re-store our na-tion; Come, ir-ri-gate dry souls,

They thought that they were dream-ing, But soon they turned to laugh-ing
They cried, "O see this mar-vel!" "God's work," re-plied the peo-ple,
That those who sow in sad-ness May reap their sheaves with glad-ness

And sang the song of joy, And sang the song of joy.
And so they sang for joy, And so they sang for joy.
And sing the song of joy, And sing the song of joy.

Unless the Lord the House Shall Build 238

BOURBON LM

The Psalter, 1912, alt.

Attr. Freeman Lewis, 1825
Harm. John Leon Hooker, 1984

1. Un - less the Lord the house shall build, The
2. In vain you rise at morn - ing break, And
3. Yes, chil - dren are a great re - ward, A
4. How blest are those whose lives are cheered By

wea - ry build - ers toil in vain; Un - less the Lord the
late your night - ly vig - ils keep, And wea - ry days of
gift from God in ver - y truth; As quiv - er full of
chil - dren's growth in strength and grace. With - in their house no

cit - y shield, The guards a use - less watch main - tain.
toil par - take; For God's be - lov - ed there is sleep.
ar - rows stored Are chil - dren given in days of youth.
foes are feared, For God keeps watch with - in that place.

239 How Happy Is Each Child of God

WINCHESTER OLD   CM

Dwyn M. Mounger, 1986

Este's *Psalmes,* 1592

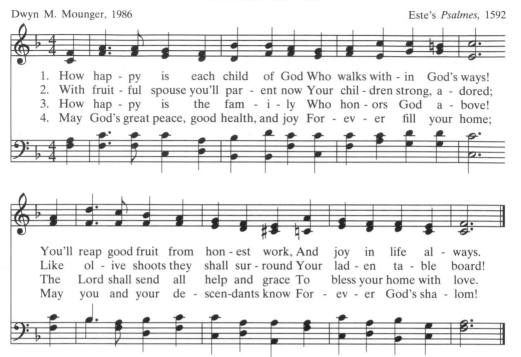

1. How hap - py is each child of God Who walks with - in God's ways!
2. With fruit - ful spouse you'll par - ent now Your chil - dren strong, a - dored;
3. How hap - py is the fam - i - ly Who hon - ors God a - bove!
4. May God's great peace, good health, and joy For - ev - er fill your home;

You'll reap good fruit from hon - est work, And joy in life al - ways.
Like ol - ive shoots they shall sur - round Your lad - en ta - ble board!
The Lord shall send all help and grace To bless your home with love.
May you and your de - scen-dants know For - ev - er God's sha - lom!

This tune with descant, 58

Out of the Depths

240

AUS TIEFER NOT   8.7.8.7.8.8.7

Martin Luther, 1524
Trans. Richard Massie, 1854; alt.

Martin Luther, 1524
Harm. Johann Sebastian Bach, 1740

1. Out of the depths to Thee I raise The voice of lam-en-ta-tion;
2. To wash a-way the crim-son stain Grace, grace a-lone pre-vail-eth.
3. There-fore my trust is in the Lord, And not in mine own mer-it.
4. What though I wait the live-long night, And till the dawn ap-pear-eth,

Lord, turn a gra-cious ear to me, And hear my sup-pli-ca-tion.
Our works, a-las! are all in vain; In much the best life fail-eth.
On God my soul shall rest; God's word Up-holds my faint-ing spir-it.
My heart still trust-eth in God's might; It doubt-eth not nor fear-eth:

If Thou shouldst count our ev-ery sin, Each e-vil deed or
For none can glo-ry in Thy sight, All must a-like con-
God's prom-ised mer-cy is my fort, My com-fort, and my
So let the Is-rael-ites in heart, Born of the Spir-it,

thought with-in, O who could stand be-fore Thee?
fess Thy might And live a-lone by mer-cy.
strong sup-port; I wait for it with pa-tience.
do their part, And wait till God ap-pear-eth.

241 Behold the Goodness of Our Lord

CRIMOND CM

Fred R. Anderson, 1986

Jessie Seymour Irvine, 1872
Harm. T. C. L. Pritchard, 1929

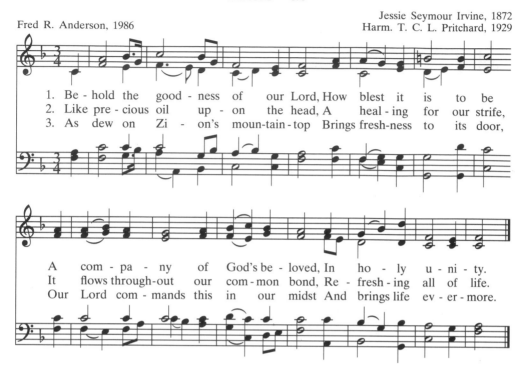

1. Be - hold the good - ness of our Lord, How blest it is to be
2. Like pre - cious oil up - on the head, A heal - ing for our strife,
3. As dew on Zi - on's moun-tain-top Brings fresh-ness to its door,

A com - pa - ny of God's be - loved, In ho - ly u - ni - ty.
It flows through-out our com - mon bond, Re - fresh - ing all of life.
Our Lord com - mands this in our midst And brings life ev - er - more.

Come, All You Servants of the Lord 242

DANBY LM

Arlo D. Duba, 1984

English folk melody
Harm. Arthur Hutchings, 1981

1. Come, all you ser - vants of the Lord, Who work and pray by night, by day, Come, bless the Lord with - in this place; With lift - ed hands your hom - age pay.

2. The Lord now bless from heaven a - bove And shine on you with ra - diant face; The Lord who heaven and earth has made Il - lu - mine you with peace and grace.

243 We Thank You, Lord, for You Are Good

WAS GOTT TUT   8.7.8.7.44.8.7

John G. Dunn, 1985

Severus Gastorius, 1681
Harm. *Common Service Book,* 1917

1. We thank You, Lord, for You are good;
2. You, Lord, a - lone did won-drous deeds; Your mer-cy lives for - ev - er.
3. You made the star - ry lights to rise;
4. You res - cue us from ev - ery foe;

Your kind-ness from of old has stood;
From You a - lone all good pro - ceeds; Your love will keep us ev - er.
Your glo - ries shine in ra - diant skies;
You feed Your crea-tures here be - low;

O God of gods, O sov - ereign Lord, We bless You
Your wis - dom made the heavens to be; You formed the
Your glow - ing moon en - hanc - es night. Your sun brings
We give You thanks, Cre - a - tor, Lord; We sing the

now with one ac - cord:
earth a - bove the sea: Your love is ev - er - last - ing.
forth each morn-ing's light:
glo - ries of Your Word.

Let Us with a Gladsome Mind

244

MONKLAND 7.7.7.7

John Milton, 1623; alt.

Freylinghausen's *Geistreiches Gesangbuch*, 1704
Arr. John B. Wilkes, 1861

1. Let us with a glad - some mind Praise the Lord who is so kind:
2. God, with all-com - mand-ing might, Filled the new-made world with light:
3. All things liv - ing God does feed, With full mea-sure meets their need:
4. Let us with a glad - some mind Praise the Lord who is so kind:

For God's mer-cies shall en - dure, Ev - er faith-ful, ev - er sure.

By the Waters of Babylon

245

Jewish melody

By the wa - ters, the wa - ters of Bab - y - lon,

We sat down and wept, and wept for Zi - on.

We re-mem-ber, we re-mem-ber, we re-mem-ber Zi - on.

May be sung as a canon.

246 By the Babylonian Rivers

KAS DZIEDAJA   8.7.8.7

Ewald Bash, 1964

Latvian melody
Harm. Geoffrey Laycock, b. 1927

1. By the Bab-y-lo-nian riv-ers We sat
2. There our cap-tors in de-ri-sion Did re-
3. How shall we sing the Lord's song In a

down in grief and wept; Hung our harps up-on the
quire of us a song; So we sat with star-ing
strange and bit-ter land; Can our voic-es veil the

wil-low, Mourned for Zi-on when we slept.
vi-sion, And the days were hard and long.
sor-row? Lord God, help Your ho-ly band.

I Will Give Thanks with My Whole Heart 247

HERR JESU CHRIST   LM

Christopher L. Webber, 1986, 1988

Cantionale Germanicum, 1628
Arr. Johann Sebastian Bach, c. 1708

1. I will give thanks with my whole heart, Be-
2. A - bove all things, O Lord, my God, You
3. All kings on earth who hear Your words, O
4. The Lord is high, yet scorns the proud, Pro-

fore the gods my praise ex - press; I will bow down be-
glo - ri - fied Your name and Word; I called and then You
Lord, will give You thanks and praise And tell how great Your
tects the low - ly on their path; Al - though I walk in

fore Your throne And praise Your love and faith - ful - ness.
an - swered me And gave me in - creased strength, O Lord.
glo - ry is, And they will sing of all Your ways.
trou - ble, Lord, You keep me safe from my foe's wrath.

5. Lord, Your right hand shall save my life
And make Your purpose for me sure;
Do not forsake what You have made;
Your love forever will endure.

248

You Are Before Me, Lord

SURSUM CORDA (Smith)   10.10.10.10

Ian Pitt-Watson, 1973, 1989

Alfred Morton Smith, 1941

1. You are be - fore me, Lord, You are be - hind, And o - ver
   me You have spread out Your hand; Such knowl-edge is too
   won-der - ful for me, Too high to grasp, too great to un - der - stand.

2. Then from Your Spir - it where, Lord, shall I go; And from Your
   pres - ence where, Lord, shall I fly? If I as - cend to
   heav-en You are there, And still are with me if in hell I lie.

3. If I should take my flight in - to the dawn, If I should
   dwell on o - cean's far - thest shore, Your might - y hand will
   rest up - on me still, And Your right hand will guard me ev - er - more.

4. If I should say, "Let dark - ness cov - er me, And I shall
   hide with - in the veil of night," Sure - ly the dark - ness
   is not dark to You: The night is as the day, the dark-ness light.

5. Search me, O God, search me and know my heart; Try me, O
   God, my mind and spir - it try; Keep me from an - y
   path that gives You pain, And lead me in the ev - er - last - ing way.

O Lord, Make Haste to Hear My Cry 249

CANNONS   LM

The Psalter, 1912; alt.

Adapted from George Frederick Handel, c. 1750

1. O Lord, make haste to hear my cry. To
2. When in the morn - ing un - to You I
3. When un - to You I look and pray With
4. O guard my thoughts, I now im - plore, And

You I call, on You re - ly. In - cline to me a
call in sup - pli - ca - tion new, Then let my prayer as
lift - ed hands at close of day, Then as the eve - ning
of my lips O keep the door; Nor leave my sin - ful

gra - cious ear, And when I call, in mer - cy hear.
in - cense rise To God en - throned a - bove the skies.
sac - ri - fice Let my re - quest ac - cept - ed rise.
heart to stray Where e - vil foot - steps lead the way.

250 When Morning Lights the Eastern Skies

ST. STEPHEN   CM

The Psalter, 1912   William Jones, 1789

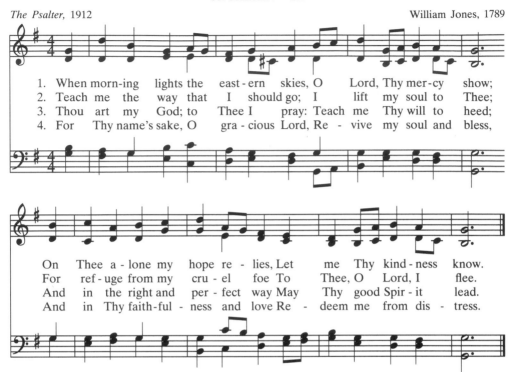

1. When morn-ing   lights the   east-ern   skies, O   Lord, Thy mer-cy   show;
2. Teach me   the   way that   I   should go; I   lift   my soul to   Thee;
3. Thou   art   my   God; to   Thee I   pray: Teach me   Thy will to   heed;
4. For   Thy name's sake, O   gra-cious Lord, Re - vive   my soul and   bless,

On   Thee a - lone my   hope re - lies, Let   me Thy kind - ness   know.
For   ref - uge from my   cru - el   foe To   Thee, O   Lord, I   flee.
And   in   the right and   per - fect   way May   Thy good Spir - it   lead.
And   in   Thy faith-ful - ness and   love Re - deem me   from dis - tress.

Your Faithfulness, O Lord, Is Sure

251

WINCHESTER NEW   LM

Para. Joy F. Patterson, 1989

Musikalisches Handbuch, 1690
Harm. William Henry Monk, 1847; alt.

1. Your faith - ful - ness, O Lord, is sure In
2. The eyes of all are fixed on You; By
3. Lord, You are just in all Your ways, And
4. My mouth shall speak Your praise, O Lord, My

all Your words, Your gra - cious deeds; You gen - tly lift all
You their wants are all sup - plied; Your o - pen hand is
kind in ev - ery - thing You do; For - ev - er near You
soul shall bless Your ho - ly name; Let all things liv - ing

bur dened souls And well pro - vide for all our needs.
boun - ti - ful And ev - ery soul is sat - is - fied.
stand to hear And help all those who call on You.
join the song Of praise, from age to age the same.

252 O Lord, You Are My God and King

JERUSALEM LMD

C. Hubert H. Parry, 1916
Harm. Richard Proulx, 1986

The Psalter, 1912; alt.

1. O Lord, You are my God and King, And I will ev - er bless Your name;
2. How rich in grace are You, O Lord, Full of com - pas - sion, mer - ci - ful,
3. Your works will give You thanks, O Lord, Your saints Your might - y acts will show,

I will ex - tol You ev - ery day, And ev - er - more Your praise pro -
Your an - ger al - ways slow to rise; Your stead - fast love You show to
Till all the peo - ples of the earth Your king - dom, pow - er, glo - ry

Harmony

claim.   You, Lord,   are   great - ly   to   be praised,   Your great-ness
all,   For   You   are   good   in   all   Your ways,   Your crea-tures
know.   E - ter - nal   is   Your king - dom, Lord,   For - ev - er

is   be - yond our   thoughts; All   gen - er - a - tions shall   tell
know   Your con-stant care.   To   all Your works   Your love   ex -
strong,   for - ev - er   sure;   While gen-er - a - tions rise   and

forth   The might - y   won-ders You have wrought.
tends,   All   souls Your ten - der mer - cies share.
die,   Your high do - min - ion will en - (dure.)

dure.

I'll Praise My Maker

253

OLD 113TH   8.8.8.8.8.8

Isaac Watts
Adapt. John Wesley, 1736; alt. 1988

Attr. Matthäus Greiter (c. 1500–1552)
Harm. V. Earle Copes, 1964

1. I'll praise my Mak-er while I've breath; And when my voice
2. How hap-py they whose hopes re-ly On Is-rael's God,
3. The Lord pours eye-sight on the blind; The Lord sup-ports
4. I'll praise my Mak-er while I've breath; And when my voice

is lost in death, Praise shall em-ploy my no-bler powers.
who made the sky And earth and seas with all their train;
the faint-ing mind And sends the la-boring con-science peace.
is lost in death, Praise shall em-ploy my no-bler powers.

My days of praise shall ne'er be past While life and thought
Whose truth for-ev-er stands se-cure, Who saves the op-pressed
God helps the strang-er in dis-tress, The wid-owed and
My days of praise shall ne'er be past While life and thought

and be-ing last, Or im-mor-tal-i-ty en-dures.
and feeds the poor, And none shall find God's prom-ise vain.
the par-ent-less, And grants the pris-oner sweet re-lease.
and be-ing last, Or im-mor-tal-i-ty en-dures.

PSALM 146

Psalm tone: Howard Hughes, 1986
Refrain: John Schiavone, 1986

I will praise my God all the days of my life.

⁵Happy are those whose help is the God òf Jacob,
  whose hope is in the Lord théir God,
⁶who made heaven ànd earth,
  the sea, and all that is ín them;

⁷**who keeps faith fòrever;** *(omit phrase b)*
  who executes justice for the òppressed;
  who gives food to thé hungry. *(R)*

⁸The Lord sets the prisonèrs free;
  the Lord opens the eyes of thé blind.
The Lord lifts up those who are bòwed down;
  the Lord loves thé righteous.

⁹**The Lord watches over thè strangers,** *(omit phrase b)*
  He upholds the widow ànd the orphan;
  but the way of the wicked He brings tó ruin. *(R)*

¹⁰The Lord will reign fòrever, *(omit phrase b)*
  your God, O Zion, to all genèrations.
Praise thé Lord! *(R)*

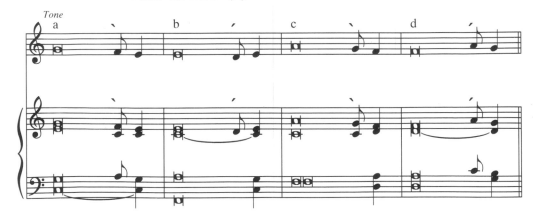

Now Praise the Lord

255

ST. ANNE   CM

Fred R. Anderson, 1986

Attr. William Croft, 1708
A Supplement to the New Version
of the Psalms, 1708

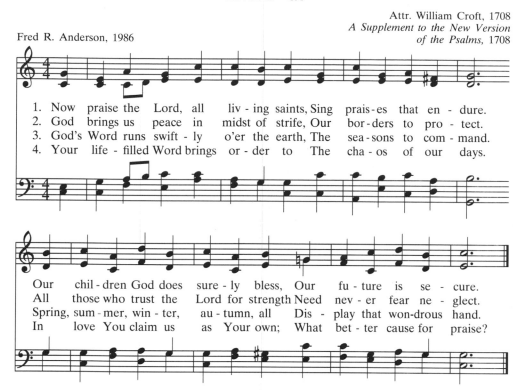

1. Now praise the Lord, all liv - ing saints, Sing prais - es that en - dure.
2. God brings us peace in midst of strife, Our bor - ders to pro - tect.
3. God's Word runs swift - ly o'er the earth, The sea - sons to com - mand.
4. Your life - filled Word brings or - der to The cha - os of our days.

Our chil - dren God does sure - ly bless, Our fu - ture is se - cure.
All those who trust the Lord for strength Need nev - er fear ne - glect.
Spring, sum - mer, win - ter, au - tumn, all Dis - play that won-drous hand.
In love You claim us as Your own; What bet - ter cause for praise?

5. Instruction, guidance, holy law,
   Some common names are these
   For God's own rule for living life.
   What other word can please?

6. No other people are so graced,
   No nation is so blest,
   As those who know God's living Word
   And this one name confess.

Text: © 1986 Fred R. Anderson; from *Singing Psalms of Joy and Praise.* Used by permission.

256 Let the Whole Creation Cry

SALZBURG 7.7.7.7 D

Jacob Hintze, 1678
Harm. Johann Sebastian Bach (1685–1750)
As in *Hymns Ancient and Modern,* 1861

Stopford A. Brooke, 1881

1. Let the whole cre - a - tion cry, "Glo-ry to the Lord on high."
2. Men and wom-en, young and old, Raise the an-them man-i-fold;

Heaven and earth, a - wake and sing, "God is our e - ter-nal King."
Join with chil-dren's songs of praise, Wor-ship God through length of days.

Praise God, all ye hosts a - bove, Ev - er shin-ing forth in love;
From the north to south-ern pole Let the might-y cho-rus roll:

Sun and moon, up - lift your voice; Night and stars, in God re - joice!
"Ho-ly, ho - ly, ho - ly One, Glo-ry be to God a - lone!"

Give Praise to the Lord

257

LAUDATE DOMINUM   10.10.11.11

The Psalter, 1912; alt. 1984

C. Hubert H. Parry, c. 1915

1. Give praise to the Lord, and sing a new song,
2. With tim-brel and harp and joy-ful ac-claim,
3. In glo-ry ex-ult, all saints of the Lord;
4. For this is God's word: the saints shall not fail,

A-mid all the saints God's prais-es pro-long;
With glad-ness and mirth, we praise Your great name;
With song in the night high prais-es ac-cord;
But o-ver the earth their power shall pre-vail;

A song to your mak-er and rul-er now raise,
For now in Your peo-ple good plea-sure You seek,
Go forth in God's ser-vice and strong in God's might
All king-doms and na-tions shall yield to their sway.

All chil-dren of Zi-on, re-joice and give praise.
With robes of sal-va-tion You cov-er the meek.
To con-quer all e-vil and stand for the right.
To God give the glo-ry; sing prais-es for aye.

258   Praise Ye the Lord

J. Jefferson Cleveland, 1981   J. Jefferson Cleveland, 1981

Choir or Congregation: Praise ye the Lord,   Hal-le-lu - jah!

Ev-ery-bod-y praise the Lord.   Lord.

Omit final time

♩=112–120

TOPICAL HYMNS

Psalm 46

259 A Mighty Fortress Is Our God

EIN' FESTE BURG (rhythmic)   8.7.8.7.6.6.6.6.7

Omer Westendorf, 1964
Stanza 1, lines 1–2, Martin Luther, 1529
Trans. Frederick Henry Hedge, 1852

Martin Luther, 1529
Harm. Hans Leo Hassler (1564–1612); alt.

1. A might-y for-tress is our God, A bul-wark
2. The wa-ters of God's good-ness flow Through-out the
3. Be-hold what won-drous deeds of peace God does for

nev-er fail - ing; Pro-tect-ing us with staff and rod,
ho-ly cit - y, And glad-den hearts of those who know
our sal-va - tion; God knows our wars and makes them cease

And pow-er all-pre-vail - ing. What if the na - tions rage
God's ten-der - ness and pit - y. Though na - tions stand un - sure,
In ev - ery land and na - tion. The war - rior's spear and lance

And surg - ing seas ram - page; What though the moun - tains fall,
God's king - dom shall en - dure; God's pow - er shall re - main,
Are splin - tered by God's glance; The guns and nu - clear might

The Lord is God of all; The Lord of hosts is with us.
And peace shall ev - er reign, The Lord of hosts is with us.
Stand with - ered in God's sight; The Lord of hosts is with us.

Isometric version, 260

260 A Mighty Fortress Is Our God

EIN' FESTE BURG (isometric)   8.7.8.7.6.6.6.6.7

Martin Luther, 1529
Trans. Frederick Henry Hedge, 1852

Martin Luther, 1529

1. A might-y for-tress is our God, A bul-wark nev-er fail-ing;
2. Did we in our own strength con-fide, Our striv-ing would be los-ing;
3. And though this world, with dev - ils filled, Should threat-en to un-do us,
4. That word a - bove all earth - ly powers, No thanks to them, a - bid - eth;

Our help-er He a - mid the flood Of mor-tal ills pre - vail - ing.
Were not the right Man on our side, The Man of God's own choos - ing.
We will not fear, for God hath willed His truth to tri - umph through us.
The Spir-it and the gifts are ours Through Him who with us sid - eth;

For still our an - cient foe Doth seek to work us woe; His craft and
Dost ask who that may be? Christ Je - sus, it is He, Lord Sab - a -
The prince of dark - ness grim, We trem-ble not for him; His rage we
Let goods and kin - dred go, This mor-tal life al - so; The bod - y

power are great, And, armed with cru - el hate, On earth is not his e - qual.
oth His name, From age to age the same, And He must win the bat - tle.
can en - dure, For lo! his doom is sure, One lit - tle word shall fell him.
they may kill, God's truth a - bid-eth still, His king-dom is for-ev - er.

Rhythmic version, 259

God of Compassion, in Mercy Befriend Us 261

O QUANTA QUALIA   11.11.11.11

John J. Moment, 1933

Paris *Antiphoner*, 1681
As in La Feillée's *Méthode du plain-chant*, 1808

1. God of com - pas - sion, in mer - cy be - friend us;
2. Wan - dering and lost, Thou hast sought us and found us,
3. How shall we stray, with Thy hand to di - rect us,

Giv - er of grace for our needs all - a - vail - ing,
Stilled our rude hearts with Thy word of con - sol - ing;
Thou who the stars in their cours - es art guid - ing?

Wis - dom and strength for each day do Thou send us,
Wrap now Thy peace, like a man - tle, a - round us,
What shall we fear, with Thy power to pro - tect us,

Pa - tience un - tir - ing and cour - age un - fail - ing.
Guard - ing our thoughts and our pas - sions con - trol - ling.
We who walk forth in Thy great - ness con - fid - ing?

262 God of the Ages, Whose Almighty Hand

NATIONAL HYMN   10.10.10.10

Daniel Crane Roberts, 1876; alt.   George William Warren, 1892

Trumpets may
be played
with each stanza

1. God of the a - ges, whose al - might-y hand
2. Thy love di - vine hath led us in the past;
3. From war's a - larms, from dead - ly pes - ti - lence,
4. Re - fresh Thy peo - ple on their toil-some way,

Leads forth in beau - ty all the star - ry band
In this free land by Thee our lot is cast;
Be Thy strong arm our ev - er sure de - fense;
Lead us from night to nev - er - end - ing day;

Of shin - ing worlds in splen-dor through the skies,
Be Thou our rul - er, guard-ian, guide, and stay;
Thy true re - li - gion in our hearts in - crease;
Fill all our lives with love and grace di - vine,

Our grate - ful songs be - fore Thy throne a - rise.
Thy word our law, Thy paths our cho - sen way.
Thy boun - teous good - ness nour - ish us in peace.
And glo - ry, laud, and praise be ev - er Thine.

Immortal, Invisible, God Only Wise 263

ST. DENIO   11.11.11.11

Walter Chalmers Smith, 1867; alt. 1987

Welsh folk melody
Adapted in *Caniadau y Cyssegr*, 1839

1. Im - mor - tal, in - vis - i - ble, God on - ly wise,
2. Un - rest - ing, un - hast - ing, and si - lent as light,
3. To all, life Thou giv - est, to both great and small;
4. Thou reign - est in glo - ry, Thou rul - est in light,

In light in - ac - ces - si - ble hid from our eyes,
Nor want - ing, nor wast - ing, Thou rul - est in might;
In all life Thou liv - est, the true life of all;
Thine an - gels a - dore Thee, all veil - ing their sight;

Most bless - ed, most glo - rious, the An - cient of Days,
Thy jus - tice like moun - tains high soar - ing a - bove
We blos - som and flour - ish like leaves on the tree,
All praise we would ren - der; O help us to see

Al - might - y, vic - to - rious, Thy great name we praise.
Thy clouds, which are foun - tains of good - ness and love.
Then with - er and per - ish; but naught chang - eth Thee.
'Tis on - ly the splen - dor of light hid - eth Thee!

264 When in Our Music God Is Glorified

ENGELBERG   10.10.10.4

Fred Pratt Green, 1972

Charles Villiers Stanford, 1904

1. When in our mu - sic God is glo - ri - fied, And a - do -
2. How of - ten, mak - ing mu - sic, we have found A new di -
3. So has the church, in lit - ur - gy and song, In faith and
4. Let ev - ery in - stru-ment be tuned for praise! Let all re -

ra - tion leaves no room for pride, It is as
men - sion in the world of sound, As wor - ship
love, through cen - tu - ries of wrong, Borne wit - ness
joice who have a voice to raise! And may God

though the whole cre - a - tion cried: Al - le - lu - ia!
moved us to a more pro - found Al - le - lu - ia!
to the truth in ev - ery tongue: Al - le - lu - ia!
give us faith to sing al - ways:

Final ending

Al - le - lu - ia! A - men.

♩=46–50

Great God, We Sing That Mighty Hand 265

WAREHAM   LM

Philip Doddridge, 1702–1751
Orton's *Hymns Founded on Various Texts*, 1755; alt.

William Knapp, 1738

1. Great God, we sing that might - y hand By which sup -
2. With grate - ful hearts the past we own; The fu - ture,
3. In scenes ex - alt - ed or de - pressed, You are our

port - ed still we stand; The o - pening year Your
all to us un - known, We to Your guard - ian
joy, and You our rest; Your good - ness all our

mer - cy shows; That mer - cy crowns it till it close.
care com - mit, And peace - ful leave be - fore Your feet.
hopes shall raise, A - dored through all our chang - ing days.

Another harmonization of this tune, 421

266 Thank You, God, for Water, Soil, and Air

AMSTEIN 9.10.10.9

Brian Wren, 1973

John Weaver, 1988

1. Thank you, God, for wa - ter, soil, and air, Large gifts sup-port-ing
2. Thank you, God, for min - er - als and ores, The ba - sis of all
3. Thank you, God, for price-less en - er - gy, Stored in each at - om,
4. Thank you, God, for weav-ing na - ture's life In - to a seam-less
5. Thank you, God, for mak - ing plan - et earth A home for us and

ev - ery-thing that lives. For - give our spoil - ing and a - buse of
build-ing, wealth, and speed. For - give our reck - less plun-der - ing and
gath-ered from the sun. For - give our greed and care-less - ness of
robe, a frag - ile whole. For - give our haste that tam-pers un - a -
a - ges yet un - born. Help us to share, con - sid - er, save, and

them. Help us re - new the face of the earth.
waste. Help us re - new the face of the earth.
power. Help us re - new the face of the earth.
ware. Help us re - new the face of the earth.
store. Come and re - new the face of the earth.

♩=96–104

All Things Bright and Beautiful

267

ROYAL OAK   7.6.7.6 with refrain

English melody, 17th century
Adapt. Martin Shaw, 1915
Harm. for *The Hymnbook*, 1953

Cecil Frances Alexander, 1848

Refrain

All things bright and   beau-ti-ful, All   crea-tures great and   small,

Fine

All things wise and   won-der-ful: The   Lord God made them   all.

1. Each lit-tle flower that   o-pens,   Each lit-tle bird that   sings:
2. The pur-ple-head-ed   moun-tain,   The riv-er run-ning   by,
3. The cold wind in the   win-ter,   The pleas-ant sum-mer   sun,
4. God gave us eyes to   see them,   And lips that we might   tell

God made their glow-ing   col-ors,   God made their ti-ny   wings.
The sun-set, and the   morn-ing   That bright-ens up the   sky,
The ripe fruits in the   gar-den: God made them ev-ery   one.
How great is God Al-   might-y,   Who has made all things well.*

*Repeat Refrain.

Music: Harmonization copyright, MCMLV, by John Ribble; renewed 1983; from *The Hymnbook*, published by Westminster Press.

268 God, Who Stretched the Spangled Heavens

HOLY MANNA 8.7.8.7 D

Catherine Arnott Cameron, 1967; alt.

Attr. William Moore, 1825
Harm. Charles Anders, 1969

1. God, who stretched the span-gled heav-ens In-fi-nite in time and place, Flung the suns in burn-ing ra-diance Through the si-lent fields of space: We, Your chil-dren
2. We have ven-tured worlds un-dreamed of Since the child-hood of our race; Known the ec-sta-sy of wing-ing Through un-trav-eled realms of space; Probed the se-crets
3. As each far ho-ri-zon beck-ons, May it chal-lenge us a-new: Chil-dren of cre-a-tive pur-pose, Serv-ing oth-ers, hon-oring You. May our dreams prove

in Your like - ness, Share in - ven - tive powers with You;
of the at - om, Yield - ing un - i - mag - ined power,
rich with prom - ise, Each en - deav - or well be - gun;

Great Cre - a - tor, still cre - at - ing, Show us what we yet may do.
Fac - ing us with life's de - struc - tion Or our most tri - um - phant hour.
Great Cre - a - tor, give us guid - ance Till our goals and Yours are one.

269 O God of Bethel, by Whose Hand

Philip Doddridge (1702–1751)
John Logan, 1781; alt.

DUNDEE   CM

Scottish Psalter, 1615

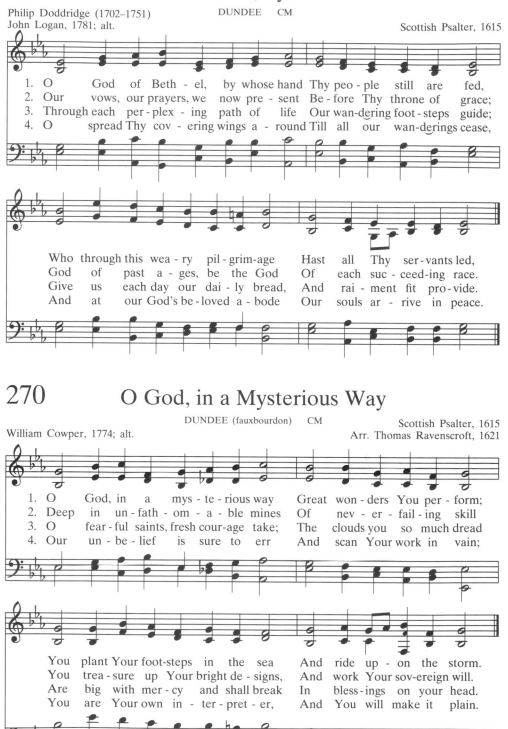

1. O God of Beth - el, by whose hand Thy peo - ple still are fed,
2. Our vows, our prayers, we now pre - sent Be - fore Thy throne of grace;
3. Through each per - plex - ing path of life Our wan-dering foot - steps guide;
4. O spread Thy cov - ering wings a - round Till all our wan-derings cease,

Who through this wea - ry pil - grim-age Hast all Thy ser - vants led,
God of past a - ges, be the God Of each suc - ceed-ing race.
Give us each day our dai - ly bread, And rai - ment fit pro - vide.
And at our God's be - loved a - bode Our souls ar - rive in peace.

270 O God, in a Mysterious Way

DUNDEE (fauxbourdon)   CM

William Cowper, 1774; alt.

Scottish Psalter, 1615
Arr. Thomas Ravenscroft, 1621

1. O God, in a mys - te - rious way Great won - ders You per - form;
2. Deep in un - fath - om - a - ble mines Of nev - er - fail - ing skill
3. O fear - ful saints, fresh cour - age take; The clouds you so much dread
4. Our un - be - lief is sure to err And scan Your work in vain;

You plant Your foot-steps in the sea And ride up - on the storm.
You trea - sure up Your bright de - signs, And work Your sov-ereign will.
Are big with mer - cy and shall break In bless-ings on your head.
You are Your own in - ter - pret - er, And You will make it plain.

Many and Great, O God, Are Thy Things 271

LACQUIPARLE   9.6.9.9.9.6

Dakota hymn
Joseph R. Renville, 1842
Trans. F. Philip Frazier, 1953 (Sioux)

Native American melody (Dakota)
Adapt. Joseph R. Renville, 1842
Harm. J. R. Murray, 1877

1. Man - y and great, O God, are Thy things, Mak - er of
2. Grant un - to us com - mu - nion with Thee, Thou star - a -

earth and sky; Thy hands have set the heav-ens with stars,
bid - ing One; Come un - to us and dwell with us:

Thy fin - gers spread the moun - tains and plains. Lo, at Thy
With Thee are found the gifts of life. Bless us with

word the wa - ters were formed; Deep seas o - bey Thy voice.
life that has no end, E - ter - nal life with Thee.

Optional hand drum or tom-tom: ♩ ♩ ♩
                                   >

♩=76–80

272

God of the Sparrow

ROEDER   5.4.6.7.7

Jaroslav J. Vajda, 1983   Carl F. Schalk, 1983

1. God of the spar-row   God of the whale
3. God of the rain-bow   God of the cross
5. God of the neigh-bor   God of the foe

God of the swirl-ing stars   How does the crea-ture say
God of the emp-ty grave   How does the crea-ture say
God of the prun-ing hook   How does the crea-ture say

Awe   How does the crea-ture say Praise
Grace   How does the crea-ture say Thanks
Love   How does the crea-ture say Peace

Descant on stanzas 2, 4, 6

2. God of the earth-quake God of the storm God of the trum-pet
4. God of the hun-gry God of the sick God of the prod-i-
6. God of the a-ges God near at hand God of the lov-ing

blast How does the crea-ture cry Woe
gal How does the crea-ture say Care
heart How do your chil-dren say Joy

[2, 4]
How does the crea-ture cry Save
How does the crea-ture say Life

[6]
How do your chil-dren say Home

♩=108–116

273 O God the Creator

KASTAAK   Irregular

Elizabeth Haile and Cecil Corbett, 1977

Joy F. Patterson, 1989

1. O God the Cre - a - tor, the Three in One, The Cre -
2. (For the) earth is our moth - er, where all things grow, And her
3. (We are) one in the Spir - it, in the great mys - ter - y, Walk to -
4. (Send a) sense of Your pres-ence as we seek lead - er - ship. Pray that

a - tor of earth and moon and sun, You have
val - leys are green where the wa - ters flow, Gen - tle
geth - er in beau - ty as we dwell in har - mo - ny, Bring-ing
God will join us in our vi - sion quest. Wel - come

loved and pro - tect - ed us since time first be - gun,
deer and the ea - gle and the might - y buf - fa - lo, And we're
all of God's chil - dren in - to one com-mu - ni - ty,
God to come in - to our hearts as our guest,

broth - ers and sis - ters in God's love, in God's love, And we're

| 1–3 | 4 |

broth-ers and sis-ters in God's love.

2. For the
3. We are
4. Send a

love.

♩=96–104

274 O God of Earth and Space

LEONI   6.6.8.4 D

Jane Parker Huber, 1980

Hebrew melody
Adapt. Thomas Olivers and Meyer Lyon, 1770

1. O God of earth and space, Of sea and fire and air,
Your prov-i-dence sur-rounds us here And ev-ery-where.
In fruit and grain and tree, In shel-ter from the cold,
In cool-ing breez-es, flow-ing wells, Now as of old.

2. Where faith-ful-ness is shown, Where love and truth a-bound,
Where beau-ty grac-es hu-man life, There You are found.
In-spir-er of all thought! Cre-a-tive force of art!
The mel-o-dy on ev-ery tongue, In ev-ery heart!

3. Wher-ev-er free-dom reigns, Where sin is o-ver-thrown,
Where jus-tice fused with mer-cy rules, There You are known.
Give us the cour-age clear To make the earth a home
For all to live in har-mo-ny In Christ's sha-lom.

4. Your word com-mands re-sponse And sum-mons us to life.
We fol-low, strength-ened by Your grace, In calm or strife.
Our ev-er-pres-ent help, Our chal-lenge and our prod,
We praise You now and to life's end, E-ter-nal God.

God of Our Life

SANDON   10.4.10.4.10.10

Hugh Thomson Kerr, 1916; alt. 1928

Charles Henry Purday, 1860
Harm. John Weaver, 1986

1. God of our life, through all the cir-cling years, We trust in Thee;
2. God of the past, our times are in Thy hand; With us a-bide.
3. God of the com-ing years, through paths un-known We fol-low Thee;

In all the past, through all our hopes and fears, Thy hand we see.
Lead us by faith to hope's true prom-ised land; Be Thou our guide.
When we are strong, Lord, leave us not a-lone; Our ref-uge be.

With each new day, when morn-ing lifts the veil,
With Thee to bless, the dark-ness shines as light,
Be Thou for us in life our dai-ly bread,

We own Thy mer - cies, Lord, which nev-er fail.
And faith's fair vi - sion chan-ges in-to sight.
Our heart's true home when all our years have sped.

276 Great Is Thy Faithfulness

FAITHFULNESS   11.10.11.10 with refrain

Thomas Obediah Chisholm, 1923

William Marion Runyan, 1923

1. *Great is Thy faith - ful - ness, O God my Fa - ther,
2. Sum - mer and win - ter, and spring-time and har - vest,
3. Par - don for sin and a peace that en - dur - eth,

There is no shad - ow of turn - ing with Thee;
Sun, moon, and stars in their cours - es a - bove
Thine own dear pres - ence to cheer and to guide;

Thou chang - est not, Thy com - pas - sions they fail not;
Join with all na - ture in man - i - fold wit - ness
Strength for to - day and bright hope for to - mor - row,

As Thou hast been Thou for - ev - er wilt be.
To Thy great faith - ful - ness, mer - cy, and love.
Bless - ings all mine, with ten thou - sand be - side!

*Or "Great is Thy faithfulness, O God, Creator."

Refrain

Great is Thy faith-ful-ness! Great is Thy faith-ful-ness!

Morn-ing by morn-ing new mer-cies I see; All I have need-ed Thy

hand hath pro-vid-ed; Great is Thy faith-ful-ness, Lord, un-to me!

277 O God, Our Faithful God

O GOTT, DU FROMMER GOTT   6.7.6.7.6.6.6.6

Johann Heermann, 1630
Trans. Catherine Winkworth, 1858; alt.

Neu ordentlich Gesangbuch, 1646
Harm. Johann Sebastian Bach (1685–1750); alt.

1. O God, our faith - ful God, O foun-tain ev - er flow-ing,
2. God, grant us strength to do With read - y heart and will - ing,
3. If dan - gers gath - er round, Still keep us calm and fear-less;

With - out whom noth-ing is, All per - fect gifts be - stow-ing,
What - ev - er You com - mand, Our call - ing here ful - fill - ing;
Help us to bear the cross When life is bleak and cheer-less,

Grant us a faith - ful life, And give us, Lord, with - in,
And do it when we ought, With zeal and joy - ful - ness;
To o - ver-come our foes With words and ac - tions kind;

Com - mit - ment free from strife, A soul un - hurt by sin.
And bless the work we've wrought, For You must give suc - cess.
O God, Your will dis - close, Your coun-sel let us find.

Alternate tune: WAS FRAG' ICH NACH DER WELT, 278

Our God, to Whom We Turn

278

WAS FRAG' ICH NACH DER WELT   6.7.6.7.6.6.6.6

Ahasuerus Fritsch, 1679
Harm. Johann Sebastian Bach, 1724

Edward Grubb, 1925

1. Our God, to whom we turn When wea-ry with il-lu-sion,
2. Thou art Thy-self the truth; Though we, who fain would find Thee,
3. All beau-ty speaks of Thee: The moun-tains and the riv-ers,
4. Thou hid-den fount of love, Of peace, and truth, and beau-ty,

Whose stars se-rene-ly burn A-bove this earth's con-fu-sion,
Have tried, with thoughts un-couth, In fee-ble words to bind Thee,
The line of lift-ed sea, Where spread-ing moon-light quiv-ers,
In-spire us from a-bove With joy and strength for du-ty;

Thine is the might-y plan, The stead-fast or-der sure,
It is be-cause Thou art We're driv-en to the quest;
The deep-toned or-gan blast That rolls through arch-es dim,
May Thy fresh light a-rise With-in each cloud-ed heart,

In which the world be-gan, En-dures, and shall en-dure.
Till truth from false-hood part, Our souls can find no rest.
Hints of the mu-sic vast Of Thine e-ter-nal hymn.
And give us o-pen eyes To see Thee as Thou art.

Text: Used by permission of the executors of the estate of Mrs. M. Walsh.

279 Lord of Our Growing Years

LITTLE CORNARD   6.6.6.6.8.8

David Mowbray (b. 1938)   Martin Shaw, 1915

1. Lord of our grow-ing years, With us from in-fan-cy,
2. Lord of our strong-est years, Stretch-ing our youth-ful powers,
3. Lord of our mid-dle years, Giv-er of stead-fast-ness,
4. Lord of our old-er years, Steep though the road may be,

Laugh-ter and quick-dried tears, Fresh-ness and en-er-gy:
Lov-ers and pi-o-neers When all the world seems ours:
Cour-age that per-se-veres When there is small suc-cess:
Rid us of fool-ish fears, Bring us se-ren-i-ty:

Refrain

Your grace sur-rounds us all our days;

For all Your gifts we bring our praise.

5. Lord of our closing years,
   Always Your promise stands;
   Hold us, when death appears,
   Safely within Your hands: *(Refrain)*

Amazing Grace, How Sweet the Sound 280

AMAZING GRACE CM

Stanzas 1–4, John Newton, 1779
Stanza 5, *A Collection of Sacred Ballads,* 1790

Virginia Harmony, 1831
Arr. Edwin O. Excell, 1900

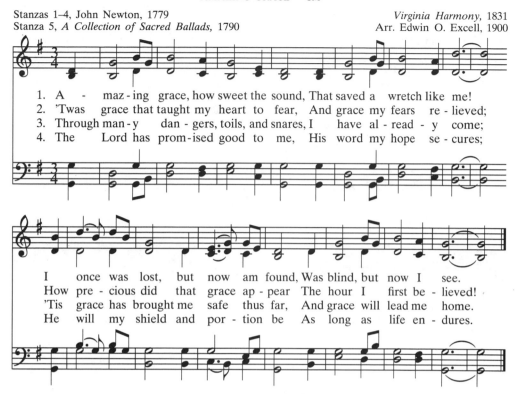

1. A - maz - ing grace, how sweet the sound, That saved a wretch like me!
2. 'Twas grace that taught my heart to fear, And grace my fears re - lieved;
3. Through man - y dan - gers, toils, and snares, I have al - read - y come;
4. The Lord has prom - ised good to me, His word my hope se - cures;

I once was lost, but now am found, Was blind, but now I see.
How pre - cious did that grace ap - pear The hour I first be - lieved!
'Tis grace has brought me safe thus far, And grace will lead me home.
He will my shield and por - tion be As long as life en - dures.

5. When we've been there ten thousand
   years,
   Bright shining as the sun,
   We've no less days to sing God's praise
   Than when we'd first begun.

Kiowa
Daw k'ee da ha dawtsahy he tsow'haw
Daw k'ee da ha dawtsahy hee.
Bay dawtsahy taw, gaw aym ow thah t'aw,
Daw k'ee da ha dawtsahy h'ee.

Creek
Po ya fek cha he thlat ah tet
Ah non ah cha pa kas
Cha fcc kcc o funnan la kus
Um e ha ta la yus.

Choctaw
Shilombish holitopa ma!
Ishmminti pulla cha
Hatak ilbusha pia ha
Is pi yukpalashke

Cherokee
Ooh nay thla nah, hee oo way gee'.
E gah gwoo yah hay ee.
Naw gwoo joe sah, we you low say,
E gah gwoo yah ho nah.

Navaho
Nizhóníígo jooba' diits' a'
Yisdáshíítinigíí,
Lałı yóóiiyá, k'ad shénáhoosdzin,
Doo eesh'íí da ńt'éé.

Text: Phonetic transcription Cherokee, Kiowa, Creek, and Choctaw: Oklahoma Indian Missionary Conference;
Navaho: phonetic transcription by Albert Tsosie.

281 Guide Me, O Thou Great Jehovah

CWM RHONDDA   8.7.8.7.8.7.7

William Williams, 1745
Stanza 1 trans. Peter Williams, 1771
Stanzas 2–3 trans. William Williams, 1772

John Hughes, 1907

1. Guide me, O Thou great Je - ho - vah, Pil - grim through this
2. O - pen now the crys - tal foun - tain, Whence the heal - ing
3. When I tread the verge of Jor - dan, Bid my anx - ious

bar - ren land; I am weak, but Thou art might - y; Hold me
stream doth flow; Let the fire and cloud - y pil - lar Lead me
fears sub - side; Death of death, and hell's de - struc - tion, Land me

with Thy power - ful hand; Bread of heav - en, bread of heav - en,
all my jour - ney through; Strong de - liv - erer, strong de - liv - erer,
safe on Ca - naan's side; Songs of prais - es, songs of prais - es

Feed me till I want no more,   Feed me till I want no more.
Be Thou still my strength and shield,   Be Thou still my strength and shield.
I will ev - er give to Thee,   I will ev - er give to Thee.

If Thou but Trust in God to Guide Thee 282

WER NUR DEN LIEBEN GOTT   9.8.9.8.8.8

Georg Neumark, 1657
Trans. Catherine Winkworth, 1855, 1863; alt. 1987   Georg Neumark, 1657

1. If thou but trust in God to guide thee, With hope-ful
2. On-ly be still, and wait God's lei-sure In cheer-ful
3. Sing, pray, and swerve not from God's ways, But do thine

heart through all thy ways, God will give strength, what-e'er be-tide thee,
hope, with heart con-tent To take what-e'er thy Keep-er's plea-sure
own part faith-ful-ly; Trust the rich prom-is-es of grace,

To bear thee through the e-vil days. Who trusts in God's un-
And all-dis-cern-ing love hath sent. No doubt our in-most
So shall they be ful-filled in thee. God nev-er yet for-

chang-ing love Builds on the rock that nought can move.
wants are clear To One who holds us al-ways dear.
sook at need The soul se-cured by trust in-deed.

283 God Marked a Line and Told the Sea

KEDRON LM

Attr. Elkanah Kelsay Dare
As in Pilsbury's *United States Harmony,* 1799

Thomas H. Troeger, 1986

1. God marked a line and told the sea Its
2. God set one lim - it in the glade Where
3. The line, the lim - it, and the law Are
4. But, dis - con - tent with fi - nite powers, We

surg - ing tides and waves were free To trav - el up the
tempt - ing, fruit - ed branch - es swayed, And that first lim - it
pat - terns meant to help us draw A bound be - tween what
reach to take what is not ours And then de - fend our

slop - ing strand But not to o - ver - take the land.
stands be - hind The lim - its that the law de - fined.
life re - quires And all the things our heart de - sires.
claim by force And swerve from life's in - tend - ed course.

5. We are not free when we're confined
   To every wish that sweeps the mind,
   But free when freely we accept
   The sacred bounds that must be kept.

♩=58–63

Text: © 1989, Oxford University Press, Inc. By permission.

O God, What You Ordain Is Right

WAS GOTT TUT   8.7.8.7.4.4.8.8

284

Samuel Rodigast, c. 1675
Trans. Catherine Winkworth, 1858, 1863; alt.

Severus Gastorius, 1679
Harm. *Common Service Book*, 1917

1. O God, what You or-dain is right, Your ho-ly will a-bid-ing; I shall be still, what-e'er You do, And fol-low where You are guid-ing. You are my God; Though dark my road, You hold me that I shall not fall; Where-fore to You I leave it all.

2. O God, what You or-dain is right; You nev-er will de-ceive me. You lead me by the prop-er path; I know You will not leave me. And take, con-tent, What You have sent; Your hand can turn my griefs a-way, And pa-tient-ly I wait Your day.

3. O God, what You or-dain is right; Here shall my stand be tak-en. Though sor-row, need, or death be mine, Yet I am not for-sak-en. Your watch-ful care Is round me there; You hold me that I shall not fall, And so to You I leave it all.

285 God, You Spin the Whirling Planets

AUSTRIAN HYMN   8.7.8.7 D

Jane Parker Huber, 1978

Franz Joseph Haydn, 1797

1. God, You spin the whirl-ing plan-ets, Fill the seas and spread the plain,
2. You have called us to be faith-ful In our life and min - is - try.
3. God, Your word is still cre-at-ing, Call-ing us to life made new.

Mold the moun-tains, fash-ion blos-soms, Call forth sun-shine, wind, and rain.
We re-spond in grate-ful wor-ship Joined in one com-mu-ni-ty.
Now re-veal to us fresh vis-tas Where there's work to dare and do.

We, cre-at-ed in Your im-age, Would a true re-flec-tion be
When we blur Your gra-cious im-age, Fo-cus us and make us whole.
Keep us clear of all dis-tor-tion. Pol-ish us with lov-ing care.

Of Your jus - tice, grace, and mer-cy And the truth that makes us free.
Healed and strength-ened as Your peo-ple, We move on-ward toward Your goal.
Thus, new crea-tures in Your im-age, We'll pro-claim Christ ev-ery-where.

Give to the Winds Thy Fears

ST. BRIDE SM

286

Paul Gerhardt, 1656
Trans. John Wesley, 1739; alt.

Samuel Howard, 1762; alt.

1. Give to the winds thy fears; Hope and be un - dis - mayed:
2. Through waves and clouds and storms God gent - ly clears thy way;
3. Leave to God's sov - ereign sway To choose and to com - mand;
4. On God the Lord re - ly, And safe shalt thou go on;

God hears thy sighs and counts thy tears, God shall lift up thy head.
Wait pa - tient - ly; so shall this night Soon end in joy - ous day.
So shalt thou, won-dering, own God's way, How wise, how strong God's hand!
Fix on God's work thy stead - fast eye, So shall thy work be done.

Alternate harmonization, 198

287 God Folds the Mountains Out of Rock

Thomas H. Troeger, 1985

REVISION   LMD

Carol Doran, 1985

1. God folds the moun-tains out of rock And fus - es el - e - men - tal powers In ores and at - oms we un - lock To claim as if their wealth were ours.

2. Our in - stru - ments can probe and sound The fold - ed moun-tain's po - tent core, But wis - dom's ways are nev - er found A - mong the lodes of bur - ied ore,

3. Lord, grant us what we can - not mine, What sci - ence can - not plumb or chart: Your wis - dom and your truth di - vine En - fold - ed in a faith - ful heart.

Text and Music: From *New Hymns for the Lectionary;* © 1985, Oxford University Press, Inc. By permission.

From veins of stone we lift up fire, And too im-
Yet wis - dom is the great - er need, And wis - dom
Then we like moun - tains rich - ly veined Will be a

pressed by our own skill We use the flame that we
is the great - er source, For lack - ing wis - dom we
source of light and flame Whose en - er - gies have been

ac - quire, Not think - ing of the Mak - er's will.
pro - ceed To waste God's oth - er gifts on force.
or - dained To glo - ri - fy the Mak - er's name.

♩=100–108

288 I Sing the Mighty Power of God

ELLACOMBE   CMD

Isaac Watts, 1715; alt.

*Gesangbuch der Herzogl. Wirtembergischen
Katholischen Hofkapelle, 1784; alt. 1868*

1. I sing the might-y power of God That made the moun-tains rise;
2. I sing the good-ness of the Lord That filled the earth with food;
3. There's not a plant or flower be-low But makes Thy glo - ries known;

That spread the flow-ing seas a - broad And built the loft - y skies.
God formed the crea-tures with a word And then pro-nounced them good.
And clouds a - rise, and tem-pests blow, By or - der from Thy throne;

I sing the wis-dom that or - dained The sun to rule the day;
Lord, how Thy won-ders are dis - played, Wher - e'er I turn my eyes;
While all that bor-rows life from Thee Is ev - er in Thy care,

The moon shines full at God's com-mand, And all the stars o - bey.
If I sur - vey the ground I tread, Or gaze up - on the skies!
And ev - ery-where that we can be, Thou, God, art pres-ent there.

Alternate tune: FOREST GREEN, 292

O God of Every Nation

LLANGLOFFAN   7.6.7.6 D

Welsh folk melody
Evans' *Hymnau a Thonau,* 1865
As in *English Hymnal,* 1906

William W. Reid, Jr., 1958; alt. 1972

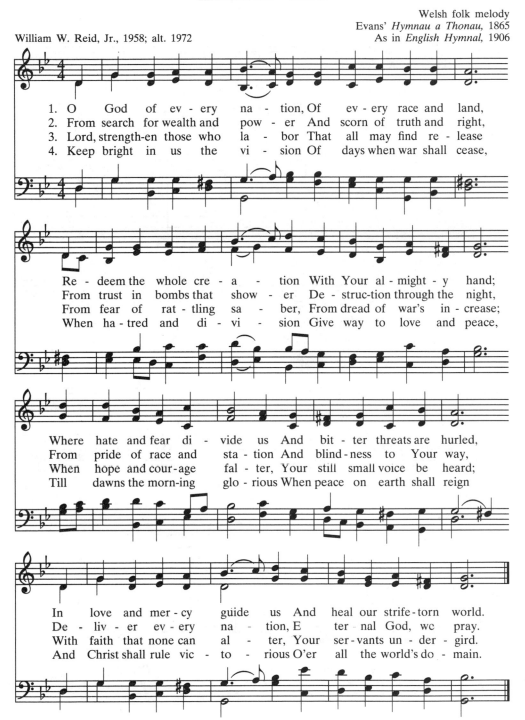

1. O God of ev - ery na - tion, Of ev - ery race and land,
2. From search for wealth and pow - er And scorn of truth and right,
3. Lord, strength-en those who la - bor That all may find re - lease
4. Keep bright in us the vi - sion Of days when war shall cease,

Re - deem the whole cre - a - tion With Your al - might - y hand;
From trust in bombs that show - er De - struc-tion through the night,
From fear of rat - tling sa - ber, From dread of war's in - crease;
When ha - tred and di - vi - sion Give way to love and peace,

Where hate and fear di - vide us And bit - ter threats are hurled,
From pride of race and sta - tion And blind - ness to Your way,
When hope and cour-age fal - ter, Your still small voice be heard;
Till dawns the morn-ing glo - rious When peace on earth shall reign

In love and mer - cy guide us And heal our strife - torn world.
De - liv - er ev - ery na - tion, E - ter - nal God, we pray.
With faith that none can al - ter, Your ser - vants un - der - gird.
And Christ shall rule vic - to - rious O'er all the world's do - main.

290 God Created Heaven and Earth

TŌA-SĪA   7.7.7.7

Taiwanese hymn
Trans. Boris and Clare Anderson, 1981

Pi-po melody
Harm. I-to Loh, 1963; rev. 1982

1. God cre - a - ted heaven and earth, All things per - fect
2. Let us praise God's mer - cy great, All our needs that
3. God is one, will ev - er be: I - dols are mere
4. But God's grace be - yond com - pare Saves us all from

brought to birth; God's great power made
love a - wait; God, who fash - ions
van - i - ty; Hand-made gods of
death's de - spair; So earth's crea - tures

dark and light, Earth re - volv-ing day and night.
all that lives, To each one a bless - ing gives.
wood and clay Can - not help us when we pray.
small and great Give thanks for that bless - ed state.

♩=88–96

O God of Earth and Altar

291

LLANGLOFFAN   7.6.7.6 D

Stanzas 1–2, Gilbert Keith Chesterton, 1906
Stanza 2 alt. Jane Parker Huber, 1985
Stanza 3, Jane Parker Huber, 1985

Welsh folk melody
Evans' *Hymnau a Thonau,* 1865
As in *English Hymnal,* 1906

1. O God of earth and al - tar, Bow down and hear our cry;
2. From all that ter - ror teach - es, From lies of pen and voice,
3. A - wak - en us to ac - tion And forge us in - to one,

Our earth-ly rul - ers fal - ter, Our peo - ple drift and die;
From all the eas - y speech - es That make our hearts re - joice,
De - fy - ing sect and fac - tion; O God, Your will be done!

The walls of gold en - tomb us, The swords of scorn di - vide;
From sale and pro - fa - na - tion Of hon - or and the sword,
Op - pres-sive sys-tems snare us; Our ap - a - thies in - crease.

Take not Your thun - der from us, But take a - way our pride.
From sleep and from dam - na - tion, De - liv - er us, good Lord!
Great God, in mer - cy spare us For jus - tice and for peace!

Text: Stanza 3 © 1985 Jane Parker Huber. Used by permission.

292 All Beautiful the March of Days

FOREST GREEN   CMD

Frances Whitmarsh Wile, 1911; alt.

English folk melody
Arr. Ralph Vaughan Williams, 1906

1. All beau-ti-ful the march of days, As sea-sons come and go;
2. O'er white ex-pans-es spar-kling pure The ra-diant morns un-fold;
3. O Thou from whose un-fath-omed law The year in beau-ty flows,

The hand that shaped the rose hath wrought The crys-tal of the snow;
The sol-emn splen-dors of the night Burn bright-er through the cold;
Thy-self the vi-sion pass-ing by In crys-tal and in rose,

Hath sent the hoar-y frost of heaven, The flow-ing wa-ters sealed,
Life mounts in ev-ery throb-bing vein, Love deep-ens round the hearth,
Day un-to day doth ut-ter speech, And night to night pro-claim,

And laid a si-lent love-li-ness On hill and wood and field.
And clear-er sounds the an-gel hymn, "Good will to all on earth."
In ev-er-chang-ing words of light, The won-der of Thy name.

This tune in a lower key, 414

This Is My Father's World

TERRA BEATA   SMD

Franklin L. Sheppard, 1915
Harm. 1953 for *The Hymnbook;* alt. 1988

Maltbie Davenport Babcock, 1901

1. This is my Fa-ther's world, And to my lis-tening ears All na - ture sings, and round me rings The mu - sic of the spheres. This is my Fa-ther's world: I rest me in the thought Of rocks and trees, of skies and seas; His hand the won - ders wrought.

2. This is my Fa-ther's world: Oh, let me ne'er for - get That though the wrong seems oft so strong, God is the Rul - er yet. This is my Fa-ther's world: The bat - tle is not done; Je - sus who died shall be sat - is - fied, And earth and heaven be one.

294

Wherever I May Wander

NEW ENGLAND   7.6.8.6 D

Ann B. Snow, 1959

New England folk melody

1. Wher - ev - er I may wan - der, Wher - ev - er I may be,
2. Through-out the whole cre - a - tion I see God's lov - ing care

I'm cer - tain of my Mak - er's love; God's care is o - ver me.
For ev - ery - one in ev - ery land, God's chil - dren ev - ery - where.

God made the great high moun-tains, And made the wide blue sea;
Wher - ev - er I may wan - der, Wher - ev - er I may be,

God made the sky where air-planes fly; God made the world, and me.
I'm cer - tain of my Mak-er's love; God's care is o - ver me.

O God of Love, O God of Peace 295

DU MEINER SEELEN   LM

Henry Williams Baker, 1860; alt. 1987

Cantica Spiritualia, 1847

1. O God of love, O God of peace, Make wars through-
out the world to cease; The wrath of na - tions
now re - strain:

2. Re - mem-ber, Lord, Thy works of old, The won - ders
that Thy peo - ple told; Re - mem-ber not our
sin's deep stain:

3. Whom shall we trust but Thee, O Lord? Where rest but
on Thy faith - ful word? None ev - er called on
Thee in vain:

4. Where saints and an - gels dwell a - bove, All hearts are
knit in ho - ly love; O bind us in that
heaven - ly chain:

Give peace, O God, give peace a - gain!

Alternate tune: QUEBEC, 510

296

Camina, Pueblo de Dios
Walk On, O People of God

NUEVA CREACIÓN   Irregular

Cesáreo Gabaráin
Trans. George Lockwood, 1987

Cesáreo Gabaráin

Estribillo
Refrain

Ca - mi - na, pue-blo de Dios, ca - mi - na, pue-blo de Dios,
Walk on, O peo-ple of God; walk on, O peo-ple of God!

nue-va ley, nue - va a - lian-za, en la nue-va cre - a - ción.
A new law, God's new al - li - ance, all cre - a - tion is re - born.

Ca - mi - na, pue-blo de Dios, ca - mi - na, pue-blo de Dios.
Walk on, O peo-ple of God; walk on, O peo-ple of God.

1. Mi - ra a - llá en el Cal - va - rio en la
2. Cris - to to - ma en su cuer - po el pe -
3. Cie - lo y tie - rra se a - bra - zan, nues - tra

1. Look on Cal - va - ry's sum - mit; on the
2. Christ takes in - to His bod - y all our
3. Heaven and earth are em - brac - ing, and our

ro - ca hay u - na cruz; muer - te que en - gen - dra la
ca - do, la es - cla - vi - tud. Al des - tru - ir - los, nos
al - ma ha - ya el per - dón. Vuel - ven a a - brir - se los

rock there tow - ers a cross; death that gives birth to new
sin, en - slave - ment, and pain; as He de - stroys them He
souls find par - don at last. Now heav-en's gates are re -

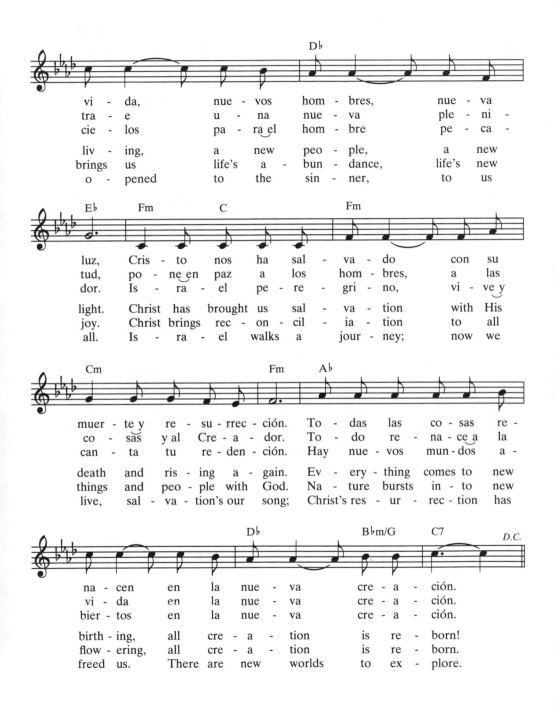

297 O Lord of Every Shining Constellation

VICAR   11.10.11.10

Albert F. Bayly, 1950; alt.   V. Earle Copes, 1963

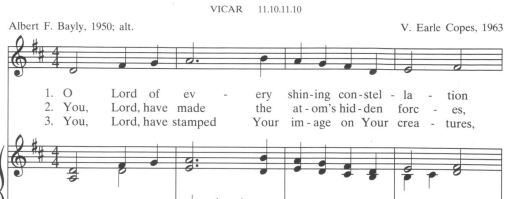

1. O Lord of ev - ery shin-ing con-stel - la - tion
2. You, Lord, have made the at - om's hid - den forc - es,
3. You, Lord, have stamped Your im - age on Your crea - tures,

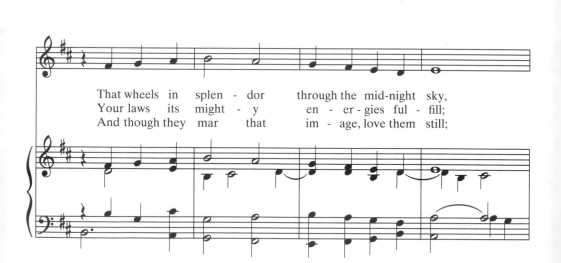

That wheels in splen - dor through the mid-night sky,
Your laws its might - y en - er - gies ful - fill;
And though they mar that im - age, love them still;

Grant us Your Spir - it's   true il - lu - mi - na - tion
Teach us, to whom You   give such rich re - sourc - es,
Lift up our eyes to   Christ, that in His fea - tures

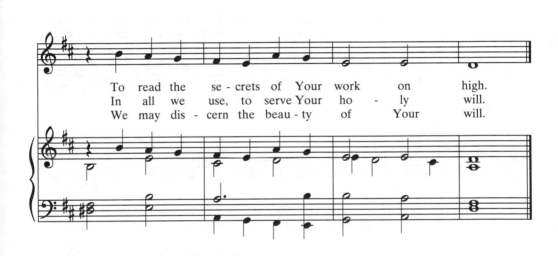

To read the se - crets of Your work on high.
In all we use, to serve Your ho - ly will.
We may dis - cern the beau - ty of Your will.

298 There's a Wideness in God's Mercy

IN BABILONE   8.7.8.7 D

Frederick William Faber, 1854; alt.

Dutch melody
Arr. Julius Röntgen (1855–1933)

1. There's a wide-ness in God's mer - cy, Like the wide-ness of the sea;
2. For the love of God is broad-er Than the mea-sures of the mind;

There's a kind-ness in God's jus-tice, Which is more than lib - er - ty.
And the heart of the E - ter-nal Is most won-der - ful - ly kind.

There is no place where earth's sor-rows Are more felt than up in heaven;
If our love were but more faith-ful, We would glad-ly trust God's Word;

There is no place where earth's fail-ings Have such kind - ly judg - ment given.
And our lives re - flect thanks-giv-ing For the good-ness of our Lord.

Amen, Amen

Irregular

African-American spiritual
Arr. Nelsie T. Johnson, 1988

African-American spiritual

Congregation

A - men, A - men, A - men, A - men, A -

Leader

1. See the lit-tle ba-by   ly - ing in a man-ger   on
2. See Him in the tem-ple   talk - ing to the el - ders;   how

3. See Him at the sea-shore   preach-ing to the peo-ple,
4. See Him in the gar-den   pray - ing to the Fa - ther   in

5. See Him on the cross   bear - ing all my sins   in
6. Yes, He died to save us   and He rose on Eas-ter;
7. ——— Al - le - lu - ia!   Je - sus is my Sav-ior,

Congregation

men!   A - men,   A -

Christ - mas morn - ing.
they all mar - veled!

heal - ing all the sick ones!
deep - est sor - row!

bit - ter ag - o - ny!
Now He lives for-ev - er!
And He lives for-ev - er!

Last time

men,   A - men, A - men, A - men!

300

Down to Earth, as a Dove

PERSONENT HODIE 6.6.6.6.6 with refrain

Piae Cantiones, 1582

Fred Kaan, 1968

Arr. Gustav Theodore Holst, 1924

1. Down to earth, as a dove, Came to light ho - ly love: Je - sus Christ from a - bove Bring-ing great sal - va - tion Meant for ev - ery na - tion.
2. This is love come to light, Now is fear put to flight. God de - feats dark-est night, Giv - ing for our sor - rows Hope of new to - mor - rows.
3. Christ the Lord comes to feed Hun - gry peo - ple in need; In the house there is bread: Je - sus in a sta - ble, In the church a ta - ble.

Refrain

Let us sing, sing, sing,

R.H.
L.H.
R.H.

Dance and spring, spring, spring, Christ is here, Ev-er near! Glo-ria in ex - cel-sis.

Lord Jesus, Think on Me 301

SOUTHWELL SM

Synesius of Cyrene (c. 370–c. 414)
Trans. Allen W. Chatfield, 1876

Daman's *Psalmes*, 1579; alt.

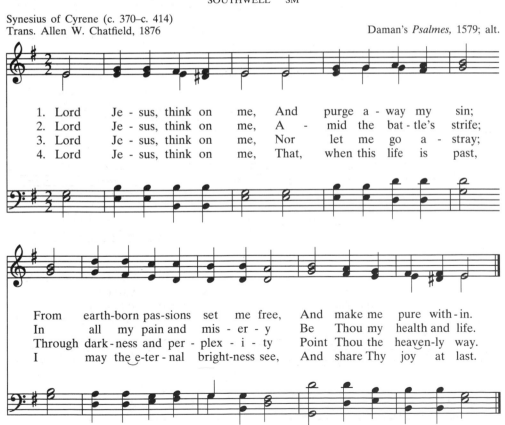

1. Lord Je - sus, think on me, And purge a - way my sin;
2. Lord Je - sus, think on me, A - mid the bat - tle's strife;
3. Lord Je - sus, think on me, Nor let me go a - stray;
4. Lord Je - sus, think on me, That, when this life is past,

From earth-born pas-sions set me free, And make me pure with - in.
In all my pain and mis - er - y Be Thou my health and life.
Through dark - ness and per - plex - i - ty Point Thou the heaven-ly way.
I may the e-ter - nal bright-ness see, And share Thy joy at last.

302 I Danced in the Morning

SIMPLE GIFTS Irregular with refrain

Sydney Carter, 1963

American Shaker melody
Harm. Sydney Carter, 1963

1. I danced in the morn - ing when the world was be - gun, And I danced in the moon and the stars and the sun, And I came down from heav - en and I danced on the earth,

2. I danced for the scribe and the Phar - i - see, But they would not dance and they would not fol - low Me; I danced for the fish - er - men, for

3. I danced on the Sab - bath and I cured the lame; The ho - ly peo - ple said it was a shame. They whipped and they stripped and they

4. I danced on a Fri - day when the sky turned black; It's hard to dance with the dev - il on your back. They bur - ied My bod - y and they

5. They cut Me down and I leap up high; I am the life that will nev - er, nev - er die; I'll live in you if you'll

303 Jesus, Lover of My Soul

ABERYSTWYTH   7.7.7.7 D

Charles Wesley, 1740   Joseph Parry, 1879

1. Je - sus, lov - er   of my   soul, Let me to Thy   bos - om fly,
2. Oth - er   ref - uge   have I   none; Hangs my help-less   soul on Thee;
3. Thou, O   Christ, art   all I   want; More than all in   Thee I find:
4. Plen - teous grace with   Thee is   found, Grace to cov - er   all   my sin;

While   the   near - er   wa - ters roll, While the tem-pest still is   high:
Leave, ah!   leave me   not a - lone, Still sup - port and com-fort   me.
Raise   the   fall - en,   cheer the faint, Heal the sick, and   lead the blind.
Let   the   heal - ing   streams a - bound; Make and keep me   pure with - in.

Hide me, O   my   Sav - ior, hide,   Till the storm of   life   is   past;
All my trust   on   Thee is stayed, All my help from   Thee   I   bring;
Just and ho - ly   is Thy name;   I am all un - righ - teous-ness;
Thou of life   the   foun - tain art,   Free - ly let me   take   of   Thee;

Safe   in - to the   ha - ven guide;   O   re - ceive my   soul at   last!
Cov - er   my de - fense-less head   With the   shad - ow   of Thy   wing.
False and full of   sin I am,   Thou   art   full of   truth and   grace.
Spring Thou up with - in   my heart,   Rise to   all   e - ter - ni - ty.

This tune in a lower key, 20

Jesus Loves Me!   304

JESUS LOVES ME   7.7.7.7 with refrain

Anna Bartlett Warner, 1859   William Batchelder Bradbury, 1861

1. Je - sus loves me! This I know, For the Bi - ble tells me so;
2. Je - sus loves me! This I know, As He loved so long a - go,

Lit - tle ones to Him be - long; They are weak, but He is strong.
Tak - ing chil - dren on His knee, Say - ing, "Let them come to Me."

Refrain

Yes, Je - sus loves me! Yes, Je - sus loves me!

Yes, Je - sus loves me! The Bi - ble tells me so.

305 Jesus, Our Divine Companion

PLEADING SAVIOR   8.7.8.7 D

Henry van Dyke, 1909; alt.

American melody, 1830
Harm. Richard Proulx, 1986

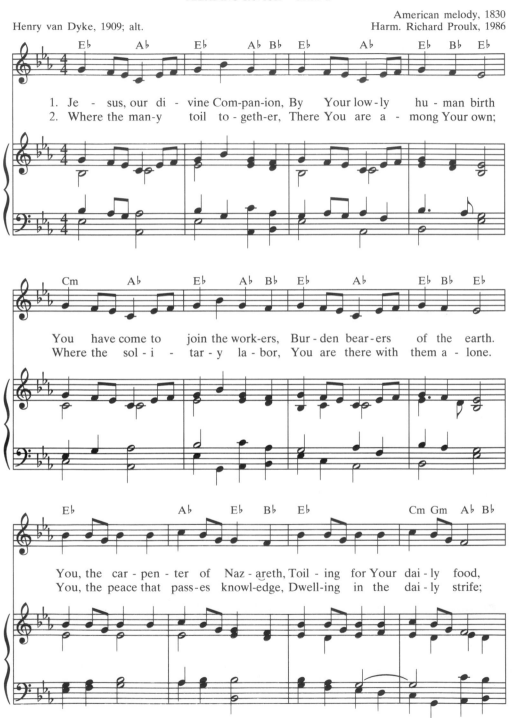

1. Je - sus, our di - vine Com-pan-ion, By Your low-ly hu - man birth
2. Where the man-y toil to - geth-er, There You are a - mong Your own;

You have come to join the work-ers, Bur - den bear-ers of the earth.
Where the sol - i - tar-y la - bor, You are there with them a - lone.

You, the car - pen - ter of Naz - areth, Toil - ing for Your dai - ly food,
You, the peace that pass - es knowl-edge, Dwell-ing in the dai - ly strife;

♩=48–52

By Your pa - tience and Your cour-age You have taught us work is good.
You, the Bread of heaven, are bro-ken In the sac - ra - ment of life.

Fairest Lord Jesus

306

CRUSADERS' HYMN   5.6.8.5.5.8

Münster *Gesangbuch,* 1677
Trans. *Church Chorals and Choir Studies,* 1850; alt.

Silesian folk melody
In *Schlesische Volkslieder,* 1842

1. Fair - est Lord Je - sus, Rul - er of all na - ture,
2. Fair are the mead - ows, Fair - er still the wood - lands,
3. Fair is the sun - shine, Fair - er still the moon - light,

O Thou of God to earth come down, Thee will I cher - ish,
Robed in the bloom - ing garb of spring: Je - sus is fair - er,
And all the twin - kling, star - ry host: Je - sus shines bright - er,

Thee will I hon - or, Thou, my soul's glo - ry, joy, and crown.
Je - sus is pur - er, Who makes the woe-ful heart to sing.
Je - sus shines pur - er, Than all the an - gels heaven can boast.

307 Fight the Good Fight

DUKE STREET   LM

John Samuel Bewley Monsell, 1863; alt.

John Hatton (d. 1793)

1. Fight the good fight with all thy might; Christ is thy
2. Run the straight race through God's good grace, Lift up thine
3. Cast care a - side, lean on thy guide; God's bound-less
4. Faint not nor fear, God's arms are near; God chang-eth

strength and Christ thy right; Lay hold on life, and
eyes, and seek Christ's face; Life with its way be -
mer - cy will pro - vide; Trust, and thy trust - ing
not, and thou art dear; On - ly be - lieve, and

it shall be Thy joy and crown e - ter - nal - ly.
fore us lies, Christ is the path, and Christ the prize.
soul shall prove Christ is its life, and Christ its love.
thou shalt see That Christ is all in all to thee.

O Sing a Song of Bethlehem

KINGSFOLD   CMD

English Country Songs, 1893

Louis FitzGerald Benson, 1899

Arr. and harm. Ralph Vaughan Williams, 1906

308

1. O sing a song of Beth-le-hem, Of shep-herds watch-ing there,
2. O sing a song of Naz-a-reth, Of sun-ny days of joy,
3. O sing a song of Gal-i-lee, Of lake and woods and hill,
4. O sing a song of Cal-va-ry, Its glo-ry and dis-may;

And of the news that came to them From an-gels in the air:
O sing of fra-grant flow-ers' breath, And of the sin-less Boy:
Of Him who walked up-on the sea And bade its waves be still:
Of Him who hung up-on the tree, And took our sins a-way:

The light that shone on Beth-le-hem Fills all the world to-day;
For now the flowers of Naz-a-reth In ev-ery heart may grow;
For though, like waves on Gal-i-lee, Dark seas of trou-ble roll,
For He who died on Cal-va-ry Is ris-en from the grave,

Of Je-sus' birth and peace on earth The an-gels sing al-way.
Now spreads the fame of His dear name On all the winds that blow.
When faith has heard the Mas-ter's word, Falls peace up-on the soul.
And Christ, our Lord, by heaven a-dored, Is might-y now to save.

309 Of the Father's Love Begotten

DIVINUM MYSTERIUM   8.7.8.7.8.7.7

Aurelius Clemens Prudentius (348–413)
Trans. John Mason Neale, 1854,
and Henry Williams Baker, 1859

Plainsong, Mode V
Harm. C. Winfred Douglas, 1940

1. Of the Father's love begotten, Ere the worlds began to be,
2. O ye heights of heaven adore Him; Angel hosts, His praises sing;
3. Christ, to Thee with God the Father, And, O Holy Ghost, to Thee,

He is Alpha and Omega, He the source, the ending He,
Powers, dominions, bow before Him, And extol our God and King;
Hymn and chant and high thanksgiving And unwearied praises be:

Of the things that are, that have been, And that future years shall see,
Let no tongue on earth be silent, Every voice in concert ring,
Honor, glory, and dominion, And eternal victory,

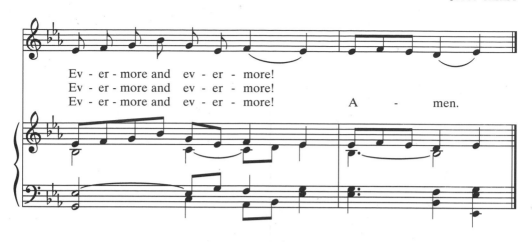

Ev - er - more and ev - er - more!
Ev - er - more and ev - er - more!
Ev - er - more and ev - er - more! A - men.

Jesus, the Very Thought of Thee   310

ST. AGNES   CM

Attr. Bernard of Clairvaux (1091–1153)
Trans. Edward Caswall, 1849; alt. 1987

John Bacchus Dykes, 1866

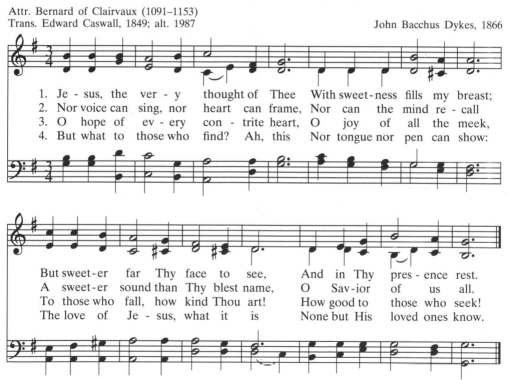

1. Je - sus, the ver - y thought of Thee With sweet-ness fills my breast;
2. Nor voice can sing, nor heart can frame, Nor can the mind re - call
3. O hope of ev - ery con - trite heart, O joy of all the meek,
4. But what to those who find? Ah, this Nor tongue nor pen can show:

But sweet-er far Thy face to see, And in Thy pres - ence rest.
A sweet-er sound than Thy blest name, O Sav-ior of us all.
To those who fall, how kind Thou art! How good to those who seek!
The love of Je - sus, what it is None but His loved ones know.

5. Jesus, our only joy be Thou,
   As Thou our prize wilt be;
   Jesus, be Thou our glory now,
   And through eternity.

311

We Meet You, O Christ

NORMANDY 10.10.11.11

Basque carol
Harm. George Mims, 1979

Fred Kaan, 1966

1. We meet You, O Christ, in man - y a guise:
2. In mil - lions a - live, a - way and a - broad;
3. We hear You, O Christ, in ag - o - ny cry.
4. You choose to be made at one with the earth;

Your im - age we see in sim - ple and wise.
In - volved in our life, You live down the road.
For free - dom You march, in ri - ots You die.
The dark of the grave pre - pares for Your birth.

You live in a pal - ace, ex - ist in a shack.
Im - pris - oned in sys - tems, You long to be free.
Your face in the pa - pers we read and we see.
Your death is Your ris - ing, cre - a - tive Your word:

We see You, the gar-dener, a tree on Your back.
We see You, Lord Je - sus, still bear-ing Your tree.
The tree must be plant-ed by hu - man de - cree.
The tree springs to life and our hope is re - stored.

♩=96–104

John 11:35

When Jesus Wept

WHEN JESUS WEPT   LM

312

William Billings, 1770
As in *New England Psalm Singer,* 1770

William Billings, 1770

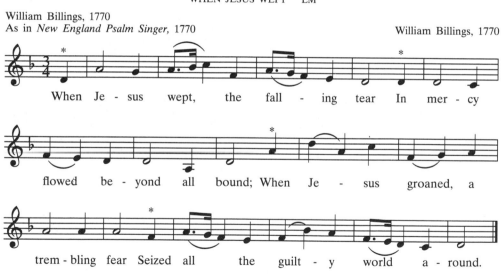

When Je - sus wept, the fall - ing tear In mer - cy flowed be - yond all bound; When Je - sus groaned, a trem - bling fear Seized all the guilt - y world a - round.

*May be sung as a canon.

♩=96–104

John 14:23,26

313 Come Down, O Love Divine

DOWN AMPNEY   6.6.11 D

Bianco da Siena (d. 1434)
Trans. Richard Frederick Littledale, 1867; alt.

Ralph Vaughan Williams, 1906

1. Come down, O Love di - vine, Seek out this soul of mine
2. O let it free - ly burn, Till earth - ly pas - sions turn
3. And so the yearn - ing strong With which the soul will long

And vis - it it with Your own ar - dor glow - ing;
To dust and ash - es in its heat con - sum - ing;
Shall far out - pass the power of hu - man tell - ing;

O Com-fort - er, draw near, With - in my heart ap - pear,
And let Your glo - rious light Shine ev - er on my sight,
For none can guess God's grace, Till Love cre - ates a place

And kin - dle it, Your ho - ly flame be - stow - ing.
And clothe me round, the while my path il - lum - ing.
Where - in the Ho - ly Spir - it makes a dwell - ing.

Music: From the *English Hymnal*, 1906. Used by permission of Oxford University Press.

Like the Murmur of the Dove's Song 314

BRIDEGROOM 8.7.8.7.6

Carl P. Daw, Jr., 1982

Peter Cutts, 1969

1. Like the mur-mur of the dove's song, Like the chal-lenge of her flight, Like the vig-or of the wind's rush, Like the new flame's ea-ger might:
2. To the mem-bers of Christ's bod-y, To the branch-es of the Vine, To the church in faith as-sem-bled, To her midst as gift and sign:
3. With the heal-ing of di-vi-sion, With the cease-less voice of prayer, With the power to love and wit-ness, With the peace be-yond com-pare:

Come, Ho-ly Spir-it, come.

♩=88–92

315 Every Time I Feel the Spirit

PENTECOST   Irregular

African-American spiritual
Arr. Joseph T. Jones (1902–1983)
Adapt. Melva W. Costen, 1989

Music: Adaptation © 1990 Melva W. Costen. All rights reserved. Used by permission.

mouth came fire and smoke. Looked all a-round me,
bod - y but not the soul. There is but one train

it looked so fine, Till I asked my Lord if all was mine.
up-on this track; It runs to heav-en and then right back.

D.C.

Breathe on Me, Breath of God 316

Edwin Hatch, 1886   TRENTHAM SM   Robert Jackson, 1894

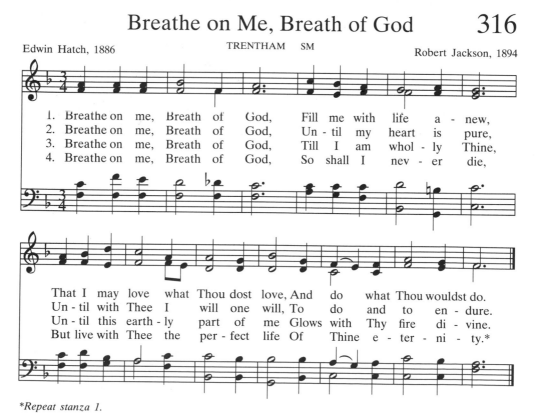

1. Breathe on me, Breath of God, Fill me with life a - new,
2. Breathe on me, Breath of God, Un - til my heart is pure,
3. Breathe on me, Breath of God, Till I am whol - ly Thine,
4. Breathe on me, Breath of God, So shall I nev - er die,

That I may love what Thou dost love, And do what Thou wouldst do.
Un - til with Thee I will one will, To do and to en - dure.
Un - til this earth - ly part of me Glows with Thy fire di - vine.
But live with Thee the per - fect life Of Thine e - ter - ni - ty.*

*Repeat stanza 1.

317 Holy Ghost, Dispel Our Sadness

GENEVA   8.7.8.7 D

Paul Gerhardt, 1648
Trans. John Christian Jacobi, c. 1725; alt.

George Henry Day, 1940

1. Ho-ly Ghost, dis-pel our sad - ness; Pierce the clouds of na - ture's night;
2. Au-thor of the new cre - a - tion, Come, a - noint us with Your power.

Come, O source of joy and glad-ness, Breathe Your life, and spread Your light.
Make our hearts Your hab-i - ta - tion; With Your grace our spir - its shower.

From the height which knows no mea - sure, As a gra - cious shower de - scend,
Hear, O hear our sup - pli - ca - tion, Bless-ed Spir - it, God of peace!

Bring-ing down the rich-est trea-sure We can wish, or God can send.
Rest up-on this con-gre-ga-tion With the full-ness of Your grace.

1 Corinthians 13

Gracious Spirit, Holy Ghost

318

ANDERSON 7.7.7.5

Christopher Wordsworth, 1862

Jane Manton Marshall, 1985

1. Gra-cious Spir-it, Ho-ly Ghost, Taught by You, we cov-et most,
2. Love is kind and suf-fers long; Love is meek and thinks no wrong;
3. Proph-e-cy will fade a-way, Melt-ing in the light of day;
4. Faith and hope and love we see, Join-ing hand in hand a-gree,

Of Your gifts at Pen-te-cost, Ho-ly, heaven-ly love.
Love than death it-self more strong; There-fore give us love.
Love will ev-er with us stay; There-fore give us love.
But the great-est of the three, And the best, is love.

319 Spirit

James K. Manley, 1975   James K. Manley, 1975

Spir - it, spir - it of gen - tle-ness, Blow through the wil - der-ness, call - ing and free, Spir - it, spir - it of rest - less - ness, Stir me from plac - id-ness, Wind, wind on the sea.

1. You moved on the wa - ters, You called to the deep, Then You coaxed up the moun - tains From the
2. You swept through the des - ert, You stung with the sand, And You gift - ed your peo - ple With a
3. You sang in a sta - ble, You cried from a hill, Then You whis - pered in si - lence When the
4. You call from to - mor - row, You break an - cient schemes, From the bond - age of sor - row The

val - leys   of   sleep,   And   o - ver   the   e -
law   and   a   land,   And   when   they   were   blind -
whole world was   still,   And   down   in   the   cit -
cap - tives dream   dreams;   Our   wom - en   see   vi -

ons   You   called   to   each   thing,   "A -
ed   With their   i - dols   and   lies,   Then You
y   You   called   once   a - gain   When You
sions,   Our   men   clear   their   eyes.   With

wake   from   your   slum - bers   And
spoke   through   Your   proph - ets   To
blew   through   Your   peo - ple   On   the
bold   new   de - ci - sions   Your

rise   on   your   wings."
o - pen   their   eyes.
rush   of   the   wind.
peo - ple   a - rise.

D.C. al Fine

♩=116–126

320 The Lone, Wild Bird

PROSPECT LM

Henry Richard McFadyen, 1925; alt.

As in *Twelve Folksongs and Spirituals,* 1968
Harm. David N. Johnson, 1968

1. The lone, wild bird in loft - y flight Is still with Thee, nor
2. The ends of earth are in Thy hand, The sea's dark deep and

leaves Thy sight. And I am Thine! I rest in
far - off land.

Thee. Great Spir - it, come, and rest in me.

Text: Copyright 1927 by *The Homiletic and Pastoral Review,* published by Catholic Polls, Inc. Used by permission.
Music: Harmonization copyright © 1968 Augsburg Publishing House. Used by permission.

321 Holy Spirit, Truth Divine

Samuel Longfellow, 1864; alt. 1987

SONG 13   7.7.7.7

Orlando Gibbons, 1623; alt.

1. Ho - ly Spir - it, truth di - vine, Dawn up - on this soul of mine;
2. Ho - ly Spir - it, love di - vine, Glow with - in this heart of mine;
3. Ho - ly Spir - it, power di - vine, Fill and nerve this will of mine;
4. Ho - ly Spir - it, right di - vine, Make my con - science whol - ly Thine;

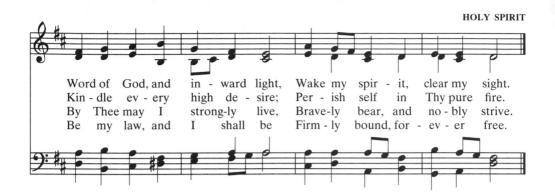

Word of God, and in - ward light, Wake my spir - it, clear my sight.
Kin - dle ev - ery high de - sire; Per - ish self in Thy pure fire.
By Thee may I strong-ly live, Brave-ly bear, and no - bly strive.
Be my law, and I shall be Firm - ly bound, for - ev - er free.

Spirit of the Living God 322

LIVING GOD   Irregular

Daniel Iverson, 1935; adapted

Daniel Iverson, 1935

Spir - it of the liv - ing God, Fall a-fresh on me;

Spir - it of the liv - ing God, Fall a-fresh on me.

Melt me, mold me, Fill me, use me.

Spir - it of the liv - ing God, Fall a-fresh on me.

323 Loving Spirit

OMNI DIE   8.7.8.7

Shirley Erena Murray, 1987

Corner's *Gross Catholisch Gesangbuch*, 1631
Arr. William Smith Rockstro (1823–1895)

1. Lov-ing Spir-it, Ho-ly Spir-it, You have cho-sen me to be;
2. Like a moth-er You en-fold me, Hold my life with-in Your own,
3. Like a fa-ther You pro-tect me, Teach me the dis-cern-ing eye,
4. Lov-ing Spir-it, in Your close-ness I am known and held and blest:

You have drawn me to Your won-der, You have set Your sign on me.
Feed me with Your ver-y bod-y, Form me of Your flesh and bone.
Hoist me up up-on Your shoul-der, Let me see the world from high.
In Your prom-ise is my com-fort, In Your pres-ence I may rest.

Text: Coyright © 1987 by The Hymn Society, Texas Christian University, Fort Worth, TX 76129.
All rights reserved. Used by permission.

♩=60–66

324 Open My Eyes That I May See

Psalm 119:18

OPEN MY EYES   8.8.9.8 with refrain

Clara H. Scott, 1895

Clara H. Scott, 1895

1. O-pen my eyes, that I may see Glimps-es of truth Thou hast for me;
2. O-pen my ears, that I may hear Voic-es of truth Thou send-est clear;
3. O-pen my mouth, and let me bear Glad-ly the warm truth ev-ery-where;

Place in my hands the won-der-ful key That shall un-clasp and set me free.
And while the wave notes fall on my ear, Ev-ery-thing false will dis-ap-pear.
O-pen my heart, and let me pre-pare Love with Thy chil-dren thus to share.

Refrain

Si-lent-ly now I wait for Thee, Read-y, my God, Thy will to see;

eyes,
O-pen my ears, il - lu - mine me, Spir - it di - vine!
heart,

Spirit Divine, Attend Our Prayers 325

NUN DANKET ALL' UND BRINGET EHR'   CM

Andrew Reed, 1829; alt.   Johann Crüger, 1647

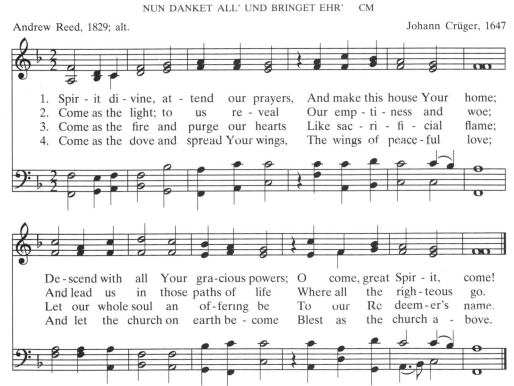

1. Spir - it di - vine, at - tend our prayers, And make this house Your home;
2. Come as the light; to us re - veal Our emp - ti - ness and woe;
3. Come as the fire and purge our hearts Like sac - ri - fi - cial flame;
4. Come as the dove and spread Your wings, The wings of peace - ful love;

De - scend with all Your gra-cious powers; O come, great Spir - it, come!
And lead us in those paths of life Where all the righ-teous go.
Let our whole soul an of-fering be To our Re deem-er's name.
And let the church on earth be - come Blest as the church a - bove.

5. Spirit divine, attend our prayers;
   Make a lost world Your home;
   Descend with all Your gracious powers;
   O come, great Spirit, come!

326 Spirit of God, Descend Upon My Heart

MORECAMBE   10.10.10.10

George Croly, 1854

Frederick Cook Atkinson, 1870

1. Spir - it of God, de - scend up - on my heart;
2. Hast Thou not bid us love Thee, God and King;
3. Teach me to feel that Thou art al - ways nigh;
4. Teach me to love Thee as Thine an - gels love,

Wean it from earth, through all its puls - es move;
All, all Thine own: soul, heart, and strength, and mind?
Teach me the strug - gles of the soul to bear,
One ho - ly pas - sion fill - ing all my frame;

Stoop to my weak - ness, might - y as Thou art,
I see Thy cross, there teach my heart to cling.
To check the ris - ing doubt, the reb - el sigh;
The bap - tism of the heaven-de - scend - ed Dove,

And make me love Thee as I ought to love.
O let me seek Thee, and O let me find!
Teach me the pa - tience of un - an - swered prayer.
My heart an al - tar, and Thy love the flame.

O Word of God Incarnate

327

MUNICH 7.6.7.6 D

William Walsham How, 1867
As in *Psalter Hymnal,* 1987

Neuvermehrtes Meiningisches Gesangbuch, 1693
Adapt. Felix Mendelssohn, 1847

1. O Word of God in-car-nate, O Wis-dom from on high,
   O Truth un-changed, un-chang-ing, O Light of our dark sky:
   We praise You for the ra-diance That from the hal-lowed page,
   A lan-tern to our foot-steps, Shines on from age to age.

2. The church from You, dear Sav-ior, Re-ceived this gift di-vine,
   And still that light is lift-ed On all the earth to shine.
   It is the chart and com-pass That, all life's voy-age through,
   A-mid the rocks and quick-sands, Still guides, O Christ, to You.

3. O make Your church, dear Sav-ior, A lamp of pur-est gold
   To bear be-fore the na-tions Your true light, as of old;
   O teach Your wan-dering pil-grims By this our path to trace,
   Till, clouds and storms thus end-ed, We see You face to face.

328 All Praise to God for Song God Gives

SACRED SONG   8.8.8.8 with refrain

Carlton C. Buck, 1986   Dale Wood, 1986

1. All praise to God for song God gives, For music
2. The word gives both the life and light, And guides us
3. In song let God be glo - ri - fied, For God is
4. All praise to God, whose sa - cred word Has brought good

and a hope that lives; God's sa - cred word is
through the shades of night, So let the mu - sic
a - ble to pro - vide The mu - sic for the
news to all who heard. We wor - ship God and

so pro - found, We sing and let the truth re - sound.
sound God's praise As hymns bring glad - ness to our days.
sing - ers' art As song God plac - es in the heart.
sing with joy, And in - stru - ments of praise em - ploy.

Refrain

God gave us mu - sic, gave us voice; Sing

Ped.

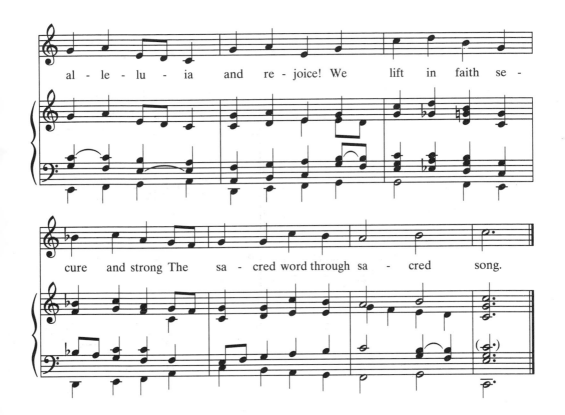

al - le - lu - ia and re - joice! We lift in faith se -

cure and strong The sa - cred word through sa - cred song.

329 Break Thou the Bread of Life

BREAD OF LIFE   6.4.6.4 D

Mary Artemesia Lathbury, 1877; alt.

William Fiske Sherwin, 1877; alt.

1. Break Thou the bread of life, Dear Lord, to me,
2. Bless Thou the truth, dear Lord, Now un - to me,

As Thou didst break the loaves Be - side the sea;
As Thou didst bless the bread By Gal - i - lee;

Be - yond the sa - cred page I seek Thee, Lord;
Then shall all bond - age cease, All fet - ters fall;

My spir - it pants for Thee, O liv - ing Word!
And I shall find my peace, My all in all.

Deep in the Shadows of the Past 330

SHEPHERDS' PIPES   CMD

Brian Wren, 1973

Annabeth McClelland Gay, 1952

1. Deep in the shad-ows of the past, Far out from set-tled lands,
2. While oth-ers bowed to change-less gods They met a mys-ter-y:
3. From A-bra-ham to Naz-a-reth The prom-ise changed and grew,
4. For all the writ-ings that sur-vived, For lead-ers, long a-go,

Some no-mads trav-eled with their God A-cross the des-ert sands.
God with an un-com-plet-ed name, "I am what I will be";
While some, re-mem-ber-ing the past, Re-cord-ed what they knew,
Who sift-ed, chose, and then pre-served The Bi-ble that we know,

The dawn of hope for hu-man-kind Was glimpsed by them a-lone:
And by their tents, a-round their fires, In sto-ry, song, and law
And some, in let-ters or la-ments, In proph-e-cy and praise,
Give thanks, and find its prom-ise yet Our com-fort, strength, and call,

A prom-ise call-ing them a-head, A fu-ture yet un-known.
They praised, re-mem-bered, hand-ed on A past that prom-ised more.
Re-cov-ered, held, and re-ex-pressed New hope for chang-ing days.
The work-ing mod-el for our faith, A-live with hope for all.

331 Thanks to God Whose Word Was Written

WYLDE GREEN   8.7.8.7.4.7

R. T. Brooks, 1954; alt.   Peter Cutts,1966

1. Thanks to God whose word was writ-ten In the Bi-ble's sa-cred page, Rec-ord of the rev-e-la-tion Show-ing God to ev-ery age. God has spo-ken:

2. Thanks to God whose word is pub-lished In the tongues of ev-ery race. See its glo-ry un-di-min-ished By the change of time or place. God has spo-ken:

3. Thanks to God whose Word In-car-nate Heights and depths of life did share. Deeds and words and death and ris-ing, Grace in hu-man form de-clare. God has spo-ken:

4. Thanks to God whose Word is an-swered By the Spir-it's voice with-in. Here we drink of joy un-mea-sured, Life re-deemed from death and sin. God is speak-ing:

Praise God for the liv - ing Word.

Luke 4:16–20

Live Into Hope

332

TRURO LM

Thomas Williams, 1789
Harm. Lowell Mason (1792–1872)

Jane Parker Huber, 1976

1. Live in - to hope of cap - tives freed, Of sight re -
2. Live in - to hope the blind shall see With in - sight
3. Live in - to hope of lib - er - ty, The right to
4. Live in - to hope of cap - tives freed From chains of

gained, the end of greed. The op-pressed shall be the
and with clar - i - ty, Re - mov - ing shades of
speak, the right to be, The right to have one's
fear or want or greed. God now pro - claims our

first to see The year of God's own ju - bi - lee!
pride and fear — A vi - sion of our God brought near.
dai - ly bread, To hear God's word and thus be fed.
full re - lease To faith and hope and joy and peace.

Text: © 1980 Jane Parker Huber; from *A Singing Faith.* Used by permission.

333

Seek Ye First

LAFFERTY   Irregular

Karen Lafferty (b. 1948)

Karen Lafferty (b. 1948)

When Israel Was in Egypt's Land 334

GO DOWN MOSES 8.5.8.5 with refrain

African-American spiritual
Arr. Melva W. Costen, 1989

African-American spiritual

1. When Is-rael was in E-gypt's land, Let my peo-ple go!
2. "Thus saith the Lord," bold Mo-ses said: Let my peo-ple go!
3. "No more shall they in bond-age toil," Let my peo-ple go!

Op-pressed so hard they could not stand, Let my peo-ple go!
"If not, I'll smite your first-born dead," Let my peo-ple go!
"Let them come out with E-gypt's spoil," Let my peo-ple go!

Refrain

Go down, Mo-ses,
Mo-ses, Way down in E-gypt's land,
Go down, go down, Mo-ses,

Tell old Phar-aoh, Let my peo-ple go!

Music: Arrangement © 1990 Melva W. Costen. All rights reserved. Used by permission.

335 Though I May Speak

O WALY WALY   LM

Hal Hopson, 1972

English folk melody
Harm. John Weaver, 1988

1. Though I may speak with brav-est fire, And have the gift to all in-spire, And have not love, my words are vain; As sound-ing brass, and hope-less gain.
2. Though I may give all I pos-sess, And striv-ing so my love pro-fess, But not be given by love with-in, The prof-it soon turns strange-ly thin.
3. Come, Spir-it, come, our hearts con-trol, Our spir-its long to be made whole. Let in-ward love guide ev-ery deed; By this we wor-ship and are freed.

As a Chalice Cast of Gold

336

INWARD LIGHT   7.7.7 D

Thomas H. Troeger, 1984

Carol Doran, 1984

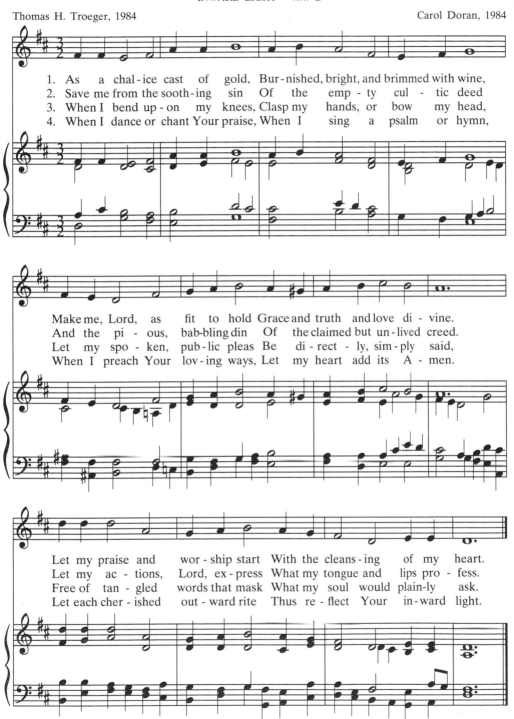

1. As a chal-ice cast of gold, Bur-nished, bright, and brimmed with wine,
2. Save me from the sooth-ing sin Of the emp-ty cul-tic deed
3. When I bend up-on my knees, Clasp my hands, or bow my head,
4. When I dance or chant Your praise, When I sing a psalm or hymn,

Make me, Lord, as fit to hold Grace and truth and love di-vine.
And the pi-ous, bab-bling din Of the claimed but un-lived creed.
Let my spo-ken, pub-lic pleas Be di-rect-ly, sim-ply said,
When I preach Your lov-ing ways, Let my heart add its A-men.

Let my praise and wor-ship start With the cleans-ing of my heart.
Let my ac-tions, Lord, ex-press What my tongue and lips pro-fess.
Free of tan-gled words that mask What my soul would plain-ly ask.
Let each cher-ished out-ward rite Thus re-flect Your in-ward light.

Text and Music: From New Hymns for the Lectionary; © 1985, Oxford University Press, Inc. By permission.

♩=66-72

337 Isaiah the Prophet Has Written of Old

SAMANTHRA 11.8.11.8 D

Joy F. Patterson, 1982

American folk melody
Arr. Alice Parker and Robert Shaw

1. I - sa - iah the proph - et has writ - ten of old How
2. Yet na - tions still prey on the meek of the world, And

God's earth-ly king-dom shall come, In - stead of the thorn tree the
con - flict turns par - ent from child. Your peo - ple de-spoil all the

fir tree shall grow; The wolf shall lie down with the lamb. The
sweet - ness of earth; The brier and the thorn grow wild. The

moun - tains and hills shall break forth in - to song, The
has - ten to bring in Your king - dom on earth, When

peo-ples be led forth in peace, For the earth shall be filled with the
no one shall hurt or de - stroy, When wis - dom and jus - tice shall

knowl - edge of God As the wa - ters cov - er the seas.
reign in the land And Your peo - ple shall go forth in joy.

♪=80–88

Kum ba Yah

338

8.8.8.5

African-American spiritual

African melody

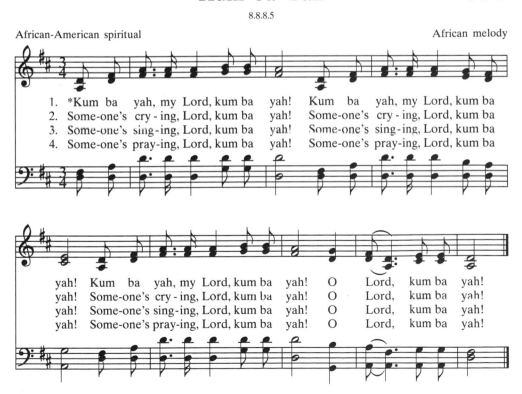

1. *Kum ba yah, my Lord, kum ba yah! Kum ba yah, my Lord, kum ba
2. Some-one's cry - ing, Lord, kum ba yah! Some-one's cry - ing, Lord, kum ba
3. Some-one's sing-ing, Lord, kum ba yah! Some-one's sing-ing, Lord, kum ba
4. Some-one's pray-ing, Lord, kum ba yah! Some-one's pray-ing, Lord, kum ba

yah! Kum ba yah, my Lord, kum ba yah! O Lord, kum ba yah!
yah! Some-one's cry - ing, Lord, kum ba yah! O Lord, kum ba yah!
yah! Some-one's sing-ing, Lord, kum ba yah! O Lord, kum ba yah!
yah! Some-one's pray-ing, Lord, kum ba yah! O Lord, kum ba yah!

* Come by here.

339 Be Thou My Vision

SLANE   10.10.9.10

Ancient Irish poem
Trans. Mary E. Byrne, 1905
Vers. Eleanor Hull, 1912; alt.

Irish ballad
Harm. David Evans, 1927

1. Be Thou my vi - sion, O Lord of my heart;
2. Rich - es I heed not, nor vain, emp - ty praise,
3. Be Thou my wis - dom, and Thou my true word;

Nought be all else to me, save that Thou art—
Thou mine in - her - i - tance, now and al - ways:
I ev - er with Thee and Thou with me, Lord;

Thou my best thought, by day or by night,
Thou and Thou on - ly, first in my heart,
Heart of my own heart, what - ev - er be - fall,

Music: Harmonization from the *Revised Church Hymnary 1927.* Used by permission of Oxford University Press.

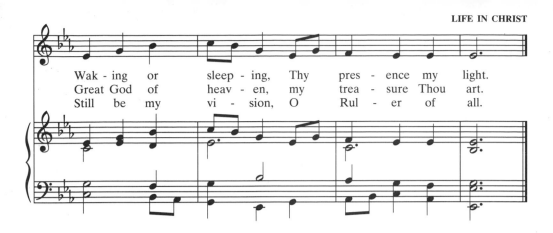

Wak - ing or sleep - ing, Thy pres - ence my light.
Great God of heav - en, my trea - sure Thou art.
Still be my vi - sion, O Rul - er of all.

Eternal Light, Shine in My Heart 340

JACOB LM

Alcuin (c. 735–804)
Para. Christopher Idle (b. 1938)

Jane Manton Marshall (b. 1924)

1. E - ter - nal light, shine in my heart; E - ter - nal hope, lift
2. E - ter - nal life, raise me from death; E - ter - nal bright - ness,
3. Un - til by Your most cost - ly grace, In - vit - ed by Your

up my eyes; E - ter - nal power, be my sup - port;
help me see; E - ter - nal Spir - it, give me breath;
ho - ly word, At last I come be - fore Your face

E - ter - nal wis - dom, make me wise.
E - ter - nal Sav - ior, come to me:
To know You, my e - ter - nal God.

♩=96–104

341 Whak Shil Hahn Nah Eh Kahn Jeung
Blessed Assurance, Jesus Is Mine!

ASSURANCE   9.10.9.9 with refrain

Fanny Jane Crosby, 1873
Transliteration of Korean: Myung Ja Yue, 1989

Phoebe Palmer Knapp, 1873

1. Ye su rul nae ga joo ro mee duh   Sung nyung gwa
2. Ye su keh maat kin nah eh ma um   Sa rahng eh

1. Bless-ed as - sur - ance, Je - sus is mine!   O what a
2. Per - fect sub - mis - sion, per - fect de - light,   Vi - sions of

pee   ro   ssuh kuh dum nah   nee   Seh sahng eh   in   nun
sok   sah   gim tu ru myun   suh   Heen oh sul   ee   bun

fore - taste of glo - ry di - vine!   Heir of sal - va - tion,
rap - ture now burst on my sight;   An - gels, de - scend - ing,

nae young hon   ee   Ha nu reh young gwang noo   ree doh   dah
chun sah dul   gwa   Shin bee hahn whan sahng bo   ree ro   dah

pur - chase of   God,   Born of His Spir - it, washed in His   blood.
bring from a - bove   Ech-oes of mer - cy, whis - pers of   love.

Hooryum
Refrain

Ee go she nah eh kahn jeung ee yo   Ee go she
This is my sto - ry, this is my song,   Prais-ing my

nah eh chan song ee rah   Nah sah nun dong ahn
Sav - ior all the day long;   This is my sto - ry,

ggeun im up see Ye su eh ee rum chan song hah ree
this is my song, Prais-ing my Sav - ior all the day long.

3. Joo ahn eh ees suh jeul guh wuh rah
Ma um eh Poong nahng ee jahm jah
  doh dah
Seh sahng doh up go na doh up go
Sa rahng eh joo mahn bo ee doh dah
Hooryum

3. Perfect submission, all is at rest,
I in my Savior am happy and blest,
Watching and waiting, looking above,
Filled with His goodness, lost in His
  love.
Refrain

342

By Gracious Powers

INTERCESSOR 11.10.11.10

Dietrich Bonhoeffer, 1944
Trans. Fred Pratt Green, 1972

C. Hubert H. Parry, 1904

1. By gra - cious powers so won - der - ful - ly shel - tered,
2. Yet is this heart by its old foe tor - ment - ed,
3. And when this cup You give is filled to brim - ming
4. Yet when a - gain in this same world You give us

And con - fi - dent - ly wait - ing, come what may,
Still e - vil days bring bur - dens hard to bear;
With bit - ter suf - fering, hard to un - der - stand,
The joy we had, the bright - ness of Your sun,

We know that God is with us night and morn - ing
O give our fright - ened souls the sure sal - va - tion
We take it thank - ful - ly and with - out trem - bling,
We shall re - mem - ber all the days we lived through,

And nev - er fails to greet us each new day.
For which, O Lord, You taught us to pre - pare.
Out of so good and so be - loved a hand.
And our whole life shall then be Yours a - lone.

Called as Partners in Christ's Service 343

BEECHER 8.7.8.7 D

Jane Parker Huber, 1981   John Zundel, 1870

1. Called as part-ners in Christ's ser-vice, Called to min-is-tries of grace,
2. Christ's ex-am-ple, Christ's in-spir-ing, Christ's clear call to work and worth,
3. Thus new pat-terns for Christ's mis-sion, In a small or glob-al sense,
4. So God grant us for to-mor-row Ways to or-der hu-man life

We re-spond with deep com-mit-ment Fresh new lines of faith to trace.
Let us fol-low, nev-er fal-tering, Rec-on-cil-ing folk on earth.
Help us bear each oth-er's bur-dens, Break-ing down each wall or fence.
That sur-round each per-son's sor-row With a calm that con-quers strife.

May we learn the art of shar-ing, Side by side and friend with friend,
Men and wom-en, rich-er, poor-er, All God's peo-ple, young and old,
Words of com-fort, words of vi-sion, Words of chal-lenge, said with care,
Make us part-ners in our liv-ing, Our com-pas-sion to in-crease,

E-qual part-ners in our car-ing To ful-fill God's cho-sen end.
Blend-ing hu-man skills to-geth-er Gra-cious gifts from God un-fold.
Bring new power and strength for ac-tion, Make us col-leagues, free and fair.
Mes-sen-gers of faith, thus giv-ing Hope and con-fi-dence and peace.

Text: © 1981 Jane Parker Huber; from *A Singing Faith.* Used by permission.

344 Christ of the Upward Way

SURSUM CORDA (Lomas)   6.4.6.4.10.10

Walter John Mathams, c. 1915; alt.   George Lomas, 1876

1. Christ of the up-ward way, My guide di - vine,
2. Give me the heart to hear Your voice and will,
3. Christ of the up-ward way, My guide di - vine,

Where You have set Your feet May I place mine;
That with - out fault or fear I may ful - fill
Where You have set Your feet May I place mine;

And move and march wher-ev - er You have trod,
Your pur - pose with a glad and ho - ly zest,
And when Your last call comes se - rene and clear,

Keep - ing face for - ward up the hill of God.
Like one who would not bring less than the best.
Calm may my an - swer be, "Lord, I am here."

Dear Lord and Father of Mankind 345

REST   8.6.8.8.6

John Greenleaf Whittier, 1872

Frederick Charles Maker, 1887

1. *Dear Lord and Fa - ther of man - kind, For - give our fool - ish
2. In sim - ple trust like theirs who heard, Be - side the Syr - ian
3. O Sab - bath rest by Gal - i - lee, O calm of hills a -
4. Drop Thy still dews of qui - et - ness, Till all our striv - ings

ways; Re - clothe us in our right - ful mind, In
sea, The gra - cious call - ing of the Lord, Let
bove, Where Je - sus knelt to share with Thee The
cease; Take from our souls the strain and stress, And

pur - er lives Thy ser - vice find, In deep - er rev - erence, praise.
us, like them, with - out a word Rise up and fol - low Thee.
si - lence of e - ter - ni - ty, In - ter - pret - ed by love!
let our or - dered lives con - fess The beau - ty of Thy peace.

*Or "Dear Lord, Creator good and kind."

5. Breathe through the heats of our desire
   Thy coolness and Thy balm;
   Let sense be dumb, let flesh retire;
   Speak through the earthquake, wind, and fire,
   O still, small voice of calm!

Alternate tune: REPTON, 419

Colossians 1:15–18

346 Christ, You Are the Fullness

ARIRANG   Irregular

Vers. Bert Polman, 1986

Korean melody
Harm. Dale Grotenhuis, 1986

1. Christ, You are the full - ness of God, first - born of ev - ery-thing.
2. Since we have been raised with You, Lord, help keep our hearts and minds
3. Help us live in peace as true mem - bers of Your bod - y.

For by You all things were made; You hold them up.
Pure and set on things that build Your rule o'er all the earth.
Let Your word dwell rich - ly in us as we teach and sing.

You are head of the church, which is Your bod - y.
All our life is now hid - den with You in God.
Thanks and praise be to God through You, Lord Je - sus.

First - born from the dead, You in all things are su - preme!
When You come a - gain, we will share Your glo - ry.
In what-e'er we do let Your name re - ceive the praise!

Forgive Our Sins as We Forgive 347

DETROIT CM

Rosamond E. Herklots, 1969, 1983

Supplement to Kentucky Harmony, 1820
Harm. Margaret W. Mealy (b. 1922)

1. "For - give our sins as we for - give," You taught us, Lord, to pray,
2. How can Your par - don reach and bless The un - for - giv - ing heart
3. In blaz - ing light Your cross re - veals The truth we dim - ly knew:
4. Lord, cleanse the depths with - in our souls And bid re - sent-ment cease.

But You a - lone can grant us grace To live the words we say.
That broods on wrongs and will not let Old bit - ter - ness de - part?
What triv - ial debts are owed to us, How great our debt to You!
Then, bound to all in bonds of love, Our lives will spread Your peace.

348 Christian Women, Christian Men

HUNTSVILLE   Irregular

Dorothy Diemer Hendry, 1986

Emma Lou Diemer, 1986

1. Chris-tian wom - en, Chris-tian men, Have we ears to hear
2. Down a grim - y cit - y street Have we eyes to see
3. When Sa - tan - ic gloom as-sails, Have we strength to hold
4. Chris-tian wom - en, Chris-tian men, Have we hearts to love

The cry - ing of a home-less child Hun-gry and in fear?
The fac - es of the aged and ill Lost in pov - er - ty?
The for - tress of our liv - ing faith Till God's day dawns gold?
Our neigh-bors as we love our-selves, Serv-ing God a - bove?

In the name of Je - sus, yes, We have ears to hear!
In the name of Je - sus, yes, We have eyes to see!
In the name of Je - sus, yes, We have strength to hold!
In the name of Je - sus, yes, We have hearts to love!

* *May be sung by leader.*
** *May be sung as a response.*

Text: © 1990 Dorothy Diemer Hendry. Used by permission.
Music: © 1990 Emma Lou Diemer. Used by permission.

In the name of Je - sus, yes, We hear! We hear!
In the name of Je - sus, yes, We see! We see!
In the name of Je - sus, yes, We hold! We hold!
In the name of Je - sus, yes, We love! We love!

Matthew 6:9

Let All Who Pray the Prayer Christ Taught 349

CHESHIRE CM

Thomas H. Troeger, 1985

Este's *Psalmes*, 1592; alt.

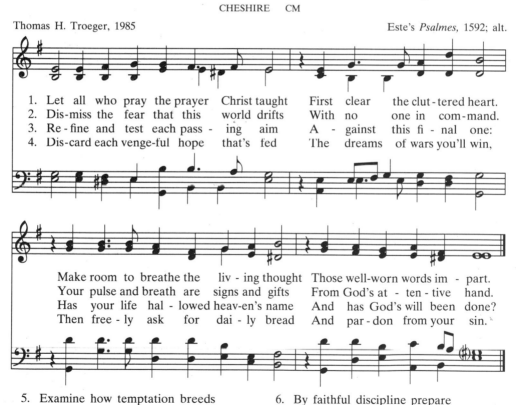

1. Let all who pray the prayer Christ taught First clear the clut-tered heart.
2. Dis-miss the fear that this world drifts With no one in com-mand.
3. Re - fine and test each pass - ing aim A - gainst this fi - nal one:
4. Dis-card each venge-ful hope that's fed The dreams of wars you'll win,

Make room to breathe the liv - ing thought Those well-worn words im - part.
Your pulse and breath are signs and gifts From God's at - ten - tive hand.
Has your life hal - lowed heav-en's name And has God's will been done?
Then free - ly ask for dai - ly bread And par - don from your sin.

5. Examine how temptation breeds
   Inside the mind's dark maze,
   Acknowledging that your life needs
   Deliverance from its ways.

6. By faithful discipline prepare
   An inward holy space
   That when you offer Jesus' prayer
   Your heart may fill with grace.

Text: From New Songs of Praise Book 2; © 1986, Oxford University Press. By permission.

350 Fill My Cup

FILL MY CUP   8.7.8.7 with refrain

Isaiah Jones, Jr., 1969   Isaiah Jones, Jr., 1969

Fill my cup, let it o-ver-flow;

Fill my cup, let it o-ver-flow; Fill my cup, let it

o-ver-flow; let it o-ver-flow with love. love.

1. Lord, let me be Your in-stru-ment, Spread-ing sun-shine in the land; Let peo-ple see Your works in me; Help me live the best I can.

2. It's my de-sire to live for You And to al-ways walk up-right; Give me the strength to face each day; Stay with me through each dark night.

351 Give to Me, Lord, a Thankful Heart

GATESCARTH 8.6.8.8.6

Caryl Micklem, 1973

Caryl Micklem, 1973

1. Give to me, Lord, a thank-ful heart And a dis-cern-ing
2. When, in the rush of days, my will Is hab-it-bound and
3. By Your di-vine and ur-gent claim, And by Your hu-man
4. Je-sus, with all Your church I long To see Your king-dom

mind; Give, as I play the Chris-tian's part, The strength to
slow, Help me to keep in vi-sion still What love and
face, Kin-dle our sink-ing hearts to flame, And as You
come: Show me Your way of right-ing wrong And turn-ing

fin-ish what I start And act on what I find.
power and peace can fill A life that trusts in You.
teach the world Your name Let it be-come Your place.
sor-row in-to song Un-til You bring me home.

Great Are Your Mercies, O My Maker   352

SONG OF THE HOE   Irregular

Tzu-chen Chao, 1931
Trans. Frank W. Price, 1953

Chinese folk song
Harm. W. H. Wong, 1977

1. Great are Your mer - cies, O my Mak - er,
2. Be not so anx - ious, O dis - ci - ples,
3. Birds of the air fly here and yon - der,
4. Could Sol - o - mon in all his glo - ry

Food and rai - ment You free - ly be - stow.
What you dai - ly eat and what you wear.
Lil - ies bloom, ar - rayed by na - ture thus;
Match these bril - liant birds and love - ly flowers?

Let me praise You al - ways, Serve You all my days.
Our Mak - er sees and knows All our wants and woes.
They sow not, nor reap in, Nei - ther do they spin.
Dis - ci - ples, do not fret; God's love fails not yet.

You the spring wind, I the grass; On me blow!
Hum - bly let us work and trust God's great care.
Yet our Mak - er cares for them. More for us!
This world is made for your home, Yours and ours.

353 Great God, Your Love Has Called Us Here

DAS NEUGEBORNE KINDELEIN   8.8.8.8.8.8.8

Brian Wren, 1973   Melchior Vulpius, 1609

1. Great God, Your love has called us here As we, by
2. We come with self - in - flict - ed pains Of bro - ken
3. Great God, in Christ You call our name And then re -
4. Then take the towel, and break the bread, And hum - ble
5. Great God, in Christ You set us free Your life to

love, for love were made. Your liv - ing like - ness still we
trust and cho - sen wrong, Half-free, half - bound by in - ner
ceive us as Your own Not through some mer - it, right, or
us, and call us friends. Suf - fer and serve till all are
live, Your joy to share. Give us Your Spir - it's lib - er -

bear, Though marred, dis - hon - ored, dis - o - beyed. We come, with
chains, By so - cial forc - es swept a - long, By powers and
claim But by Your gra - cious love a - lone. We strain to
fed And show how grand - ly love in - tends To work till
ty To turn from guilt and dull de - spair And of - fer

all our heart and mind Your call to hear, Your love to find.
sys - tems close con - fined Yet seek-ing hope for hu - man-kind.
glimpse Your mer - cy seat And find You kneel - ing at our feet.
all cre - a - tion sings, To fill all worlds, to crown all things.
all that faith can do While love is mak - ing all things new.

Guide My Feet

354

GUIDE MY FEET   8.8.8.10

African-American spiritual

African-American spiritual
Harm. Wendell Whalum (1932–1987)

1. Guide my feet
2. Hold my hand
3. Stand by me
4. I'm Your child

while I run this race,

yes, my Lord!

Guide my feet
Hold my hand
Stand by me
I'm Your child

while I run this race,

yes, my Lord!

Guide my feet
Hold my hand
Stand by me
I'm Your child

while I run this race, For I

don't want to run this race in vain! (race in vain!)

5. Search my heart . . .

6. Guide my feet . . .

Music: Harmonization © by the estate of Wendell Whalum. Used by permission.

Wotanin Waste Nahon Po
355 Hear the Good News of Salvation

1 Corinthians 15:3

NETTLETON 8.7.8.7 D

Native American (Dakota)
John B. Renville, 1879
Trans. Emma Tibbets, 1955
Vers. Jane Parker Huber, 1989

Wyeth's *Repository of Sacred Music,* 1813

1. Wo - tan - in wa - ste na - hon po, Je - sus he wa - i - hdu - sna:
2. Wo - a - hta - ni kin e - ca - mon, Hdu - ha Je - sus si - ha en,

1. Hear the good news of sal - va - tion: Je - sus died to show God's love.
2. All the sins I have com - mit - ted To my Sav - ior now I bring.

To - wa - o - si - da kin tan - ka, He de - han i - yo - ma - hi.
Kun i - wa - hpa - mda wa - ce - ya, Je - sus on - śi - ma - da ce.

Such great kind - ness! Such great mer - cy! Come to us from heaven a - bove.
I bow down with tears of an - guish; Christ for - gives and so I sing:

Je - sus Christ wa - ste - wa - da - ka, Je - sus Christ ni - ma - yan: Han, Wa -
Je - sus Christ, how much I love You! Je - sus Christ, You save from sin!

ste - wa - da - ke a - ma - ton - we Is e - ya wa - ste - ma - da.
How I love You! Look up - on me. Love me still and cleanse with - in.

Come, Thou Fount of Every Blessing 356

Robert Robinson, c. 1758

1. Come, Thou Fount of every blessing,
   Tune my heart to sing Thy grace;
   Streams of mercy, never ceasing,
   Call for songs of loudest praise.
   Teach me some melodious sonnet,
   Sung by flaming tongues above;
   Praise the mount! I'm fixed upon it,
   Mount of God's unchanging love!

2. Here I raise my Ebenezer,
   Hither by Thy help I'm come;
   And I hope, by Thy good pleasure,
   Safely to arrive at home.

Jesus sought me when a stranger,
Wandering from the fold of God;
He, to rescue me from danger,
Interposed His precious blood.

3. O to grace how great a debtor
   Daily I'm constrained to be!
   Let that grace now, like a fetter,
   Bind my wandering heart to Thee:
   Prone to wander, Lord, I feel it,
   Prone to leave the God I love;
   Here's my heart, O take and seal it,
   Seal it for Thy courts above.

Tune: NETTLETON, opposite.

O Master, Let Me Walk with Thee 357

Washington Gladden, 1879   MARYTON LM   Henry Percy Smith, 1874

1. O Master, let me walk with Thee In lowly paths of service free; Tell me Thy secret; help me bear The strain of toil, the fret of care.

2. Help me the slow of heart to move By some clear, winning word of love; Teach me the wayward feet to stay, And guide them in the homeward way.

3. Teach me Thy patience; still with Thee In closer, dearer company, In work that keeps faith sweet and strong, In trust that triumphs over wrong.

4. In hope that sends a shining ray Far down the future's broadening way; In peace that only Thou canst give, With Thee, O Master, let me live.

358 Help Us Accept Each Other

BARONITA 7.6.7.6 D

Fred Kaan, 1975

Doreen Potter, 1975

1. Help us ac - cept each oth - er As Christ ac - cept-ed us;
2. Teach us, O Lord, Your les - sons, As in our dai - ly life
3. Let Your ac - cep - tance change us, So that we may be moved
4. Lord, for to - day's en - coun - ters With all who are in need,

Teach us as sis - ter, broth-er, Each per - son to em - brace.
We strug - gle to be hu - man And search for hope and faith.
In liv - ing sit - u - a - tions To do the truth in love;
Who hun - ger for ac - cep-tance, For righ - teous - ness and bread,

Be pres - ent, Lord, a - mong us And bring us to be - lieve
Teach us to care for peo - ple, For all, not just for some,
To prac - tice Your ac - cep-tance Un - til we know by heart
We need new eyes for see - ing, New hands for hold - ing on:

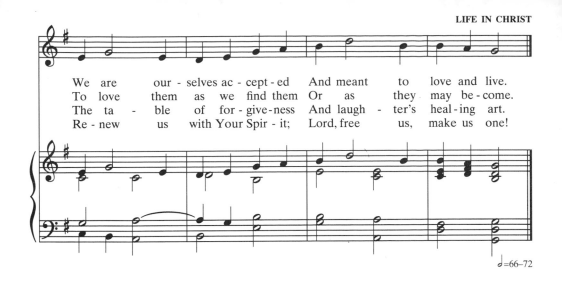

We are our-selves ac-cept-ed And meant to love and live.
To love them as we find them Or as they may be-come.
The ta-ble of for-give-ness And laugh-ter's heal-ing art.
Re-new us with Your Spir-it; Lord, free us, make us one!

♩=66–72

More Love to Thee, O Christ 359

MORE LOVE TO THEE   6.4.6.4.6.6.4.4

Elizabeth Payson Prentiss, 1856   William Howard Doane, 1870

1. More love to Thee, O Christ, More love to Thee! Hear Thou the
2. Once earth-ly joy I craved, Sought peace and rest; Now Thee a-
3. Then shall my lat-est breath Whis-per Thy praise; This be the

prayer I make On bend-ed knee. This is my ear-nest plea:
lone I seek, Give what is best. This all my prayer shall be:
part-ing cry My heart shall raise. This still its prayer shall be:

More love, O Christ, to Thee, More love to Thee, More love to Thee!

360 Hope of the World

Georgia Harkness, 1954

DONNE SECOURS   11.10.11.10

Genevan Psalter, 1551

1. Hope of the world, Thou Christ of great com-pas-sion,
   Speak to our fear-ful hearts by con-flict rent.
   Save us, Thy peo-ple, from con-sum-ing pas-sion,
   Who by our own false hopes and aims are spent.

2. Hope of the world, God's gift from high-est heav-en,
   Bring-ing to hun-gry souls the bread of life,
   Still let Thy Spir-it un-to us be giv-en
   To heal earth's wounds and end our bit-ter strife.

3. Hope of the world, a-foot on dust-y high-ways,
   Show-ing to wan-dering souls the path of light;
   Walk Thou be-side us lest the tempt-ing by-ways
   Lure us a-way from Thee to end-less night.

4. Hope of the world, who by Thy cross didst save us
   From death and deep de-spair, from sin and guilt;
   We ren-der back the love Thy mer-cy gave us;
   Take Thou our lives and use them as Thou wilt.

5. Hope of the world, O Christ, o'er death vic-to-rious,
   Who by this sign didst con-quer grief and pain,
   We would be faith-ful to Thy gos-pel glo-rious:
   Thou art our Lord! Thou dost for-ev-er reign!

How Firm a Foundation

361

FOUNDATION   11.11.11.11

"K" in *A Selection of Hymns*, 1787
Ed. John Rippon; alt.

American folk melody
Funk's *Genuine Church Music*, 1832

1. How firm a foun - da - tion, ye saints of the Lord,
2. "Fear not, I am with thee, O be not dis - mayed,
3. "When through the deep wa - ters I call thee to go,
4. "When through fi - ery tri - als thy path - way shall lie,

Is laid for your faith in God's ex - cel - lent Word!
For I am thy God, and will still give thee aid;
The riv - ers of sor - row shall not o - ver - flow;
My grace, all - suf - fi - cient, shall be thy sup - ply;

What more can be said than to you God hath said,
I'll strength - en thee, help thee, and cause thee to stand,
For I will be near thee, thy trou - bles to bless,
The flame shall not hurt thee; I on - ly de - sign

To you who for ref - uge to Je - sus have fled?
Up - held by My righ - teous, om - nip - o - tent hand.
And sanc - ti - fy to thee thy deep - est dis - tress.
Thy dross to con - sume, and thy gold to re - fine.

5. "The soul that on Jesus hath leaned for repose,
   I will not, I will not desert to its foes;
   That soul, though all hell should endeavor to shake,
   I'll never, no, never, no, never forsake."

362   I Love the Lord, Who Heard My Cry

CM

Isaac Watts, 1719

African-American spiritual
Arr. Richard Smallwood, 1975

1. I love the Lord,   who heard my   cry
2. I love the Lord,   who heard my   cry

And pit - ied   ev -   ery   groan.
And chased my   grief   a -   way.

Long as I   live   and trou-bles   rise,
O   let my   heart   no more de - spair

I'll has - ten   to   God's throne.
While I have   breath   to   pray.

I Want Jesus to Walk with Me

SOJOURNER   Irregular

African-American spiritual   African-American spiritual

1. I want Je - sus to walk with me; (Walk with me)
2. In my tri - als, Lord, walk with me;
3. When I'm in trou - ble, Lord, walk with me; When

I want Je - sus to walk with me; (Walk with me)
In my tri - als, Lord, walk with me;
I'm in trou - ble, Lord, walk with me;

All a - long my pil - grim jour - ney,
When my heart is al - most break - ing,
When my head is bowed in sor - row,

1.2.3. Lord, I want Je - sus to walk with me. (with me)

Music: Arrangement © 1990 Westminster/John Knox Press.

364 I Sing a Song of the Saints of God

GRAND ISLE   Irregular

Lesbia Scott, 1929; adapted

John Henry Hopkins, 1940
As in *The Hymnal 1940*

1. I sing a song of the saints of God, Pa - tient and
2. They loved their Lord so dear, so dear, And God's love
3. They lived not on - ly in a - ges past, There are hun - dreds of

brave and true, Who toiled and fought and lived and died
made them strong; And they fol - lowed the right, for Je - sus' sake,
thou - sands still; The world is bright with the joy - ous saints

For the Lord they loved and knew. And one was a
The whole of their good lives long. And one was a
Who love to do Je - sus' will. You can meet them in

doc - tor, and one was a queen, And one was a shep - herd-ess
sol - dier, and one was a priest, And one was slain by a
school, or in lanes, or at sea, In church, or in trains, or in

on the green: They were all of them saints of
fierce wild beast: And there's not an - y rea - son,
shops, or at tea; For the saints of God are just

God, and I mean, God help - ing, to be one too.
no, not the least, Why I should - n't be one too.
folk like me, And I mean to be one too.

♩=58–63

365 Jesus, Priceless Treasure

JESU, MEINE FREUDE   6.6.5.6.6.5.7.8.6

Johann Franck, 1650
Trans. Catherine Winkworth, 1863

Johann Crüger, 1653
Harm. Johann Sebastian Bach, 1723

1. Je - sus, price - less trea - sure, Source of pur - est plea - sure,
2. In Thine arm I rest me; Foes who would op - press me
3. Hence, all thoughts of sad - ness! For the Lord of glad - ness,

Tru - est friend to me; Long my heart hath pant - ed, Till it well - nigh
Can-not reach me here. Though the earth be shak - ing, Ev - ery heart be
Je - sus, en - ters in: Those who love the Fa - ther, Though the storms may

faint - ed, Thirst-ing af - ter Thee. Thine I am, O spot-less Lamb,
quak - ing, God dis - pels our fear; Sin and hell in con - flict fell
gath - er, Still have peace with - in; Yea, what-e'er we here must bear,

I will suf - fer nought to hide Thee, Ask for nought be - side Thee.
With their heav-iest storms as - sail us: Je - sus will not fail us.
Still in Thee lies pur - est plea - sure, Je - sus, price - less trea - sure!

Jesus, Thy Boundless Love to Me 366

ST. CATHERINE   8.8.8.8.8.8

Paul Gerhardt, 1653
Trans. John Wesley, c. 1739; alt.

Henri Frederick Hemy, 1864
Alt. James George Walton, 1874

1. Je - sus, Thy bound - less love to me No thought can reach, no tongue de - clare; O knit my thank - ful heart to Thee, And reign with - out a ri - val there! Thine whol - ly, Thine a - lone, I'd live, My - self to Thee en - tire - ly give.

2. O grant that noth - ing in my soul May dwell, but Thy pure love a - lone; O may Thy love pos - sess me whole, My joy, my trea - sure, and my crown! All cold - ness from my heart re - move; May ev - ery act, word, thought be love.

3. O Love, how gra - cious is Thy way! All fear be - fore Thy pres - ence flies; Care, an - guish, sor - row melt a - way, Wher - e'er Thy heal - ing beams a - rise. O Je - sus, noth - ing may I see, Noth - ing de - sire, or seek, but Thee.

367 Jesu, Jesu, Fill Us with Your Love

CHEREPONI   Irregular with refrain

Ghanaian folk song
Trans. Tom Colvin, 1969

Ghanaian folk melody
Adapt. Tom Colvin, 1963
Arr. Jane Marshall, 1982

Je - su, Je - su, fill us with Your love, Show

Fine

us how to serve the neigh-bors we have from You.

1. Kneels at the feet of His friends, Si - lent - ly wash - es their
2. Neigh-bors are rich and poor, Var - ied in col - or and
3. These are the ones we should serve, These are the ones we should
4. Lov - ing puts us on our knees, Serv - ing as though we are
5. Kneel at the feet of our friends, Si - lent - ly wash - ing their

D.C.

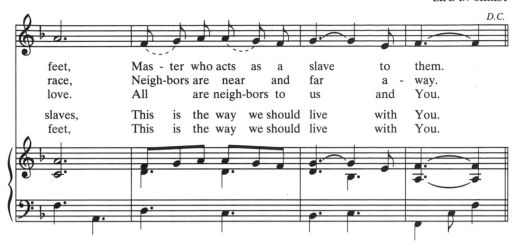

feet,	Mas - ter who acts as a slave to them.
race,	Neigh-bors are near and far a - way.
love.	All are neigh-bors to us and You.
slaves,	This is the way we should live with You.
feet,	This is the way we should live with You.

I've Got Peace Like a River 368

African-American spiritual   7.7.11   African-American spiritual

1. I've got peace like a riv - er, I've got peace like a
2. I've got joy like a foun-tain, I've got joy like a
3. I've got love like an o - cean, I've got love like an

riv - er, I've got peace like a riv - er in - a my
foun-tain, I've got joy like a foun-tain in - a my
o - cean, I've got love like an o - cean in - a my

soul.   I've got riv - er in - a my soul.
soul.   I've got foun-tain in - a my soul.
soul.   I've got o - cean in - a my soul.

369 I'm Gonna Live So God Can Use Me

I'M GONNA LIVE   Irregular

African-American spiritual

African-American spiritual
Arr. Wendell Whalum (1932–1987)

1. I'm gon-na live so (live so)
2. I'm gon-na work so (work so) God can use me   an-y - where, Lord,
3. I'm gon-na pray so (pray so)
4. I'm gon-na sing so (sing so)

an-y - time!   I'm gon-na live so (live so)
(an-y - time!) I'm gon-na work so (work so) God can
                      I'm gon-na pray so (pray so)
                      I'm gon-na sing so (sing so)

use   me   an-y - where, Lord,   an-y - time!
                      (my   Lord,)   (an-y - time!)

Music: Arrangement © by the estate of Wendell Whalum. Used by permission.

Just as I Am, Without One Plea 370

WOODWORTH LM

William Batchelder Bradbury, 1849
Harm. *The Hymnbook*, 1955

Charlotte Elliott, 1834

1. Just as I am, with-out one plea But that Thy
2. Just as I am, though tossed a-bout With man-y a
3. Just as I am, Thou wilt re-ceive, Wilt wel-come,
4. Just as I am, Thy love un-known Has bro-ken

blood was shed for me, And that Thou biddest me
con - flict, man - y a doubt, Fight - ings and fears with -
par - don, cleanse, re - lieve; Be - cause Thy prom - ise
ev - ery bar - rier down; Now to be Thine, yea,

come to Thee,
in, with - out,
I be - lieve, O Lamb of God, I come, I come!
Thine a - lone,

Music: Harmonization copyright, MCMLV, by John Ribble; renewed 1983; from *The Hymnbook*, published by Westminster Press.

371 Lift High the Cross

CRUCIFER 10.10 with refrain

George William Kitchin (1827–1912)
Rev. by Michael Robert Newbolt, 1916; alt.

Sidney Hugo Nicholson, 1916
Desc. Richard Proulx (b. 1937)

Lift high the cross, the love of Christ pro - claim

Till all the world a - dore His sa - cred name.

Till all the world a - dore His sa - cred name.

Fine

1. Come, Chris - tians, fol - low where our Sav - ior trod,
2. Each new - born ser - vant of the Cru - ci - fied
3. O Lord, once lift - ed on the glo - rious tree,
4. So shall our song of tri - umph ev - er be:

Repeat Refrain

The Lamb vic - to - rious, Christ, the Son of God.
Bears on the brow the seal of Christ who died.
Your death has brought us life e - ter - nal - ly.
Praise to the Cru - ci - fied for vic - to - ry.

Lord, I Want to Be a Christian

I WANT TO BE A CHRISTIAN   Irregular

African-American spiritual   African-American spiritual

1. Lord, I want to be a Chris-tian In-a my heart, in-a my heart,
2. Lord, I want to be more lov-ing In-a my heart, in-a my heart,
3. Lord, I want to be more ho-ly In-a my heart, in-a my heart,
4. Lord, I want to be like Je-sus In-a my heart, in-a my heart,

Lord, I want to be a Chris-tian In-a my heart.
Lord, I want to be more lov-ing In-a my heart.
Lord, I want to be more ho-ly In-a my heart.
Lord, I want to be like Je-sus In-a my heart.

In-a my heart, In-a my heart, In-a my heart, In-a my heart,

Lord, I want to be a Chris-tian In-a my heart.
Lord, I want to be more lov-ing In-a my heart.
Lord, I want to be more ho-ly In-a my heart.
Lord, I want to be like Je-sus In-a my heart.

Kahm Kahm hahn Bom Sanaoon
Lonely the Boat

373

BAI   Irregular

Helen Kim, 1927
Transliteration: Samuel Yun, 1989
Trans. Hae Jong Kim (b. 1935)
Vers. Hope C. Kawashima, 1987

Dong Hoon Lee, 1967

1. Kahm Kahm hahn bom Sa - na - oon pa - ram bu -
2. Pee pah rah mee moo - sup keh mo - la

1. Lone - ly the boat, sail - ing at sea, tossed on a
2. Strong winds a - rose in all their rage, toss - ing the

ool thae Mahn-kyung chang-pa mahng - mahng
chi - koh Gue nol lan mool keu eun pa-doh

cold, storm-y night; Cru - el the sea which seemed so wide,
ti - ny lone boat; Waves bil - lowing high, toss - ing the boat,

hahn pa - da eh Oe ro un
yee il tae eh Juh bat sa

with waves so high. This sin - gle ship
lost and a - float. The sail - or stood

bae hahn chuch - i thuh - na ga ni Ah - we
kong uh - zul jool mo - la hah nee Oh - ka
sailed the deep sea, straight in - to the gale; O Lord,
all a - lone, won - dering what to do; O Lord,

tae ha koo nah we - tae ha koo nah.
ryun ha koo na ka - ryun ha koo na.
great is the per - il, dan - gers do all as - sail.
so help - less was he, won - der - ing what to do.

3. Jeul mahng joong eh keuhsa kong
   thuh ul myon seueu do
   Hahn jool ki ae par al keun bit
   poko suh
   Pae ahn eh do Hah Nah Nim
   Kehshim mit koh
   Ohki do all lin dah ki do all lin
   dah.

4. Ah buh jee yuh yee geoi yin
   koopuh posah
   Sung nahn poong rahng jahan jahn
   keh hahshigo
   Yee pool ssang hahn yinsang eul
   sahli so suh
   Ohwoo ree Hah Nah Nim wooree
   Hah Nah Nim.

5. Mo jin pah ram tdoh hum hahn
   keunmool kyuli
   Jeh ah moo ree sungnae uh duh up
   chuh do
   Kwon neung eh sohn keuhno reul
   juheu si nee
   Ohmar keun pa da rah markeun pa
   da rah.

3. Trembling with fear, deep in despair,
   looking for help all around,
   The sailor saw light from above.
   "Help can be found;
   My God is here in my small boat,
   standing by my side;
   O I trust in the Savior; now in
   my life abide.

4. "Pleading for Your mercy, O Lord,
   even a sinner like me;
   Command, O Lord, calm to the sea,
   as in Galilee!
   Please save my life from all danger,
   grant a peaceful life;
   O please be merciful, Lord, in times
   of calm and strife.

5. "Storms in our lives, cruel and cold,
   surely will arise again,
   Threatening lives, threatening us on
   life's wild sea.
   Powerful and great, God's hand is
   there, firmly in control.
   O Lord, calm peace comes from You,
   peace comes to my lone soul."

374 Lord, Make Us Servants of Your Peace

DICKINSON COLLEGE   LM

Francis of Assisi (1181/2–1226)
Para. James Quinn (b. 1919)

Lee Hastings Bristol, Jr., 1962

1. Lord, make us ser - vants of Your peace: Where there is
2. Where all is doubt, may we sow faith; Where all is
3. Je - sus, our Lord, may we not seek To be con -
4. May we not look for love's re - turn, But seek to

hate, may we sow love; Where there is hurt, may we for -
gloom, may we sow hope; Where all is night, may we sow
soled, but to con - sole, Nor look to un - der - stand-ing
love un - self - ish - ly, For in our giv - ing we re -

give; Where there is strife, may we make one.
light; Where all is tears, may we sow joy.
hearts, But look for hearts to un - der - stand.
ceive, And in for - giv - ing are for - given.

5. Dying, we live, and are reborn
   Through death's dark night to endless day:
   Lord, make us servants of Your peace
   To wake at last in heaven's light.

♩=104–112

Text: © James Quinn, S.J. Reprinted by permission of Geoffrey Chapman, a division of Cassell Publishers Ltd., London.
Music: Copyright © 1962, Theodore Presser Co. Used by permission of the publisher.

Lord of All Good

TOULON   10.10.10.10

375

Albert F. Bayly, 1962; alt.

Genevan Psalter, 1551
Adapt. from Genevan 124

1. Lord of all good, our gifts we bring to You;
2. We give our minds to un-der-stand Your ways,
3. Fa-ther, whose boun-ty all cre-a-tion shows;

Use them Your ho-ly pur-pose to ful-fill;
Hands, eyes, and voice to serve Your great de-sign,
Christ, by whose will-ing sac-ri-fice we live;

To-kens of love and pledg-es brought a-new,
Heart with the flame of Your own love a-blaze,
Spir-it, from whom all life in full-ness flows:

That our whole life is of-fered to Your will.
Till for Your glo-ry all our powers com-bine.
To You with grate-ful hearts our-selves we give.

♩=92–100

376 Love Divine, All Loves Excelling

HYFRYDOL   8.7.8.7 D

Charles Wesley, 1747   Rowland Hugh Prichard, 1831

1. Love di - vine, all loves ex - cel - ling, Joy of heaven, to
2. Breathe, O breathe Thy lov - ing Spir - it In - to ev - ery
3. Come, Al - might - y to de - liv - er, Let us all Thy
4. Fin - ish, then, Thy new cre - a - tion; Pure and spot - less

earth come down, Fix in us Thy hum - ble dwell - ing,
trou - bled breast! Let us all in Thee in - her - it,
life re - ceive; Sud - den - ly re - turn, and nev - er,
let us be; Let us see Thy great sal - va - tion

All Thy faith - ful mer - cies crown! Je - sus, Thou art all com -
Let us find the prom - ised rest; Take a - way the love of
Nev - er - more Thy tem - ples leave. Thee we would be al - ways
Per - fect - ly re - stored in Thee; Changed from glo - ry in - to

pas - sion, Pure, un - bound - ed love Thou art; Vis - it us with
sin - ning; Al - pha and O - me - ga be; End of faith, as
bless - ing, Serve Thee as Thy hosts a - bove; Pray, and praise Thee
glo - ry, Till in heaven we take our place, Till we cast our

Thy sal - va - tion, En - ter ev - ery trem-bling heart.
its be - gin - ning, Set our hearts at lib - er - ty.
with - out ceas - ing, Glo - ry in Thy per - fect love.
crowns be - fore Thee, Lost in won - der, love, and praise.

Alternate tune: BEECHER, 343

Tú Has Venido a la Orilla
Lord, You Have Come to the Lakeshore 377

PESCADOR DE HOMBRES   8.10.10 with refrain

Cesáreo Gabaráin, 1979
Trans. Gertrude Suppe, George Lockwood,
and Raquel Achón, 1988; alt.

Cesáreo Gabaráin
Harm. Skinner Chávez-Melo

1. Tú   has ve - ni-do a la o - ri - lla,
2. Tú   sa - bes bien lo que ten - go:

1. You   have come up to the lake - shore,
2. You   know that I own so lit - tle,

No has bus - ca - do   ni a sa - bios ni a ri - cos,   Tan
En mi bar - ca   no hay o - ro ni es-pa - das,   Tan

Look - ing nei - ther   for wise nor for wealth - y.   You
In my boat there's   no mon-ey nor weap - ons,   You'll

só - lo quie - res   que yo te si - ga.
só - lo re - des   y mi tra - ba - jo.

on - ly want - ed   that I should fol - low.
on - ly find there   my nets and la - bor.

Estribillo
Refrain

Se - ñor,   me has mi - ra - do_a los o - jos

O Lord,   with Your eyes You have searched me,

y son - rien - do   has di - cho mi nom - bre;

And, while smil - ing,   have called out my name.

en la_a - re - na   he de - ja - do mi bar - ca;

Now my boat's left   on the shore - line be - hind me,

jun - to_a ti   bus-ca - ré   o - tro   mar.
Now with You   I will seek oth-er   seas.

3. Tú necesitas mis manos,
   Mi cansancio que_a otros descanse,
   Amor que quiera seguir amando.
   Estribillo

4. Tú, pescador de_otros mares,
   Ansia_eterna de almas que_esperan,
   Amigo bueno, que_así me llamas.
   Estribillo

3. You need the caring of my hands.
   Through my tiredness, may others find resting.
   You need a love that just goes on loving.
   Refrain

4. You, who have fished other oceans,
   Ever longed for by souls that are waiting,
   My dear and good friend, as thus You call me.
   Refrain

Make Me a Captive, Lord 378

ST. BRIDE   SM

George Matheson, 1890

Samuel Howard, 1762
Harm. David Evans, 1927

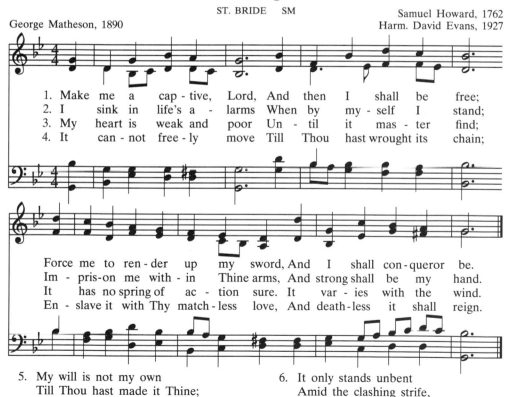

1. Make me a cap - tive, Lord, And then I shall be free;
2. I sink in life's a - larms When by my - self I stand;
3. My heart is weak and poor Un - til it mas - ter find;
4. It can - not free - ly move Till Thou hast wrought its chain;

Force me to ren - der up my sword, And I shall con - queror be.
Im - pris-on me with - in Thine arms, And strong shall be my hand.
It has no spring of ac - tion sure. It var - ies with the wind.
En - slave it with Thy match - less love, And death-less it shall reign.

5. My will is not my own
   Till Thou hast made it Thine;
   If it would reach a monarch's throne,
   It must its crown resign;

6. It only stands unbent
   Amid the clashing strife,
   When on Thy bosom it has leant,
   And found in Thee its life.

Alternate harmonization: 198

Music: Harmonization from the *Revised Church Hymnary 1927;* by permission of Oxford University Press.

379 My Hope Is Built on Nothing Less

SOLID ROCK   LM with refrain

Edward Mote, c. 1834

William Batchelder Bradbury, 1863

1. My hope is built on noth-ing less Than Je-sus' blood and
2. When dark-ness veils His love-ly face, I rest on His un-
3. His oath, His cov-e-nant, His blood Sup-port me in the
4. When He shall come with trum-pet sound, O may I then in

righ-teous-ness; I dare not trust the sweet-est frame, But whol-ly
chang-ing grace; In ev-ery high and storm-y gale, My an-chor
whelm-ing flood; When all a-round my soul gives way, He then is
Him be found, Dressed in His righ-teous-ness a-lone, Fault-less to

Refrain

lean on Je-sus' name.
holds with-in the veil. On Christ, the sol-id Rock, I stand; All
all my hope and stay.
stand be-fore the throne.

oth-er ground is sink-ing sand, All oth-er ground is sink-ing sand.

Alternate tune: MELITA, 562

O Christ, the Healer

380

ERHALT UNS, HERR   LM

Klug's *Geistliche Lieder*, 1543
Harm. Johann Sebastian Bach (1725)

Fred Pratt Green, 1969

1. O Christ, the heal - er, we have come To pray for
2. From ev - ery ail - ment flesh en - dures Our bod - ies
3. How strong, O Lord, are our de - sires, How weak our
4. In con - flicts that de - stroy our health We rec - og -
5. Grant that we all, made one in faith, In Your com -

health, to plead for friends. How can we fail to
clam - or to be freed; Yet in our hearts we
knowl - edge of our - selves! Re - lease in us those
nize the world's dis - ease; Our com - mon life de -
mu - ni - ty may find The whole - ness that, en -

be re - stored, When reached by love that nev - er ends?
would con - fess That whole - ness is our deep - est need.
heal - ing truths Un - con - scious pride re - sists or shelves.
clares our ills: Is there no cure, O Christ, for these?
rich - ing us, Shall reach the whole of hu - man - kind.

Text: Copyright © 1969 by Hope Publishing Company, Carol Stream, IL 60188. All rights reserved. Used by permission.   ♩=76–84

381 O Come Unto the Lord

KOREA Irregular

Young tăik Chun, 1943
Trans. Steve S. Shim, 1976; alt. 1989

Chai Hoon Park, 1949

Refrain

O come un-to the Lord, O come back to the Lord;

1. No
2. Our
3. No

mat - ter how heav-y And how great your sins may be, There are no
Sav - ior is wait-ing Your re - turn both night and day: Je-sus
mat - ter how bur-dened And how beat - en you may be, The

sins that Christ our Sav - ior Can-not bear, can-not ac - cept. The great
anx - ious - ly a - waits you,With doors kept o - pen wide, As
Lord will com-fort you great - ly, With hands that touch and heal. Come

depth of Je - sus' lov - ing heart Is far deep - er than the seas.
One who waits through-out the night For a lost child to come back home.
un - to Christ, who loves you so. Please come home, please come back home.

Somebody's Knocking at Your Door 382

SOMEBODY'S KNOCKIN'   Irregular

African-American spiritual
Arr. Joy F. Patterson, 1989

African-American spiritual

Some-bod-y's knock-ing at your door;   Some-bod-y's knock-ing at your

door;   O   sin-ner, why don't you an-swer? Some-bod-y's knock-ing

at your   door.

1. Knocks like   Je - sus,
2. Can't   you   hear Him? Some-bod - y's knock-ing
3. An - swer   Je - sus.

Knocks like   Je - sus,
at your door; Can't   you   hear Him? Some-bod-y's knock-ing at your door;
An - swer   Je - sus.

O   sin-ner, why don't you an-swer? Some-bod-y's knock-ing at your door.

383 My Faith Looks Up to Thee

OLIVET   6.6.4.6.6.6.4

Ray Palmer, 1830   Lowell Mason, 1831

1. My faith looks up to Thee, Thou Lamb of Cal - va - ry,
2. May Thy rich grace im - part Strength to my faint - ing heart,
3. While life's dark maze I tread, And griefs a - round me spread,
4. When ends life's tran - sient dream, When death's cold, sul - len stream

Sav - ior di - vine: Now hear me while I pray, Take all my
My zeal in - spire; As Thou hast died for me, O may my
Be Thou my guide; Bid dark-ness turn to day, Wipe sor-row's
Shall o'er me roll, Blest Sav - ior, then, in love, Fear and dis -

guilt a - way, O let me from this day Be whol - ly Thine!
love to Thee Pure, warm, and change-less be, A liv - ing fire!
tears a - way, Nor let me ev - er stray From Thee a - side.
trust re-move; O bear me safe a - bove, A ran - somed soul!

O Love That Wilt Not Let Me Go

384

ST. MARGARET   8.8.8.8.6

George Matheson, 1882

Albert Lister Peace, 1884

1. O love that wilt not let me go,
   I rest my wea-ry soul in Thee;
   I give Thee back the life I owe,
   That in Thine o-cean depths its flow
   May rich-er, full-er be.

2. O light that fol-lowest all my way,
   I yield my flick-ering torch to Thee;
   My heart re-stores its bor-rowed ray,
   That in Thy sun-shine's blaze its day
   May bright-er, fair-er be.

3. O joy that seek-est me through pain,
   I can-not close my heart to Thee;
   I trace the rain-bow through the rain,
   And feel the prom-ise is not vain
   That morn shall tear-less be.

4. O cross that lift-est up my head,
   I dare not ask to fly from Thee;
   I lay in dust life's glo-ry dead,
   And from the ground there blos-soms red
   Life that shall end-less be.

385 O God, We Bear the Imprint of Your Face

SONG 1   10.10.10.10.10.10

Melody and bass: Orlando Gibbons (1583–1625)
Harm. Ralph Vaughan Williams, 1906
As in *The English Hymnal*, 1906

Shirley Erena Murray, 1987

1. O God, we bear the im - print of Your face:
2. Where we are torn and pulled a - part by hate
3. O God, we share the im - age of Your Son

The col - ors of our skin are Your de - sign,
Be - cause our race, our skin is not the same;
Whose flesh and blood are ours, what - ev - er skin,

And what we have of beau - ty in our race
While we are judged un - e - qual by the state
In His hu - man - i - ty we find our own,

As man or wom - an, You a - lone de - fine,
And vic - tims made be - cause we own our name,
And in His fam - i - ly our prop - er kin:

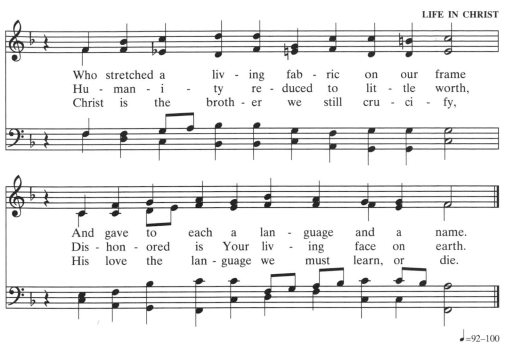

Who stretched a liv - ing fab - ric on our frame
Hu - man - i - ty re - duced to lit - tle worth,
Christ is the broth - er we still cru - ci - fy,

And gave to each a lan - guage and a name.
Dis - hon - ored is Your liv - ing face on earth.
His love the lan - guage we must learn, or die.

♩=92–100

O for a World 386

AZMON CM

Miriam Therese Winter, 1987

Carl Gotthelf Gläser, 1828
Arr. Lowell Mason, 1839

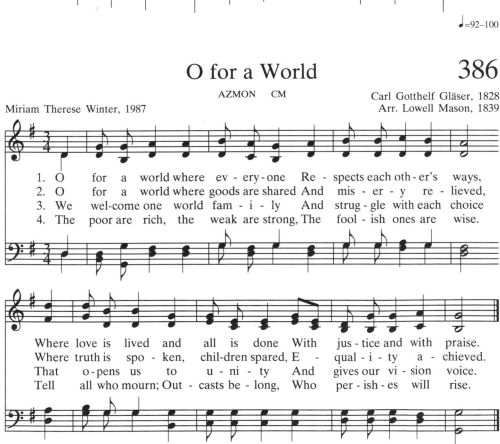

1. O for a world where ev - ery-one Re - spects each oth - er's ways,
2. O for a world where goods are shared And mis - er - y re - lieved,
3. We wel-come one world fam - i - ly And strug - gle with each choice
4. The poor are rich, the weak are strong, The fool - ish ones are wise.

Where love is lived and all is done With jus - tice and with praise.
Where truth is spo - ken, chil-dren spared, E - qual - i - ty a - chieved.
That o - pens us to u - ni - ty And gives our vi - sion voice.
Tell all who mourn; Out - casts be - long, Who per - ish - es will rise.

5. O for a world preparing for
   God's glorious reign of peace,

Where time and tears will be no more,
And all but love will cease.

Alternate version, 466

387   Savior, Like a Shepherd Lead Us

BRADBURY   8.7.8.7 D

Thrupp's *Hymns for the Young,* 1836   William Batchelder Bradbury, 1859

1. Sav - ior, like a shep-herd lead us,   Much we need Thy ten - der care;
2. Thou hast prom-ised to re - ceive us,   Poor and sin - ful though we be;
3. Ear - ly let us seek Thy fa - vor;   Ear - ly let us do Thy will;

In Thy pleas-ant pas-tures feed us,   For our use Thy folds pre-pare:
Thou hast mer - cy to re - lieve us,   Grace to cleanse, and power to free:
Bless - ed Lord and on - ly Sav - ior,   With Thy love our bo - soms fill:

Bless-ed Je - sus, bless-ed Je - sus,   Thou hast bought us, Thine we are;
Bless-ed Je - sus, bless-ed Je - sus,   Ear - ly let us turn to Thee;
Bless-ed Je - sus, bless-ed Je - sus,   Thou hast loved us, love us still;

Bless-ed Je - sus, bless-ed Je - sus,   Thou hast bought us, Thine we are.
Bless-ed Je - sus, bless-ed Je - sus,   Ear - ly let us turn to Thee.
Bless-ed Je - sus, bless-ed Je - sus,   Thou hast loved us, love us still.

Alternate tune: SICILIAN MARINERS, 538

O Jesus, I Have Promised

388

ANGEL'S STORY   7.6.7.6 D

John Ernest Bode, 1868

Arthur Henry Mann, 1881

1. O Je-sus, I have prom-ised To serve Thee to the end;
2. O let me feel Thee near me! The world is ev-er near;
3. O let me hear Thee speak-ing In ac-cents clear and still,
4. O Je-sus, Thou hast prom-ised To all who fol-low Thee

Be Thou for-ev-er near me, My Mas-ter and my friend;
I see the sights that daz-zle, The tempt-ing sounds I hear;
A-bove the storms of pas-sion, The mur-murs of self-will;
That where Thou art in glo-ry There shall Thy ser-vant be;

I shall not fear the bat-tle If Thou art by my side,
My foes are ev-er near me, A-round me and with-in;
O speak to re-as-sure me, To has-ten or con-trol;
And, Je-sus, I have prom-ised To serve Thee to the end;

Nor wan-der from the path-way If Thou wilt be my guide.
But, Je-sus, draw Thou near-er And shield my soul from sin.
O speak, and make me lis-ten, Thou guard-ian of my soul.
O give me grace to fol-low, My Mas-ter and my friend.

Alternate tune: NYLAND, 389

389

O Jesus, I Have Promised

NYLAND   7.6.7.6 D

John Ernest Bode, 1866

Finnish folk melody
Adapt. and harm. David Evans, 1927

1. O   Je - sus,   I   have   prom - ised   To   serve Thee   to   the   end;
2. O   let   me   feel   Thee   near   me!   The   world   is   ev - er   near;
3. O   let   me   hear   Thee   speak - ing   In   ac - cents clear and   still,
4. O   Je - sus,   Thou hast   prom - ised   To   all   who fol - low   Thee

Be   Thou   for - ev - er   near   me,   My   Mas - ter   and   my   friend;
I   see   the sights that   daz - zle,   The   tempt - ing   sounds   I   hear;
A - bove   the storms of   pas - sion, The   mur - murs   of   self - will;
That where Thou art   in   glo - ry   There shall   Thy   ser - vant   be;

I   shall not   fear   the   bat - tle   If   Thou art   by   my   side,
My   foes are   ev - er   near   me,   A - round me and   with - in;
O   speak to   re - as - sure   me,   To   has - ten or   con - trol;
And,   Je - sus,   I   have   prom - ised   To   serve Thee to   the   end;

Alternate tune: ANGEL'S STORY, 388

Music: Adaptation and harmonization from the *Revised Church Hymnary 1927;* used by permission of Oxford University Press.

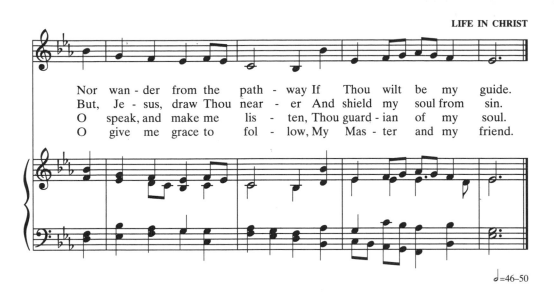

Nor wan-der from the path-way If Thou wilt be my guide.
But, Je-sus, draw Thou near-er And shield my soul from sin.
O speak, and make me lis-ten, Thou guard-ian of my soul.
O give me grace to fol-low, My Mas-ter and my friend.

♩=46–50

O Savior, in This Quiet Place 390

ST. STEPHEN   CM

Fred Pratt Green, 1974; alt. 1988   William Jones, 1789

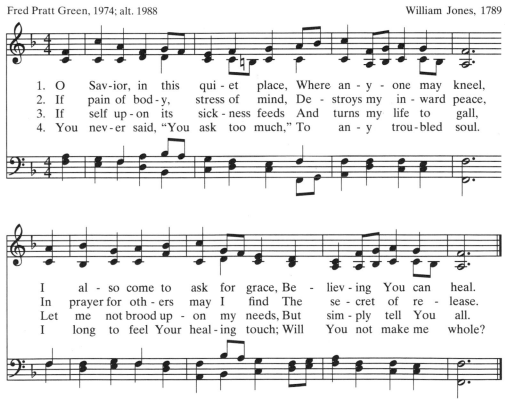

1. O   Sav-ior, in this qui-et place, Where an-y-one may kneel,
2. If   pain of bod-y, stress of mind, De-stroys my in-ward peace,
3. If   self up-on its sick-ness feeds And turns my life to gall,
4. You nev-er said, "You ask too much," To an-y trou-bled soul.

I   al-so come to ask for grace, Be-liev-ing You can heal.
In   prayer for oth-ers may I find The se-cret of re-lease.
Let me not brood up-on my needs, But sim-ply tell You all.
I   long to feel Your heal-ing touch; Will You not make me whole?

5. But if the thing I most desire
   Is not Your way for me,
   May faith, when tested in the fire,
   Prove its integrity.

6. Of all my prayers, may this be chief:
   Till faith is fully grown,
   Lord, disbelieve my unbelief,
   And claim me as Your own.

391

Take My Life

HENDON 7.7.7.7

Frances Ridley Havergal, 1874

H. A. César Malan, 1827

1. Take my life, and let it be Con-se-crat-ed, Lord, to Thee.
   Take my mo-ments and my days; Let them flow in cease-less praise, Let them flow in cease-less praise.

2. Take my hands, and let them move At the im-pulse of Thy love.
   Take my feet, and let them be Swift and beau-ti-ful for Thee, Swift and beau-ti-ful for Thee.

3. Take my voice, and let me sing, Al-ways, on-ly, for my King.
   Take my lips, and let them be Filled with mes-sa-ges from Thee, Filled with mes-sa-ges from Thee.

4. Take my sil-ver and my gold, Not a mite would I with-hold;
   Take my in-tel-lect, and use Ev-ery power as Thou shalt choose, Ev-ery power as Thou shalt choose.

5. Take my will, and make it Thine;
   It shall be no longer mine.
   Take my heart, it is Thine own;
   It shall be Thy royal throne,
   It shall be Thy royal throne.

6. Take my love; my Lord, I pour
   At Thy feet its treasure store.
   Take myself, and I will be
   Ever, only, all for Thee,
   Ever, only, all for Thee.

Take Thou Our Minds, Dear Lord

392

HALL   10.10.10.10

William H. Foulkes
Stanzas 1–3, 1918
Stanza 4, c. 1920

Calvin Weiss Laufer, 1918

1. Take Thou our minds, dear Lord, we hum-bly pray;
2. Take Thou our hearts, O Christ, they are Thine own;
3. Take Thou our wills, Most High! Hold Thou full sway;
4. Take Thou our-selves, O Lord, heart, mind, and will;

Give us the mind of Christ each pass-ing day;
Come Thou with-in our souls and claim Thy throne;
Have in our in-most souls Thy per-fect way;
Through our sur-ren-dered souls Thy plans ful-fill.

Teach us to know the truth that sets us free;
Help us to shed a-broad Thy death-less love;
Guard Thou each sa-cred hour from self-ish ease;
We yield our-selves to Thee— time, tal-ents, all;

Grant us in all our thoughts to hon-or Thee.
Use us to make the earth like heav-en a-bove.
Guide Thou our or-dered lives as Thou dost please.
We hear, and hence-forth heed, Thy sov-ereign call.

393 Take Up Your Cross, the Savior Said

BOURBON LM

Charles William Everest, 1833; alt.

Attr. Freeman Lewis, 1825
Harm. John Leon Hooker, 1984

1. Take up your cross, the Sav - ior said, If
2. Take up your cross, let not its weight Fill
3. Take up your cross, heed not the shame, And
4. Take up your cross, then, in Christ's strength, And

you would My dis - ci - ple be; Take up your cross with
your weak spir - it with a - larm; Christ's strength shall bear your
let your fool - ish heart be still; The Lord for you ac -
calm - ly ev - ery dan - ger brave: It guides you to a -

will - ing heart, And hum - bly fol - low af - ter Me.
spir - it up And brace your heart and nerve your arm.
cept - ed death Up - on a cross, on Cal - vary's hill.
bun - dant life And leads to vic - tory o'er the grave.

There Is a Balm in Gilead

394

BALM IN GILEAD 7.6.7.6. with refrain

African-American spiritual
Arr. Melva W. Costen, 1989; alt.

African-American spiritual

There is a balm in Gil-e-ad to make the wound-ed whole.

There is a balm in Gil-e-ad to heal the sin-sick soul.

1. Some-times I feel dis-cour-aged, And think my work's in vain, But
2. Don't ev-er feel dis-cour-aged, For Je-sus is your friend, And
3. If you can-not preach like Pe-ter, If you can-not pray like Paul, You can

then the Ho-ly Spir-it Re-vives my soul a-gain. There is a
if you lack for knowl-edge He'll not re-fuse to lend. There is a
tell the love of Je-sus And say, "He died for all." There is a

Piedad
Have Mercy, Lord, on Me

395

PIEDAD   7.6.7.6 D

Marcelino Montoya
Trans. George P. Simmonds, 1968

Marcelino Montoya
Harm. Norman Parish, Jr. (b. 1932)
Arr. George P. Simmonds, 1964

1. Se - ñor, por tu cle - men - cia, Te - ned de mí pie - dad,
2. Se - ñor Om - ni - po - ten - te, Es - cu - cha mi o - ra - ción,

1. Take pit - y, Lord, I pray Thee, Thy mer - cy show to me,
2. O ho - ly Lord Al - might - y, My need to Thee I bear,

De - lan - te tu pre - sen - cia Con - fie - so mi mal - dad;
Y sé a mí cle - men - te, In - dig - no pe - ca - dor;

My sins and my wrong-do - ing I now con - fess to Thee;
Al - though un - done, un - wor - thy, I pray Thee, hear my prayer;

De to - dos mis pe - ca - dos Me re - di - mis - te Tú
Cor - de - ro in - ma - cu - la - do, Di - vi - no Re - den - tor,

From all of my trans-gres - sions Thou, Lord, hast set me free,
O Lamb for sin - ners wound - ed, Re - deem - er of man - kind,

Con san - gre tan pre - cio - sa Ver - ti - da en la cruz.
Tú e - res quien me has da - do La e - ter - na sal - va - ción.

Thy blood so pre - cious shed - ding Up - on the cru - el tree.
E - ter - nal life and par - don My soul in Thee doth find.

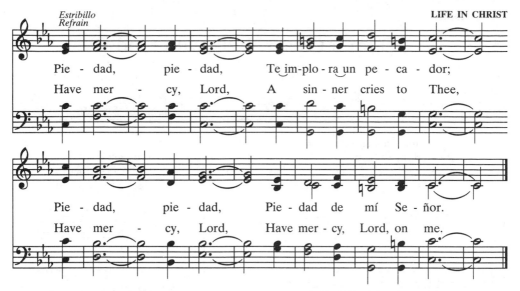

Estribillo / Refrain

Pie - dad, pie - dad, Te im-plo - ra un pe - ca - dor;
Have mer - cy, Lord, A sin - ner cries to Thee,

Pie - dad, pie - dad, Pie - dad de mí Se - ñor.
Have mer - cy, Lord, Have mer - cy, Lord, on me.

3. Señor, que en el Calvario
Me diste redención,
Muriendo voluntario
Por mí, vil pecador;
Bendito sea tu nombre
Por la eternidad,
Que agonizante fuiste,
Señor, por mi maldad. *(Estribillo)*

3. Lord, willingly Thou gavest
Thyself for all to die,
And purchase full redemption
For sinners such as I;
O blessed be Thy name, Lord,
Through all eternity
For bearing shame and anguish
Upon the cross for me. *(Refrain)*

O for a Closer Walk with God 396

CAITHNESS CM

William Cowper, 1772

Scottish Psalter, 1635
Harm. *The English Hymnal,* 1906; alt.

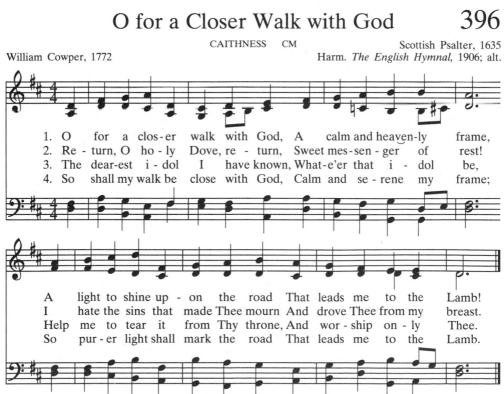

1. O for a clos-er walk with God, A calm and heaven-ly frame,
2. Re - turn, O ho - ly Dove, re - turn, Sweet mes-sen - ger of rest!
3. The dear-est i - dol I have known, What-e'er that i - dol be,
4. So shall my walk be close with God, Calm and se - rene my frame;

A light to shine up - on the road That leads me to the Lamb!
I hate the sins that made Thee mourn And drove Thee from my breast.
Help me to tear it from Thy throne, And wor - ship on - ly Thee.
So pur - er light shall mark the road That leads me to the Lamb.

397 O for a Closer Walk with God

DALEHURST CM

William Cowper, 1772

Arthur Cottman, 1874

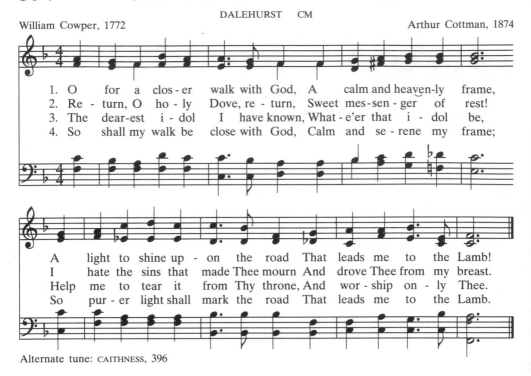

1. O for a clos-er walk with God, A calm and heaven-ly frame,
2. Re-turn, O ho-ly Dove, re-turn, Sweet mes-sen-ger of rest!
3. The dear-est i-dol I have known, What-e'er that i-dol be,
4. So shall my walk be close with God, Calm and se-rene my frame;

A light to shine up-on the road That leads me to the Lamb!
I hate the sins that made Thee mourn And drove Thee from my breast.
Help me to tear it from Thy throne, And wor-ship on-ly Thee.
So pur-er light shall mark the road That leads me to the Lamb.

Alternate tune: CAITHNESS, 396

398 There's a Sweet, Sweet Spirit

SWEET, SWEET SPIRIT   9.11.9.11 with refrain

Doris Akers, 1962

Doris Akers, 1962

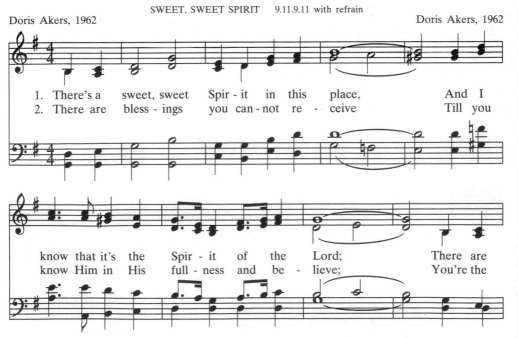

1. There's a sweet, sweet Spir-it in this place, And I
2. There are bless-ings you can-not re-ceive Till you

know that it's the Spir-it of the Lord; There are
know Him in His full-ness and be-lieve; You're the

sweet ex - pres-sions on each face, And I know they feel the
one to prof - it when you say, "I am going to walk with

pres-ence of the Lord. Sweet Ho - ly Spir - it,
Je - sus all the way."

Sweet heav-en-ly Dove, Stay right here with us, Fill-ing us

with Your love; And for these bless-ings We lift our hearts in

praise. With - out a doubt we'll know that we have

been re - vived When we shall leave this place.

399   We Walk by Faith and Not by Sight

DUNLAP'S CREEK   CM

Samuel McFarland, c. 1816
Harm. Richard Proulx, 1986

Henry Alford, 1844; alt.

1. We walk by faith and not by sight; No gra-cious words we hear From Christ, who spoke as none e'er spoke; But we be-lieve Him near.

2. We may not touch His hands and side, Nor fol-low where He trod; But in His prom-ise we re-joice, And cry, "My Lord and God!"

3. Help then, O Lord, our un-be-lief; And may our faith a-bound To call on You when You are near And seek where You are found:

4. That, when our life of faith is done, In realms of clear-er light We may be-hold You as You are, With full and end-less sight.

Pues Si Vivimos
When We Are Living

SOMOS DEL SEÑOR   10.10.10.10

Stanza 1 trans. Elise S. Eslinger, 1983
Stanzas 2–4, Roberto Escamilla, 1983;
trans. George Lockwood, 1987

Spanish melody

1. Pues si vi - vi - mos pa - ra Él vi - vi - mos
2. En es - ta vi - da, fru - tos he - mos de dar
3. En la tris - te - za y en el do - lor,
4. En es - te mun - do, he - mos de en - con - trar

1. When we are liv - ing, it is in Christ Je - sus,
2. Through all our liv - ing, we our fruits must give.
3. Mid times of sor - row and in times of pain,
4. A - cross this wide world, we shall al - ways find

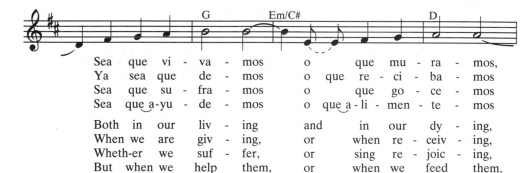

Y si mo - ri - mos pa - ra Él mo - ri - mos.
Las o - bras bue - nas son pa - ra o - fren - dar.
En la be - lle - za y en el a - mor,
Gen - te que llo - ra y sin con - so - lar.

And when we're dy - ing, it is in the Lord.
Good works of ser - vice are for of - fer - ing.
When sens - ing beau - ty or in love's em - brace,
Those who are cry - ing with no peace of mind,

Sea que vi - va - mos o que mu - ra - mos,
Ya sea que de - mos o que re - ci - ba - mos
Sea que su - fra - mos o que go - ce - mos
Sea que a-yu - de - mos o que a-li - men - te - mos

Both in our liv - ing and in our dy - ing,
When we are giv - ing, or when re - ceiv - ing,
Wheth-er we suf - fer, or sing re - joic - ing,
But when we help them, or when we feed them,

Refrain

So - mos del Se - ñor, so - mos del Se - ñor.
We be - long to God. we be - long to God.

Text: Translation copyright © 1989 The United Methodist Publishing House. Used by permission.

401 When Will People Cease Their Fighting?

RUSTINGTON 8.7.8.7 D

Constance Cherry, 1986

C. Hubert H. Parry, 1897

1. When will peo-ple cease their fight-ing? When will ar-mies wage no war, Na-tions con-quer not their neigh-bor, Weap-ons id-le, used no more? When will guns and bombs be si-lent? When will cap-tives be set free? All cre-

2. Floods and earth-quakes, drought and fam-ine Plague the world with awe-some ill, But far great-er is war's hor-ror Caused by hu-man, stub-born will. Blest are those who, work-ing, pray-ing, Pur-pose in their hearts to be In-stru-

3. As we strive for peace with vig-or, Hop-ing to be shown the way, We are strength-ened in the knowl-edge Of a fu-ture, per-fect day; For we know that deep-er, rich-er Peace is ours when Christ shall reign: Then will

a - tion groans in long - ing For the world's true lib - er - ty.
ments of peace, com - mit - ted To the na - tions' har - mo - ny.
all our swords be plow-shares And God's chil - dren free from pain.

♩=88–96

Now Praise the Hidden God of Love 402

DICKINSON COLLEGE   LM

Fred Pratt Green, 1975

Lee Hastings Bristol, Jr., 1962

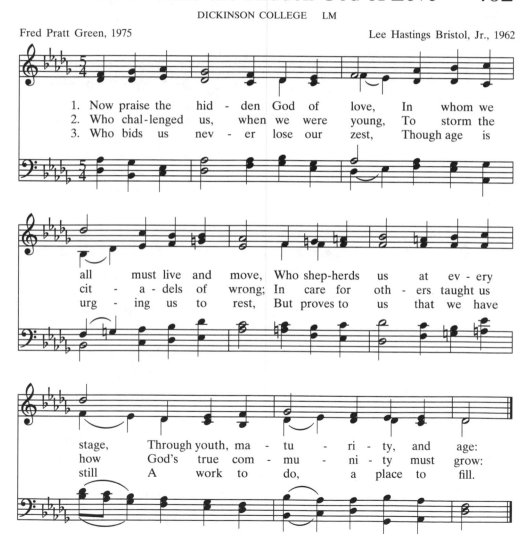

1. Now praise the hid - den God of love, In whom we
2. Who chal - lenged us, when we were young, To storm the
3. Who bids us nev - er lose our zest, Though age is

all must live and move, Who shep-herds us at ev - ery
cit - a - dels of wrong; In care for oth - ers taught us
urg - ing us to rest, But proves to us that we have

stage, Through youth, ma - tu - ri - ty, and age:
how God's true com - mu - ni - ty must grow:
still A work to do, a place to fill.

Jin Shil Ha Shin Chin Goo
403 What a Friend We Have in Jesus

CONVERSE   8.7.8.7 D

Joseph Scriven, c. 1855
Transliteration of Korean: Myung Ja Yue

Charles Crozat Converse, 1868

1. Chway jim ma tun oo ree goo joo   Uh jjee joh un chin goon jee
2. She hum guhk juhng mo dun kway rom   Um nun sah rahm noo goon gah

1. What a friend we have in Je - sus,   All our sins and griefs to bear!
2. Have we tri - als and temp-ta - tions?   Is there trou-ble an - y - where?

Kuhk juhng keun shim moo guh oon jim   Oo ree joo ggeh mat ggee seh
Boo jil up see nahk shim mahl go   Kee doh duh ryuh ah ray seh

What a priv - i - lege to car - ry   Ev - ery-thing to God in prayer!
We should nev - er be dis - cour - aged: Take it to the Lord in prayer!

Joo ggeh sah juhng ah ray jahn ah   Pyung wha uht jee mot ha neh
Ee run jin shil ha shin chin goo   Uh dee dah shi iss ul ggah

O what peace we of - ten for - feit,   O what need-less pain we bear,
Can we find a friend so faith - ful,   Who will all our sor-rows share?

Oo ree du ree uht jjee ha yuh   Ah rel joo rul mo rul kka
Oo ree yak ham ah shi oh nee   Uh jjee ah nee ah rel kka

All be-cause we do not car - ry   Ev - ery-thing to God in prayer!
Je - sus knows our ev-ery weak - ness;   Take it to the Lord in prayer!

3. Kuhn shim guhk juhng moo guh ooh jim
   Ah nee jin jah noo goon gah
   Pee nahn chuh nun oo ree Ye su
   Joo ggeh kee doh duh ree seh
   Seh sahng chin goo myul see ha go
   Nuh rul joh rong ha yuh doh
   Joo eh poo meh ahn gee uh suh
   Cham dwen wee ro baat get neh.

3. Are we weak and heavy laden,
   Cumbered with a load of care?
   Precious Savior, still our refuge—
   Take it to the Lord in prayer!
   Do thy friends despise, forsake thee?
   Take it to the Lord in prayer!
   In His arms He'll take and shield thee,
   Thou wilt find a solace there.

Precious Lord, Take My Hand 404

PRECIOUS LORD   6.6.9 D

Thomas A. Dorsey, 1938

George N. Allen, 1844
Arr. Thomas A. Dorsey, 1938

1. Pre - cious Lord, take my hand, Lead me on, help me stand; I am
2. When my way grows drear, Pre - cious Lord, lin - ger near; When my

tired, I am weak, I am worn; Through the storm, through the night, Lead me
life is al - most gone, Hear my cry, hear my call, Hold my

on to the light; Take my hand, pre - cious Lord, lead me home.
hand lest I fall; Take my hand, pre - cious Lord, lead me home.

Micah 6:6–8

405   What Does the Lord Require

SHARPTHORNE   6.6.6.6.33.6

Albert F. Bayly, 1949, 1982

Erik Routley, 1968

1. What does the Lord re-quire For praise and of - fer - ing?
2. Rul - ers of earth, give ear! Should you not jus - tice know?
3. How shall our life ful - fill God's law so hard and high?

What sac - ri - fice de - sire, Or trib - ute bid you bring?
Will God your plead - ing hear, While crime and cruel - ty grow?
Let Christ en - due our will With grace to for - ti - fy.

Do just - ly; love mer - cy; Walk
Do just - ly; love mer - cy; Walk
Then just - ly, in mer - cy, We'll

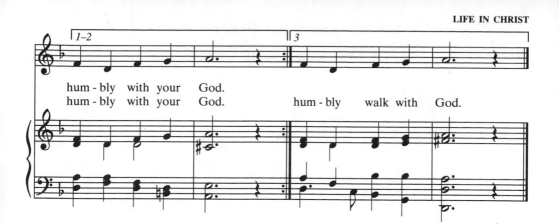

hum - bly with your God.
hum - bly with your God. hum - bly walk with God.

♩=84–92

Matthew 27:46

Why Has God Forsaken Me?

406

SHIMPI   7.7.7.7

Bill Wallace, 1980

Taihei Sato, 1981

1. "Why has God for - sak - en me?" Cried our Sav - ior from the cross
2. At the tomb of Laz - a - rus Je - sus wept with o - pen grief:
3. As His life ex - pired, our Lord Placed Him - self with - in God's care:
4. Mys - tery shrouds our life and death But we need not be a - fraid,

As He shared the lone - li - ness Of our deep - est grief and loss.
Grant us, Lord, the tears which heal All our pain and un - be - lief.
At our dy - ing, Lord, may we Trust the love which con - quers fear.
For the mys - tery's heart is love, God's great love which Christ dis - played.

♩=69–76

Cuando el Pobre
When a Poor One

407

EL CAMINO   12.11.12 with refrain

J. A. Olivar and Miguel Manzano, 1976
English trans. George Lockwood, 1989; alt.

J. A. Olivar and Miguel Manzano, 1976
Arr. Alvin Schutmaat

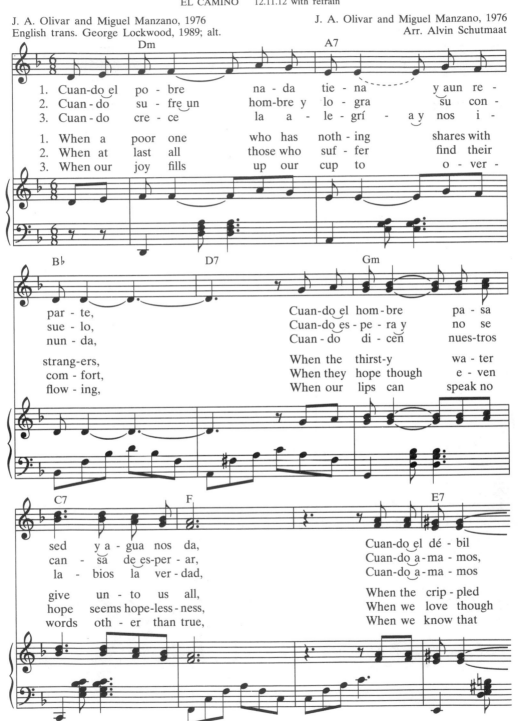

a su her-ma - no for - ta - le - ce,
aun-que_el o - di - o nos ro - dee,
el sen - tir de los sen - ci - llos,

in their weak-ness strength-en oth - ers,
hate at times seems all a - round us,
love for sim - ple things is bet - ter,

Estribillo
Refrain

Va Dios mis - mo_en nues-tro mis - mo ca - mi - nar,

Then we know that God still goes that road with us,

Va Dios mis - mo_en nues-tro mis - mo ca - mi - nar.

Then we know that God still goes that road with us.

4. Cuando a bunda el bien y llena los hogares,
   Cuando un hombre donde hay guerra pone paz,
   Cuando "hermano" le llamamos al extraño, *(Estribillo)*

4. When our homes are filled with goodness in abundance,
   When we learn how to make peace instead of war,
   When each stranger that we meet is called a neighbor, *(Refrain)*

408 Where Cross the Crowded Ways of Life

GERMANY LM

Attr. Ludwig van Beethoven (1770–1827)
Gardiner's *Sacred Melodies*, 1815

Frank Mason North, 1905; alt.

1. Where cross the crowd-ed ways of life, Where sound the
   cries of race and clan, A - bove the noise of
   self - ish strife, We hear Thy voice, O Son of Man.

2. In haunts of wretch-ed - ness and need, On shad - owed
   thresh - olds fraught with fears, From paths where hide the
   lures of greed, We catch the vi - sion of Thy tears.

3. From ten - der child - hood's help - less - ness, From hu - man
   grief and bur - dened toil, From fam - ished souls, from
   sor - row's stress, Thy heart has nev - er known re - coil.

4. The cup of wa - ter given for Thee Still holds the
   fresh - ness of Thy grace; Yet long these mul - ti -
   tudes to see The sweet com - pas - sion of Thy face.

5. O Master, from the mountainside,
   Make haste to heal these hearts of pain;
   Among these restless throngs abide,
   O tread the city's streets again;

6. Till all the world shall learn Thy love,
   And follow where Thy feet have trod;
   Till glorious from Thy heaven above
   Shall come the city of our God.

Wild and Lone the Prophet's Voice 409

ABERYSTWYTH 7.7.7.7 D

Carl P. Daw, Jr., 1989

Joseph Parry, 1879

1. Wild and lone the proph-et's voice Ech-oes through the des - ert still,
2. "Bear the fruit re - pent-ance sows: Lives of jus - tice, truth, and love.
3. With such preach-ing stark and bold John pro-claimed sal - va - tion near,

Call - ing us to make a choice, Bid - ding us to do God's will:
Trust no oth - er claim than those; Set your heart on things a - bove.
And his time-less warn-ings hold Words of hope to all who hear.

"Turn from sin and be bap-tized; Cleanse your heart and mind and soul.
Soon the Lord will come in power, Burn - ing clean the thresh - ing floor:
So we dare to jour - ney on, Led by faith through ways un - trod,

Quit-ting all the sins you prized, Yield your life to God's con - trol.
Then will flames the chaff de - vour; Wheat a - lone shall fill God's store."
Till we come at last like John To be - hold the Lamb of God.

This tune in a lower key, 20

410 Yee Jun Ae Joo Nim Eul Nae Ka Mol La
When I Had Not Yet Learned of Jesus

10.10.10.10

Yongchul Chung, 1967
Transliteration of Korean: Samuel Yun, 1989
Para. Jane Parker Huber, 1989

Yoosun Lee, 1967

1. Yee   jun ae   Joo   Nim eul   nae   ka   mol   la
2. Nah   bah deun   tal - ent   ul   mah   run   kah

1. When   I   had   not   yet learned   of   Je - sus   Christ,
2. What - ev - er   tal - ent God   has   giv - en   me

Young kwang ae   Joo   Nim eul   bee   pahng   hat - da
Nah   hym sshuh gue   kuh seul   nahm   ki   uh - suh

When   I   re - fused   to   lis - ten   to   God's   call,
I   pledge to   use   in ser - vice   and   in   love.

Jee   keuk   hahn   keu - eun   hye   nae   keh   num   chuh
Kop   jul   roh   Joo - Nim   keh   bah   chi   oh   myon

I   was   de - fi - ant   then,   till   God   broke   through;
Joined with   my   God   to   lift   my   neigh - bor's   load,

Nul   bull   luh   joo   si   nee   koh   ma   wah   rah
Chung sung   doen   jong   yee rah   sahng   joo   si - ri

Now   by   God's   grace   Christ is   my   all   in   all.
New   strength and   hope   are   giv - en   from   a - bove.

Text: Paraphrase © 1990 Jane Parker Huber. Transliteration © 1990 Westminster/John Knox Press. All rights reserved.

♩=92–100

3. Chun ha go moo neung hahn nah eh
   keh do
   Gui joong hahn jik poon eul maht kee
   syut dah
   Gue eun hye gomahb go go mah wah
   rah
   Yee sang myong bah chyuh seo chung
   sung ha ri

4. Nae hah neun yil deu li hah do juh
   guh
   Keun yeol mae noon up peh ahn veh
   uhdo
   Joo Nim keh joogdo roke chung sung
   ha myon
   Sang myong eui myol ryu kwan uh
   duh ri rah

3. To be God's servant in this
   earthly life,
   No matter if the task is great
   or small,
   This is my charge: to witness
   faithfully,
   Strengthened by Christ who is
   my all in all.

Isaiah 61:1–2 📖   CHURCH: MISSION

Arise, Your Light Is Come!   411

FESTAL SONG   SM

Ruth Duck, 1974   William H. Walter, 1894

1. A - rise, your light is come! The Spir - it's call o - bey;
2. A - rise, your light is come! Fling wide the pris - on door;
3. A - rise, your light is come! All you in sor - row born,
4. A - rise, your light is come! The moun-tains burst in song!

Show forth the glo - ry of your God, Which shines on you to - day.
Pro - claim the cap-tives' lib - er - ty, Good ti - dings to the poor.
Bind up the bro - ken - heart-ed ones And com - fort those who mourn.
Rise up like ea - gles on the wing; God's power will make us strong.

412   Eternal God, Whose Power Upholds

FOREST GREEN   CMD

English folk melody

Henry Hallam Tweedy, 1929   Arr. Ralph Vaughan Williams, 1906

1. E - ter-nal God, whose power up - holds Both flower and flam - ing star,
2. O God of love, whose Spir - it wakes In ev - ery hu - man breast,
3. O God of truth, whom sci - ence seeks And rev - erent souls a - dore,
4. O God of beau - ty, oft re - vealed In dreams of hu - man art,
5. O God of righ - teous - ness and grace, Seen in the Christ, Thy Son,

To whom there is no here nor there, No time, no near nor far,
Whom love, and love a - lone, can know, In whom all hearts find rest:
Who light - est ev - ery ear - nest mind Of ev - ery clime and shore:
In speech that flows to mel - o - dy, In ho - li - ness of heart:
Whose life and death re - veal Thy face, By whom Thy will was done:

No a - lien race, no for - eign shore, No child un-sought, un - known:
Help us to spread Thy gra - cious reign Till greed and hate shall cease,
Dis - pel the gloom of er - ror's night, Of ig - no-rance and fear,
Teach us to turn from sin - ful - ness That shuts our hearts to Thee,
In - spire Thy her - alds of good news To live Thy life di - vine,

This tune in a higher key, 292

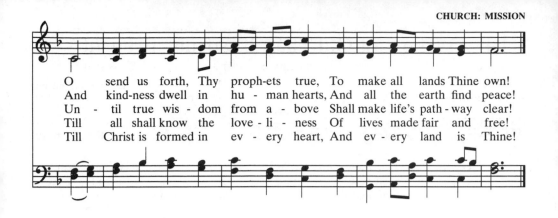

O send us forth, Thy proph-ets true, To make all lands Thine own!
And kind-ness dwell in hu - man hearts, And all the earth find peace!
Un - til true wis - dom from a - bove Shall make life's path - way clear!
Till all shall know the love - li - ness Of lives made fair and free!
Till Christ is formed in ev - ery heart, And ev - ery land is Thine!

John 9:4

All Who Love and Serve Your City 413

CHARLESTOWN   8.7.8.7

The United States Sacred Harmony, 1799
Harm. Carlton R. Young, 1964

Erik Routley, 1966

1. All who love and serve your cit - y, All who bear its dai - ly stress,
2. In your day of wealth and plen - ty, Wast - ed work and wast - ed play,
3. For all days are days of judg-ment, And the Lord is wait - ing still,
4. Ris - en Lord, shall yet the cit - y Be the cit - y of de - spair?

All who cry for peace and jus - tice, All who curse and all who bless:
Call to mind the word of Je - sus, "You must work while it is day."
Draw - ing near a world that spurns Him, Of - fering peace from Cal-vary's hill.
Come to - day, our judge, our glo - ry. Be its name "The Lord is there!"

414 As Those of Old Their Firstfruits Brought

FOREST GREEN   CMD

Frank von Christierson, 1960; alt.

English folk melody
Arr. Ralph Vaughan Williams, 1906

1. As those of old their first-fruits brought Of vine-yard, flock, and field
2. A world in need now sum-mons us To la-bor, love, and give,
3. With grat-i-tude and hum-ble trust We bring our best to You,

To God, the giv-er of all good, The source of boun-teous yield,
To make our life an of-fer-ing To God that all may live.
Not just to serve Your cause, but share Your love with neigh-bors too.

So we to-day our first-fruits bring, The wealth of this good land:
The church of Christ is call-ing us To make the dream come true:
O God who gave Your-self to us In Je-sus Christ Your Son,

Of farm and mar-ket, shop and home, Of mind and heart and hand.
A world re-deemed by Christ-like love, All life in Christ made new.
Help us to give our-selves each day Un-til life's work is done.

Come, Labor On

415

ORA LABORA   4.10.10.10.4

Jane Laurie Borthwick, 1859; rev. 1863; alt.   Thomas Tertius Noble, 1918

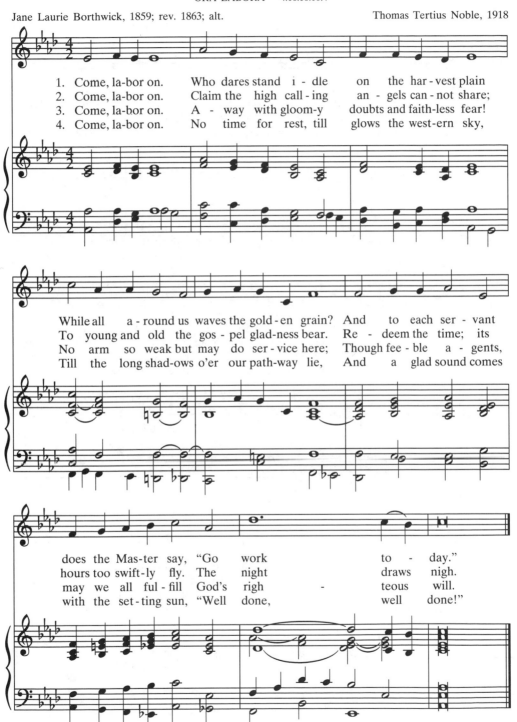

1. Come, la-bor on. Who dares stand i - dle on the har - vest plain
2. Come, la-bor on. Claim the high call - ing an - gels can - not share;
3. Come, la-bor on. A - way with gloom-y doubts and faith-less fear!
4. Come, la-bor on. No time for rest, till glows the west-ern sky,

While all a - round us waves the gold - en grain? And to each ser - vant
To young and old the gos - pel glad-ness bear. Re - deem the time; its
No arm so weak but may do ser - vice here; Though fee - ble a - gents,
Till the long shad-ows o'er our path-way lie, And a glad sound comes

does the Mas-ter say, "Go work to - day."
hours too swift-ly fly. The night draws nigh.
may we all ful - fill God's righ - teous will.
with the set-ting sun, "Well done, well done!"

416   Christ Is Made the Sure Foundation

WESTMINSTER ABBEY   8.7.8.7.8.7

7th century, Latin
Trans. John Mason Neale, 1851; alt. 1861, 1972

Henry Purcell (1659–1695), adapt.

1. Christ is made the sure foun-da-tion, Christ the head and cor-ner-stone,
2. To this tem-ple, where we call You, Come, O Lord of Hosts, to-day;
3. Here be-stow on all Your ser-vants What they ask of You to gain,
4. Laud and hon-or to the Fa-ther, Laud and hon-or to the Son,

Cho-sen of the Lord and pre-cious, Bind-ing all the church in one;
With Your wont-ed lov-ing-kind-ness Hear Your peo-ple as they pray,
What they gain from You for-ev-er With the bless-ed to re-tain,
Laud and hon-or to the Spir-it, Ev-er three and ev-er one;

Ho-ly Zi-on's help for-ev-er, And our con-fi-dence a-lone.
And Your full-est ben-e-dic-tion Shed with-in its walls al-way.
And here-af-ter in Your glo-ry Ev-er-more with You to reign.
One in might and one in glo-ry While un-end-ing a-ges run.

Christ Is Made the Sure Foundation 417

REGENT SQUARE   8.7.8.7.8.7

7th century, Latin
Trans. John Mason Neale, 1851; alt. 1861, 1972

Henry Thomas Smart, 1867

1. Christ is made the sure foun-da - tion, Christ the head and
2. To this tem - ple, where we call You, Come, O Lord of
3. Here be - stow on all Your ser - vants What they ask of
4. Laud and hon - or to the Fa - ther, Laud and hon - or

cor - ner - stone, Cho - sen of the Lord and pre - cious,
Hosts, to - day; With Your wont - ed lov - ing - kind - ness
You to gain, What they gain from You for - ev - er
to the Son, Laud and hon - or to the Spir - it,

Bind - ing all the church in one; Ho - ly Zi - on's
Hear Your peo - ple as they pray, And Your full - est
With the bless - ed to re - tain, And here - af - ter
Ev - er three and ev - er one; One in might and

help for - ev - er, And our con - fi - dence a - lone.
ben - e - dic - tion Shed with - in its walls al - way.
in Your glo - ry Ev - er - more with You to reign.
one in glo - ry While un - end - ing a - ges run.

418 God, Bless Your Church with Strength!

ICH HALTE TREULICH STILL   SMD

John A. Dalles, 1984

Attr. Johann Sebastian Bach, 1736

1. God, bless Your church with strength! Wher-ev-er we may be,
2. God, bless Your church with life! May all our branch-es thrive,
3. God, bless Your church with hope! De-spite cha-ot-ic days,

Up-build Your ser-vants as we work In com-mon min-is-try.
Un-blem-ished, whole-some, bear-ing fruit, A-bun-dant-ly a-live.
May we in cha-os shine to light A path-way through life's maze.

Urge us from fledg-ling faith To ven-ture and to soar Through
From You, one ho-ly vine, In free-dom may we grow; Sus-
May jus-tice be our aim, And kind-ness ours to share, In

o-pen skies, to sing the praise Of Christ whom we a-dore.
tain us in our mis-sion, Lord, Your love and peace to show.
hum-ble-ness O may we walk, As-sured our God is there!

Alternate tune: DIADEMATA, 151

How Clear Is Our Vocation, Lord

419

REPTON   8.6.8.8.6.6

Fred Pratt Green, 1981

C. Hubert H. Parry, 1888

1. How clear is our vo-ca-tion, Lord, When once we heed Your call:
2. But if, for-get-ful, we should find Your yoke is hard to bear,
3. We mark Your saints, how they be-came In hin-dranc-es more sure,
4. In what You give us, Lord, to do, To-geth-er or a-lone,

To live ac-cord-ing to Your word, And dai-ly learn, re-freshed, re - stored,
If world-ly pres-sures fray the mind And love it - self can-not un - wind
Whose joy-ful vir-tues put to shame The cas-ual way we wear Your name,
In old rou-tines or ven-tures new, May we not cease to look to You—

That You are Lord of all And will not let us fall.
Its tan-gled skein of care: Our in-ward life re - pair.
And by our faults ob - scure Your power to cleanse and cure.
The cross You hung up - on— All You en-deav - ored done.

420 God of Grace and God of Glory

CWM RHONDDA   8.7.8.7.8.7.7

Harry Emerson Fosdick, 1930; alt.

John Hughes, 1907

1. God of grace and God of glo - ry, On Thy peo - ple pour Thy power; Crown Thine an - cient chur - ch's sto - ry; Bring its bud to glo - rious flower. Grant us wis - dom, grant us cour - age, For the fac - ing of this hour, For the fac - ing of this hour.

2. Lo! the hosts of e - vil round us Scorn Thy Christ, as - sail Thy ways! From the fears that long have bound us Free our hearts to faith and praise. Grant us wis - dom, grant us cour - age, For the liv - ing of these days, For the liv - ing of these days.

3. Cure Thy chil - dren's war - ring mad - ness, Bend our pride to Thy con - trol; Shame our wan - ton, self - ish glad - ness, Rich in things and poor in soul. Grant us wis - dom, grant us cour - age, Lest we miss Thy king-dom's goal, Lest we miss Thy king-dom's goal.

4. Set our feet on loft - y pla - ces; Gird our lives that they may be Ar - mored with all Christ - like gra - ces, Pledged to set all cap-tives free. Grant us wis - dom, grant us cour - age, That we fail not them nor Thee! That we fail not them nor Thee!

Text: Used by permission of Elinor Fosdick Downs.

5. Save us from weak resignation
   To the evils we deplore;
   Let the gift of Thy salvation
   Be our glory evermore.

Grant us wisdom, grant us courage,
Serving Thee whom we adore,
Serving Thee whom we adore.

The Church of Christ in Every Age 421

WAREHAM LM

Fred Pratt Green, 1969

William Knapp, 1738

1. The church of Christ in ev - ery age, Be - set by
2. A - cross the world, a - cross the street, The vic - tims
3. Then let the ser - vant church a - rise, A car - ing
4. For Christ a - lone, whose blood was shed, Can cure the

change but Spir - it led, Must claim and test its
of in - jus - tice cry For shel - ter and for
church that longs to be A part - ner in Christ's
fe - ver in our blood, And teach us how to

her - i - tage And keep on ris - ing from the dead.
bread to eat, And nev - er live un - til they die.
sac - ri - fice, And clothed in Christ's hu - man - i - ty.
share our bread And feed the starv - ing mul - ti - tude.

5. We have no mission but to serve
   In full obedience to our Lord:

To care for all, without reserve,
And spread Christ's liberating word.

Another harmonization of this tune, 265

422 God, Whose Giving Knows No Ending

BEACH SPRING   8.7.8.7 D

Robert L. Edwards, 1961

The Sacred Harp, 1844
Harm. James H. Wood, 1958

1. God, whose giv - ing knows no end - ing, From Your rich and
2. Skills and time are ours for press - ing Toward the goals of
3. Trea - sure too You have en - trust - ed, Gain through powers Your

end - less store, Na - ture's won - der, Je - sus' wis - dom,
Christ, Your Son: All at peace in health and free - dom,
grace con - ferred; Ours to use for home and kin - dred,

Cost - ly cross, grave's shat - tered door: Gift - ed by You, we turn
Rac - es joined, the church made one. Now di - rect our dai - ly
And to spread the gos - pel Word. O - pen wide our hands, in

to You, Of-fering up our - selves in praise; Thank-ful
la - bor, Lest we strive for self a - lone; Born with
shar - ing, As we heed Christ's age - less call, Heal - ing,

song shall rise for - ev - er, Gra-cious do - nor of our days.
tal - ents, make us ser - vants Fit to an - swer at Your throne.
teach - ing, and re - claim - ing, Serv-ing You by lov - ing all.

423 Jesus Shall Reign Where'er the Sun

DUKE STREET LM

Isaac Watts, 1719, alt.

John Hatton (d. 1793)
Desc. David McKinley Williams, 1959

5. Let ev-ery crea-ture rise and bring Hon-ors pe-

1. Je - sus shall reign where - e'er the sun Does its suc-
2. To Him shall end - less prayer be made, And prais-es
3. Peo - ple and realms of ev - ery tongue Dwell on His
4. Bless - ings a - bound wher - e'er He reigns; The pris-oners

cu - liar to our King; An - gels de - scend with

ces - sive jour - neys run, His king-dom stretch from
throng to crown His head; His name, like sweet per -
love with sweet - est song, And in - fant voic - es
leap to lose their chains, The wea - ry find e -

songs a - gain, And earth re - peat the loud A - men!

shore to shore, Till moons shall wax and wane no more.
fume, shall rise With ev - ery morn - ing sac - ri - fice.
shall pro - claim Their ear - ly bless - ings on His name.
ter - nal rest, And all who suf - fer want are blest.

5. Let every creature rise and bring
Honors peculiar to our King;

Angels descend with songs again,
And earth repeat the loud Amen!

O Jesus Christ, May Grateful Hymns Be Rising

424

CHARTERHOUSE 11.10.11.10

Bradford Gray Webster, 1954

David Evans, 1927

1. O Jesus Christ, may grateful hymns be rising, In every city for Your love and care; Inspire our worship, grant the glad surprising That Your blest Spirit rouses everywhere.

2. Grant us new courage, sacrificial, humble, Strong in Your strength to venture and to dare; To lift the fallen, guide the feet that stumble, Seek out the lonely and God's mercy share.

3. Show us Your Spirit, brooding o'er each city, As You once wept above Jerusalem, Seeking to gather all in love and pity, And healing those who touch Your garment's hem.

♩=48–52

425 Lord of Light, Your Name Outshining

Howell Elvet Lewis, 1916; alt. ABBOT'S LEIGH 8.7.8.7 D Cyril Vincent Taylor, 1941

1. Lord of light, Your name out-shin-ing All the stars and
2. By the toil of faith-ful work-ers In some far out-
3. Grant that knowl-edge, still in-creas-ing, At Your feet may
4. By the prayers of faith-ful watch-ers, Nev-er si - lent

suns of space, Use our tal-ents in Your king-dom As the
ly - ing field, By the cour-age where the ra-diance Of the
low-ly kneel; With Your grace our tri - umphs hal-low, With Your
day or night; By the cross of Je - sus, bring-ing Peace to

ser - vants of Your grace; Use us to ful-fill Your pur - pose
cross is still re-vealed, By the vic - to-ries of meek-ness,
char - i - ty our zeal; Lift the na-tions from the shad-ows
all and heal-ing light; By the love that pass - es knowl-edge,

Refrain

In the gift of Christ Your Son:
Through re - proach and suf - fer-ing won: Ab - ba, as in
To the glad - ness of the sun:
Mak - ing all Your chil - dren one:

high - est heav - en, So on earth Your will be done.

♩=88–96

Lord, Speak to Me, That I May Speak 426

Frances Ridley Havergal, 1872   CANONBURY   LM   Robert Schumann, 1839

1. Lord, speak to me, that I may speak In liv - ing
2. O lead me, Lord, that I may lead The wan - dering
3. O teach me, Lord, that I may teach The pre - cious
4. O fill me with Thy full - ness, Lord, Un - til my

ech - oes of Thy tone; As Thou hast sought, so
and the wa - vering feet; O feed me, Lord, that
things Thou dost im - part; And wing my words, that
ver - y heart o'er - flow In kin - dling thought and

let me seek Thine err - ing chil - dren lost and lone.
I may feed Thy hun - gering ones with man - na sweet.
they may reach The hid - den depths of man - y a heart.
glow - ing word, Thy love to tell, Thy praise to show.

5. O use me, Lord, use even me,
   Just as Thou wilt, and when, and where;
   Until Thy blessed face I see,
   Thy rest, Thy joy, Thy glory share.

427 Lord, Whose Love Through Humble Service

BLAENHAFREN   8.7.8.7 D

Albert F. Bayly, 1961; alt.

Welsh melody

1. Lord, whose love through hum-ble ser-vice Bore the weight of
2. Still Your chil-dren wan-der home-less; Still the hun-gry
3. As we wor-ship, grant us vi-sion, Till Your love's re-
4. Called from wor-ship to Your ser-vice, Forth in Your dear

hu-man need, Who up-on the cross, for-sak-en, Of-fered
cry for bread; Still the cap-tives long for free-dom; Still in
veal-ing light, In its height and depth and great-ness, Dawns up-
name we go, To the child, the youth, the a-ged, Love in

mer-cy's per-fect deed, We, Your ser-vants, bring the wor-ship
grief we mourn our dead. As, O Lord, Your deep com-pas-sion
on our quick-ened sight, Mak-ing known the needs and bur-dens
liv-ing deeds to show; Hope and health, good-will and com-fort,

Not of voice a-lone, but heart, Con-se-crat-ing
Healed the sick and freed the soul, Use the love Your
Your com-pas-sion bids us bear, Stir-ring us to
Coun-sel, aid, and peace we give, That Your ser-vants,

Text: Used by permission of Oxford University Press.

to Your pur - pose Ev - ery gift that You im - part.
Spir - it kin - dles Still to save and make us whole.
tire - less striv - ing, Your a - bun - dant life to share.
Lord, in free - dom May Your mer - cy know and live.

♩ =92–100

We Give Thee but Thine Own 428

SCHUMANN SM

William Walsham How, c. 1858

Mason and Webb's *Cantica Laudis,* 1850

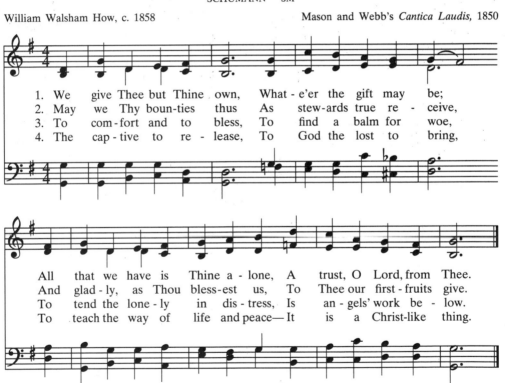

1. We give Thee but Thine own, What - e'er the gift may be;
2. May we Thy boun-ties thus As stew-ards true re - ceive,
3. To com-fort and to bless, To find a balm for woe,
4. The cap - tive to re - lease, To God the lost to bring,

All that we have is Thine a - lone, A trust, O Lord, from Thee.
And glad - ly, as Thou bless-est us, To Thee our first - fruits give.
To tend the lone - ly in dis - tress, Is an - gels' work be - low.
To teach the way of life and peace—It is a Christ-like thing.

5. And we believe Thy Word,
   Though dim our faith may be;
   Whate'er for Thine we do, O Lord,
   We do it unto Thee.

429 Lord, You Give the Great Commission

ABBOT'S LEIGH 8.7.8.7 D

Jeffery W. Rowthorn, 1978

Cyril Vincent Taylor, 1941

1. Lord, you give the great com-mis-sion: "Heal the sick and
2. Lord, you call us to your ser-vice: "In my name bap-
3. Lord, you make the com-mon ho-ly: "This my bod-y,
4. Lord, you show us love's true mea-sure: "Fa-ther, what they

preach the word." Lest the church ne-glect its mis-sion, And the
tize and teach." That the world may trust your prom-ise, Life a-
this my blood." Let us all, for earth's true glo-ry, Dai-ly
do, for-give." Yet we hoard as pri-vate trea-sure All that

gos-pel go un-heard, Help us wit-ness to your pur-pose
bun-dant meant for each, Give us all new fer-vor, draw us
lift life heav-en-ward, Ask-ing that the world a-round us
you so free-ly give. May your care and mer-cy lead us

With re-newed in-teg-ri-ty; With the Spir-it's
Clos-er in com-mu-ni-ty;
Share your chil-dren's lib-er-ty;
To a just so-ci-e-ty;

gifts em-power us For the work of min - is - try.

♩=88–96

5. Lord, you bless with words assuring:
"I am with you to the end."
Faith and hope and love restoring,
May we serve as you intend,

And, amid the cares that claim us,
Hold in mind eternity;
With the Spirit's gifts empower us
For the work of ministry.

Come Sing, O Church, in Joy! 430

DARWALL'S 148TH   6.6.6.6.8.8

Brian Dill, 1988   John Darwall, 1770

1. Come sing, O church, in joy! Come join, O church, in song!
2. Long years have come and gone, And still God reigns su - preme,
3. Let cour - age be our friend, Let wis - dom be our guide,
4. Come sing, O church, in joy! Come join, O church, in song!

For Christ the Lord has led us through the a - ges long!
Em - power-ing us to catch the vi - sion, dream the dream!
As we in mis - sion mag - ni - fy the Cru - ci - fied!
For Christ the Lord has tri-umphed o'er the a - ges long!

In bold ac - cord, come cel - e-brate the jour-ney now and praise the Lord!

This tune in a lower key, 155

431 O Lord, You Gave Your Servant John

ST. PATRICK'S BREASTPLATE   LMD

Joy F. Patterson, 1988

Irish melody
Adapt. Charles Villiers Stanford, 1902

1. O Lord, You gave Your ser - vant John A vi - sion
2. Our cit - ies, Lord, wear shrouds of pain; Be - neath our
3. Come, Lord, make real John's vi - sion fair; Come, dwell with

of the world to come: A ra - diant cit - y
gleam - ing towers of wealth The home - less crouch in
us, make all things new; We try in vain to

filled with light, Where You with us will make Your home;
rain and snow, The poor cry out for strength and health.
save our world Un - less our help shall come from You.

Where nei - ther grief nor pain shall dwell, Since for - mer
Youth's hope is dimmed by ig - no - rance; Un - will - ing,
Come, strength - en us to live in love; Bid ha - tred,

things have passed a - way, And where they need no
work - ers i - dled stand; In - dif - ference walks un -
greed, in - jus - tice cease. Your glo - ry all the

sun nor moon; Your glo - ry lights e - ter - nal day.
heed - ing by As hun - ger stretch - es out its hand.
light we need, Let all our cit - ies shine forth peace.

Canto de Esperanza
Song of Hope

432

ARGENTINA   11.11.11.11 with refrain

Alvin Schutmaat, 1984

Argentine folk melody

¡Dios de la es-pe - ran - za, da - nos go - zo y paz! Al mun-do en
May the God of hope go with us ev - ery day, Fill-ing all our

cri - sis, ha - bla tu ver - dad. Dios de la jus - ti - cia, mán - da -
lives with love and joy and peace. May the God of jus-tice speed us

nos tu luz, Luz y es-pe - ran - za en la os - cu - ri - dad.
on our way, Bring-ing light and hope to ev - ery land and race.

Refrain

O - re - mos por la paz, Can - te - mos de tu a-mor.
Pray-ing, let us work for peace, Sing-ing, share our joy with all,

Lu - che - mos por la paz, Fie - les a Ti, Se - ñor.
Work-ing for a world that's new, Faith-ful when we hear Christ's call.

433 There's a Spirit in the Air

LAUDS 7.7.7.7

Brian Wren, 1969; rev. 1987

John W. Wilson, 1967

Descant

Praise the love! Praise the love!

1. There's a spir - it in the air, Tell - ing Chris - tians ev - ery-where:
2. Lose your shy - ness, find your tongue, Tell the world what God has done:
3. When be - liev - ers break the bread, When a hun - gry child is fed,
4. Still the Spir - it gives us light, See - ing wrong and set - ting right:

Al - le - lu - ia! Al - le - lu - ia!

"Praise the love that Christ re-vealed, Liv - ing, work - ing in our world."
God in Christ has come to stay. Live to - mor - row's life to - day!
Praise the love that Christ re-vealed, Liv - ing, work - ing in our world.
God in Christ has come to stay. Live to - mor - row's life to - day!

♩.=50–54

5. When a stranger's not alone,
   Where the homeless find a home;
   Praise the love that Christ revealed,
   Living, working in our world.

6. May the Spirit fill our praise,
   Guide our thoughts and change our ways.
   God in Christ has come to stay.
   Live tomorrow's life today!

7. There's a Spirit in the air,
   Calling people everywhere;
   Praise the love that Christ revealed,
   Living, working in our world.

Today We All Are Called to Be Disciples 434

KINGSFOLD   CMD

English Country Songs, 1893
Arr. and harm. Ralph Vaughan Williams, 1906

H. Kenn Carmichael, 1985

1. To - day we all are called to be Dis - ci - ples of the Lord,
2. God made the world and at its birth Or - dained our hu - man race
3. Pray jus - tice may come roll - ing down As in a might - y stream,
4. May we in ser - vice to our God Act out the liv - ing Word,

To help to set the cap - tive free, Make plow-share out of sword,
To live as stew-ards of the earth, Re - spond-ing to God's grace.
With righ-teous - ness in field and town To cleanse us and re - deem.
And walk the road the saints have trod Till all have seen and heard.

To feed the hun-gry, quench their thirst, Make love and peace our fast,
But we are vain and sad - ly proud, We sow not peace but strife,
For God is long-ing to re - store An earth where con - flicts cease,
As stew-ards of the earth may we Give thanks in one ac - cord

To serve the poor and home-less first, Our ease and com-fort last.
Our dis - cord spreads a dead - ly cloud That threat-ens all of life.
A world that was cre - at - ed for A har - mo - ny of peace.
To God who calls us all to be Dis - ci - ples of the Lord.

435 We All Are One in Mission

ES FLOG EIN KLEINS WALDVÖGELEIN   7.6.7.6 D

Rusty Edwards, 1986; alt.

Memmingen ms., 17th century
Harm. George Ratcliffe Woodward, 1904

1. We all are one in mis - sion, We all are one in call,
2. We all are called for ser - vice To wit - ness in God's name;
3. Now let us be u - nit - ed And let our song be heard.

Our var - ied gifts u - nit - ed By Christ, the Lord of all.
Our min - is - tries are dif - ferent, Our pur - pose is the same:
Now let us be a ves - sel For God's re - deem - ing word.

A sin - gle, great com - mis - sion Com - pels us from a - bove
To touch the lives of oth - ers By God's sur - pris - ing grace
We all are one in mis - sion, We all are one in call,

To plan and work to - geth - er That all may know Christ's love.
So ev - ery folk and na - tion May feel God's warm em - brace.
Our var - ied gifts u - nit - ed By Christ, the Lord of all.

Text: © 1986 Howard M. Edwards III. All rights reserved. Used by permission.

♩=52–56

We Are Your People

436

WHITFIELD   Irregular

Brian Wren, 1973

John W. Wilson, 1980

1. We are Your peo - ple: Lord, by Your grace,
2. Called to por - tray You, help us to live
3. Glad of tra - di - tion, Help us to see
4. Joined in com - mu - ni - ty, break - ing Your bread,
5. Lord, as we min - is - ter in dif - ferent ways,

You dare to make us Christ to our neigh - bors of ev - ery
Clos - er than neigh - bors, o - pen to stran - gers, a - ble to
In all life's chang - ing where You are lead - ing, Where our best
May we dis - cov - er gifts in each oth - er, will - ing to
May all we're do - ing show that You're liv - ing, meet - ing Your

1,5
1. na - tion and race.
5. love with our praise.

2,3,4
2. clash and for - give.
3. ef - forts should be.
4. lead and be led.

D.C.

♩=92–100

437 Our Cities Cry to You, O God

SALVATION   CMD

Kentucky Harmony, 1816
Harm. *Songs for Liturgy and
More Hymns and Spiritual Songs*, 1971

Margaret Clarkson, 1981

1. Our   cit - ies cry to You, O God, From out their pain and strife;
2. Yet   still You walk our streets, O Christ! We   know Your pres - ence here
3. Your   peo-ple are Your hands and feet To serve Your world to - day,
4. O   heal-ing Sav - ior, Prince of Peace, Sal - va - tion's source and sum,

You   made us for Your-self a - lone, But we choose al - ien   life.
Where   hum-ble Chris-tians love and serve In   god - ly grace and   fear.
Our   lives the book our   cit - ies read To help them find Your way.
For   You our bro - ken   cit - ies cry: O   come, Lord Je - sus, come!

Our   goals are plea - sure, gold, and power; In - jus - tice stalks our earth;
O   Word made flesh, be   seen in us! May all we say and do
O   pour Your sov - ereign Spir-it out On heart and will and brain:
With   truth Your roy - al   di - a - dem, With right-teous-ness Your rod,

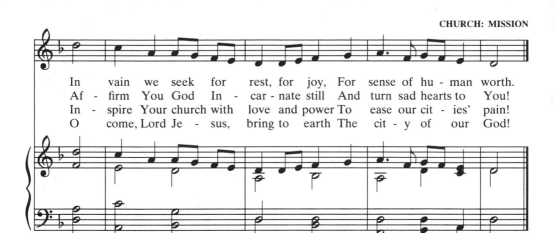

In vain we seek for rest, for joy, For sense of hu - man worth.
Af - firm You God In - car - nate still And turn sad hearts to You!
In - spire Your church with love and power To ease our cit - ies' pain!
O come, Lord Je - sus, bring to earth The cit - y of our God!

♩=52–56

Blest Be the Tie That Binds 438

DENNIS SM

Johann Georg Nägeli (1773–1836)
Arr. Lowell Mason, 1845

John Fawcett, 1782

1. Blest be the tie that binds Our hearts in Chris - tian love:
2. Be - fore our *Fa - ther's throne We pour our ar - dent prayers;
3. We share our mu - tual woes, Our mu - tual bur - dens bear,
4. From sor - row, toil, and pain, And sin we shall be free;

The fel - low - ship of kin - dred minds Is like to that a - bove.
Our fears, our hopes, our aims are one, Our com - forts and our cares.
And of - ten for each oth - er flows The sym - pa - thiz - ing tear.
And per - fect love and friend-ship reign Through all e - ter - ni - ty.

*Or "Maker's."

439 In Christ There Is No East or West

ST. PETER   CM

John Oxenham, 1908; alt.

Alexander Robert Reinagle, 1836

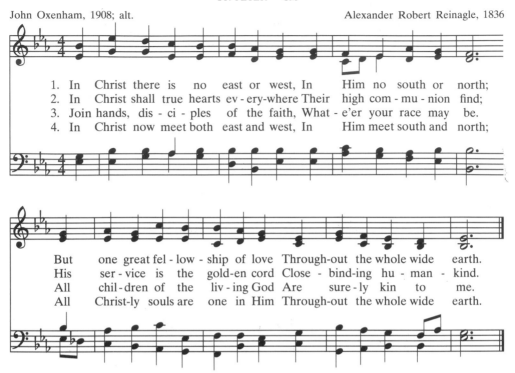

1. In Christ there is no east or west, In Him no south or north;
2. In Christ shall true hearts ev-ery-where Their high com-mu-nion find;
3. Join hands, dis-ci-ples of the faith, What-e'er your race may be.
4. In Christ now meet both east and west, In Him meet south and north;

But one great fel-low-ship of love Through-out the whole wide earth.
His ser-vice is the gold-en cord Close-bind-ing hu-man-kind.
All chil-dren of the liv-ing God Are sure-ly kin to me.
All Christ-ly souls are one in Him Through-out the whole wide earth.

Text: Reprinted by permission of the American Tract Society, Garland, Texas.

Luke 13:29

440 In Christ There Is No East or West

MC KEE   CM

African-American spiritual
Jubilee Songs, 1884
Adapt. Harry T. Burleigh, 1940

John Oxenham, 1908; alt.

C   G   C   F   Bb   F   C   F   Am Dm7 G7   C   F   C

1. In Christ there is no east or west, In Him no south or north;
2. In Christ shall true hearts ev-ery-where Their high com-mu-ni-on find;
3. Join hands, dis-ci-ples of the faith, What-e'er your race may be.
4. In Christ now meet both east and west, In Him meet south and north;

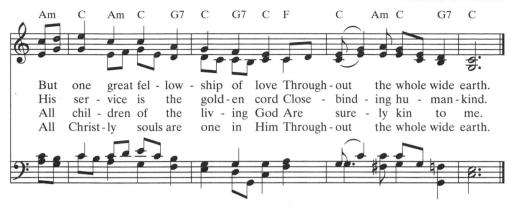

But one great fel - low - ship of love Through - out the whole wide earth.
His ser - vice is the gold - en cord Close - bind - ing hu - man - kind.
All chil - dren of the liv - ing God Are sure - ly kin to me.
All Christ - ly souls are one in Him Through - out the whole wide earth.

Text: Reprinted by permission of the American Tract Society, Garland, Texas.

I Love Thy Kingdom, Lord 441

ST. THOMAS SM

Timothy Dwight, 1800

The Universal Psalmodist, 1763
Adapt. Aaron Williams, 1770

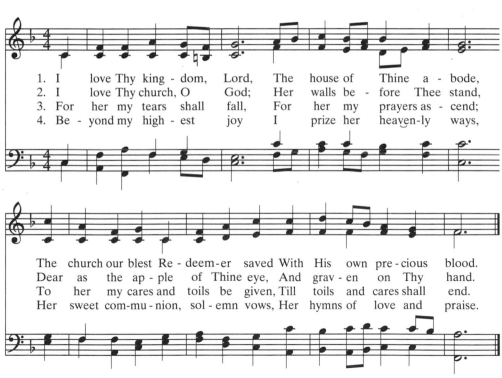

1. I love Thy king - dom, Lord, The house of Thine a - bode,
2. I love Thy church, O God; Her walls be - fore Thee stand,
3. For her my tears shall fall, For her my prayers as - cend;
4. Be - yond my high - est joy I prize her heaven - ly ways,

The church our blest Re - deem - er saved With His own pre - cious blood.
Dear as the ap - ple of Thine eye, And grav - en on Thy hand.
To her my cares and toils be given, Till toils and cares shall end.
Her sweet com - mu - nion, sol - emn vows, Her hymns of love and praise.

5. Sure as Thy truth shall last,
   To Zion shall be given
   The brightest glories earth can yield,
   And brighter bliss of heaven.

442 The Church's One Foundation

Samuel John Stone, 1866; alt.

AURELIA 7.6.7.6 D

Samuel Sebastian Wesley, 1864

1. The church's one foun - da - tion Is Je - sus Christ her Lord;
2. E - lect from ev - ery na - tion, Yet one o'er all the earth,
3. Though with a scorn - ful won - der This world sees her op - pressed,
4. Mid toil and trib - u - la - tion, And tu - mult of her war,

She is His new cre - a - tion By wa - ter and the word;
Her char - ter of sal - va - tion One Lord, one faith, one birth;
By schis - ms rent a - sun - der, By her - e - sies dis - tressed,
She waits the con - sum - ma - tion Of peace for - ev - er - more;

From heaven He came and sought her To be His ho - ly bride;
One ho - ly name she bless - es, Par - takes one ho - ly food,
Yet saints their watch are keep - ing; Their cry goes up: "How long?"
Till with the vi - sion glo - rious Her long - ing eyes are blest,

With His own blood He bought her, And for her life He died.
And to one hope she press - es, With ev - ery grace en - dued.
And soon the night of weep - ing Shall be the morn of song.
And the great church vic - to - rious Shall be the church at rest.

5. Yet she on earth has union
   With God the Three in One,
   And mystic sweet communion
   With those whose rest is won:
   O happy ones and holy!
   Lord, give us grace that we,
   Like them, the meek and lowly,
   May live eternally.

O Christ, the Great Foundation 443

AURELIA   7.6.7.6 D

Timothy T'ingfang Lew, 1933; alt.
Trans. Mildred A. Wiant, 1966

Samuel Sebastian Wesley, 1864

1. O Christ, the great foun - da - tion On which Your peo - ple stand
2. Bap - tized in one con - fes - sion, One church in all the earth,
3. Where ty - rants' hold is tight - ened, Where strong de - vour the weak,
4. This is the mo - ment glo - rious When He who once was dead

To preach Your true sal - va - tion In ev - ery age and land:
We bear our Lord's im - pres - sion, The sign of sec - ond birth:
Where in - no - cents are fright - ened, The righ - teous fear to speak,
Shall lead His church vic - to - rious, Their cham - pion and their head.

Pour out Your Ho - ly Spir - it To make us strong and pure,
One ho - ly peo - ple gath - ered In love be - yond our own,
There let Your church a - wak - ing At - tack the powers of sin
The Lord of all cre - a - tion His heaven - ly king - dom brings,

To keep the faith un - bro - ken As long as worlds en - dure.
By grace we were in - vit - ed, By grace we make You known.
And, all their ram - parts break - ing, With You the vic - tory win.
The fi - nal con - sum - ma - tion, The glo - ry of all things.

444 We Gather Here to Bid Farewell

WINCHESTER NEW   LM

Margaret Clarkson, 1987

Musikalisches Handbuch, 1690
Harm. William Henry Monk, 1847

1. We gath-er here to bid fare-well To friends who leave for oth-er parts; Our prayers we pledge, our love we tell, And lift to God our grate-ful hearts.

2. We bless the hand that brought you here And rich-ly blest us all in you: As now you leave for wid-er sphere God's cov-enant mer-cies we re-view.

3. In friend-ship's bonds our souls u-nite In prayer and praise and ho-ly vow: To God's great heart of love and light Your kin in Christ com-mit you now.

4. God guide you, keep you, lead you on From hope to hope, from strength to strength, Un-til, in God's all glo-rious dawn, We meet be-fore the throne at length.

Great Day!

445

Irregular

African-American spiritual
Arr. Joseph T. Jones (1902–1983)
Adapt. Melva W. Costen, 1989

African-American spiritual

Great day! Great day, the right-teous march-ing, Great day!

God's going to build up Zi - on's walls. Oh, Zi - on's walls. 1. The
2. This

1. char-i-ot rode on the moun-tain-top, God's going to build up Zi-on's walls.
2. is the day of Ju - bi - lee,

My God spoke and the char-iot did stop. God's going to build up Zi-on's walls. Oh,
God shall set the peo - ple free.

446   Glorious Things of Thee Are Spoken

AUSTRIAN HYMN   8.7.8.7 D

John Newton, 1779; alt.

Franz Joseph Haydn, 1797
Desc. Michael E. Young, 1979

3. Round each hab - i - ta - tion hov - ering, See the cloud and

1. Glo - rious things of thee are spo - ken, Zi - on, cit - y
2. See, the streams of liv - ing wa - ters, Spring-ing from e -
3. Round each hab - i - ta - tion hov - ering, See the cloud and

fire ap - pear   For a glo - ry

of our God; God, whose word can - not be
ter - nal love, Well sup - ply thy sons and
fire ap - pear For a glo - ry and a

cov - ering, Show - ing that the Lord is near.

bro - ken, Formed thee for a blest a - bode.
daugh - ters And all fear of want re - move.
cov - ering, Show - ing that the Lord is near.

Thus de-riv-ing light by night and

On the rock of a - ges found-ed, What can shake thy
Who can faint while such a riv - er Ev - er flows their
Thus de - riv - ing from their ban - ner Light by night and

shade by day, Safe they feed on

sure re - pose? With sal - va - tion's walls sur -
thirst to as - suage? Grace, which like the Lord the
shade by day, Safe they feed up - on the

man - na Which God gives them when they pray.

round - ed, Thou may'st smile at all thy foes.
giv - er, Nev - er fails from age to age.
man - na Which God gives them when they pray.

Alternate tune: ABBOT'S LEIGH, 461

447 Lead On, O King Eternal

LANCASHIRE   7.6.7.6 D

Ernest W. Shurtleff, 1888   Henry Thomas Smart, c. 1835

1. Lead on, O King e - ter - nal, The day of march has come;
2. Lead on, O King e - ter - nal, Till sin's fierce war shall cease,
3. Lead on, O King e - ter - nal: We fol - low, not with fears;

Hence-forth in fields of con - quest Thy tents shall be our home:
And ho - li - ness shall whis - per The sweet a - men of peace;
For glad-ness breaks like morn - ing Wher - e'er Thy face ap - pears;

Through days of prep - a - ra - tion Thy grace has made us strong,
For not with swords' loud clash - ing, Nor roll of stir-ring drums;
Thy cross is lift - ed o'er us; We jour-ney in its light:

And now, O King e - ter - nal, We lift our bat - tle song.
With deeds of love and mer - cy The heaven-ly king-dom comes.
The crown a - waits the con - quest; Lead on, O God of might.

Lead On, O King Eternal

LLANGLOFFAN   7.6.7.6 D

Ernest W. Shurtleff, 1888

Welsh folk melody
Evans' *Hymnau a Thonau,* 1865
As in *English Hymnal,* 1906

1. Lead on, O King e - ter - nal, The day of march has come;
2. Lead on, O King e - ter - nal, Till sin's fierce war shall cease,
3. Lead on, O King e - ter - nal: We fol - low, not with fears;

Hence - forth in fields of con - quest Thy tents shall be our home:
And ho - li - ness shall whis - per The sweet a - men of peace;
For glad - ness breaks like morn - ing Wher - e'er Thy face ap - pears;

Through days of prep - a - ra - tion Thy grace has made us strong,
For not with swords' loud clash - ing, Nor roll of stir - ring drums;
Thy cross is lift - ed o'er us; We jour - ney in its light:

And now, O King e - ter - nal, We lift our bat - tle song.
With deeds of love and mer - cy The heaven - ly king - dom comes.
The crown a - waits the con - quest; Lead on, O God of might.

449 My Lord! What a Morning

Irregular

African-American spiritual

African-American spiritual
Arr. Melva W. Costen, 1989

Refrain

My Lord! what a morn-ing, My Lord! what a morn-ing,

Oh, my Lord! what a morn-ing, When the stars be-gin to

Fine

fall, When the stars be-gin to fall.
1. You will hear the trum-pet
2. You will hear the sin - ner
3. You will hear the Chris-tian

sound
cry To wake the na - tions un - der - ground,
shout

D.C.

Look-ing to my God's right hand When the stars be-gin to fall.

O Day of Peace

450

JERUSALEM LMD

Carl P. Daw, Jr., 1982

C. Hubert H. Parry, 1916
Harm. Richard Proulx, 1986

Unison

1. O day of peace that dim-ly shines
2. Then shall the wolf dwell with the lamb,

Through all our hopes and prayers and dreams, Guide us to jus - tice,
Nor shall the fierce de - vour the small; As beasts and cat - tle

truth, and love, De - liv - ered from our self - ish schemes. May swords of
calm - ly graze, A lit - tle child shall lead them all. Then en - e-

Harmony

hate fall from our hands, Our hearts from en - vy find
mies shall learn to love, All crea - tures find their true

re - lease, Till by God's grace our war - ring
ac - cord; The hope of peace shall be ful -

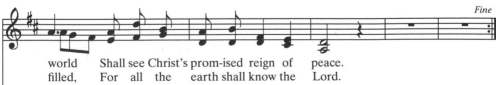

Fine

world Shall see Christ's prom-ised reign of peace.
filled, For all the earth shall know the Lord.

Accompaniment for this tune, 252

♩=48–52

451   Ye Watchers and Ye Holy Ones

LASST UNS ERFREUEN   LM with alleluias

Geistliche Kirchengesäng, 1623; alt.
Harm. Ralph Vaughan Williams, 1906

John Athelstan Laurie Riley, 1906

1. Ye watch-ers and ye ho-ly ones, Bright ser-aphs, cher-u-bim, and thrones, Raise the glad strain, Al-le-lu-ia! Cry out, do-min-ions, prince-doms, powers, Vir-tues, arch-an-gels, an-gels' choirs, Al-le-lu-ia! Al-le-lu-ia!

2. O high-er than the cher-u-bim, More glo-rious than the ser-a-phim, Lead their prais-es, Al-le-lu-ia! Thou bear-er of the e-ter-nal Word, Most gra-cious, mag-ni-fy the Lord, Al-le-lu-ia! Al-le-lu-ia!

3. Re-spond, ye souls in end-less rest, Ye pa-tri-archs and proph-ets blest, Al-le-lu-ia, Al-le-lu-ia! Ye ho-ly twelve, ye mar-tyrs strong, All saints tri-um-phant, raise the song, Al-le-lu-ia! Al-le-lu-ia!

4. O friends, in glad-ness let us sing, Su-per-nal an-thems ech-o-ing, Al-le-lu-ia, Al-le-lu-ia! To God the Fa-ther, God the Son, And God the Spir-it, Three in One, Al-le-lu-ia! Al-le-lu-ia!

Text and Music: From the *English Hymnal,* 1906. Used by permission of Oxford University Press.

Unison

Al - le - lu - ia! Al - le - lu - ia! Al - le - lu - ia!

O Day of God, Draw Nigh 452

ST. MICHAEL SM

Robert B. Y. Scott, 1937, 1939; alt. 1972

Genevan Psalter, 1551
Adapt. William Crotch, 1836

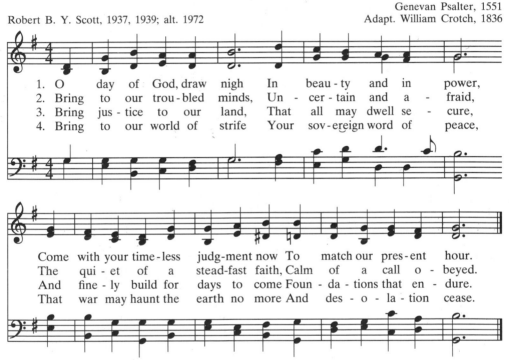

1. O day of God, draw nigh In beau - ty and in power,
2. Bring to our trou - bled minds, Un - cer - tain and a - fraid,
3. Bring jus - tice to our land, That all may dwell se - cure,
4. Bring to our world of strife Your sov - ereign word of peace,

Come with your time - less judg-ment now To match our pres - ent hour.
The qui - et of a stead-fast faith, Calm of a call o - beyed.
And fine - ly build for days to come Foun - da - tions that en - dure.
That war may haunt the earth no more And des - o - la - tion cease.

5. O day of God, draw nigh
   As at creation's birth;
   Let there be light again, and set
   Your judgments in the earth.

453 O Holy City, Seen of John

MORNING SONG   8.6.8.6.8.6.

Walter Russell Bowie, 1909; alt.

Wyeth's *Repository of Sacred Music,* 1813
Harm. C. Winfred Douglas, 1940

1. O ho-ly cit-y, seen of John, Where Christ, the Lamb, does reign,
2. O shame to us who rest con-tent While lust and greed for gain
3. Give us, O God, the strength to build The cit-y that has stood
4. Al-read-y in the mind of God That cit-y ris-es fair.

With-in whose four-square walls shall come No night, nor need, nor pain,
In street and shop and ten-e-ment Wring gold from hu-man pain,
Too long a dream, whose laws are love, Whose ways are ser-vant-hood,
Lo, how its splen-dor chal-len-ges The souls that great-ly dare,

And where the tears are wiped from eyes That shall not weep a-gain!
And bit-ter lips in blind de-spair Cry, "Christ has died in vain!"
And where the sun that shines be-comes God's grace for hu-man good.
And bids us seize the whole of life And build its glo-ry there.

Music: Harmonization © 1943, 1961, 1985 Church Pension Fund. Used by permission.

♩=88–96

Blessed Jesus, at Your Word

454

LIEBSTER JESU   7.8.7.8.8.8

Tobias Clausnitzer, 1663
Trans. Catherine Winkworth, 1858; alt. 1972

Johann Rudolph Ahle, 1664
Harm. Johann Sebastian Bach (1685–1750); alt.

1. Bless - ed Je - sus, at Your word We are gath - ered
2. All our knowl-edge, sense, and sight Lie in deep - est
3. Glo - rious Lord, Your - self im - part! Light of light, from

all to hear You; Let our hearts and souls be stirred
dark-ness shroud - ed, Till Your Spir - it breaks our night
God pro - ceed - ing, O - pen now our ears and heart,

Now to seek and love and fear You; By Your teach-ings
With the beams of truth un - cloud - ed; You a - lone to
Help us by Your Spir - it's plead - ing; Hear the cry that

true and ho - ly, Drawn from earth to love You sole - ly.
God can win us, You must work all good with - in us.
we are rais - ing; Hear, and bless our prayers and prais - ing.

455   All Creatures of Our God and King

LASST UNS ERFREUEN   LM with alleluias

Francis of Assisi, 1225
Trans. and para. William Henry Draper, c. 1910; alt.

Geistliche Kirchengesäng, 1623; alt.
Harm. Ralph Vaughan Williams, 1906

Unison

1. All creatures of our God and King, Lift up your voice
2. Thou rush-ing wind that art so strong, Ye clouds that sail
3. Thou flow-ing wa - ter, pure and clear, Make mu - sic for
4. Thou fer - tile earth, that day by day Un - fold - est bless-

Harmony

and with us sing, Al - le - lu - ia! Al - le - lu - ia!
in heaven a - long, O sing ye! Al - le - lu - ia!
thy Lord to hear, Al - le - lu - ia! Al - le - lu - ia!
ings on your way, O sing ye! Al - le - lu - ia!

Unison

Thou burn - ing sun with gold - en beam, Thou sil - ver moon with
Thou ris - ing morn, in praise re - joice, Ye lights of eve - ning,
Thou fire so mas - ter - ful and bright, That giv - est us both
The flowers and fruits that in thee grow, Let them God's glo - ry

Harmony

soft - er gleam,
find a voice! Al - le - lu - ia! Al - le - lu - ia!
warmth and light,
al - so show!

Text: Copyright © 1926 (Renewed) J. Curwen & Sons Ltd. International copyright secured. All rights reserved. Reprinted by permission of G. Schirmer, Inc.
Music: From the *English Hymnal,* 1906. Used by permission of Oxford University Press.

Unison

Al - le - lu - ia! Al - le - lu - ia! Al - le - lu - ia!

5. And everyone of tender heart,
   Forgiving others, take your part.
   O sing ye! Alleluia!
   Ye who long pain and sorrow bear,
   Praise God and cast on God your care!
   Alleluia! Alleluia!
   Alleluia! Alleluia! Alleluia!

6. All creatures, your Creator bless,
   And worship God in humbleness.
   O sing ye! Alleluia!
   Praise, praise the Father, praise the Son,
   And praise the Spirit, Three in One!
   Alleluia! Alleluia!
   Alleluia! Alleluia! Alleluia!

Awake, My Soul, and with the Sun   456

MORNING HYMN   LM

François Hippolyte Barthélémon, 1785
As in *The Church Hymnal
for the Christian Year*, 1917

Thomas Ken, 1695; alt.

1. A - wake, my soul, and with the sun your
2. Lord, I my vows to You re - new. Dis -
3. Di - rect, con - trol, sug - gest, this day, All

dai - ly stage of du - ty run; Shake off dull sloth, and
perse my sins as morn-ing dew; Guard my first springs of
I de - sign or do or say; That all my powers, with

joy - ful rise To pay your morn - ing sac - ri - fice.
thought and will, And with Your - self my spir - it fill.
all their might, In Your sole glo - ry may u - nite.

♩=96–104

457 I Greet Thee, Who My Sure Redeemer Art

TOULON 10.10.10.10

Attr. John Calvin
French Psalter, Strassburg, 1545
Trans. Elizabeth Lee Smith, 1868

Adapt. from Genevan 124
Genevan Psalter, 1551

1. I greet Thee, who my sure Re-deem-er art,
2. Thou art the King of mer-cy and of grace,
3. Thou art the life, by which a-lone we live,
4. Thou hast the true and per-fect gen-tle-ness,

My on-ly trust and Sav-ior of my heart,
Reign-ing om-nip-o-tent in ev-ery place:
And all our sub-stance and our strength re-ceive;
No harsh-ness hast Thou and no bit-ter-ness:

Who pain didst un-der-go for my poor sake;
So come, O King, and our whole be-ing sway;
Sus-tain us by Thy faith and by Thy power,
O grant to us the grace we find in Thee,

I pray Thee from our hearts all cares to take.
Shine on us with the light of Thy pure day.
And give us strength in ev-ery try-ing hour.
That we may dwell in per-fect u-ni-ty.

5. Our hope is in no other save in Thee;
   Our faith is built upon Thy promise free;
   Lord, give us peace, and make us calm and sure,
   That in Thy strength we evermore endure.

Earth and All Stars

458

DEXTER   4.5.7 D with refrain

Herbert Frederick Brokering, 1964

David N. Johnson, 1968

1. Earth and all stars, Loud rush-ing plan - ets Sing to the
2. Steel and ma - chines, Loud pound-ing ham - mers Sing to the
3. Class - rooms and labs, Loud boil - ing test tubes Sing to the
4. Knowl-edge and truth, Loud sound-ing wis - dom Sing to the

Lord   a new song! Hail, wind, and rain, Loud blow-ing snow-storm
Lord   a new song! Lime-stone and beams, Loud build-ing work - ers
Lord   a new song! Ath - lete and band, Loud cheer-ing peo - ple
Lord   a new song! Daugh-ter and son, Loud pray-ing mem - bers

Sing to the Lord   a new song!
Sing to the Lord   a new song!
Sing to the Lord   a new song!   God has done
Sing to the Lord   a new song!

mar - vel-ous things. We will sing prais-es with a new song!

♩=116–126

459 Father, We Praise Thee

CHRISTE SANCTORUM 11.11.11.5

Attr. Gregory the Great (540–604)
Trans. Percy Dearmer, 1906

Paris *Antiphoner,* 1681
Harm. David Evans, 1927

1. Fa - ther, we praise Thee, now the night is o - ver; Ac - tive and
2. Mon - arch of all things, fit us for Thy man - sions; Ban - ish our
3. All - ho - ly Fa - ther, Son, and e - qual Spir - it, Trin - i - ty

watch - ful, stand we all be - fore Thee; Sing - ing, we of - fer
weak - ness, health and whole-ness send - ing; Bring us to heav - en,
bless - ed, send us Thy sal - va - tion; Thine is the glo - ry,

prayer and med - i - ta - tion: Thus we a - dore Thee.
where Thy saints u - nit - ed Joy with-out end - ing.
gleam-ing and re - sound-ing Through all cre - a - tion.

Music: Harmonization from the *Revised Church Hymnary 1927.* Used by permission of Oxford University Press.

Holy God, We Praise Your Name

460

GROSSER GOTT, WIR LOBEN DICH   7.8.7.8.7.7

Attr. Ignaz Franz, c. 1774
Trans. Clarence Alphonsus Walworth, 1858; alt.

Allgemeines Katholisches Gesangbuch, c. 1774
Alt. Johann Gottfried Schicht, 1819

1. Ho - ly God, we praise Your name; Lord of all, we
2. Hark, the glad ce - les - tial hymn An - gel choirs a -
3. All a - pos - tles join the strain As Your sa - cred
4. Ho - ly Fa - ther, Ho - ly Son, Ho - ly Spir - it:

bow be - fore You; All on earth Your scep - ter claim,
bove are rais - ing; Cher - u - bim and ser - a - phim,
name they hal - low; Proph - ets swell the glad re - frain,
Three we name You, While in es - sence on - ly One;

All in heaven a - bove a - dore You. In - fi - nite Your
In un - ceas - ing cho - rus prais - ing, Fill the heavens with
And the bless - ed mar - tyrs fol - low, And from morn to
Un - di - vid - ed God we claim You, And a - dor - ing

vast do - main, Ev - er - last - ing is Your reign.
sweet ac - cord: Ho - ly, ho - ly, ho - ly Lord.
set of sun, Through the church the song goes on.
bend the knee While we own the mys - ter - y.

461 God Is Here!

ABBOT'S LEIGH   8.7.8.7 D

Fred Pratt Green, 1979; rev. 1988

Cyril Vincent Taylor, 1941

1. God is here! As we Your peo-ple Meet to of - fer
2. Here are sym-bols to re - mind us Of our life - long
3. Here our chil - dren find a wel-come In the Shep _ herd's
4. Lord of all, of church and king-dom, In an age of

praise and prayer, May we find in ful - ler mea-sure What it
need of grace; Here are ta - ble, font, and pul - pit; Here the
flock and fold, Here, as bread and wine are tak - en, Christ sus-
change and doubt Keep us faith - ful to the gos - pel, Help us

is in Christ we share. Here, as in the world a - round us,
cross has cen - tral place. Here in hon - es - ty of preach-ing,
tains us as of old. Here the ser - vants of the Ser - vant
work Your pur - pose out. Here, in this day's ded - i - ca - tion,

All our var - ied skills and arts Wait the com - ing
Here in si - lence, as in speech, Here, in new - ness
Seek in wor - ship to ex - plore What it means in
All we have to give, re - ceive: We, who can - not

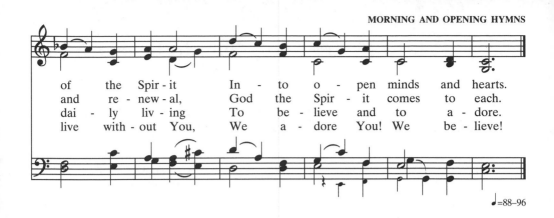

of the Spir - it   In - to o - pen minds and hearts.
and re - new - al,   God the Spir - it comes to each.
dai - ly liv - ing   To be - lieve and to a - dore.
live with - out You,   We a - dore You! We be - lieve!

♩=88–96

Christ, Whose Glory Fills the Skies   462

RATISBON   7.7.7.7.7.7

Freylinghausen's *Gesangbuch,* 1704
Rev. in Werner's *Choralbuch,* 1815
As in *Old Church Psalmody,* 1847

Charles Wesley, 1740

1. Christ, whose glo - ry fills the skies, Christ, the true, the on - ly light,
2. Dark and cheer-less is the morn Un - ac - com - pa - nied by Thee;
3. Vis - it then this soul of mine; Pierce the gloom of sin and grief;

Sun of Righ-teous - ness, a - rise, Tri - umph o'er the shades of night;
Joy - less is the day's re - turn Till Thy mer - cy's beams I see,
Fill me, ra - dian - cy di - vine; Scat - ter all my un - be - lief;

Day-spring from on high, be near; Day - star, in my heart ap - pear.
Till they in - ward light im - part, Cheer my eyes and warm my heart.
More and more Thy - self dis - play, Shin - ing to the per - fect day.

Alternate tune: CHRIST WHOSE GLORY, 463

463 Christ, Whose Glory Fills the Skies

CHRIST WHOSE GLORY   7.7.7.7.7.7

Charles Wesley, 1740   Malcolm Williamson (b. 1931)

1. Christ, whose glo - ry fills the skies, Christ, the true, the on - ly light,
2. Dark and cheer-less is the morn Un - ac - com - pa-nied by Thee;
3. Vis - it then this soul of mine; Pierce the gloom of sin and grief;

Sun of Righ-teous-ness, a - rise, Tri-umph o'er the shades of night;
Joy-less is the day's re - turn Till Thy mer-cy's beams I see,
Fill me, ra - dian - cy di - vine; Scat-ter all my un - be - lief;

Day-spring from on high, be near; Day - star, in my heart ap - pear.
Till they in - ward light im-part, Cheer my eyes and warm my heart.
More and more Thy - self dis-play, Shin - ing to the per - fect day.

Alternate tune: RATISBON, 462

Joyful, Joyful, We Adore Thee   464

HYMN TO JOY   8.7.8.7 D

Ludwig van Beethoven, 1824
Adapt. Edward Hodges (1796–1867); alt.

Henry van Dyke, 1907; alt.

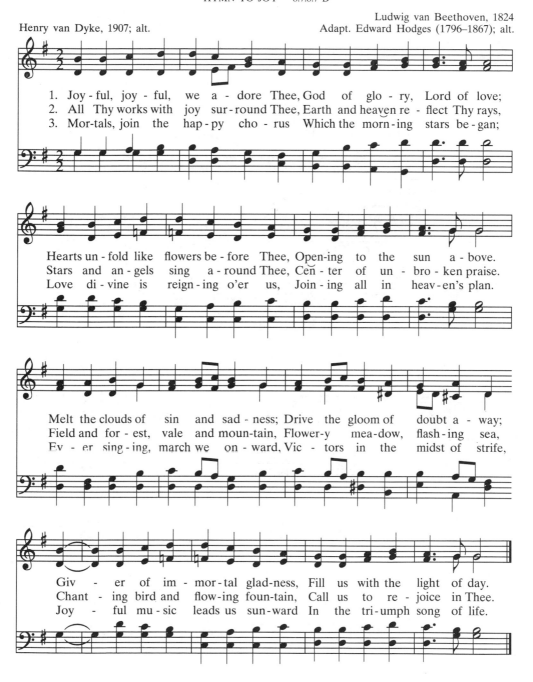

1. Joy-ful, joy-ful, we a-dore Thee, God of glo-ry, Lord of love;
2. All Thy works with joy sur-round Thee, Earth and heaven re-flect Thy rays,
3. Mor-tals, join the hap-py cho-rus Which the morn-ing stars be-gan;

Hearts un-fold like flowers be-fore Thee, Open-ing to the sun a-bove.
Stars and an-gels sing a-round Thee, Cen-ter of un-bro-ken praise.
Love di-vine is reign-ing o'er us, Join-ing all in heav-en's plan.

Melt the clouds of sin and sad-ness; Drive the gloom of doubt a-way;
Field and for-est, vale and moun-tain, Flower-y mea-dow, flash-ing sea,
Ev-er sing-ing, march we on-ward, Vic-tors in the midst of strife,

Giv-er of im-mor-tal glad-ness, Fill us with the light of day.
Chant-ing bird and flow-ing foun-tain, Call us to re-joice in Thee.
Joy-ful mu-sic leads us sun-ward In the tri-umph song of life.

465   Here, O Lord, Your Servants Gather

TŌKYŌ   7.5.7.5 D

Tokuo Yamaguchi, 1958
Trans. Everett M. Stowe, 1958; alt. 1972

Japanese gagaku mode
Isao Koizumi, 1958

1. Here, O Lord, Your ser-vants gath - er, Hand we link with hand;
2. Man - y are the tongues we speak, Scat - tered are the lands,
3. Na - ture's se - crets o - pen wide, Chang-es nev - er cease;
4. Grant, O God, an age re - newed, Filled with death-less love;

Look - ing toward our Sav-ior's cross, Joined in love we stand.
Yet our hearts are one in God, One in love's de - mands.
Where, O where, can wea - ry souls Find the source of peace?
Help us as we work and pray, Send us from a - bove

As we seek the realm of God, We u - nite to pray:
E'en in dark - ness hope ap - pears, Call - ing age and youth:
Un - to all those sore dis - tressed, Torn by end-less strife:
Truth and cour - age, faith and power Need-ed in our strife:

Je - sus, Sav - ior, guide our steps, For You are the Way.
Je - sus, teach - er, dwell with us, For You are the Truth.
Je - sus, heal - er, bring Your balm, For You are the Life.
Je - sus, Sav - ior, be our way, Be our truth, our life.

O for a Thousand Tongues to Sing   466

AZMON   CM

Charles Wesley, 1738; alt.

Carl Gotthelf Gläser, 1828
Arr. Lowell Mason, 1839

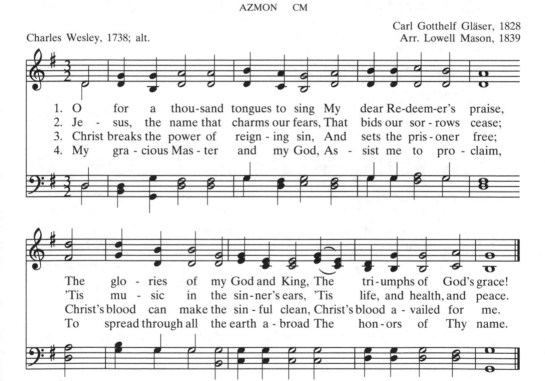

1. O for a thou-sand tongues to sing My dear Re-deem-er's praise,
2. Je - sus, the name that charms our fears, That bids our sor - rows cease;
3. Christ breaks the power of reign - ing sin, And sets the pris - oner free;
4. My gra - cious Mas - ter and my God, As - sist me to pro - claim,

The glo - ries of my God and King, The tri - umphs of God's grace!
'Tis mu - sic in the sin-ner's ears, 'Tis life, and health, and peace.
Christ's blood can make the sin - ful clean, Christ's blood a - vailed for me.
To spread through all the earth a - broad The hon - ors of Thy name.

467

How Great Thou Art

O STORE GUD   11.10.11.10 with refrain

Carl Gustav Boberg, 1885
English version: Stuart K. Hine, 1953
Transliteration of Korean: Myung Ja Yue, 1989

Swedish folk melody
Harm. Stuart K. Hine, 1949

1. Joo ha nah nim jee eu shin mo dun seh geh Nae ma um
2. Soop sok ee nah hum hahn sahn gol jjak eh suh Jee juh gee

1. O Lord my God! when I in awe-some won - der Con-sid-er
2. When through the woods and for - est glades I wan - der And hear the

so geh geu ree uh bol ttae Ha neul eh byul ool
nun juh sae so ree deul gwa Ko yo ha geh heu

all the *worlds Thy hands have made, I see the stars, I
birds sing sweet-ly in the trees; When I look down from

lyuh paw jee nun nweh sung Joo nim eh kwon nung oo joo eh chan
reu nun see nae moo reun Joo nim eh som ssee no rae ha doh

hear the *roll - ing thun - der, Thy power through-out the u - ni-verse dis -
loft - y moun-tain gran - deur And hear the brook and feel the gen - tle

Hooryum
Refrain

neh
dah

Joo nim eh nop go wee dae ha shim ul

played;
breeze;

Then sings my soul, my Sav - ior God, to Thee,

Nae young hon ee chan yahng ha neh Joo nim eh nop go
How great Thou art, how great Thou art! Then sings my soul, my

wee dae ha shim eul Nae young hon ee chan yahng ha neh
Sav - ior God, to Thee, How great Thou art, how great Thou art!

3. Joo ha nah nim tok seng ja ak kim up
   see
   Oo ree rul wee hae ddang eh bo nae uh
   Seep ja ga eh pee heul lyuh juk keh ha
   sa
   Nae mo dun chway rul goo sok ha shun
   neh
   Hooryum

3. And when I think that God, His Son
   not sparing,
   Sent Him to die, I scarce can take it in;
   That on the cross, my burden gladly
   bearing,
   He bled and died to take away my sin;
   Refrain

4. Nae joo Ye su seh sahng eh dah see ol
   ttae
   Juh chun goo geu ro nal in doh ha ree
   Na kyum son hee up deu ryuh kyung
   bae ha myuh
   Young won hee joo rul chan yahng ha
   ree rah
   Hooryum

4. When Christ shall come with shout
   of acclamation
   And take me home, what joy shall
   fill my heart!
   Then I shall bow in humble adoration,
   And there proclaim, my God,
   how great Thou art!
   Refrain

*Original English words were "works" and "mighty."

468 Let All the World in Every Corner Sing

AUGUSTINE   10.4.6.6.6.6.10.4

George Herbert (1593–1632)
As in *The Temple*, 1633

Erik Routley, 1964

1. Let all the world in ev-ery cor-ner sing, My God and King!

1. The heavens are not too high, God's praise may thith-er fly; (The)
2. The church with psalms must shout: No door can keep them out; (But)

The earth is not too low, God's prais-es there may grow.
But, a-bove all, the heart Must bear the long-est part.

Let all the world in ev-ery cor-ner sing, My God and King! My God and King!

Music: Copyright © 1976 by Hinshaw Music, Inc. Reprinted by permission.

♩=112–120

Morning Has Broken

469

BUNESSAN. 5.5.5.4 D

Gaelic melody
Arr. Dale Grotenhuis, 1985

Eleanor Farjeon, 1931

1. Morn-ing has bro - ken Like the first morn - ing, Black-bird has
2. Sweet the rain's new fall Sun - lit from heav - en, Like the first
3. Mine is the sun - light! Mine is the morn - ing Born of the

spo - ken Like the first bird. Praise for the sing - ing! Praise for the
dew - fall On the first grass. Praise for the sweet - ness Of the wet
one light E - den saw play! Praise with e - la - tion, Praise ev - ery

morn - ing! Praise for them, spring - ing Fresh from the Word!
gar - den, Sprung in com - plete - ness Where God's feet pass.
morn - ing, God's re - cre - a - tion Of the new day!

470 O Day of Radiant Gladness

ES FLOG EIN KLEINS WALDVÖGELEIN   7.6.7.6 D

Stanzas 1–2, Christopher Wordsworth, 1862; alt.
Stanza 3, Charles P. Price, 1980
Stanza 4, *The Hymnal 1982*

Memmingen ms., 17th century
Harm. George Ratcliffe Woodward, 1904

1. O day of ra-diant glad-ness, O day of joy and light,
2. This day at the cre-a-tion The light first had its birth;
3. This day God's peo-ple, meet-ing, The Ho-ly Scrip-ture hear;
4. That light our hope sus-tain-ing, We walk the pil-grim way,

O balm of care and sad-ness, Most beau-ti-ful, most bright;
This day for our sal-va-tion Christ rose from depths of earth;
Christ's liv-ing pres-ence greet-ing, Through bread and wine made near.
At length our rest at-tain-ing, Our end-less Sab-bath day.

This day the high and low-ly, Through a-ges joined in tune,
This day our Lord vic-to-rious The Spir-it sent from heaven,
We jour-ney on, be-liev-ing, Re-newed with heaven-ly might,
We sing to You our prais-es, O Fa-ther, Spir-it, Son;

Sing "Ho-ly, ho-ly, ho-ly" To the great God tri-une.
And thus this day most glo-rious A tri-ple light was given.
From grace more grace re-ceiv-ing On this blest day of light.
The church its voice up-rais-es To You, blest Three in One.

O Praise the Gracious Power

471

Thomas H. Troeger, 1984   CHRISTPRAISE RAY   SM with refrain   Carol Doran, 1984

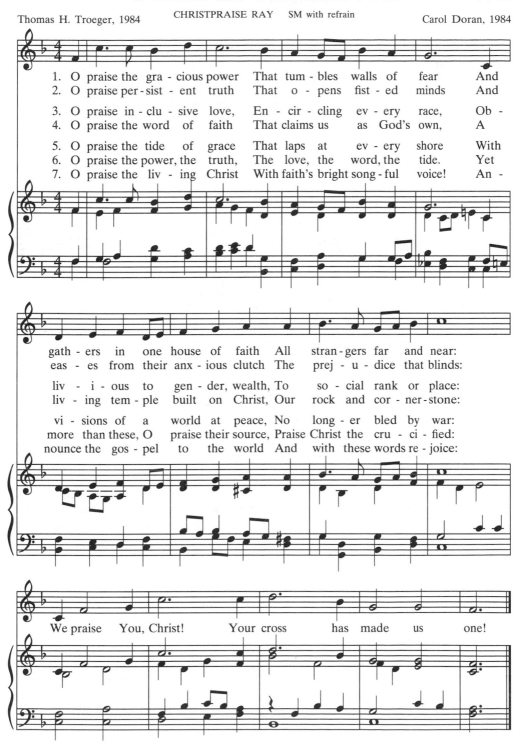

1. O praise the gra - cious power That tum - bles walls of fear And
2. O praise per - sist - ent truth That o - pens fist - ed minds And
3. O praise in - clu - sive love, En - cir - cling ev - ery race, Ob -
4. O praise the word of faith That claims us as God's own, A
5. O praise the tide of grace That laps at ev - ery shore With
6. O praise the power, the truth, The love, the word, the tide. Yet
7. O praise the liv - ing Christ With faith's bright song - ful voice! An -

gath - ers in one house of faith All stran - gers far and near:
eas - es from their anx - ious clutch The prej - u - dice that blinds:
liv - i - ous to gen - der, wealth, To so - cial rank or place:
liv - ing tem - ple built on Christ, Our rock and cor - ner - stone:
vi - sions of a world at peace, No long - er bled by war:
more than these, O praise their source, Praise Christ the cru - ci - fied:
nounce the gos - pel to the world And with these words re - joice:

We praise You, Christ! Your cross has made us one!

♩=120–132

Cantad al Señor
O Sing to the Lord

11.11.11.10

Brazilian folk song
Trans. Gerhard Cartford (b. 1923)

Brazilian folk melody

1. Can - tad al Se - ñor un cán - ti - co nue - vo,
2. Por - que el Se - ñor ha he - cho pro - di - gios,
3. Can - tad al Se - ñor, ala - bad - le con ar - pa,

1. O sing to the Lord, O sing God a new song.
2. By His ho - ly power our God has done won - ders.
3. So dance for our God and blow all the trum - pets.

Can - tad al Se - ñor un cán - ti - co nue - vo,
Por - que el Se - ñor ha he - cho pro - di - gios,
Can - tad al Se - ñor, ala - bad - le con ar - pa,

O sing to the Lord, O sing God a new song.
By His ho - ly power our God has done won - ders.
So dance for our God and blow all the trum - pets.

Can - tad al Se - ñor un cán - ti - co nue - vo,
Por - que el Se - ñor ha he - cho pro - di - gios,
Can - tad al Se - ñor, ala - bad - le con ar - pa,

O sing to the Lord, O sing God a new song.
By His ho - ly power our God has done won - ders.
So dance for our God and blow all the trum - pets.

472

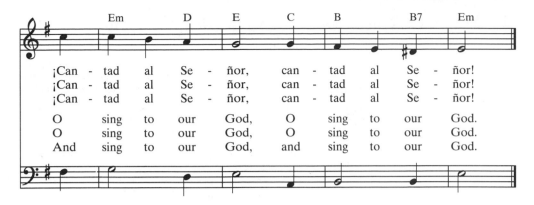

¡Can - tad al Se - ñor, can - tad al Se - ñor!
¡Can - tad al Se - ñor, can - tad al Se - ñor!
¡Can - tad al Se - ñor, can - tad al Se - ñor!

O sing to our God, O sing to our God.
O sing to our God, O sing to our God.
And sing to our God, and sing to our God.

For the Beauty of the Earth 473

DIX 7.7.7.7.7.7

Conrad Kocher, 1838
Abr. William Henry Monk, 1861
Harm. *The English Hymnal,* 1906

Folliott Sandford Pierpoint, 1864

1. For the beau - ty of the earth, For the glo - ry of the skies,
2. For the won - der of each hour Of the day and of the night,
3. For the joy of ear and eye, For the heart and mind's de - light,
4. For the joy of hu - man love, Broth-er, sis - ter, par - ent, child,

For the love which from our birth O - ver and a - round us lies,
Hill and vale, and tree and flower, Sun and moon, and stars of light,
For the mys - tic har - mo - ny Link-ing sense to sound and sight,
Friends on earth, and friends a - bove, For all gen - tle thoughts and mild,

Refrain

Lord of all, to Thee we raise This our hymn of grate-ful praise.

5. For Thy church that evermore
   Lifteth holy hands above,
   Offering up on every shore

Her pure sacrifice of love,
Lord of all, to Thee we raise
This our hymn of grateful praise.

474   O Splendor of God's Glory Bright

PUER NOBIS NASCITUR   LM

Trier ms., 15th century

Ambrose of Milan, c. 374

Trans. composite, *Rejoice in the Lord,* 1985

Adapt. Michael Praetorius, 1609

Harm. George Ratcliffe Woodward, 1902

1. O splen-dor of God's glo-ry bright, From light e-ter-nal bring-ing light; Thou light of life, light's liv-ing spring, True day, all days il-lu-min-ing:

2. Come, Ho-ly Sun of heaven-ly love, Shower down Thy ra-diance from a-bove, And to our in-ward hearts con-vey The Ho-ly Spir-it's cloud-less ray.

3. O joy-ful be the pass-ing day With thoughts as clear as morn-ing's ray, With faith like noon-tide shin-ing bright, Our souls un-shad-owed by the night.

4. O Lord, with each re-turn-ing morn Thine im-age to our hearts is born; O may we ev-er clear-ly see Our Sav-ior and our God in Thee!

Alternate tune: WAREHAM, 421

O That I Had a Thousand Voices

475

O DASS ICH TAUSEND ZUNGEN HÄTTE   9.8.9.8.8.8

Johann Mentzer, 1704
Trans. *The Lutheran Hymnal,* 1941; alt.

Attr. Johann Balthasar König, 1738
Harmonischer Liederschatz, 1738

1. O that I had a thou-sand voic - es   To praise my God with thou-sand tongues!   My heart, which in the Lord re-joic - es,   Would then pro-claim in grate-ful songs   To all, wher-ev - er I might be,   What great things God has done for me!

2. O all you powers that God im-plant-ed,   A - rise, keep si - lence now no more;   Put forth the strength that God has grant - ed!   Your no - blest work is to a - dore!   O soul and bod - y, join to raise   With heart-felt joy our Mak-er's praise!

3. You for - est leaves so green and ten - der   That dance for joy in sum - mer air,   You mead - ow grass - es, bright and slen - der,   You flowers so fra - grant and so fair,   You live to show God's praise a - lone.   Join me to make God's glo - ry known!

4. All crea-tures that have breath and mo - tion,   That throng the earth, the sea, the sky,   Come, share with me my heart's de - vo - tion,   Help me to sing God's prais - es high!   My ut - most powers can nev - er quite   De - clare the won - ders of God's might!

476 O Worship the King, All Glorious Above!

LYONS   10.10.11.11

Robert Grant, 1833; alt.

Attr. Johann Michael Haydn (1737–1806); alt.

1. O wor - ship the King, all glo - rious a - bove!
2. O tell of God's might, O sing of God's grace,
3. The earth with its store of won - ders un - told,
4. Thy boun - ti - ful care what tongue can re - cite?

O grate - ful - ly sing God's power and God's love;
Whose robe is the light, whose can - o - py space.
Al - might - y, Thy power hath found - ed of old;
It breathes in the air, it shines in the light;

Our shield and de - fend - er, the An - cient of Days, Pa -
The char - iots of heaven the deep thun - der - clouds form, And
Hath stab - lished it fast by a change-less de - cree, And
It streams from the hills, it de - scends to the plain, And

vil - ioned in splen - dor and gird - ed with praise.
bright is God's path on the wings of the storm.
round it hath cast, like a man - tle, the sea.
sweet - ly dis - tills in the dew and the rain.

5. Frail children of dust, and feeble as frail,
   In Thee do we trust, nor find Thee to fail;
   Thy mercies how tender, how firm to the end,
   Our maker, defender, redeemer, and friend.

Ye Servants of God, Your Master Proclaim 477

HANOVER　　10.10.11.11

Attr. William Croft, 1708
A Supplement to the New Version of the Psalms, 1708

Charles Wesley, 1744

1. Ye ser-vants of God, your Mas-ter pro-claim,
2. God rul-eth on high, al-might-y to save;
3. "Sal-va-tion to God, who sits on the throne,"
4. Then let us a-dore, and give Him His right,

And pub-lish a-broad His won-der-ful name;
And still He is nigh— His pres-ence we have;
Let all cry a-loud, and hon-or the Son;
All glo-ry and power, all wis-dom and might,

The name all-vic-to-rious of Je-sus ex-tol;
The great con-gre-ga-tion His tri-umph shall sing,
The prais-es of Je-sus the an-gels pro-claim,
All hon-or and bless-ing, with an-gels a-bove,

His king-dom is glo-rious, He rules o-ver all.
As-crib-ing sal-va-tion to Je-sus our King.
Fall down on their fac-es, and wor-ship the Lamb.
And thanks nev-er ceas-ing, and in-fi-nite love.

478 Praise, My Soul, the King of Heaven

LAUDA ANIMA   8.7.8.7.8.7

Henry Francis Lyte, 1834; alt.   John Goss, 1869

1. Praise, my soul, the King of heav - en; To His feet thy
2. Praise Him for His grace and fa - vor To His peo - ple
3. Fa - ther - like He tends and spares us; Well our fee - ble
4. An - gels, help us to a - dore Him: Ye be - hold Him

trib - ute bring; Ran - somed, healed, re - stored, for - giv - en,
in dis - tress; Praise Him still the same as ev - er,
frame He knows; In His hands He gen - tly bears us,
face to face; Sun and moon, bow down be - fore Him,

Ev - er - more His prais - es sing: Al - le - lu - ia!
Slow to chide, and swift to bless: Al - le - lu - ia!
Res - cues us from all our foes. Al - le - lu - ia!
Dwell - ers all in time and space. Al - le - lu - ia!

Al - le - lu - ia! Praise the ev - er - last - ing King.
Al - le - lu - ia! Glo - rious in His faith - ful - ness.
Al - le - lu - ia! Wide - ly yet His mer - cy flows.
Al - le - lu - ia! Praise with us the God of grace.

♩=48-52

Praise, My Soul, the King of Heaven

LAUDA ANIMA   8.7.8.7.8.7

John Goss, 1869

Alternate harmony

Praise, My Soul, the God of Heaven 479

Henry Francis Lyte, 1834; alt.
Adapt. Ecumenical Women's Center, 1974

1. Praise, my soul, the God of heaven,
   Glad of heart your carols raise;
   Ransomed, healed, restored, forgiven,
   Who, like me, should sing God's praise?
   Alleluia! Alleluia!
   Praise the Maker all your days!

2. Praise God for the grace and favor
   Shown our forebears in distress;
   God is still the same forever,
   Slow to chide, and swift to bless.
   Alleluia! Alleluia!
   Sing our Maker's faithfulness!

3. Like a loving parent caring,
   God knows well our feeble frame;
   Gladly all our burdens bearing,
   Still to countless years the same.
   Alleluia! Alleluia!
   All within me, praise God's name!

4. Angels, teach us adoration,
   You behold God face to face;
   Sun and moon and all creation,
   Dwellers all in time and space.
   Alleluia! Alleluia!
   Praise with us the God of grace!

480 Praise Our God Above

HSUAN P'ING   5.5.5.5 D

Chinese hymn
Tzu-chen Chao, 1931
Trans. Frank W. Price, 1953

Confucian chant
Harm. W. H. Wong, 1973

1. Praise our God a - bove, Source of bound-less love: Spring wind, sum - mer
2. God's care like a cloak Wraps us coun - try folk, Makes all green things

rain, Then the har - vest grain; Pearl - y rice and corn, Fra - grant
grow, Rip - ens what we sow. Through God we are strong; Sing our

au - tumn morn. Though our work is hard, God gives us re - ward.
har - vest song. Sing praise, field and flower, Praise God's might-y power.

Text and Music: From *Hymns of Universal Praise,* revised edition. Copyright © 1977 by the Chinese Christian Literature Council Ltd., Hong Kong.

♩=66–72

Praise the Lord, God's Glories Show 481

LLANFAIR   7.7.7.7 with alleluias

Henry Francis Lyte, 1834; alt.

Robert Williams, 1817
Harm. David Evans, 1927

1. Praise the Lord, God's glo - ries show,
2. Earth to heaven and heaven to earth, Al - le - lu - ia!
3. Praise the Lord, great mer - cies trace,

Saints with - in God's courts be - low,
Tell the won - ders, sing God's worth, Al - le - lu - ia!
Praise this prov - i - dence and grace,

An - gels round the throne a - bove,
Age to age and shore to shore, Al - le - lu - ia!
All that God for us has done,

All that see and share God's love.
Praise God, praise for - ev - er - more! Al - le - lu - ia!
All God sends us through the Son.

Music: Harmonization from the *Revised Church Hymnary 1927.* Used by permission of Oxford University Press.

482 Praise Ye the Lord, the Almighty

LOBE DEN HERREN 14.14.4.7.8

Joachim Neander, 1680
Trans. Catherine Winkworth, 1863; alt.

Stralsund *Ernewerten Gesangbuch,* 1665
Harm. *The Chorale Book for England,* 1863
Desc. Craig Sellar Lang, 1953

Music: Descant from *20 Hymn Tune Descants* (C. S. Lang). Reproduced by permission of Novello and Company Limited.

prais - es be - fore Him! Let the a - men Sound from His

health and sal - va - tion! All ye who hear, Now to His
gen - tly sus - tain - eth! Hast thou not seen How thy de -
prais - es be - fore Him! Let the a - men Sound from His

peo-ple a - gain; Glad - ly for aye we a - dore Him.

tem - ple draw near; Join me in glad ad - o - ra - tion!
sires e'er have been Grant-ed in what He or - dain - eth?
peo - ple a - gain; Glad - ly for aye we a - dore Him.

483 Sing Praise to God, Who Reigns Above

MIT FREUDEN ZART   8.7.8.7.8.8.7

Johann Jacob Schütz, 1675
Trans. Frances Elizabeth Cox, 1864; alt.

Bohemian Brethren's *Kirchengesang*, 1566

1. Sing praise to God, who reigns above, The God of all cre-a-tion, The God of power, the God of love, The God of our sal-va-tion; With heal-ing balm my soul is filled, And ev-ery faith-less mur-mur stilled:

2. What God's al-might-y power hath made, God's gra-cious mer-cy keep-eth; By morn-ing glow or eve-ning shade God's watch-ful eye ne'er sleep-eth; With-in the king-dom of God's might, Lo! all is just and all is right:

3. The Lord is nev-er far a-way, But through all grief dis-tress-ing, An ev-er pres-ent help and stay, Our peace, and joy, and bless-ing; As with a moth-er's ten-der hand, God gent-ly leads the cho-sen band:

4. Thus all my glad-some way a-long, I sing a-loud Thy prais-es That all may hear the grate-ful song My voice un-wea-ried rais-es. Be joy-ful in the Lord, my heart, Both soul and bod-y take your part:

To God all praise and glo-ry!

May be sung in unison.

This tune in a lower key, 7

Sing with Hearts

INTAKO   11.10.11.9 with refrain

Jonathan Malicsi, 1983   Kalinga melody

Optional Introduction

Sing with hearts, sing with souls, Dance with joy to God, To whom we

of - fer prais-es, To whom we sing with glad - ness.

1. Let all our
2. Let all our
3. Let all our

hearts o - pen up to the Lord God, Let all the heavens hear how our
bod - ies sway to God's mu - sic, Let all the earth move with our
souls shine out with God's beau - ty, Let all cre - a - tion feel our

hearts re - joice; For it is God who has giv - en us grac - es,
feet and hands; For it is God who in - spires and up - lifts us,
love for God; For it is God who has grant - ed us wis - dom,

From whom comes the mu - sic in our voice. O Lord, we sing
From whom flows all rhythm in our dance.
In whom we find re - al - i - ty and dream.

with joy-ful hearts, with soul and bod - y of-fer we our arts.

♩=92–100

485 To God Be the Glory

TO GOD BE THE GLORY   11.11.11.11 with refrain

Fanny Jane Crosby, 1875

William Howard Doane, 1875

1. To God be the glo - ry, great things He hath done!
2. Great things He hath taught us, great things He hath done,

So loved He the world that He gave us His Son,
And great our re - joic - ing through Je - sus the Son;

Who yield - ed His life an a - tone - ment for sin,
But pur - er, and high - er, and great - er will be

And o - pened the life - gate that all may go in.
Our won - der, our trans - port, when Je - sus we see.

Refrain

Praise the Lord, praise the Lord, Let the earth hear His voice!

Praise the Lord, praise the Lord, Let the peo - ple re - joice!

O come to the Fa - ther through Je - sus the Son,

And give Him the glo - ry: great things He hath done!

486   When the Morning Stars Together

WEISSE FLAGGEN   8.7.8.7 D

Albert F. Bayly, 1969; alt.   As in *Tochter Sion,* Cologne, 1741

1. When the morn-ing stars to-geth-er Their Cre-a-tor's glo-ry sang,
2. When in syn-a-gogue and tem-ple Voic-es raised the psalm-ists' songs,
3. Voice and in-stru-ment in u-nion Through the a-ges spoke Your praise,
4. Lord, we bring our gift of mu-sic; Touch our lips and fire our hearts,

And the an-gel host all shout-ed Till with joy the heav-ens rang,
Of-fer-ing the a-do-ra-tion Which a-lone to You be-longs,
Plain-song, tune-ful hymns, and an-thems Told Your faith-ful, gra-cious ways.
Teach our minds and train our sens-es, Fit us for these sa-cred arts.

Then Your wis-dom and Your great-ness Their ex-ul-tant mu-sic told,
When the sing-ers and the cym-bals With the trum-pet made ac-cord,
Choir and or-ches-tra and or-gan Each a sa-cred of-fer-ing brought,
Then with skill and con-se-cra-tion We would serve You, Lord, and give

All the beau-ty and the splen-dor Which Your might-y works un-fold.
Glo-ry filled the house of wor-ship, And all knew Your pres-ence, Lord.
While, in-spired by Your own Spir-it, Po-et and com-pos-er wrought.
All our powers to glo-ri-fy You, And in serv-ing ful-ly live.

When Morning Gilds the Skies

487

LAUDES DOMINI 6.6.6 D

German hymn, c. 1800
Trans. Edward Caswall, 1853, 1858; alt.

Joseph Barnby, 1868

1. When morn-ing gilds the skies, My heart a-wak-ing cries:
2. Does sad-ness fill my mind? A sol-ace here I find:
3. Let earth's wide cir-cle round In joy-ful notes re-sound:
4. Be this, while life is mine, My can-ti-cle di-vine:

May Je-sus Christ be praised! A-like at work and prayer
May Je-sus Christ be praised! Or fades my earth-ly bliss?
May Je-sus Christ be praised! Let air and sea and sky
May Je-sus Christ be praised! Be this the e-ter-nal song

To Je-sus I re-pair: May Je-sus Christ be praised!
My com-fort still is this: May Je-sus Christ be praised!
From depth to height re-ply: May Je-sus Christ be praised!
Through all the a-ges long: May Je-sus Christ be praised!

488 The God of Abraham Praise

LEONI   6.6.8.4 D

Daniel ben Judah, 1404
Trans. Max Landsberg and Newton Mann, 1885; alt.

Hebrew melody
Adapt. Thomas Olivers
and Meyer Lyon, 1770

1. The God of A-braham praise, Who reigns en-throned a - bove;
2. Your spir - it still flows free, High surg - ing where it will;
3. You have e - ter - nal life Im - plant - ed in the soul;

The an - cient of e - ter - nal days, The God of love!
In proph-et's word You spoke of old And You speak still.
Your love shall be our strength and stay, While a - ges roll.

The Lord, the great I Am, By earth and heaven con - fessed,
Es - tab - lished is Your law, And change-less it shall stand,
We praise You, liv - ing God! We praise Your ho - ly name;

We bow be - fore Your ho - ly name, For - ev - er blest.
Deep writ up - on the hu - man heart, On sea, or land.
The first, the last, be - yond all thought, And still the same!

Open Now Thy Gates of Beauty

489

UNSER HERRSCHER   8.7.8.7.7.7

Benjamin Schmolck, 1732
Trans. Catherine Winkworth, 1863

Joachim Neander, 1680
Harm. *The Chorale Book for England,* 1863; alt.
Desc. John Dykes Bower (1905–1981)

Descant

3. Speak, O Lord, and I will hear Thee, Let Thy will be done in - deed;

1. O - pen now thy gates of beau - ty, Zi - on, let me en - ter there,
2. Gra - cious God, I come be - fore Thee, Come Thou al - so down to me;
3. Speak, O Lord, and I will hear Thee, Let Thy will be done in - deed;

May I un - dis - turbed draw near Thee, While Thou dost Thy peo - ple feed.

Where my soul in joy - ful du - ty Waits for God who an - swers prayer;
Where we find Thee and a - dore Thee, There a heaven on earth must be;
May I un - dis - turbed draw near Thee, While Thou dost Thy peo - ple feed.

Here of life the foun - tain flows, Here is balm for all our woes.

O how bless - ed is this place, Filled with sol - ace, light, and grace.
To my heart O en - ter Thou, Let it be Thy tem - ple now.
Here of life the foun - tain flows, Here is balm for all our woes.

Ephesians 5:15–20

490 With Glad, Exuberant Carolings

CAROL'S GIFT   8.6.8.6.8.6

Thomas H. Troeger, 1984

Carol Doran, 1984

1. With glad, ex-u-berant car-ol-ings, With
2. Through song-ful wor-ship, know that truth Bare
3. Through mu-sic blend the po-ten-cies Of
4. O brim the bar-reled lungs with joy And
5. By day, by night, at work, at prayer, Through

hymns and psalms of praise, Give thanks through Christ for
words can-not en-fold. In rap-tured mel-o-
mind and heart and soul And with their fu-sioned
emp-ty out this song: "Our breath, our pulse, our
storms and times of calm Let all your deeds and

ev-ery-thing, Give thanks to God al-ways!
dies of prayer Your God be-hold, be-hold!
en-er-gies Your God ex-tol, ex-tol!
lives, our gifts To Christ the Lord be-long!
words com-pose A con-stant, liv-ing psalm!

Give thanks through Christ for ev - ery - thing,
In rap - tured mel - o - dies of prayer
And with their fu - sioned en - er - gies

Our breath, our pulse, our lives, our gifts
Let all your deeds and words com - pose

Give thanks to God al - ways!
Your God be - hold, be - hold!
Your God ex - tol, ex - tol!

To Christ the Lord be - long!"
A con - stant, liv - ing psalm!

♩=116–126

491   Stand Up and Bless the Lord

CARLISLE   SM

James Montgomery, 1824; alt.

Charles Lockhart, 1769
Desc. Sydney Nicholson (1875–1947)

5. Stand up and bless the Lord; The Lord your God adore;

1. Stand up and bless the Lord, Ye people of God's choice; Stand up and bless the Lord your God With heart and soul and voice.
2. Though high above all praise, Above all blessing high, Who would not fear God's holy name, And laud and magnify?
3. O for the living flame From God's own altar brought, To touch our lips, our minds inspire, And wing to heaven our thought!
4. God is our strength and song, Now is salvation ours; Then be God's love in Christ proclaimed With all our ransomed powers.

5. Stand up and bless the Lord;
   The Lord your God adore;

Stand up and bless God's glorious name,
Henceforth forevermore.

Baptized in Water

492

BUNESSAN   5.5.8.5.5.9

Gaelic melody
Arr. Dale Grotenhuis, 1985

Michael A. Saward, 1981

1. Bap-tized in   wa - ter, Sealed by the Spir - it, Cleansed by the
2. Bap-tized in   wa - ter, Sealed by the Spir - it, Dead   in the
3. Bap-tized in   wa - ter, Sealed by the Spir - it, Marked with the

blood   of   Christ, our   King;   Heirs of sal - va - tion, Trust-ing the
tomb   with   Christ, our   King;   One with His   ris - ing, Freed and for -
sign   of   Christ, our   King;   Born of the Spir - it,   We   are God's

prom - ise,   Faith-ful - ly   now   God's   prais-es   we   sing.
giv - en,   Thank-ful - ly   now   God's   prais-es   we   sing.
chil - dren, Joy-ful - ly   now   God's   prais-es   we   sing.

493 Dearest Jesus, We Are Here

LIEBSTER JESU   7.8.7.8.8.8

Benjamin Schmolck, 1704
Trans. Catherine Winkworth, 1858; alt.

Johann Rudolph Ahle, 1664
Harm. Johann Sebastian Bach (1685–1750); alt.

1. Dearest Jesus, we are here, Gladly Your command obeying. With this child we now draw near In response to Your own saying That to You it shall be given As a child and heir of heaven.

2. Your command is clear and plain, And we would obey it duly: "You must all be born again, Heart and life renewing truly, Born of water and the Spirit, And My kingdom thus inherit."

3. This is why we come to You, In our arms this infant bearing; Lord, to us Your glory show; Let this child, Your mercy sharing, In Your arms be shielded ever, Yours on earth and Yours forever.

4. Gracious Lord, Your member own; Shepherd, take Your lamb and feed it; Prince of Peace, make here Your throne; Way of life, to heaven lead it; Precious vine, let nothing sever From Your side this branch forever.

Out of Deep, Unordered Water

494

RUSTINGTON   8.7.8.7 D

Fred Kaan, 1965   C. Hubert H. Parry, 1897

1. Out of deep, un-or-dered wa-ter God cre-at-ed light and land,
2. Wa-ter on the hu-man fore-head, Birth-mark of the love of God,
3. Stand-ing round the font re-minds us Of the He-brews' climb a-shore.

World of bird and beast and, lat-er, In God's im-age, wom-an, man.
Is the sign of death and ris-ing; Through the seas there runs a road.
Life is hal-lowed by the knowl-edge: God has been this way be-fore.

There is wa-ter in the riv-er Bring-ing life to tree and plant.

Let cre-a-tion praise its giv-er: There is wa-ter in the font.

Alternate tune: WEISSE FLAGGEN, 486   ♩=92–100

495 We Know That Christ Is Raised

ENGELBERG   10.10.10.4

John Brownlow Geyer, 1969

Charles Villiers Stanford, 1904

1. We know that Christ is raised and dies no more. Em-braced by
2. We share by wa-ter in His sav-ing death. Re-born we
3. The Fa-ther's splen-dor clothes the Son with life. The Spir-it's
4. A new cre-a-tion comes to life and grows As Christ's new

death He broke its fear-ful hold; And our de-spair He turned to
share with Him an Eas-ter life As liv-ing mem-bers of a
pow-er shakes the church of God. Bap-tized we live with God the
bod-y takes on flesh and blood. The u-ni-verse, re-stored and

1–3

blaz-ing joy.
liv-ing Christ.   Al - le - lu - ia!
Three in One.
whole, will sing:

Al - le - lu - ia! A - men.

♩=46–50

Lord Jesus Christ, Our Lord Most Dear 496

VOM HIMMEL HOCH   LM

Heinrich von Laufenberg, 1429
Trans. Catherine Winkworth, 1869; alt.

Schumann's *Geistliche Lieder,* 1539

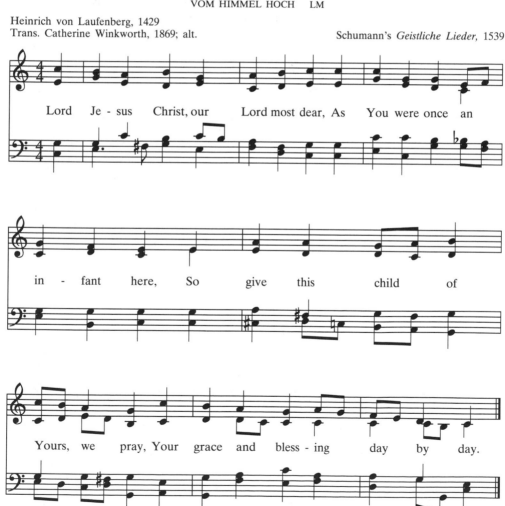

Lord Je - sus Christ, our Lord most dear, As You were once an

in - fant here, So give this child of

Yours, we pray, Your grace and bless - ing day by day.

497 With Grateful Hearts Our Faith Professing

Fred Kaan, c. 1963; alt. ST. CLEMENT 9.8.9.8 Clement Cotterill Scholefield, 1874

1. With grate-ful hearts our faith pro-fess-ing, We ask You,
2. We know that in Your true pro-vid-ing The young and
3. Give to the par-ents love and pa-tience, Each home with
4. Ac-cept, O Lord, our ded-i-ca-tion To fill with

Lord, come to our aid, That we, our com-mon
old to Christ be-long; Lord, help us to be
Chris-tian grac-es fill. Pro-tect our chil-dren
love the grow-ing mind, That in this church and

faith con-fess-ing, May keep the vows that we have made.
wise in guid-ing, And make us in ex-am-ple strong.
in temp-ta-tions, And keep them safe in child-hood's ill.
con-gre-ga-tion The young a faith for life may find.

This tune in a higher key, 546

498 Child of Blessing, Child of Promise

Ronald S. Cole-Turner, 1980 KINGDOM 8.7.8.7 V. Earle Copes, 1959

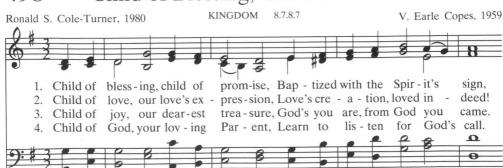

1. Child of bless-ing, child of prom-ise, Bap-tized with the Spir-it's sign,
2. Child of love, our love's ex-pres-sion, Love's cre-a-tion, loved in-deed!
3. Child of joy, our dear-est trea-sure, God's you are, from God you came.
4. Child of God, your lov-ing Par-ent, Learn to lis-ten for God's call.

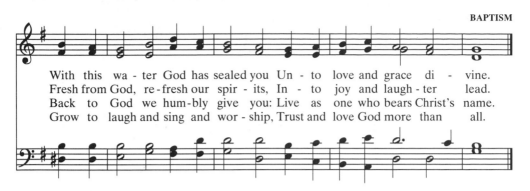

With this wa - ter God has sealed you Un - to love and grace di - vine.
Fresh from God, re-fresh our spir - its, In - to joy and laugh-ter lead.
Back to God we hum-bly give you: Live as one who bears Christ's name.
Grow to laugh and sing and wor - ship, Trust and love God more than all.

Wonder of Wonders, Here Revealed 499

PENTECOST (Boyd)   LM

Jane Parker Huber, 1980   William Boyd, 1864

1. Won - der of won - ders, here re - vealed; God's cov - e -
2. Here in this sac - ra - ment we see God's grace un -
3. This child of God, though young or old, We wel - come
4. Now we our vow of faith re - new, Stretch wide our

nant with us is sealed. And long be - fore we
bound, for all, for me! May we re - spond with
now in - to Christ's fold, To know with us God's
sights to glo - bal view, And claim with Chris - tians

know or pray, God's love en - folds us ev - ery day.
joy - ful praise In lov - ing ser - vice all our days.
lov - ing care; Here all our joys and sor - rows share.
far and near A larg - er fam - i - ly held dear.

500 Become to Us the Living Bread

O FILII ET FILIAE   8.8.8 with alleluias

Miriam Drury, 1970

French melody, 15th century
Airs sur les hymnes sacrés, odes et noëls, 1623

Al - le - lu - ia! Al - le - lu - ia! Al - le - lu - ia! Al -

le - lu - ia!
1. Be - come to us the liv - ing bread
2. Be - come the nev - er - fail - ing wine,
3. May Chris - tians all with one ac - cord

By which the Chris - tian life is fed, Re - newed, and great - ly
The spring of joy that shall in - cline Our hearts to bear the
U - nite a - round the sa - cred board, To praise Your ho - ly

com - fort - ed,
cov - enant sign, Al - le - lu - ia! Al - le - lu - ia!
name, O Lord,

Text: © 1972 by The Westminster Press; from *The Worshipbook—Services and Hymns.*

Bread of Heaven, on Thee We Feed   501

ARFON   7.7.7.7.7.7

Josiah Conder, 1824; alt.

French and Welsh melody
Arr. Hugh Davies, 1906

1. Bread of heaven, on Thee we feed, For Thou art our
2. Vine of heaven, Thy love sup-plies This blest cup of

food in-deed; Ev-er may our souls be fed
sac-ri-fice; 'Tis Thy wounds our heal-ing give;

With this true and liv-ing Bread, Day by day with
To Thy cross we look and live: Thou our life! O

strength sup-plied Through the life of Christ who died.
let us be Root-ed, graft-ed, built on Thee.

502 Bread of the World in Mercy Broken

RENDEZ À DIEU   9.8.9.8 D

Reginald Heber (1783–1826)
As in *Hymns Written and Adapted,* 1827

Louis Bourgeois, 1543; rev. 1551

Bread of the world in mer-cy bro - ken, Wine of the soul in mer - cy shed,

By whom the words of life were spo - ken, And in whose death our sins are dead:

Look on the heart by sor-row bro - ken, Look on the tears by sin - ners shed;

And be Thy feast to us the to - ken That by Thy grace our souls are fed.

Come, Risen Lord

503

SURSUM CORDA (Smith)   10.10.10.10

George Wallace Briggs, 1931

Alfred Morton Smith, 1941

1. Come, ris-en Lord, and deign to be our guest; Nay, let us be Thy guests; the feast is Thine; Thy-self at Thine own board make man-i-fest In Thine own sac-ra-ment of bread and wine.

2. We meet, as in that up-per room they met, Thou at the ta-ble, bless-ing, yet dost stand; "This is My bod-y"; so Thou giv-est yet: Faith still re-ceives the cup as from Thy hand.

3. One bod-y we, one bod-y who par-take, One church u-nit-ed in com-mu-nion blest; One name we bear, one bread of life we break, With all Thy saints on earth and saints at rest.

4. One with each oth-er, Lord, for one in Thee, Who art one Sav-ior and one liv-ing head; Then o-pen Thou our eyes, that we may see; Be known to us in break-ing of the bread.

Text: From *Songs of Praise*, 1931. Used by permission of Oxford University Press.
Music: Used by permission of the estate of Doris Wright Smith.

504 Draw Us in the Spirit's Tether

UNION SEMINARY 8.7.8.7.4.4.7

Percy Dearmer, 1931; alt.

Harold Friedell, 1957

1. Draw us in the Spir-it's teth - er, For when hum - bly in Your name Two or three are met to - geth - er, You are in the midst of them; Al-le-lu - ia!

2. As dis - ci - ples used to gath - er In the name of Christ to sup, Then with thanks to God the Fa - ther Break the bread and bless the cup, Al-le-lu - ia!

3. All our meals and all our liv - ing Make as sac - ra - ments of You, That by car - ing, help-ing, giv - ing, We may be dis - ci - ples true. Al-le-lu - ia!

Al - le - lu - ia! Touch we now Your gar - ment's hem.
Al - le - lu - ia! So now bind our friend - ship up.
Al - le - lu - ia! We will serve with faith a - new.

Luke 24:30–35

Be Known to Us in Breaking Bread 505

ST. FLAVIAN   CM

James Montgomery, 1825   Day's *Psalter*, 1562

1. Be known to us in break-ing bread, But do not then de - part;
2. There sup with us in love di - vine; Thy bod - y and Thy blood,

Sav - ior, a - bide with us, and spread Thy ta - ble in our heart.
That liv - ing bread, that heaven-ly wine, Be our im - mor - tal food.

506 Deck Yourself, My Soul, with Gladness

SCHMÜCKE DICH   LMD

Johann Franck (1618–1677)
Trans. Catherine Winkworth, 1863,
and John Casper Mattes, 1913; alt.

Johann Crüger, 1649

1. Deck your-self, my soul, with glad - ness, Leave be - hind all gloom and sad - ness;
2. Sun, who all my life does bright-en; Light, who does my soul en - light - en;
3. Je - sus, source of life and plea - sure, Tru - est friend and dear - est trea - sure,

Come in - to the day-light's splen-dor, There with joy your prais-es ren - der
Joy, Your won-drous gift be - stow-ing; Fount, from which all good is flow-ing:
By Your love I am in - vit - ed, Be Your love with love re-quit-ed.

Un - to God, whose grace un-bound-ed Has this won-drous ban-quet found-ed;
At Your feet I cry, my Mak - er, Let me be a fit par-tak - er
From this ban - quet let me mea - sure, Lord, how vast and deep its trea-sure;

Come, for now the Lord most ho - ly Stoops to you in like - ness low - ly.
Of this bless-ed food from heav-en, For our good, Your glo - ry giv - en.
Through the gifts that here You give me, As Your guest in heaven re - ceive me.

I Come with Joy

507

DOVE OF PEACE   8.6.8.6.6

American folk melody
Arr. Austin C. Lovelace, 1977

Brian Wren, 1968; rev. 1977

1. I come with joy to meet my Lord, For-giv-en, loved, and free, In awe and won-der to re-call His life laid down for me, His life laid down for me.
2. I come with Chris-tians far and near To find, as all are fed, The new com-mu-ni-ty of love In Christ's com-mu-nion bread, In Christ's com-mu-nion bread.
3. As Christ breaks bread and bids us share, Each proud di-vi-sion ends. The love that made us, makes us one, And stran-gers now are friends, And stran-gers now are friends.
4. And thus with joy we meet our Lord. His pres-ence, al-ways near, Is in such friend-ship bet-ter known: We see and praise Him here, We see and praise Him here.
5. To-geth-er met, to-geth-er bound, We'll go our dif-ferent ways, And as His peo-ple in the world, We'll live and speak His praise, We'll live and speak His praise.

Alternate tune: LAND OF REST, 522

508 For the Bread Which You Have Broken

KINGDOM   8.7.8.7

Louis FitzGerald Benson, 1924; alt.   V. Earle Copes, 1959

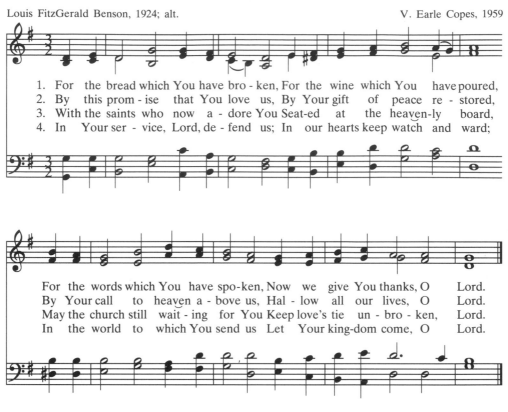

1. For the bread which You have bro - ken, For the wine which You   have poured,
2. By   this prom - ise   that You love us, By Your gift   of   peace re - stored,
3. With the saints who   now a - dore You Seat-ed   at   the heaven-ly   board,
4. In   Your ser - vice, Lord, de - fend us; In   our hearts keep watch and ward;

For the words which You have spo-ken, Now   we   give You thanks, O   Lord.
By Your call   to   heaven a - bove us, Hal - low all our lives, O   Lord.
May the church still   wait - ing for You Keep love's tie   un - bro - ken,   Lord.
In   the world to   which You send us Let   Your king-dom come, O   Lord.

509 For the Bread Which You Have Broken

CROSS OF JESUS   8.7.8.7

Louis FitzGerald Benson, 1924; alt.   John Stainer, 1887

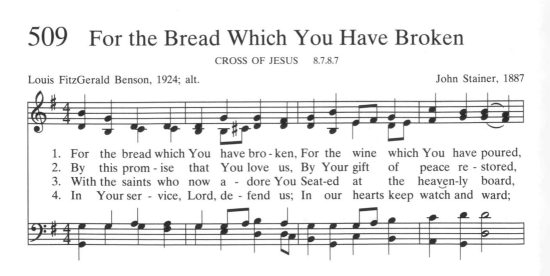

1. For the bread which You   have bro - ken, For the   wine   which You have poured,
2. By   this prom - ise   that You love us, By Your gift   of   peace re - stored,
3. With the saints who   now a - dore You Seat-ed   at   the   heaven-ly   board,
4. In   Your ser - vice, Lord, de - fend us; In   our   hearts keep watch and ward;

For the words which You have spo-ken, Now we give You thanks, O Lord.
By Your call to heaven a - bove us, Hal - low all our lives, O Lord.
May the church still wait - ing for You Keep love's tie un - bro - ken, Lord.
In the world to which You send us Let Your king-dom come, O Lord.

Jesus, Thou Joy of Loving Hearts 510

Attr. Bernard of Clairvaux (1091–1153)
Trans. Ray Palmer, 1858; alt.

QUEBEC LM

Henry Baker, 1854

1. Je - sus, Thou joy of lov - ing hearts, Thou fount of
2. Thy truth un - changed hath ev - er stood; Thou sav - est
3. We taste Thee, O Thou liv - ing bread, And long to
4. Our rest - less spir - its yearn for Thee, Wher-e'er our

life, Thou light of all, From the best bliss that
those that on Thee call; To them that seek Thee
feast up - on Thee still; We drink of Thee, the
change - ful lot is cast, Glad when Thy gra - cious

earth im - parts We turn, un - filled, to heed Thy call.
Thou art good, To them that find Thee, all in all.
foun - tain - head, And thirst our souls from Thee to fill.
smile we see, Blest when our faith can hold Thee fast.

5. O Jesus, ever with us stay,   O chase the night of sin away,
   Make all our moments calm and bright;   Shed o'er the world Thy holy light.

Alternate tune: JESU DULCIS MEMORIA, 511

511   Jesus, Thou Joy of Loving Hearts

JESU DULCIS MEMORIA   LM

Attr. Bernard of Clairvaux (1091–1153)
Trans. Ray Palmer, 1858; alt.

From plainsong, Mode II
Arr. James McGregor, 1984

1. Je - sus, Thou joy of lov - ing hearts, Thou fount of life, Thou
2. Thy truth un - changed hath ev - er stood; Thou sav - est those that
3. We taste Thee, O Thou liv - ing bread, And long to feast up -
4. Our rest - less spir - its yearn for Thee, Wher - e'er our change - ful

light of all, From the best bliss that earth im -
on Thee call; To them that seek Thee Thou art
on Thee still; We drink of Thee, the foun - tain -
lot is cast, Glad when Thy gra - cious smile we

parts   We turn, un - filled, to heed Thy call.
good,   To them that find Thee, all in all.
head,   And thirst our souls from Thee to fill.
see,   Blest when our faith can hold Thee fast.

5. O Jesus, ever with us stay,   O chase the night of sin away,
   Make all our moments calm and bright;   Shed o'er the world Thy holy light.

Alternate tune: QUEBEC, 510

Living Word of God Eternal

512

KOMM, O KOMM, DU GEIST DES LEBENS   8.7.8.7.8.7

Jeffery Rowthorn, 1983

Neuvermehrtes Meiningisches Gesangbuch, 1693

1. Liv - ing Word of God e - ter - nal, Lay - ing
2. Lov - ing Sav - ior, whose em - brac - es Our true
3. Liv - ing Bread come down from heav - en, Bro - ken,
4. Lov - ing Spir - it, pray - ing in us, Giv - ing
5. May Your Word a - mong us spo - ken, May the

claim to ev - ery age, Je - sus, speak through all our
selves a - lone un - mask, In this fel - low - ship's small
shared, dis - trib - ut - ed, Feed us, gath - ered at this
voice to all our sighs, Show the wide - ness of Your
lov - ing which we dare, May Your Bread a - mong us

speak - ing, Bring to life the Bi - ble's page; Let Your
com - pass Train us for our com - mon task: By our
ta - ble, With Your grace un - lim - it - ed, And as
mer - cy To deaf ears and blind - ed eyes; Free our
bro - ken, May the prayers in which we share Dai - ly

gos - pel, heard and heed - ed, Set our course of pil - grim - age.
love to grow more like You And to dare what You will ask.
ser - vants then em - ploy us Till this hun - gry world is fed.
tongues to come be - fore You With our neigh - bors' joys and cries.
make us faith - ful peo - ple, Liv - ing signs, Lord, of Your care.

513 Let Us Break Bread Together

LET US BREAK BREAD　10.10 with refrain　African-American spiritual

African-American spiritual

Arr. Melva Wilson Costen, 1988

1. Let us break bread to-geth-er on our knees; (on our knees;)
2. Let us drink wine to-geth-er on our knees; (on our knees;)

Let us break bread to-geth-er on our knees. (on our knees.)
Let us drink wine to-geth-er on our knees. (on our knees.)

Refrain

When I fall on my knees, With my face to the ris - ing sun,

O Lord, have mer-cy on me. (on me.)

3. Let us praise God to-geth-er on our knees; (on our knees;)

knees

Let us praise God to-geth-er on our knees.

Refrain

When I fall on my knees, With my face to the ris - ing sun,

O Lord, have mer-cy on me. (on me.)

514 Let Us Talents and Tongues Employ

LINSTEAD   LM with refrain

Fred Kaan, 1975

Jamaican folk melody
Adapt. Doreen Potter, 1975

1. Let us tal - ents and tongues em - ploy,   Reach-ing out with a
2. Christ is a - ble to make us one,   At the ta - ble He
3. Je - sus calls us in, sends us out   Bear - ing fruit in a

shout of joy: Bread is bro - ken, the wine is poured,
sets the tone,   Teach - ing peo - ple to live to bless,
world of doubt,   Gives us love to tell, bread to share:

Refrain

Christ is spo - ken and seen and heard.   Je - sus lives a - gain,
Love in word and in deed ex - press.
God (Im-man - u - el) ev - ery - where!

Maracas and other rhythm instruments may be used.

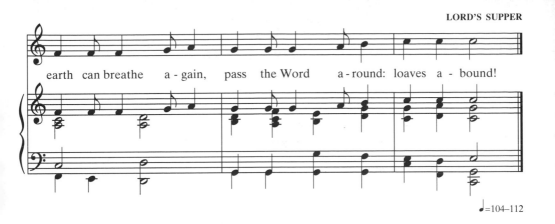

earth can breathe a-gain, pass the Word a-round: loaves a-bound!

♩=104–112

Now to Your Table Spread 515

Shirley Erena Murray, 1987   LOVE UNKNOWN   6.6.12.4.4.8   John Ireland, 1918

1. Now to Your ta-ble spread We come, each one in faith That
2. Hands of the world stretch out Your mys-ter-y to touch In
3. Here is our com-mon wealth In shar-ing what is good, As

You a-lone pro-vide the words of life and death: In
long-ing to be-lieve a truth be-yond our reach, To
though all hu-man-kind a-round one ta-ble stood, This

wine and bread, In prom-ised food We find Your lov-ing heart, O God.
sing in joy, To cry in grief, To know Your mean-ing for our life.
bread to break, This wine to taste: One peo-ple in the name of Christ.

Alternate tune: RHOSYMEDRE, 534

𝅗𝅥=52–56

516

Lord, We Have Come
at Your Own Invitation

O QUANTA QUALIA   11.10.11.10

Fred Pratt Green, 1977

Paris *Antiphoner,* 1681
As in La Feillée's *Méthode du plain-chant,* 1808

1. Lord, we have come at Your own in-vi-ta-tion,
Cho-sen by You, to be count-ed Your friends;
Yours is the strength that sus-tains ded-i-ca-tion,
Ours a com-mit-ment we know nev-er ends.

2. Here, at Your ta-ble, con-firm our in-ten-tion,
Give it Your seal of for-give-ness and grace;
Teach us to serve with-out pride or pre-ten-sion,
Lord, in Your king-dom, what-ev-er our place.

3. When, at Your ta-ble, each time of re-turn-ing,
Vows are re-newed and our cour-age re-stored:
May we in-creas-ing-ly glo-ry in learn-ing
All that it means to ac-cept You as Lord.

This tune in a higher key, 147

We Come as Guests Invited

WIE LIEBLICH IST DER MAIEN   7.6.7.6 D

517

Timothy Dudley-Smith, 1975

Johann Steurlein, 1575

1. We come as guests in - vit - ed When Je - sus bids us dine,
2. We eat and drink, re - ceiv - ing From Christ the grace we need,
3. One bread is ours for shar - ing, One sin - gle fruit-ful vine,

His friends on earth u - nit - ed To share the bread and wine;
And in our hearts be - liev - ing On Him by faith we feed;
Our fel - low-ship de - clar - ing Re - newed in bread and wine:

The bread of life is bro - ken, The wine is free - ly poured
With won - der and thanks-giv - ing For love that knows no end,
Re - newed, sus-tained, and giv - en By to - ken, sign, and word,

For us, in sol - emn to - ken Of Christ our dy - ing Lord.
We find in Je - sus liv - ing Our ev - er - pres - ent Friend.
The pledge and seal of heav - en, The love of Christ our Lord.

♩=104–112

Una Espiga
Sheaves of Summer

UNA ESPIGA   10.10.13.10

Cesáreo Gabaráin, 1973
Trans. George Lockwood, 1988

Cesáreo Gabaráin, 1973
Harm. Skinner Chávez-Melo, 1987

518

1. U - na es - pi - ga do - ra - da por el sol,
2. Com - par - ti - mos la mis - ma co - mu - nión,

1. Sheaves of sum-mer turned gold-en by the sun,
2. We are shar-ing the same com - mu-nion meal,

El ra - ci - mo que cor - ta el vi - ña - dor,
So - mos tri - go del mis - mo sem-bra - dor,

Grapes in bunch-es cut down when ripe and red,
We are wheat by the same great Sow-er sown;

Se con - vier - ten a - ho - ra en pan y vi - no de a - mor,
Un mo - li - no a la vi - da nos tri - tu - ra con do - lor,

Are con - vert - ed in - to the bread and wine of God's love
Like a mill-stone, life grinds us down with sor - row and pain,

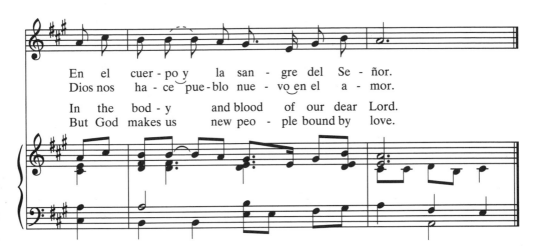

En   el   cuer - po y   la san - gre del Se - ñor.
Dios nos   ha - ce pue - blo nue - vo en el   a - mor.

In   the   bod - y   and blood   of   our   dear   Lord.
But God   makes us   new peo - ple bound by   love.

3. Como granos que han hecho el
    mismo pan,
  Como notas que tejen un cantar,
  Como gotas de agua que se funden
    en el mar,
  Los cristianos un cuerpo formarán.

4. En la mesa de Dios se sentarán,
  Como hijos su pan compartirán,
  Una misma esperanza caminando
    cantarán
  En la vida como hermanos
    se amarán.

3. Like the grains which become one
    same whole loaf,
  Like the notes that are woven into song,
  Like the droplets of water that are
    blended in the sea,
  We, as Christians, one body shall become.

4. At God's table together we shall sit.
  As God's children, Christ's body
    we will share.
  One same hope we will sing together
    as we walk along.
  Brothers, sisters, in life, in love,
    we'll be.

519 Thee We Adore, O Hidden Savior, Thee

ADORO TE DEVOTE   10.10.10.10

Thomas Aquinas (c. 1225–1274)
Trans. James Russell Woodford, 1850

Benedictine plainsong, Mode V, 13th century
As in *Hymnal for Colleges and Schools*, 1956

1. Thee we a - dore, O hid - den Sav - ior, Thee,
2. O blest me - mo - rial of our dy - ing Lord,
3. Foun - tain of good - ness, Je - sus, Lord and God,
4. O Christ, whom now be - neath a veil we see,

Who at this bless - ed feast art pleased to be;
Who liv - ing Bread to all doth here af - ford!
Cleanse us, un - clean, with Thy most cleans - ing blood;
May what we thirst for soon our por - tion be,

Both flesh and spir - it in Thy pres - ence fail,
O may our souls for - ev - er feed on Thee,
In - crease our faith and love, that we may know
To gaze on Thee un - veiled, and see Thy face,

Music: Harmonization © 1956 Yale University Press. All rights reserved. Used by permission.

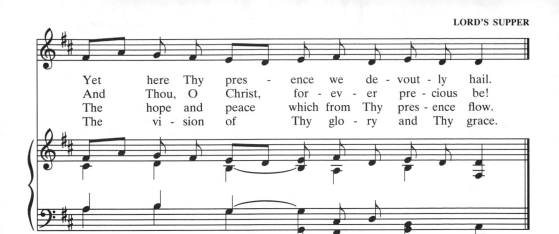

Yet   here   Thy   pres - ence   we   de - vout - ly   hail.
And   Thou, O   Christ,   for - ev - er   pre - cious   be!
The   hope   and   peace   which from Thy   pres - ence   flow.
The   vi - sion   of   Thy   glo - ry   and   Thy   grace.

Revelation 21:1–5

Here, O Our Lord,
We See You Face to Face

520

Horatius Bonar, 1855; alt. 1972

1. Here, O our Lord, we see You face to face,
   Here would we touch and handle things unseen,
   Here grasp with firmer hand eternal grace,
   And all our weariness upon You lean.

2. We have no help but Yours, nor do we need
   Another arm save Yours to lean upon.
   It is enough, O Lord, enough indeed;
   Our strength is in Your might, Your might alone.

3. This is the hour of banquet and of song;
   This is the heavenly table for us spread;
   Here let us feast and, feasting, still prolong
   The fellowship of living wine and bread.

4. Too soon we rise; the symbols disappear.
   The feast, though not the love, is past and gone;
   The bread and wine remove, but You are here,
   Nearer than ever, still our shield and sun.

5. Feast after feast thus comes and passes by,
   Yet, passing, points to that glad feast above,
   Giving sweet foretaste of the festal joy,
   The Lamb's great bridal feast of bliss and love.

Tune: ADORO TE DEVOTE, 519; MORECAMBE, 326

521 You Satisfy the Hungry Heart

FINEST WHEAT   CM with refrain

Omer Westendorf, 1976

Robert E. Kreutz, 1976

Refrain

You sat-is-fy the hun-gry heart with gift of fin-est wheat;

Come give to us, O sav-ing Lord, the bread of life to eat.

1. As when the shep-herd calls his sheep, They know and heed his voice;
2. With joy - ful lips we sing to You Our praise and grat - i - tude
3. Is not the cup we bless and share The blood of Christ out-poured?
4. The mys-tery of Your pres-ence, Lord, No mor - tal tongue can tell:
5. You give Your-self to us, O Lord; Then self - less let us be,

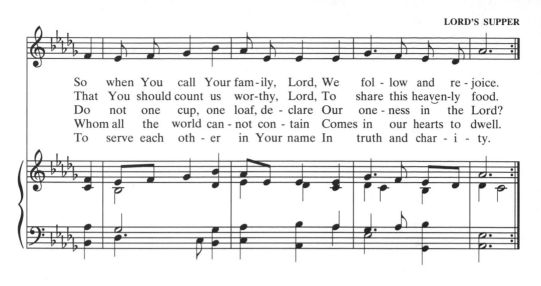

So when You call Your fam-i-ly, Lord, We fol-low and re-joice.
That You should count us wor-thy, Lord, To share this heaven-ly food.
Do not one cup, one loaf, de-clare Our one-ness in the Lord?
Whom all the world can-not con-tain Comes in our hearts to dwell.
To serve each oth-er in Your name In truth and char-i-ty.

ORDINATION AND CONFIRMATION

Lord, When I Came Into This Life 522

LAND OF REST CM

Fred Kaan, 1976

American folk melody
Arr. Annabel Morris Buchanan, 1938

1. Lord, when I came in-to this life You called me by my name;
2. With-in the cir-cle of the faith As mem-ber of Your cast,
3. In all the ten-sions of my life, Be-tween my faith and doubt,
4. So, help me in my un-be-lief And let my life be true:

To-day I come, com-mit my-self, Re-spond-ing to Your claim.
I take my place with all the saints Of fu-ture, pres-ent, past.
Let Your great Spir-it give me hope, Sus-tain me, lead me out.
Feet firm-ly plant-ed on the earth, My sights set high on You.

523 God the Spirit, Guide and Guardian

BETHANY (Smart)   8.7.8.7 D

Carl P. Daw, Jr., 1988   Henry Thomas Smart, 1867

1. God the Spir - it, guide and guard-ian, Wind - sped flame and
2. Christ our Sav - ior, Sov - ereign, Shep - herd, Word made flesh, Love
3. Great Cre - a - tor, Life - be - stow - er, Truth be - yond all
4. Tri - une God, mys - ter - ious Be - ing, Un - di - vid - ed

hov - ering dove, Breath of life and voice of proph-ets, Sign of
cru - ci - fied, Teach-er, heal - er, suf - fering Ser - vant, Friend of
thought's re - call, Fount of wis-dom, womb of mer - cy, Giv - ing
and di - verse, Deep - er than our minds can fath - om, Great-er

bless - ing, power of love: Give to those who lead Your peo - ple
sin - ners, foe of pride: In Your tend - ing may all *pas - tors
and for - giv - ing all: As You know our strength and weak-ness,
than our creeds re - hearse: Help us in our var - ied call - ings

Fresh a - noint - ing of Your grace; Send them forth as
Learn and live a Shep - herd's care; Grant them cour - age
So may those the church ex - alts O - ver - see her
Your full im - age to pro - claim, That our min - is -

*Or "elders" or "deacons."

bold a-pos-tles To Your church in ev-ery place.
and com-pas-sion Shown through word and deed and prayer.
life stead-fast-ly, Yet not o-ver-look her faults.
tries u-nit-ing May give glo-ry to Your name.

Holy Spirit, Lord of Love 524

SALZBURG 7.7.7.7 D

Jacob Hintze, 1678
Harm. Johann Sebastian Bach (1685–1750)
As in *Hymns Ancient and Modern,* 1861

William Dalrymple Maclagen, c. 1873; alt.

1. Ho-ly Spir-it, Lord of love, Who de-scend-ed from a-bove,
2. When the sa-cred vow is made, When the hands on them are laid,

Gifts of bless-ing to be-stow On Your wait-ing church be-low,
Come in this most sol-emn hour With Your strength-ening gift of power.

Once a-gain in love draw near To Your ser-vants gath-ered here;
Give them light Your truth to see; Give them life Your own to be,

From their bright bap-tis-mal day You have led them on their way.
Dai-ly power to con-quer sin, Pa-tient faith the crown to win.

525 Here I Am, Lord

HERE I AM, LORD   7.7.7.4 D with refrain

Daniel L. Schutte, 1981

Daniel L. Schutte, 1981; alt.

Harm. Michael Pope, Daniel L. Schutte, and John Weissrock, 1983

1. I, the Lord of sea and sky,   I have heard My peo-ple cry.
2. I, the Lord of snow and rain,   I have borne My peo-ple's pain.
3. I, the Lord of wind and flame,   I will tend the poor and lame.

All who dwell in deep-est sin   My hand will save.
I have wept for love of them,   They turn a-way.
I will set a feast for them,   My hand will save.

I who made the stars of night,   I will make their dark-ness bright.
I will break their hearts of stone,   Give them hearts for love a-lone.
Fin-est bread I will pro-vide   Till their hearts be sat-is-fied.

Who will bear My light to them? Whom shall I send?
I will speak My word to them. Whom shall I send?
I will give My life to them. Whom shall I send?

Refrain
Unison

Here I am, Lord. Is it I, Lord? I have

heard You call-ing in the night I will

go, Lord, if You lead me. I will hold Your

Fine

peo-ple in my heart.

526 For All the Saints

SINE NOMINE   10.10.10 with alleluias

William Walsham How, 1864

Ralph Vaughan Williams, 1906

1. For all the saints who from their la - bors rest, Who
2. Thou wast their rock, their for - tress, and their might;
*3. O blest com - mu - nion, fel - low - ship di - vine!
**4. From earth's wide bounds, from o - cean's far-thest coast, Through

Thee by faith be - fore the world con - fessed, Thy
Thou, Lord, their cap - tain in the well-fought fight;
We fee - bly strug - gle, they in glo - ry shine; Yet
gates of pearl streams in the count-less host,

name, O Je - sus, be for - ev - er blest.
Thou, in the dark - ness drear, their one true light.
all are one in Thee, for all are Thine.
Sing - ing to Fa - ther, Son, and Ho - ly Ghost,

Music: From the English Hymnal, *1906. Used by permission of Oxford University Press.*

Al - le - lu - ia! Al - le - lu - ia!

Harmony, stanza 3

3. O blest com - mu - nion, fel-low-ship di - vine! We fee-bly strug-gle,

they in glo-ry shine; Yet all are one in Thee, for all are

D.C. for stanza 4

Al - le - lu - ia!

Thine. Al - le - lu - ia! Al - le - lu - ia!

*(May be sung before stanza 3)

O may Thy soldiers, faithful, true, and bold,
Fight as the saints who nobly fought of old,
And win with them the victor's crown of gold.
Alleluia! Alleluia!

**(May be sung before stanza 4)

And when the strife is fierce, the warfare long,
Steals on the ear the distant triumph song,
And hearts are brave again, and arms are strong.
Alleluia! Alleluia!

527 Near to the Heart of God

MC AFEE   CM with refrain

Cleland Boyd McAfee, 1901   Cleland Boyd McAfee, 1901

1. There is a place of qui - et rest, Near to the heart of God,
2. There is a place of com - fort sweet, Near to the heart of God,
3. There is a place of full re - lease, Near to the heart of God,

A place where sin can - not mo - lest, Near to the heart of God.
A place where we our Sav - ior meet, Near to the heart of God.
A place where all is joy and peace, Near to the heart of God.

Refrain

O Je - sus, blest Re - deem - er, Sent from the heart of God,

Hold us, who wait be - fore Thee, Near to the heart of God.

Give Thanks for Life

SARUM   10.10.10.4.4

Shirley Erena Murray, 1987

Joseph Barnby, 1868

1. Give thanks for life, the mea-sure of our days;
2. Give thanks for those who made their life a light
3. And for our own, our liv-ing and our dead,

Mor - tal, we pass through beau-ty that de - cays,
Caught from the Christ-flame, burst-ing through the night,
Thanks for the love by which our life is fed,

Yet sing to God our hope, our love, our praise:
Who touched the truth, who burned for what is right:
A love not changed by time or death or dread:

Al - le - lu - ia! Al - le - lu - ia!

529 Lord of the Living

CHRISTE SANCTORUM 11.11.11.5

Fred Kaan (b. 1929)

Paris *Antiphoner,* 1681
Harm. David Evans, 1927

1. Lord of the liv - ing, in Your name as - sem - bled We join to thank You for the life re - mem - bered. O God, have mer - cy, to Your chil - dren giv - ing Hope in be - liev - ing.

2. Help us to trea - sure all that will re - mind us Of the en - rich - ment in the days be - hind us. Your love has set us in the gen - er - a - tions, God of cre - a - tion.

3. May we, when - ev - er tempt - ed to de - jec - tion, Strong - ly re - cap - ture thoughts of res - ur - rec - tion. You gave us Je - sus to de - feat our sad - ness With East - er glad - ness.

4. Lord, You can lift us from the grave of sor - row In - to the pres - ence of Your own to - mor - row; Give to Your peo - ple for the day's af - flic - tion Your ben - e - dic - tion.

O Lord of Life, Where'er They Be

530

GELOBT SEI GOTT   8.8.8 with alleluias

Melchior Vulpius, 1609
As in *Pilgrim Hymnal*, 1958

Frederick Lucian Hosmer, 1888; alt.

1. O Lord of life, wher-e'er they be, Safe in Your own e-ter-ni-ty, Now live Your chil-dren glo-rious-ly. Al-le-lu-ia! Al-le-lu-ia! Al-le-lu-ia!

2. All souls You call, both here and there, Do rest with-in Your shel-ter-ing care; One prov-i-dence a-like they share: Al-le-lu-ia! Al-le-lu-ia! Al-le-lu-ia!

3. Your word is true, Your ways are just; A-bove the chant-ed "Dust to dust" Shall rise our song of grate-ful trust: Al-le-lu-ia! Al-le-lu-ia! Al-le-lu-ia!

4. Hap-py are they in God who rest, No more by fear and doubt op-pressed; Liv-ing or dy-ing, they are blest: Al-le-lu-ia! Al-le-lu-ia! Al-le-lu-ia!

531 Not for Tongues of Heaven's Angels

Timothy Dudley-Smith, 1985

BRIDEGROOM 8.7.8.7.6

Peter Cutts, 1969

1. Not for tongues of heav-en's an-gels, Not for wis-dom to dis-
2. Love is hum-ble, love is gen-tle, Love is ten-der, true, and
3. Nev-er jeal-ous, nev-er self-ish, Love will not re-joice in
4. In the day this world is fad-ing Faith and hope will play their

cern, Not for faith that mas-ters moun-tains; For this
kind; Love is gra-cious, ev-er-pa-tient, Gen-er-
wrong; Nev-er boast-ful nor re-sent-ful, Love be-
part; But when Christ is seen in glo-ry Love shall

bet-ter gift we yearn:
ous of heart and mind:
lieves and suf-fers long: May love be ours, O Lord.
reign in ev-ery heart:

Text and Music: Text copyright © 1985, music copyright © 1969 by Hope Publishing Company, Carol Stream, IL 60188. All rights reserved. Used by permission.

♩=88–96

O God, You Give Humanity Its Name 532

Fred Kaan, 1968   SURSUM CORDA (Smith)   10.10.10.10   Alfred Morton Smith, 1941

1. O God, You give hu-man-i-ty its name, Your cov-e-
2. May through their u-nion oth-er lives be blessed, Their door be
3. Pre-serve their days from in-ward-ness of heart: To each the
4. From stage to stage on life's un-fold-ing way Bring to their
5. Lord, bless us all to whom this day brings joy, Let no e-

nant of grace re-mains the same: Be with these two who
wide to stran-ger and to guest; Give them the un-der-
gift of truth-ful-ness im-part. Their bond be strong a-
mind the vows they make this day; Your Spir-it be their
vents our u-ni-ty de-stroy, And help us, till all

now be-fore You wait; En-large the love they come to con-se-crate.
stand-ing that is kind; Grant them the bless-ing of an o-pen mind.
gainst all strain and strife A-mid the chang-es of this earth-ly life.
guide in ev-ery move, Their faith in Christ the ba-sis of their love.
sense of time is lost, To live and love and not to count the cost.

533 O Perfect Love

PERFECT LOVE   11.10.11.10

Dorothy Frances Gurney, 1883

Joseph Barnby, 1889

1. O per-fect love, all hu-man thought tran-scend-ing,
2. O per-fect life, be Thou their full as-sur-ance
3. Grant them the joy which bright-ens earth-ly sor-row;

Low-ly we kneel in prayer be-fore Thy throne,
Of ten-der char-i-ty and stead-fast faith,
Grant them the peace which calms all earth-ly strife,

That theirs may be the love which knows no end-ing,
Of pa-tient hope, and qui-et, brave en-dur-ance,
And to life's day the glo-rious un-known mor-row

Whom Thou for-ev-er-more dost join in one.
With child-like trust that fears nor pain nor death.
That dawns up-on e-ter-nal love and life.

The Grace of Life Is Theirs   534

RHOSYMEDRE   6.6.6.6.8.8.8

Fred Pratt Green, 1970   John David Edwards, 1840

1. The grace of life is theirs Who on this wed - ding day
2. Where love is, God a - bides: And God shall sure - ly bless
3. And when time lays its hand On all we hold most dear,

De - light to make their vows And for each oth - er pray.
A home where trust and care Give birth to hap - pi - ness.
And life, by life con - sumed, Ful - fills its pur - pose here,

May they, O Lord, to - geth - er prove The last - ing joy of
May they, O Lord, to - geth - er prove The last - ing joy of
May we, O Lord, to - geth - er prove The last - ing joy of

Chris - tian love, The last - ing joy of Chris - tian love.
such a love, The last - ing joy of such a love.
Chris - tian love, The last - ing joy of Chris - tian love.

Alternate tune: LOVE UNKNOWN, 76

535

Go with Us, Lord

TALLIS' CANON LM

Thomas Tallis
Mary Jackson Cathey, 1986
Adapt. Parker's *Whole Psalter*, c. 1561

Go with us, Lord, and guide the way Through this and

ev - ery com - ing day, That in Your Spir - it

strong and true Our lives may be our gift to You.

*May be sung as a canon.

536

Lord, Make Us More Holy

6.6.6.6.6.6

African-American spiritual   African-American spiritual

1. Lord, make us more ho - ly,   Lord, make us more ho - ly,
2. Lord, make us more lov - ing,   Lord, make us more lov - ing,
3. Lord, make us more pa - tient, Lord, make us more pa - tient,
4. Lord, make us more faith - ful, Lord, make us more faith - ful,

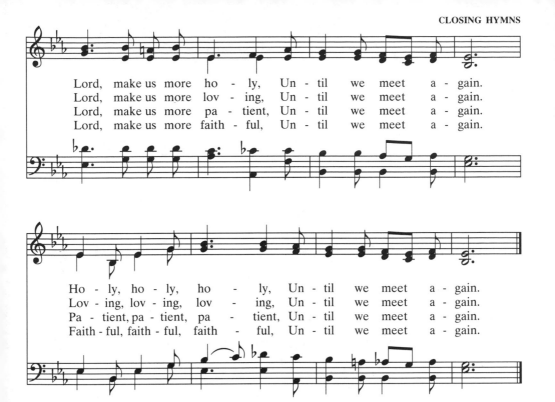

Lord, make us more ho - ly, Un - til we meet a - gain.
Lord, make us more lov - ing, Un - til we meet a - gain.
Lord, make us more pa - tient, Un - til we meet a - gain.
Lord, make us more faith - ful, Un - til we meet a - gain.

Ho - ly, ho - ly, ho - ly, Un - til we meet a - gain.
Lov - ing, lov - ing, lov - ing, Un - til we meet a - gain.
Pa - tient, pa - tient, pa - tient, Un - til we meet a - gain.
Faith - ful, faith - ful, faith - ful, Un - til we meet a - gain.

Shalom, Chaverim! 537
Farewell, Good Friends

Israeli round

Sha - lom, cha - ve - rim! Sha - lom, cha - ve - rot! Sha - lom, sha - lom!
Fare - well, good friends, Fare - well, good friends, Sha - lom, sha - lom!

Le - hit - ra - ot, le - hit - ra - ot, Sha - lom, sha - lom.
Till we meet a - gain, till we meet a - gain, Sha - lom, sha - lom.

*May be sung as a canon.

♩=100–108

538 Lord, Dismiss Us with Thy Blessing

SICILIAN MARINERS 8.7.8.7.8.7

Attr. John Fawcett, 1773
Stanza 1, line 6, alt. 1774, Conyer's *Collection of Psalms*
Stanza 3 alt. Godfrey Thring (1823–1903)

Sicilian melody

1. Lord, dis-miss us with Thy bless-ing; Fill our hearts with
2. Thanks we give and ad-o-ra-tion For Thy gos-pel's
3. So that when Thy love shall call us, Sav-ior, from the

joy and peace; Let us each, Thy love pos-sess-ing,
joy-ful sound; May the fruits of Thy sal-va-tion
world a-way, Let no fear of death ap-pall us,

Tri-umph in re-deem-ing grace. O re-fresh us,
In our hearts and lives a-bound. Ev-er faith-ful,
Glad Thy sum-mons to o-bey. May we ev-er,

O re-fresh us, Trav-eling through this wil-der-ness.
Ev-er faith-ful To the truth may we be found;
May we ev-er Reign with Thee in end-less day.

Savior, Again to Thy Dear Name We Raise 539

ELLERS   10.10.10.10

John Ellerton, 1866

Edward John Hopkins, 1869

1. Sav - ior, a - gain to Thy dear name we raise
2. Grant us Thy peace up - on our home-ward way;
3. Grant us Thy peace, Lord, through the com - ing night;
4. Grant us Thy peace through - out our earth - ly life,

With one ac - cord our part - ing hymn of praise.
With Thee be - gan, with Thee shall end the day.
Turn Thou for us its dark - ness in - to light.
Our balm in sor - row, and our stay in strife.

We stand to bless Thee ere our wor - ship cease;
Guard Thou the lips from sin, the hearts from shame,
From harm and dan - ger keep Thy chil - dren free,
Then, when Thy voice shall bid our con - flict cease,

And, now de - part - ing, wait Thy word of peace.
That in this house have called up - on Thy name.
For dark and light are both a - like to Thee.
Call us, O Lord, to Thine e - ter - nal peace.

540 God Be with You Till We Meet Again

RANDOLPH 9.8.8.9

Jeremiah Eames Rankin, 1880; alt.

Ralph Vaughan Williams, 1906

1. God be with you till we meet a-gain; Lov-ing coun-sels
2. God be with you till we meet a-gain; Un-seen wings pro-
3. God be with you till we meet a-gain; When life's per-ils
4. God be with you till we meet a-gain; Keep love's ban-ner

guide, up-hold you, With a Shep-herd's care en-fold you:
tect-ing hide you, Dai-ly man-na still pro-vide you:
thick con-found you, Put un-fail-ing arms a-round you:
float-ing o'er you, Smite death's threat-ening wave be-fore you:

God be with you till we meet a-gain.

Music: From the *English Hymnal,* 1906. Used by permission of Oxford University Press.

541 Now the Day Is Over

MERRIAL 6.5.6.5

Sabine Baring-Gould, 1865; alt.

Joseph Barnby, 1868

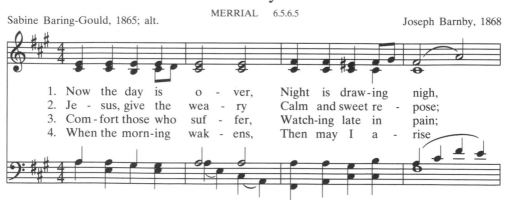

1. Now the day is o-ver, Night is draw-ing nigh,
2. Je-sus, give the wea-ry Calm and sweet re-pose;
3. Com-fort those who suf-fer, Watch-ing late in pain;
4. When the morn-ing wak-ens, Then may I a-rise

Shad - ows of the eve - ning Steal a - cross the sky.
With Thy ten - derest bless - ing May mine eye - lids close.
Those who plan some e - vil From their sin re - strain.
Pure, and fresh, and sin - less In Thy ho - ly eyes.

All Praise to Thee, My God, This Night 542

TALLIS' CANON   LM

Thomas Tallis
Adapt. Parker's *Whole Psalter,* c. 1561

Thomas Ken, 1674

1. All praise to Thee, my God, this night, For
2. For - give me, Lord, through Christ, I pray, The
3. O may my soul on Thee re - pose, And
4. Praise God, from whom all bless - ings flow; Praise

all the bless - ings of the light! Keep me, O keep me
wrong that I have done this day, That I, be - fore I
with sweet sleep mine eye - lids close; Sleep that shall me more
God, all crea - tures here be - low; Praise God a - bove, ye

safe from harm With - in the shel - ter of Thine arm!
sleep, may be At peace with neigh - bor, self, and Thee.
vi - gorous make To serve Thee, God, when I a - wake.
heaven - ly host; Praise Fa - ther, Son, and Ho - ly Ghost.

May be sung as a canon.

543

Abide with Me

Henry Francis Lyte, 1847

EVENTIDE 10.10.10.10

William Henry Monk, 1861

1. A - bide with me: fast falls the e - ven - tide;
2. Swift to its close ebbs out life's lit - tle day;
3. I need Thy pres - ence ev - ery pass - ing hour;
4. I fear no foe, with Thee at hand to bless:

The dark - ness deep - ens; Lord, with me a - bide!
Earth's joys grow dim, its glo - ries pass a - way;
What but Thy grace can foil the tempt - er's power?
Ills have no weight, and tears no bit - ter - ness.

When oth - er help - ers fail and com - forts flee,
Change and de - cay in all a - round I see.
Who, like Thy - self, my guide and stay can be?
Where is death's sting? Where, grave, Thy vic - to - ry?

Help of the help - less, O a - bide with me.
O Thou who chang - est not, a - bide with me.
Through cloud and sun - shine, Lord, a - bide with me.
I tri - umph still, if Thou a - bide with me.

5. Hold Thou Thy cross before my closing eyes;
   Shine through the gloom and point me to the skies:
   Heaven's morning breaks, and earth's vain shadows flee;
   In life, in death, O Lord, abide with me.

Day Is Done

544

AR HYD Y NOS   8.4.8.4.8.8.8.4

James Quinn, 1969

Welsh melody, c. 1784

1. Day is done, but love un-fail-ing Dwells ev - er here;
2. Dark de-scends, but light un-end-ing Shines through our night;
3. Eyes will close, but You un-sleep-ing Watch by our side;

Shad - ows fall, but hope, pre - vail - ing, Calms ev - er - y fear.
You are with us, ev - er lend-ing New strength to sight:
Death may come, in love's safe-keep-ing Still we a - bide.

God, our Mak - er, none for - sak - ing, Take our hearts, of Love's own
One in love, Your truth con - fess - ing, One in hope of heav - en's
God of love, all e - vil quell - ing, Sin for - giv - ing, fear dis -

mak-ing, Watch our sleep-ing, guard our wak - ing, Be al - ways near.
bless-ing, May we see, in love's pos-sess-ing, Love's end - less light!
pel - ling, Stay with us, our hearts in-dwell-ing, This e - ven - tide.

545 Now, on Land and Sea Descending

VESPER HYMN 8.7.8.7.8.6.8.7

Attr. Dimitri S. Bortniansky (1751–1825)
As in Stevenson's *A Selection of Popular National Airs*, 1818

Samuel Longfellow, 1859

1. Now, on land and sea de-scend-ing, Brings the night its peace pro-found;
2. Soon as dies the sun-set glo-ry, Stars of heaven shine out a-bove,
3. Now, our wants and bur-dens leav-ing To God's care who cares for all,
4. As the dark-ness deep-ens o'er us, Lo! e-ter-nal stars a-rise;

Let our ves-per hymn be blend-ing With the ho-ly calm a-round.
Tell-ing still the an-cient sto-ry— Their Cre-a-tor's change-less love.
Cease we fear-ing, cease we griev-ing: At God's touch our bur-dens fall.
Hope and faith and love rise glo-rious, Shin-ing in the Spir-it's skies.

Ju-bi-la-te! Ju-bi-la-te! Ju-bi-la-te! A-men!

Let our ves-per hymn be blend-ing With the ho-ly calm a-round.
Tell-ing still the an-cient sto-ry— Their Cre-a-tor's change-less love.
Cease we fear-ing, cease we griev-ing: At God's touch our bur-dens fall.
Hope and faith and love rise glo-rious, Shin-ing in the Spir-it's skies.

The Day Thou Gavest, Lord, Is Ended 546

ST. CLEMENT   9.8.9.8

John Ellerton, 1870   Clement Cotterill Scholefield, 1874

1. The day Thou gav - est, Lord, is end - ed, The dark - ness
2. We thank Thee that Thy church un - sleep-ing, While earth rolls
3. As o'er each con - ti - nent and is - land The dawn leads
4. The sun that bids us rest is wak-ing Thy chil - dren

falls at Thy be - hest; To Thee our morn - ing
on - ward in - to light, Through all the world a
on an - oth - er day, The voice of prayer is
'neath the west - ern sky, And hour by hour fresh

hymns as - cend-ed, Thy praise shall hal - low now our rest.
watch is keep-ing And rests not now by day or night.
nev - er si - lent, Nor dies the strain of praise a - way.
lips are mak-ing Thy won - drous do - ings heard on high.

5. So be it, Lord; Thy throne shall never,
   Like earth's proud empires, pass away;
   Thy kingdom stands, and grows forever
   Till all Thy creatures own Thy sway.

This tune in a lower key, 497

Awit Sa Dapit Hapon
When Twilight Comes

Irregular

Filipino hymn
Moises Andrade
Trans. and para. James Minchin

Francisco F. Feliciano (b. 1941)

1. Nga - yong nag - da - da - pit ha - pon
2. No - on din ay da - pit ha - pon

1. When twi - light comes and the sun sets,
2. One day the Rab - bi Lord Je - sus

at lu - mu - lu - bog ang a - raw hu - ma -
at nag - wa - wa - kas ang a - raw nag - ha -

moth - er hen pre - pares for night's rest. As her
called the Twelve to share His last meal. As the

ha - pon ang i - na - hin at ang kan - yang ma -
pu - nan ang gu - ro at pa - ti kan yang ma -

brood shel - ters un - der her wings she gives the love of
hen tends her young, so for them He spent Him - self to

G_1 *G_2*

* Accompaniment is for two guitars.

pag - pa - lang ka - may.
a - lay sa la - hat.
new to - mor - row's song.
fore the com - ing night.

3. Ngayong nagdadapit hapon
at lumulubog ang araw
ang manga magulang at ang
manga anak ay naghahapunan
nagtitipon at nagsasalo
sa ligaya't pagdiriwang
sa Ama't Anak na Diyos,
Diyos Espiritung Banal.

3. So gather round once again, friends,
touched by fading glow of sun's gold,
and recount all our frail human hopes:
the dreams of young and stories of old.
Oh! what joy to pray close together,
kneeling as one family,
by a mother's love embraced
in the blessed Trinity.

548   O Radiant Light, O Sun Divine

CONDITOR ALME SIDERUM   LM

Phos Hilaron, 3rd century
Trans. William G. Storey, c. 1970

Sarum plainsong, Mode IV, 9th century
Harm. C. Winfred Douglas, 1943
Handbell intonations by Kenneth E. Williams, 1986

Handbells needed   Optional *L.V.*   Play this cluster stanza 1 only
Handbells   Use handbells or accompaniment

Intro. Stanza 1 only
L.V.=Let Vibrate

1. O ra-diant Light, O Sun di - vine,
2. O Son of God, the source of life,
3. Lord Je - sus Christ, as day - light fades,

Of God the Fa-ther's death-less face, O i - mage of the Light sub-lime,
Praise is Your due by night and day. Our hap - py lips must raise the strain
As shine the lights of ev - en - tide, We praise the Fa-ther with the Son,

That fills the heaven - ly dwell-ing place,
Of Your es-teemed and splen-did name.
The Spir - it blest and with them one.   A - men.

549

O Gladsome Light

LE CANTIQUE DE SIMÉON   6.6.7.6.6.7

Phos Hilaron, 3rd century
Para. Robert Seymour Bridges, 1899; alt.

Genevan Psalter, 1551
Harm. Claude Goudimel, 1565

1. O glad-some light, O grace Of our Cre - a - tor's face,
2. As fades the day's last light, We see the lamps of night
3. To You of right be - longs All praise of ho - ly songs,

The e - ter - nal splen-dor wear - ing: Ce - les - tial, ho - ly, blest,
Our com - mon hymn out - pour - ing; O God of might un - known,
O Son of God, Life - giv - er; You, there-fore, O Most High,

Our Sav - ior Je - sus Christ, Joy - ful in Your ap - pear - ing.
You, the in - car - nate Son, And Spir - it blest a - dor - ing.
The world does glo - ri - fy And shall ex - alt for - ev - er.

O Light Whose Splendor Thrills

550

LES COMMANDEMENTS DE DIEU   9.8.9.8

Phos Hilaron, 3rd century
Para. Carl P. Daw, Jr., 1989

Louis Bourgeois, 1543
Harm. Claude Goudimel, 1564; alt.

1. O Light whose splen - dor thrills and glad - dens With ra - diance bright-er than the sun, Pure gleam of God's un - end-ing glo - ry, O Je - sus, blest a - noint - ed One;

2. As twi - light hov - ers near at sun - set, And lamps are lit, and chil - dren nod, In even-ing hymns we lift our voic - es To Fa - ther, Spir - it, Son: one God.

3. In all life's bril - liant, time - less mo - ments, Let faith - ful voic - es sing Your praise, O Son of God, our life - be - stow - er, Whose glo - ry light-ens end - less days.

551   Come, Ye Thankful People, Come

ST. GEORGE'S WINDSOR   7.7.7.7 D

Henry Alford, 1844; alt.

George Job Elvey, 1859

1. Come, ye thank-ful peo - ple, come, Raise the song of har - vest home:
2. All the world is God's own field, Fruit un - to God's praise to yield;
3. For the Lord our God shall come, And shall take the har - vest home;
4. E - ven so, Lord, quick - ly come To Thy fi - nal har - vest home;

All is safe - ly gath - ered in, Ere the win - ter storms be - gin;
Wheat and tares to - geth - er sown, Un - to joy or sor - row grown;
From each field shall in that day All of - fens - es purge a - way;
Gath - er Thou Thy peo - ple in, Free from sor - row, free from sin;

God, our Mak - er, doth pro - vide For our wants to be sup - plied:
First the blade, and then the ear, Then the full corn shall ap - pear:
Give the an - gels charge at last In the fire the tares to cast,
There for - ev - er pu - ri - fied, In Thy pres-ence to a - bide:

Come to God's own tem - ple, come, Raise the song of har - vest home.
Lord of har - vest, grant that we Whole-some grain and pure may be.
But the fruit - ful ears to store In God's gar - ner ev - er - more.
Come, with all Thine an - gels, come, Raise the glo - rious har - vest home.

Give Thanks, O Christian People

552

ES FLOG EIN KLEINS WALDVÖGELEIN   7.6.7.6 D

Mary Jackson Cathey, 1984

Memmingen ms., 17th century
Harm. George Ratcliffe Woodward, 1904

1. Give thanks, O Chris-tian peo - ple, For work-ers of our day
2. Give thanks, O Chris-tian peo - ple, For lead-ers of our years
3. Give thanks, O Chris-tian peo - ple, For all who love the Lord,
4. Give thanks, O Chris-tian peo - ple, For life in fel-low-ship

Who heed the call to ser - vice And make it their life's way
Who live to share with oth - ers Our joy when Christ ap - pears,
Who live each day be - liev - ing In God's e - ter - nal Word:
With all who trust our Sav - ior Their serv-ing to e - quip

To go to feed the hun - gry, To tend to those in need,
To teach the ones who seek light, To guide the fal-tering feet,
To share Christ's love in liv - ing, To wit - ness with each deed,
To ease an - oth - er's bur - dens, To cope in joy and stress,

To work for e - qual jus - tice, Till all God's folk are freed.
To lead the fol - lowers for - ward Our liv - ing Lord to meet.
To use the tal - ents giv - en To plant the gos-pel seed.
To mag - ni - fy God's mes - sage And Christ's great love con - fess.

553 For the Fruit of All Creation

EAST ACKLAM 8.4.8.4.8.8.8.4

Fred Pratt Green, 1970 Francis Jackson, 1957

1. For the fruit of all cre-a-tion, Thanks be to God.
2. In the just re-ward of la-bor, God's will be done.
3. For the har-vests of the Spir-it, Thanks be to God.

For the gifts to ev-ery na-tion, Thanks be to God.
In the help we give our neigh-bor, God's will be done.
For the good we all in-her-it, Thanks be to God.

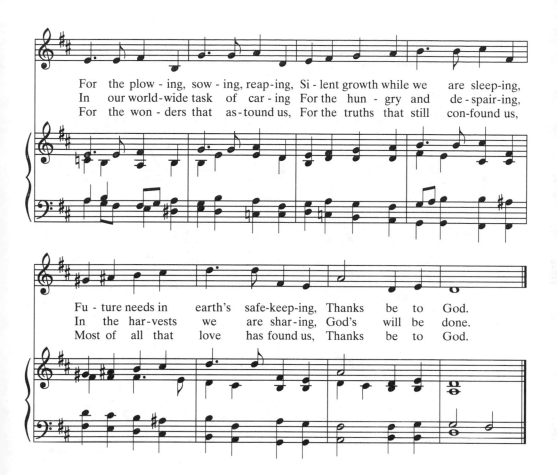

For the plow-ing, sow-ing, reap-ing, Si-lent growth while we are sleep-ing,
In our world-wide task of car-ing For the hun-gry and de-spair-ing,
For the won-ders that as-tound us, For the truths that still con-found us,

Fu-ture needs in earth's safe-keep-ing, Thanks be to God.
In the har-vests we are shar-ing, God's will be done.
Most of all that love has found us, Thanks be to God.

554 Let All Things Now Living

ASH GROVE   6.6.11.6.6.11 D

Katherine K. Davis, 1939; alt.

Welsh folk melody
Harm. Gerald H. Knight (1908–1979)

1. Let all things now liv-ing A song of thanks-giv-ing
2. By law God en-forc-es. The stars in their cours-es,

To God our Cre-a-tor tri-um-phant-ly raise;
The sun in its or-bit o-be-dient-ly shine;

Who fash-ioned and made us, Pro-tect-ed and stayed us,
The hills and the moun-tains, The riv-ers and foun-tains,

By guid-ing us on to the end of our days.
The depths of the o-cean pro-claim God di-vine.

God's ban - ners are o'er us, Pure light goes be - fore us,
We, too, should be voic - ing Our love and re - joic - ing

A pil - lar of fire shin - ing forth in the night:
With glad ad - o - ra - tion, a song let us raise:

Till shad-ows have van-ished, All fear - ful - ness ban - ished,
Till all things now liv-ing U - nite in thanks-giv - ing,

As for - ward we trav - el from light in - to Light.
To God in the high - est, ho - san - na and praise.

555　Now Thank We All Our God

NUN DANKET ALLE GOTT　6.7.6.7.6.6.6.6

Martin Rinkart, c. 1636
Trans. Catherine Winkworth, 1858; alt.
Stanza 3, *Rejoice in the Lord,* 1985

Johann Crüger, 1648
Harm. adapt. *Lobegesang,* Felix Mendelssohn, 1840

1. Now thank we all our God With heart and hands and voic - es,
2. O may this boun - teous God Through all our life be near us,
3. All praise and thanks to God, Who reigns in high - est heav - en,

Who won-drous things hath done, In whom this world re - joic - es;
With ev - er joy - ful hearts And bless - ed peace to cheer us;
To Fa - ther and to Son And Spir - it now be giv - en.

Who, from our moth - ers' arms, Hath blessed us on our way
And keep us in God's grace, And guide us when per - plexed,
The one e - ter - nal God, Whom heaven and earth a - dore,

With count-less gifts of love, And still is ours to - day.
And free us from all ills In this world and the next.
The God who was, and is, And shall be ev - er - more.

The World Abounds
with God's Free Grace

556

HALIFAX   CM with refrain

David G. Mehrtens, 1980

George Frederick Handel, 1748
Harm. C. Winfred Douglas, 1941

1. The world a-bounds with God's free grace; What
2. Give thanks for plains and val-leys spaced By
3. In full thanks-giv-ing for God's love, From
4. Give thanks in hope, re-joice, re-pent, And

won-ders bless the land! And on through bound-less
moun-tains thrust-ing high; Give thanks by fight-ing
which earth's bless-ings flow, Pro-tect the pre-cious
prac-tice all you prayed; True thanks can nev-er

star-ry space, God's match-less works ex-pand.
greed and waste That drain their trea-sures dry.
air a-bove, The wa-ters spread be-low.
be con-tent To foul the world God made.

Refrain

Lord, teach us all an at-ti-tude that thanks You all our days,

A love that shows our grat-i-tude through deeds that live our praise.

¿Con Qué Pagaremos?
O What Shall I Render?

557

GRATITUD   Irregular

Latin American hymn
Trans. George P. Simmonds, 1968

Latin American melody
Arr. Ethel Winn, 1964

1. ¿Con qué pa-ga-re-mos   A-mor tan in-men-so?   Que
2. Y cuan-do la no-che   Ex-tien-de su man-to.   Mis

1. O what shall I ren-der   For love so un-bound-ed   That
2. And when the night draw-eth   Its cur-tains of dark-ness,   My

dis-te tu vi-da   Por el pe-ca-dor;   En
o-jos en llan-to   En Ti fi-ja-ré;   Al-

led Thee, dear Sav-ior,   For sin-ners to die?   Re-
eyes view Thy glo-ries   The heav-ens de-clare;   And

cam-bio re-ci-bes   La o-fren-da hu-mil-de,
zan-do mis o-jos   Ve-ré las es-tre-llas,

ceive, I be-seech Thee,   My heart's hum-ble of-fering:
back of the star-light   I know God my Fa-ther,

La o-fren-da hu-mil-de,   Se-ñor Je-su-cris-to,   De
Yo sé que tras e-llas   Cual Pa-dre a-mo-ro-so   Tú

Thanks-giv-ing and prais-es   My glad heart up-rais-es   To
Or wak-ing or sleep-ing,   Is lov-ing-ly keep-ing   Me

mi co - ra - zón,
ve - las por mí,
Thee, Lord, on high.
in His dear care.

La o - fren - da hu - mil - de, Se -
Yo sé que tras e - llas Cual
Thanks - giv - ing and prais - es My
Or wak - ing or sleep - ing, Is

ñor Je - su - cris - to, De mi co - ra - zón.
Pa - dre a - mo - ro - so Tú ve - las por mí.
glad heart up - rais - es To Thee, Lord, on high.
lov - ing - ly keep - ing Me in His dear care.

3. No puedo pargarte
   Con oro ni plata
   El gran sacrificio
   Que hiciste por mí;
   No tengo que darte
   Por tanto amarme,
   Recibe este canto
   Mezclado con llanto,
   Y mi corazón,
   Recibe este canto
   Mezclado con llanto,
   Y mi corazón.

3. I ne'er can repay Thee
   With gold or with silver
   For all Thou didst suffer,
   Dear Savior, for me;
   There's nought I can give Thee
   For Thy love so boundless.
   For joy I am singing,
   My gratitude bringing
   An offering to Thee.
   For joy I am singing,
   My gratitude bringing
   An offering to Thee.

558 Come, Sing a Song of Harvest

CHRISTUS, DER IST MEIN LEBEN   7.6.7.6

Fred Pratt Green, 1976; alt.   Melchior Vulpius, 1609

1. Come, sing a song of har - vest, Of thanks for dai - ly food!
2. Shall we, some-times for - get - ful Of where cre - a - tion starts,
3. May God, the great Cre - a - tor, To whom all life be - longs,
4. And lest the world go hun - gry While we our-selves are fed,

To of - fer God the first - fruits Is old as grat - i - tude.
View sci - ence as our sav - ior, Lose won - der from our hearts?
Ac - cept these gifts we of - fer, Our ser - vice and our songs.
Make each of us more read - y To share our dai - ly bread.

We Gather Together

559

KREMSER 12.11.12.11

Netherlands folk hymn, 1625
Trans. Theodore Baker, 1894

Nederlandtsch Gedenckclanck, 1626
Harm. Eduard Kremser, 1877

1. We gath - er to - geth - er to ask the Lord's bless - ing;
2. Be - side us to guide us, our God with us join - ing,
3. We all do ex - tol Thee, Thou lead - er tri - um - phant,

He chas - tens and has - tens His will to make known;
Or - dain - ing, main - tain - ing His king - dom di - vine;
And pray that Thou still our de - fend - er wilt be.

The wick - ed op - press - ing now cease from dis - tress - ing,
So from the be - gin - ning the fight we were win - ning;
Let Thy con - gre - ga - tion es - cape trib - u - la - tion;

Sing prais - es to His name; He for - gets not His own.
Thou, Lord, wast at our side; All glo - ry be Thine!
Thy name be ev - er praised! O Lord, make us free!

560   We Plow the Fields and Scatter

NYLAND   7.6.7.6 D

Matthias Claudius, 1782
Trans. Jane Montgomery Campbell, 1861; alt.

Finnish folk melody
Adapt. and harm. David Evans, 1927

1. We plow the fields and scat - ter The good seed on the land,
2. You on - ly are the Mak - er Of all things near and far;
3. We thank You, then, Cre - a - tor, For all things bright and good,

But it is fed and wa - tered By God's al - might - y hand;
You paint the way - side flow - er, You light the eve - ning star;
The seed-time and the har - vest, Our life, our health, our food;

God sends the snow in win - ter, The warmth to swell the grain,
The winds and waves o - bey You, By You the birds are fed;
Ac - cept the gifts we of - fer, For all Your love im - parts,

The breez-es and the sun - shine, And soft, re - fresh-ing rain.
Much more to us, Your chil - dren, You give our dai - ly bread.
And what You most would wel - come, Our hum - ble, thank-ful hearts.

♩=46–50

561 My Country, 'Tis of Thee

AMERICA   6.6.4.6.6.6.4

Samuel Francis Smith, 1831

Thesaurus Musicus, London, c. 1740

1. My coun - try, 'tis of thee, Sweet land of lib - er - ty,
2. My na - tive coun - try, thee, Land of the no - ble free,
3. Let mu - sic swell the breeze, And ring from all the trees
4. Our *fa - thers' God, to Thee, Au - thor of lib - er - ty,

Of thee I sing; Land where my *fa - thers died, Land of the
Thy name I love; I love thy rocks and rills, Thy woods and
Sweet free-dom's song; Let mor - tal tongues a - wake, Let all that
To Thee we sing; Long may our land be bright With free-dom's

pil - grims' pride, From ev - ery moun-tain - side Let free - dom ring.
tem - pled hills; My heart with rap - ture thrills Like that a - bove.
breathe par - take, Let rocks their si - lence break, The sound pro - long.
ho - ly light; Pro - tect us by Thy might, Great God, our King.

*Or "parents."

Eternal Father, Strong to Save

562

MELITA   8.8.8.8.8.8

William Whiting, 1860; alt.

John Bacchus Dykes, 1861

1. E - ter - nal Fa - ther, strong to save, Whose arm has bound the
2. O Sav - ior, whose al - might - y word The wind and waves sub -
3. O Ho - ly Spir - it, who did brood Up - on the cha - os
4. O Trin - i - ty of love and power, All trav - elers guard in

rest - less wave, Who bade the might - y o - cean deep Its
mis - sive heard, Who walked up - on the foam - ing deep, And
wild and rude, And bade its an - gry tu - mult cease, And
dan - ger's hour; From rock and tem - pest, fire and foe, Pro -

own ap - point - ed lim - its keep: O hear us when we
calm a - mid its rage did sleep: O hear us when we
gave, for fierce con - fu - sion, peace: O hear us when we
tect them where - so - e'er they go; Thus ev - er - more shall

cry to Thee For those in per - il on the sea.
cry to Thee For those in per - il on the sea.
cry to Thee For those in per - il on the sea.
rise to Thee Glad praise from air and land and sea.

563 Lift Every Voice and Sing

LIFT EVERY VOICE Irregular

James Weldon Johnson, 1921

J. Rosamond Johnson, 1921

1. Lift ev-ery voice and sing till earth and heav-en ring, Ring with the har-mo-nies of lib - er - ty. Let our re-joic-ing rise high as the lis - tening skies; Let it re-sound loud as the roll - ing sea.

2. Ston-y the road we trod, bit-ter the chas-ten-ing rod, Felt in the days when hope un - born had died; Yet, with a stead - y beat, have not our wea - ry feet Come to the place for which our *fa - thers sighed?

3. God of our wea - ry years, God of our si - lent tears, Thou who hast brought us thus far on the way; Thou who hast by Thy might led us in - to the light; Keep us for - ev - er in the path, we pray.

*Or "parents."

Sing a song full of the faith that the dark past has taught us;
We have come o-ver a way that with tears has been wa-tered;
Lest our feet stray from the plac-es, our God, where we met Thee;

Sing a song full of the hope that the pres-ent has brought
We have come, tread-ing our path through the blood of the slaugh -
Lest, our hearts drunk with the wine of the world, we for-get

us; Fac-ing the ris-ing sun of our new day be -
tered, Out from the gloom-y past, till now we stand at
Thee; Shad-owed be-neath Thy hand may we for-ev -er

gun, Let us march on, till vic-to-ry is won.
last Where the white gleam of our bright star is cast.
stand, True to our God, true to our na-tive land.

564   O Beautiful for Spacious Skies

MATERNA   CMD

Katharine Lee Bates, 1893   Samuel Augustus Ward, 1882

1. O beau-ti-ful for spa-cious skies, For am-ber waves of grain,
2. O beau-ti-ful for pil-grim feet, Whose stern, im-pas-sioned stress
3. O beau-ti-ful for he-roes proved In lib-er-at-ing strife,
4. O beau-ti-ful for pa-triot dream That sees be-yond the years

For pur-ple moun-tain maj-es-ties A-bove the fruit-ed plain!
A thor-ough-fare for free-dom beat A-cross the wil-der-ness!
Who more than self their coun-try loved, And mer-cy more than life!
Thine al-a-bas-ter cit-ies gleam, Un-dimmed by hu-man tears!

A-mer-i-ca! A-mer-i-ca! God shed His grace on thee,
A-mer-i-ca! A-mer-i-ca! God mend thine ev-ery flaw,
A-mer-i-ca! A-mer-i-ca! May God thy gold re-fine
A-mer-i-ca! A-mer-i-ca! God shed His grace on thee

And crown thy good with *broth-er-hood From sea to shin-ing sea!
Con-firm thy soul in self-con-trol, Thy lib-er-ty in law!
Till all suc-cess be no-ble-ness And ev-ery gain di-vine!
And crown thy good with *broth-er-hood From sea to shin-ing sea!

*Or "servanthood."

SERVICE MUSIC

Lord, Have Mercy

Kyrie

565

John Weaver, 1984

Lord, have mer - cy. Christ, have mer - cy. Lord, have mer - cy.

♩=84–92

566 Glory to God in the Highest
Gloria in Excelsis

John Weaver, 1988

♩=63–69

give You thanks, we praise You for Your glo - ry. Lord Je - sus

Christ, on - ly Son of the Fa - ther, Lord God, Lamb of God,

You take a - way the sin of the world: have mer - cy

on us; *mf* You are seat - ed at the right hand of the

Fa - ther: re - ceive our prayer. For You a - lone are the

f

Ho - ly One, You a - lone are the Lord, You a -

Harmony   *Unison*

lone are the Most High, Je - sus Christ, with the Ho - ly

ff

Harmony

Spir-it, in the glo - ry of God the Fa ther.

♩=63–69

Glory to the Father
Gloria Patri

John Weaver, 1978

567

Glo-ry to the Fa-ther, and to the Son, and to the Ho-ly Spir-it: as it was in the be-gin-ning, is now, and will be for ev-er. A-men. A - men. A - men.

May be sung as a canon.

♩=58–63

568

Holy, Holy, Holy Lord
Sanctus

John Weaver, 1984

Ho - ly, ho - ly, ho - ly Lord, God of pow-er and might, heaven and earth are full of Your glo - ry.

Ho - san - na in the high - est. Bless - ed,

bless - ed is He who comes in the name of the Lord.

Ho - san - na in the high - est.

subito ***p***

♩=120–132

569

Christ Has Died
Memorial Acclamation

John Weaver, 1987

Christ will come a - gain.

♩=92–100

Amen 570

John Weaver, 1978

A-men, A - men, A - men.

𝅗𝅥=58–63

571 Our Father in Heaven

The Lord's Prayer

John Weaver, 1988

Our Fa-ther in heav-en, hal-lowed be Your name,

Your king-dom come, Your will be done, on earth as in heav-en.

Give us to-day our dai-ly bread. For-give us our sins

as we for-give those who sin a-gainst us.

Save us from the time of tri-al and de-liv-er us from e-vil.

For the king-dom, the power, and the glo-ry are Yours now

cresc.

and for ev-er. A-men.

f

♩=46–50

572 Lord, Have Mercy Upon Us
Kyrie

John Merbecke, 1550
Arr. Healey Willan, 1930

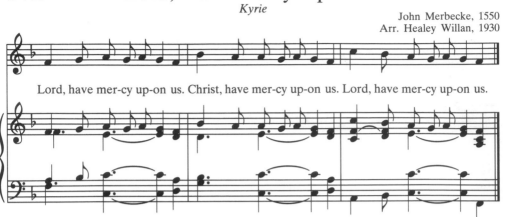

Lord, have mer-cy up-on us. Christ, have mer-cy up-on us. Lord, have mer-cy up-on us.

573 Lord, Have Mercy
Kyrie

Harm. Richard Proulx, 1984

Leader — Lord, have mer - cy. *Response* — Lord, have mer - cy. *Leader* — Christ, have mer - cy.

Man. Ped. Man.

Response — Christ, have mer - cy. *Leader* — Lord, have mer - cy. *Response* — Lord, have mer - cy.

Ped. Man. Ped.

Lord, Have Mercy Upon Us

Kyrie

574

The Worshipbook, 1972
Arr. David N. Johnson, 1972

Lord, have mer - cy up - on us.

Christ, have mer - cy up - on us.

Lord, have mer - cy up - on us.

R.H.

♩=54–58

575 Glory to God in the Highest

Gloria in Excelsis

Old Scottish chant; alt.

1. Glory to God in the highest, and peace to God's people on earth.
2. Lord God, heaven-ly King, almighty God and Fa - ther,

3. We worship You, we give You thanks, we praise You for Your glo - ry.

4. Lord Jesus Christ, only Son of the Father, Lord God, Lamb of God,
5. You take away the sin of the world: have mer - cy on us;
6. You are seated at the right hand of the Father: re - ceive our prayer.

7. For You alone are the Ho-ly One, You a - lone are the Lord,
8. You alone are the Je-sus Christ, with the Holy Spirit,
   Most High, . . . in the glory of God the Fa - ther.

Gloria, Gloria

576

Jacques Berthier, 1979

Glo - ri - a, glo - ri - a, in ex - cel - sis De - o!

Glo - ri - a, glo - ri - a, al - le - lu - ia, al - le - lu - ia!

♩=63–69

577 Glory Be to the Father

Gloria Patri

Richard K. Avery and Donald S. Marsh, 1967

Glo-ry be to the Fa-ther, and the Son, and the Ho-ly Ghost;

As it was in the be-gin-ning, is now, and ev-er shall be,

world with-out end. A - men. As it was in the be-gin-ning, is

578

Glory Be to the Father
Gloria Patri

Old Scottish chant

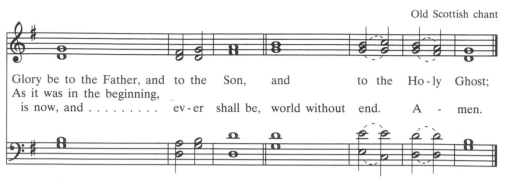

Glory be to the Father, and to the Son, and to the Ho-ly Ghost;
As it was in the beginning,
is now, and . . . . ev-er shall be, world without end. A - men.

579

Glory Be to the Father
Gloria Patri

Henry W. Greatorex, 1851

Glo - ry be to the Fa - ther, and to the Son, and to the

Ho - ly Ghost; As it was in the be - gin - ning, is

now, and ev - er shall be, world with-out end. A - men, A - men.

Holy, Holy, Holy
Sanctus

580

John Merbecke, 1550
Arr. Healey Willan, 1930

Music: Arrangement reprinted with the permission of the executor of the estate of Healey Willan.

581 Holy, Holy, Holy Lord

Sanctus

Joseph Roff, 1980

Ho - ly, ho - ly, ho - ly Lord, God of pow-er and might,

heav-en and earth are full of Your glo-ry. Ho - san - na in the

high - est. Bless-ed is He who comes in the name of the

Lord. Ho - san - na in the high - est, ho - san - na in the high - est.

Dying, You Destroyed Our Death

Memorial Acclamation

582

Joseph Roff, 1980

Dy - ing, You de - stroyed our death; Ris - ing, You re - stored our life. Lord Je - sus, come in glo - ry.

Amen

583

Marty Haugen, 1984

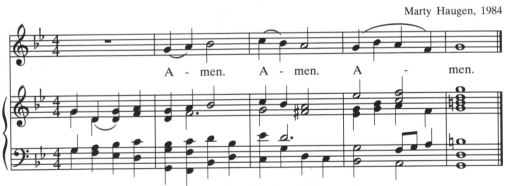

A - men. A - men. A - men.

Amen

584

Dresden
Johann G. Naumann (1741–1801)

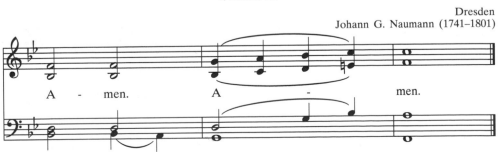

A - men. A - men.

585

Amen

McNeil Robinson II

A - men. A - men. A - men.

586

Amen

Danish

A - men. A - men. A - men.

587

Amen

African-American

A - men. A - men. A - men. A - men. A - men.

588

Amen

Joseph Roff, 1980

A - men. A - men. A - men.

Our Father, Which Art in Heaven

589

The Lord's Prayer

West Indian folk melody
Melody transcribed by Olive Pattison, 1945
Harm. for this publication, 1989

Leader

1. Our Fa - ther, which art in heav - en,
2. On earth as it is in heav - en,
3. And for - give us all our debts,
4. And lead us not in - to temp - ta - tion.
5. For Thine is the king - dom, the power, and the glo - ry.

Response

Hal - low - ed - a be Thy name.

Leader

Thy king - dom come, Thy will be done,
Give us this day our dai - ly bread,
As we for - give our debt - ors,
But de - liv - er us from e - vil,
For - ev - er and ev - er. A - men.

Response

Hal - low - ed - a be Thy name.

Music: Melody from *Edric Connor Collection of West Indian Spirituals and Folk Tunes,* copyright 1945 by Boosey and Company, Ltd.; reprinted by permission of Boosey and Hawkes, Inc. Copyright Renewed.
Harmonization © 1990 Westminster/John Knox Press.

590 Our Father, Lord of Heaven and Earth

The Lord's Prayer

VATER UNSER   8.8.8.8.8.8

Vers. Henry J. deJong, 1982

Schumann's *Geistliche Lieder,* 1539
Harm. Johann Sebastian Bach, 1723

1. Our Fa - ther, Lord of heaven and earth, Let praise and hon - or
2. For - give us, Lord, our sins and debts As we to debt - ors

clothe Your name. Your king - dom come, Your will be done;
show Your grace. Re - move us from all tempt-ing paths

Through-out the world com - plete Your reign. Teach us, O Lord,
And guard us from the dev - il's ways; For glo - ry, strength,

to trust in You For bread and breath each day a - new.
and heav-en's throne Be - long to You, and You a - lone. A - men.

Praise God, from Whom All Blessings Flow 591
Doxology

OLD HUNDREDTH   LM

Neil Weatherhogg, 1988   Genevan Psalter, 1551

Praise God, from whom all bless-ings flow; Praise Christ, all peo-ple here be-low; Praise Ho-ly Spir-it ev-er-more; Praise Tri-une God, whom we a-dore. A-men.

592 Praise God, from Whom All Blessings Flow

Doxology

OLD HUNDREDTH LM

Thomas Ken, 1695, 1709

Genevan Psalter, 1551

Praise God, from whom all bless-ings flow; Praise *Him, all crea-tures here be-low; Praise *Him a-bove, ye heaven-ly host; Praise Fa-ther, Son, and Ho-ly Ghost. A-men.

* Or "God."

593 Praise God, from Whom All Blessings Flow

Doxology

LM

Thomas Ken, 1695, 1709

Richard K. Avery and Donald S. Marsh, 1967

Praise God, from whom all bless-ings flow; Praise God, all crea-tures

594 This Is the Feast of Victory

FESTIVAL CANTICLE   Irregular

Adapt. John W. Arthur, 1978

Richard Hillert, 1978

This is the feast of vic-to-ry for our God.

To stanzas | *Last time*

Al-le - lu - ia, al-le - lu - ia, al - le - lu - ia! lu - ia!

1. — Wor - thy is Christ, the Lamb who was slain, whose
2. Pow - er, rich - es, wis - dom, and strength, and
3. Sing with all the peo - ple of God, and
4. Bless - ing, hon - or, glo - ry, and might be to
5. For the Lamb who was slain has be -

D.C.

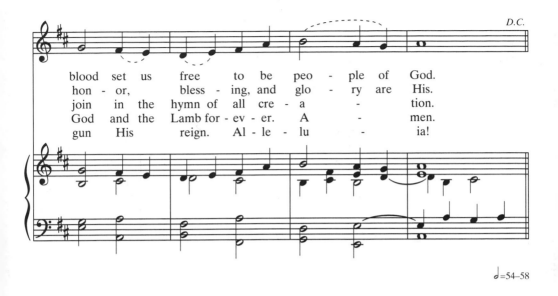

blood set us free to be peo - ple of God.
hon - or, bless - ing, and glo - ry are His.
join in the hymn of all cre - a - tion.
God and the Lamb for - ev - er. A - men.
gun His reign. Al - le - lu - ia!

♩=54–58

Heleluyan
Alleluia

595

HELELUYAN

Transcribed by Charles Webb, 1989
Native American (Muscogee)

Native American (Muscogee)

*   *

He - le - lu - yan, he - le - lu - yan; he - le, he - le - lu - yan;
Al - le - lu - ia, al - le - lu - ia; al - le, al - le - lu - ia;

he - le - lu - yan, he - le - lu - yan; he - le, he - le - lu - yan.
al - le - lu - ia, al - le - lu - ia; al - le, al - le - lu - ia.

* *May be sung as a canon.*

596 May the Lord, Mighty God

WEN-TI   Irregular

Adapted from scripture

Chinese folk tune
Attr. Pao-chen Li (1907–1979)

May the Lord, might - y God, bless and

keep you for - ev - er; Grant you peace,

Fine

per - fect peace, cour - age in ev - ery en - deav - or.

Voice I (melody)

Lift up your eyes and see God's face, full of

Voice II

Lift up and see God's face, full of

grace for - ev - er; May the Lord,

grace for - ev - er; May the Lord,

D.C.

might - y God, bless and keep you for - ev - er.

D.C.

might - y God, bless and keep you for - ev - er.

Bless the Lord, O My Soul   597

Appalachian folk melody
The Worshipbook, 1972
Arr. Richard D. Wetzel, 1972

Music: Arrangement © 1972 by The Westminster Press; from *The Worshipbook—Services and Hymns.*

598

This Is the Good News

The Worshipbook, 1972
Based on Native American (Dakota) melody
Arr. Richard D. Wetzel (b. 1935)

The Worshipbook, 1970; alt.

This is the good news which we re-ceived, in which we stand, and by which we are saved: that Christ died for our sins ac-cord-ing to the scrip-tures, that He was bur-ied, that He was raised on the third day; and that He ap-peared to the wom-en, and that He ap-peared to Pe-ter,

* *Keyboard and guitar should not sound together.*

599 Jesus, Remember Me

Jacques Berthier, 1981

Je - sus, re - mem-ber me when You come in - to Your king - dom.

Je - sus, re - mem-ber me when You come in - to Your king - dom.

Accompaniment

Flute

(Je-sus, re - mem-ber me)

♩=66–72

Song of Mary

Magnificat

MORNING SONG   CM

Para. Miriam Therese Winter, 1987

Wyeth's *Repository of Sacred Music,* 1813
Harm. C. Winfred Douglas, 1940

600

1. My soul gives glo - ry to my God, My heart pours out its praise. God lift - ed up my low - li - ness In man - y mar - vel - ous ways.
2. My God has done great things for me: Yes, ho - ly is this Name. All peo - ple will de - clare me blessed, And bless - ings they shall claim.
3. From age to age to all who fear, Such mer - cy love im - parts, Dis - pens - ing jus - tice far and near, Dis - miss - ing self - ish hearts.
4. Love casts the might - y from their thrones, Pro - motes the in - se - cure, Leaves hun - gry spir - its sat - is - fied; The rich seem sud - den - ly poor.
5. Praise God, whose lov - ing cov - e - nant Sup - ports those in dis - tress, Re - mem - ber - ing past prom - is - es With pres - ent faith - ful - ness.

Guitar and keyboard should not sound together.

♩=88–96

Luke 1:68–79

601 Song of Zechariah

Benedictus

KINGSFOLD   CMD

James Quinn, 1969; alt. 1985

English Country Songs, 1893
Arr. and harm. Ralph Vaughan Williams, 1906

1. Blest be the God of Is-ra-el, The ev-er-liv-ing Lord. You come in power to save Your own, Your peo-ple Is-ra-el. For Is-ra-el You now raise up Sal-va-tion's tower on high In
2. Through ho-ly proph-ets did You speak Your word in days of old, That You would save us from our foes And all who bear us ill. On Si-nai You gave to us Your cov-e-nant of love; So
3. Of old You gave Your sol-emn oath To fa-ther A-bra-ham: Whose seed a might-y race should be And blest for-ev-er-more. You vowed to set Your peo-ple free From fear of ev-ery foe, That
4. O ti-ny child, Your name shall be The proph-et of the Lord; The way of God You will pre-pare To make God's com-ing known. You shall pro-claim to Is-ra-el Sal-va-tion's dawn-ing day, When

Da - vid's house, who reigned as king And ser - vant of the Lord.
with us now You keep Your word In love that knows no end.
we might serve You all our days In good-ness, love, and peace.
God shall wipe a - way all sins With mer - cy and with love.

5. The rising sun shall shine on us
   To bring the light of day
   To all who sit in darkest night
   And shadow of the grave.
   Our footsteps God shall safely guide
   To walk the ways of peace,
   Whose name forevermore be blest,
   Who lives and loves and saves.

602 Song of Zechariah

Benedictus

MERLE'S TUNE   7.6.7.6 D

Michael A. Perry, 1973

Hal H. Hopson, 1983

1. Blest be the God of Is - rael, Who comes to set us free;
2. God from the house of Da - vid A child of grace has given;
3. On those who sit in dark - ness The sun be - gins to rise,

Who vis - its and re - deems us, Who grants us lib - er - ty.
A Sav - ior comes a - mong us To raise us up to heaven.
The dawn - ing of for - give - ness Up - on the sin - ner's eyes.

The proph - ets spoke of mer - cy, Of free - dom and re - lease;
Be - fore Him goes the her - ald, Fore - run - ner in the way,
God guides the feet of pil - grims A - long the paths of peace.

God shall ful-fill that prom - ise And bring the peo-ple peace.
The proph-et of sal - va - tion, The har - bin-ger of day.
O bless our God and Sav - ior With songs that nev - er cease!

Luke 2:29–32

Song of Simeon

603

Nunc Dimittis

LAND OF REST   CM

American folk melody
Arr. Annabel Morris Buchanan, 1938

Para. James Quinn (b. 1919)

C   F   Bb   F   C   Dm   C   C7   F   Am

1. Lord, bid Your ser - vant go in peace, Your word is now ful - filled.
2. This is the Sav - ior of the world, The Gen - tiles' prom-ised light,

Dm   C   Dm   Am   Bb   F   C7   F   Bb   C7   F

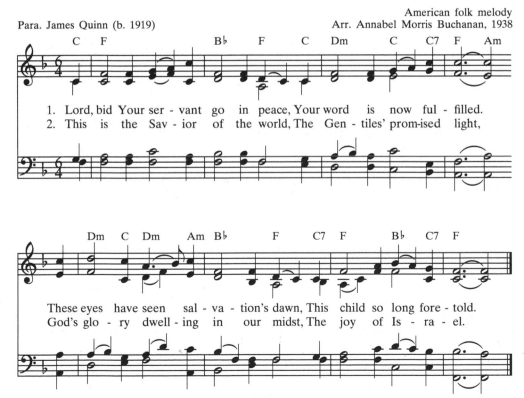

These eyes have seen sal - va - tion's dawn, This child so long fore - told.
God's glo - ry dwell - ing in our midst, The joy of Is - ra - el.

Luke 2:29–32

604

Song of Simeon

Nunc Dimittis

SONG 1   10.10.10.10.10.10

Para. Rae E. Whitney, 1982

Orlando Gibbons, 1623
Arr. Ralph Vaughan Williams, 1906

Lord God, You now have set Your ser-vant free To go in
peace as prom-ised in Your word; My eyes have seen the
Sav-ior, Christ the Lord, Pre-pared by You for all the
world to see, To shine on na-tions trapped in dark-est night,
The glo-ry of Your peo-ple, and their light.

♩=92–100

Song of Simeon

Nunc Dimittis

NUNC DIMITTIS   6.6.7 D

605

Para. Dewey Westra, 1931; alt.

Louis Bourgeois, 1551
Harm. Claude Goudimel, 1564

1. Now may Your ser - vant, Lord, Ac - cord-ing to Your word,
2. You did for all pre - pare This gift so great, so rare,

De - part in ex - ul - ta - tion. My peace shall be se - rene,
Ful - fill - ing proph-ets' sto - ry— A light to show the way

For now my eyes have seen Your won-der - ful sal - va - tion.
To Gen-tiles gone a - stray, And un - to Is - rael's glo - ry.

INDEXES

INDEX OF AUTHORS, TRANSLATORS, AND SOURCES

INDEX OF COMPOSERS, ARRANGERS, AND SOURCES

INDEX OF SCRIPTURAL ALLUSIONS

TOPICAL INDEX

METRICAL INDEX OF TUNES

ALPHABETICAL INDEX OF TUNES

INDEX OF FIRST LINES
AND COMMON TITLES